PC LEARNING LABS TEACHES AMI PRO 3.0

PLEASE NOTE—USE OF THE DISK(S) AND THE PROGRAMS INCLUDED ON THE DISK(S) PACKAGED WITH THIS BOOK AND THE PROGRAM LISTINGS INCLUDED IN THIS BOOK IS SUBJECT TO AN END-USER LICENSE AGREEMENT (THE "AGREEMENT") FOUND AT THE BACK OF THE BOOK. PLEASE READ THE AGREEMENT CAREFULLY BEFORE MAKING YOUR PURCHASE DECISION. **PURCHASE OF THE BOOK** AND USE OF THE DISKS, PROGRAMS, AND PROGRAM LISTINGS WILL CONSTITUTE ACCEPTANCE OF THE AGREEMENT.

PC LEARNING LABS TEACHES AMI PRO 3.0

LOGICAL OPERATIONS

Ziff-Davis Press
Emeryville, California

Curriculum Development	Logical Operations
Writer	Chris Benz
Editor	Carol Henry
Technical Reviewer	Lisa Biow
Project Coordinator	Bill Cassel
Proofreader	Cort Day
Production Coordinator, Logical Operations	Tary Simizon
Cover Illustration and Design	Carrie English
Book Design	Laura Lamar/MAX, San Francisco
Screen Graphics Editor	Dan Brodnitz
Word Processing	Howard Blechman, Cat Haglund, and Allison Levin
Page Layout	Anna L. Marks and M. D. Barrera
Indexer	Valerie Robbins

This book was produced on a Macintosh IIfx, with the following applications: FrameMaker®, Microsoft® Word, MacLink® *Plus*, Aldus® FreeHand™, Adobe Photoshop™, and Collage Plus™.

Ziff-Davis Press
5903 Christie Avenue
Emeryville, CA 94608

Copyright © 1993 by Ziff-Davis Press. All rights reserved.

Ziff-Davis Press, ZD Press, PC Learning Labs, and PC Learning Labs Teaches are trademarks of Ziff Communications Company.

All other product names and services identified throughout this book are trademarks or registered trademarks of their respective companies. They are used throughout this book in editorial fashion only and for the benefit of such companies. No such uses, or the use of any trade name, is intended to convey endorsement or other affiliation with the book.

No part of this publication may be reproduced in any form, or stored in a database or retrieval system, or transmitted or distributed in any form by any means, electronic, mechanical photocopying, recording, or otherwise, without the prior written permission of Ziff-Davis Press, except as permitted by the Copyright Act of 1976 and the End-User License Agreement at the back of this book and except that program listings may be entered, stored, and executed in a computer system.

EXCEPT FOR THE LIMITED WARRANTY COVERING THE PHYSICAL DISK(S) PACKAGED WITH THIS BOOK AS PROVIDED IN THE END-USER LICENSE AGREEMENT AT THE BACK OF THIS BOOK, THE INFORMATION AND MATERIAL CONTAINED IN THIS BOOK ARE PROVIDED "AS IS," WITHOUT WARRANTY OF ANY KIND, EXPRESS OR IMPLIED, INCLUDING WITHOUT LIMITATION ANY WARRANTY CONCERNING THE ACCURACY, ADEQUACY, OR COMPLETENESS OF SUCH INFORMATION OR MATERIAL OR THE RESULTS TO BE OBTAINED FROM USING SUCH INFORMATION OR MATERIAL. NEITHER ZIFF-DAVIS PRESS NOR THE AUTHOR SHALL BE RESPONSIBLE FOR ANY CLAIMS ATTRIBUTABLE TO ERRORS, OMISSIONS, OR OTHER INACCURACIES IN THE INFORMATION OR MATERIAL CONTAINED IN THIS BOOK, AND IN NO EVENT SHALL ZIFF-DAVIS PRESS OR THE AUTHOR BE LIABLE FOR DIRECT, INDIRECT, SPECIAL, INCIDENTAL, OR CONSEQUENTIAL DAMAGES ARISING OUT OF THE USE OF SUCH INFORMATION OR MATERIAL.

ISBN 1-56276-134-X

Manufactured in the United States of America
10 9 8 7 6 5 4 3 2 1

CONTENTS AT A GLANCE

Introduction xix

Chapter 1: Ami Pro Basics 1

Chapter 2: Navigating in Ami Pro 35

Chapter 3: Editing Text 71

Chapter 4: Text Formatting 103

Chapter 5: Text Enhancements 125

Chapter 6: Page Layouts 169

Chapter 7: Proofing Your Documents 197

Chapter 8: Advanced Editing and Formatting Techniques 217

Chapter 9: Paragraph Styles and Style Sheets 247

Chapter 10: Working with Tables 281

Chapter 11: Form Letters, Labels, and Envelopes 325

Chapter 12: Creating a Newsletter 359

Appendix A: Installation 389

Appendix B: Keyboard Shortcut Reference 395

Appendix C: Exchanging Documents with Other Programs 401

Index 407

TABLE OF CONTENTS

Introduction xix
    Read This Before Starting Chapter 1! xx
    Who This Book Is For xx
    How to Use This Book xx
        As a Learning Guide xx
        As a Review Tool xxi
        As a Quick Reference xxi
    What This Book Contains xxi
    The Equipment You Need xxiii
        A Computer and Monitor xxiii
        A Keyboard xxiii
        A Mouse, Trackball, or Other Pointing Device xxiv
        A Printer xxvi
    Conventions Used in This Book xxvi
    About the Illustrations in This Book xxvii
    Creating Your Work Directory xxviii
    Before You Start xxxi

Chapter 1: Ami Pro Basics 1
    Introduction to Windows 2
        Starting Windows 3
        The Program Manager Window 5

Introduction to Ami Pro 7
    Starting Ami Pro 8
    Setting Ami Pro's Defaults 9
    The Ami Pro Application and Document Windows 13
    Issuing Commands through the Menu Bar 16
    Practice Your Skills 18

The Basics of Entering Text 18
    The Typing Area 18
    Word Wrap and the Enter Key 19
    Using Tabs to Align Text 20
    Deleting Text with the Backspace Key 21
    Displaying Nonprinting Symbols 22
    Practice Your Skills 24

Saving a Document 24
    The File, Save As Command 24
    The File, Save Command 25
    Naming a Document 26

Printing a Document 28

Closing a Document 30

Creating a New Document 30

Exiting Ami Pro 31

Summary 31

A Note on How to Proceed 33

Chapter 2: Navigating in Ami Pro 35

Using File, Open to Open a Document 36

Understanding the Document Path 39
- Changing the Default Document Path 40
- Using the Document Path Button 41

Scrolling through a Document 43

Moving through a Document 46
- Using the Keyboard to Move through a Document 46
- Using Edit, Go To to Move to a Page 48
- Using the Status Bar to Move to a Page 49
- Practice Your Skills 51

Using Edit, Find & Replace to Search for Text 51
- Practice Your Skills 54

Controlling Document Magnification 55

Obtaining On-Line Help 57
- Using the Help Table of Contents 57
- Obtaining Context-Sensitive Help 59

Saving a Modified Document 61

Practice Your Skills 61

Summary 66

If You're Stopping Here 68

Chapter 3: Editing Text 71

Basic Editing Techniques 72
- Using a SmartIcon to Open a Document 72
- Deleting Text with the Delete Key 74

    Deleting Blocks of Text 76
    Replacing Text 78
    Practice Your Skills 78

More Techniques for Selecting Text 79
    Practice Your Skills 83

Using Edit, Find & Replace to Replace Found Text 85

Moving and Copying Text 88
    Understanding the Windows Clipboard 88
    Moving Text 88
    Copying Text 90

Using Edit, Undo to Undo Your Most Recent Operation 91

Practice Your Skills 92

Summary 98

If You're Stopping Here 100

Chapter 4: Text Formatting 103

Understanding Text Formatting 104

Applying Text Attributes 105
    Using the Text Menu to Apply and Remove Text Attributes 105
    Using SmartIcons to Apply and Remove Text Attributes 108
    Practice Your Skills 110

Changing Fonts 110
    Using the Font Dialog Box to Change Fonts 111
    Practice Your Skills 112
    Using the Status Bar to Change Fonts 112
    Practice Your Skills 114

Using Fast Format to Copy Text Formatting 115
    Practice Your Skills 117

Summary 121

If You're Stopping Here 122

Chapter 5: Text Enhancements 125

Understanding the Current Ruler 126
    Displaying the Current Ruler 127
    Selecting Paragraphs for Text Enhancements 129

Working with Tabs 130
    Tab Types 130
    Setting Custom Tabs in the Current Ruler 131
    Setting Various Types of Tabs 136
    Practice Your Skills 137
    Moving Custom Tabs 137
    Clearing Individual Tabs 138

Setting Indentions and Line Breaks 140
    The Current Ruler's Indent Markers 141
    Setting Indentions with the Current Ruler 142
    Setting Indentions Using the Indention Dialog Box 144
    Practice Your Skills 145
    Setting Hanging Indents 146
    Practice Your Skills 148
    Using Ctrl+Enter to Create a New Line 148

Changing Paragraph Alignment 151
    Practice Your Skills 154

Changing Line Spacing 155

Practice Your Skills 157

Summary 164

If You're Stopping Here 166

Chapter 6: Page Layouts 169

Creating Headers and Footers 170
- Creating a Header 171
- Creating a Footer 173
- Adding a Date 173
- Adding Page Numbers 175
- Editing Headers and Footers 176

Changing Document Margins 177
- Changing Document Margins through the Modify Page Layout Dialog Box 179
- Changing Document Margins through the Current Ruler 180
- Changing Header and Footer Margins 182

Paginating a Document 185
- Viewing Page Layouts in Full Page View 185
- Inserting Manual Page Breaks 187
- Practice Your Skills 189
- Removing a Manual Page Break 189

Controlling the Printing of Your Documents 190

Summary 192

If You're Stopping Here 194

Chapter 7: Proofing Your Documents 197

Checking Spelling 198
Starting Spell Check 198
Using Spell Check 199

Finding and Placing Synonyms with Thesaurus 204

Checking Grammar, Style, and Mechanics 206
Starting Grammar Check 207
Using Grammar Check 207
Readability Statistics 208

Summary 213

If You're Stopping Here 214

Chapter 8: Advanced Editing and Formatting Techniques 217

Copying and Moving Text with Drag & Drop 218

Copying Text between Documents 221

Adding Bullets 224
Practice Your Skills 226

Finding and Replacing Text Attributes 227
Practice Your Skills 229

Customizing SmartIcons and SmartIcon Sets 230
Switching SmartIcon Sets 231
Practice Your Skills 233
Positioning SmartIcon Sets 233
Changing the Order of SmartIcons Within a Set 237
Removing a SmartIcon From a Set 239
Adding a SmartIcon to a Set 241

Summary 242

If You're Stopping Here 244

Chapter 9: Paragraph Styles and Style Sheets 247

Understanding Paragraph Styles 248

Assigning Styles 249
- Assigning Styles with the Style Status Button 250
- Practice Your Skills 251
- Assigning Styles with Function Keys 252
- Practice Your Skills 253

Modifying Styles 254
- Modifying a Style's Text-Formatting Elements 255
- Practice Your Skills 257
- Modifying a Style's Spacing Elements 258
- Overriding Styles 260

Creating Styles 261
- Creating a New Style Based on Selected Text 262
- Creating a New Style Based on Another Style 263

Understanding Style Sheets 269
- Using Style Sheets 269
- Using a Style Sheet to Create a Calendar 270

Practice Your Skills 272

Summary 276

If You're Stopping Here 278

Chapter 10: Working with Tables 281

Table Basics 282
    Creating a Table 283
    Specifying Table View Preferences 284
    Moving in a Table 287
    Practice Your Skills 289
    Entering Text in a Table 289
    Practice Your Skills 290

Working with Numbers in a Table 291
    Entering Numbers 292
    Practice Your Skills 293
    Using Quick Add 295
    Practice Your Skills 296

Modifying a Table Layout 296
    Table Selection Techniques 297
    Changing Column Widths 300
    Inserting and Deleting Columns and Rows 303
    Practice Your Skills 306
    Adding Lines to Selected Cells 307
    Adding a Line around a Table 308
    Centering a Table 311

Changing the Appearance of Table Contents 311
    Applying Text Formatting and Enhancements 312
    Modifying the Table Text Style 313

Practice Your Skills 315

Summary 320

If You're Stopping Here 322

Chapter 11: Form Letters, Labels, and Envelopes 325

The Components of a Merge Operation 326
- The Merge Data File 326
- The Merge Document 328
- The Merged Documents 329

Creating Form Letters 329
- Creating a Merge Data File 330
- Editing an Existing Merge Data File 335
- Editing a Merge Document 339
- Merging the Form Letters 343
- Merging Records That Contain Blank Fields 344
- Practice Your Skills 346

Creating Mailing Labels 346
- Sorting Records in a Merge Data File 346
- Merging Mailing Labels 349

Creating an Envelope 352

Summary 355

If You're Stopping Here 357

Chapter 12: Creating a Newsletter 359

Understanding Frames 360
- Displaying the Vertical Ruler 361
- Creating a Frame 362
- Typing Text in a Frame 366
- Modifying a Frame Layout 367

Working with Multiple Columns 370
- Creating Multiple Columns 370

Specifying Gutter Width 373
Inserting a Manual Column Break 374
Practice Your Skills 375
Justifying and Hyphenating Text 376

Working with Pictures 378
Importing a Picture 379
Sizing a Picture Frame 381

Adding a Line around a Page 382

Summary 384

Appendix A: Installation 389

Preparing Your Computer for Ami Pro Installation 390

Installing Ami Pro 3.0 on Your Computer 391

Appendix B: Keyboard Shortcut Reference 395

Movement 396

Text Selection 396

Menu Commands 397

Appendix C: Exchanging Documents with Other Programs 401

Opening Non-Ami Pro 3.0 Files 402

Saving Ami Pro 3.0 Documents in Other File Formats 404

Importing and Exporting for Unsupported Programs 406

Loss of Formatting When Importing and Exporting 406

Index 407

INTRODUCTION

Welcome to *PC Learning Labs Teaches Ami Pro 3.0*, a hands-on instruction book designed to help you attain a high level of Ami Pro fluency in as short a time as possible. And congratulations on choosing Ami Pro 3.0, a powerful and feature-rich program that helps you create professional-looking documents with a minimum of work.

We at PC Learning Labs believe this book to be a unique and welcome addition to the ranks of "how-to" computer publications. Our instructional approach stems directly from over a decade of successful teaching in a hands-on classroom environment. Throughout the book, we have consistently mixed theory with practice; a topic is explained and then immediately drilled in a hands-on activity. These activities employ sample Ami Pro documents provided on the Data Disk bound into the back of the book.

When you finish working your way through this book, you will have a solid foundation of skills in these Ami Pro functions:

- *Documents*   Creating, editing, printing, storing, and retrieving text
- *Navigation*   Getting around in large documents
- *Editing*   Deleting, replacing, selecting, moving, and copying text
- *Formatting*   Controlling a document's appearance
- *Proofing*   Checking documents for spelling, grammar, and word choices
- *Styles and style sheets*   Quickly and uniformly creating and formatting complex documents

- *Tables*   Organizing text and numbers into rows and columns
- *Merging*   Generating form letters, mailing labels, and envelopes
- *Newsletters*   Working with frames, multiple-column text, pictures, and full-page borders

Note: Throughout this Introduction, we have italicized terms with which you may not be familiar. Don't worry; we'll explain them in the chapters of the book. In the interim, please bear with us.

READ THIS BEFORE STARTING CHAPTER 1!

We strongly recommend that you read through the rest of this Introduction before beginning Chapter 1. If you are eager to dive in right away, however, please work through at least the upcoming section, "Creating Your Work Directory"; it is crucial to every activity in the book.

WHO THIS BOOK IS FOR

This book was written with the beginner in mind. Though experience with word processing and personal computers will certainly be helpful to you, little or none is required. You should know how to turn on your computer, monitor, and printer; how to use your keyboard; and how to move your mouse. Everything beyond that will be explained in the text.

HOW TO USE THIS BOOK

This book is designed to be used as a learning guide, a review tool, and a quick reference.

AS A LEARNING GUIDE

Each chapter covers one broad topic or a set of related topics. Chapters are arranged in order of increasing Ami Pro proficiency; skills you acquire in one chapter are used and developed in subsequent chapters. For this reason, you should work through the chapters in strict sequence.

Each chapter is organized into explanatory topics and hands-on, step-by-step activities. Topics provide the theoretical overview you need to master Ami Pro; activities enable you to apply this understanding immediately to specific examples.

AS A REVIEW TOOL

Any method of instruction is only as effective as the time and effort you are willing to invest in it. For this reason, we encourage you to review the more challenging topics and activities presented in this book.

AS A QUICK REFERENCE

General procedures (such as opening a document or selecting text) are presented as a series of bulleted steps; you can find these bullets (•) easily as you page through the book.

At the end of every chapter, you'll find a quick reference that lists the actions required to perform the techniques introduced in that chapter.

WHAT THIS BOOK CONTAINS

The contents of this book are divided into the following 12 chapters:

Chapter 1	Ami Pro Basics
Chapter 2	Navigating in Ami Pro
Chapter 3	Editing Text
Chapter 4	Text Formatting
Chapter 5	Text Enhancements

Chapter 6   Page Layouts

Chapter 7   Proofing Your Documents

Chapter 8   Advanced Editing and Formatting Techniques

Chapter 9   Paragraph Styles and Style Sheets

Chapter 10   Working with Tables

Chapter 11   Form Letters, Labels, and Envelopes

Chapter 12   Creating a Newsletter

In addition, there are three appendices:

Appendix A   Installation

Appendix B   Keyboard Shortcut Reference

Appendix C   Exchanging Documents with Other Programs

The following features of this book are designed to facilitate your learning:

- Carefully sequenced topics that build on the knowledge you've acquired from previous topics

- Frequent hands-on activities, designed to sharpen your Ami Pro skills

- Numerous illustrations showing how your screen should look at key points during the activities

- The Data Disk, which contains all the document files you'll need to complete the activities

- A quick reference at the end of each chapter, listing in easy-to-read table form the actions required to perform the techniques introduced in the chapter

THE EQUIPMENT YOU NEED

To run Ami Pro 3.0 and complete this book, you need several pieces of computer equipment: a computer, monitor, keyboard, and a pointing device such as a mouse. A printer is strongly recommended, but optional.

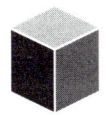

A COMPUTER AND MONITOR

To install and run Ami Pro, you need an IBM or IBM-compatible personal computer that has an 80286 or higher processor (80386, 80486, and so on) that is capable of running Microsoft Windows version 3.0 or higher. To completely install and use Ami Pro and this book's Data Disk document files, your computer's *hard disk drive* (or *hard drive*) must have at least 18 megabytes of free storage space. To run Ami Pro, your computer must have at least two megabytes of random access memory (although four megabytes or more is strongly recommended). Finally, you need an EGA or higher (VGA, SVGA, and so on) graphics card and computer monitor to display Windows and Ami Pro at their intended screen resolution.

Before starting Chapter 1, you must have DOS 3.1 (or higher) and Windows 3.0 (or higher) installed on your computer; if they are not, see your DOS and Windows documentation for instructions. Ami Pro 3.0 must also be installed, preferably *freshly* installed. After completing the "Creating Your Work Directory" section in this Introduction, see Appendix A for help on installing or reinstalling Ami Pro.

Note: Although you *can* run Ami Pro 3.0 under Windows 3.0, we *strongly* recommend that you use Windows 3.1.

A KEYBOARD

IBM-compatible computers come with various styles of keyboards; these keyboards function identically, but have different layouts. Figures I.1, I.2, and I.3 show the three most popular desktop-computer keyboard styles and their key arrangements. If you are using a portable computer, your keyboard may not exactly match any of these three keyboard styles, but should contain all of the keys necessary to run Ami Pro.

Ami Pro uses the three main areas of the keyboard:

- The *function keys* (F1, F2, and so on) enable you to use many of Ami Pro's features. On the PC-, XT-, and AT-style keyboards, there are ten function keys at the left end of the keyboard; on the PS/2-style Enhanced Keyboard, there are 12 function keys at the top of the keyboard.

- The *typing keys* are located in the main body of all the keyboards. These keys include letters, numbers, and punctuation marks, as well as the Shift, Ctrl, and Alt keys.

- The *numeric keypad* contains a group of number keys (the same ones found across the top row of the typing keys) for convenient numeric data entry. The numeric keypad also contains the *movement keys*: the Up, Down, Left, and Right Arrow keys; Home; End; PgUp (Page Up); and PgDn (Page Down).

    Pressing the Num Lock key toggles Num Lock on and off. For you to enter numeric data using the numeric keypad, Num Lock must be on. For you to use the movement keys on the keypad, Num Lock must be off. To enter numeric data when Num Lock is off, use the number keys on the top row of the typing area. The Enhanced Keyboard has an additional movement keypad to the left of the numeric keypad. This enables you to use the numeric keypad for numeric data entry (with Num Lock on) and still be able to use movement keys.

A MOUSE, TRACKBALL, OR OTHER POINTING DEVICE

You will need a mouse, trackball, or other pointing device to work through the activities in this book. Any Windows-compatible PC mouse, trackball, or other pointing device will do.

Figure I.1 **The IBM PC-style keyboard**

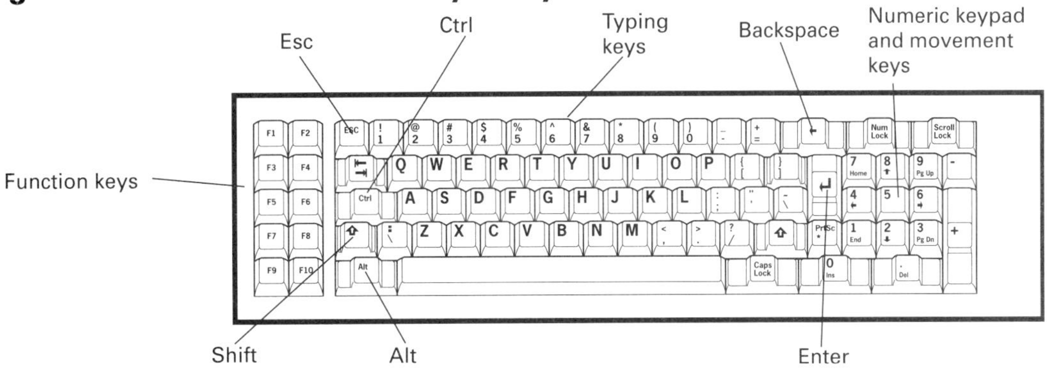

Figure I.2 **The XT/AT-style keyboard**

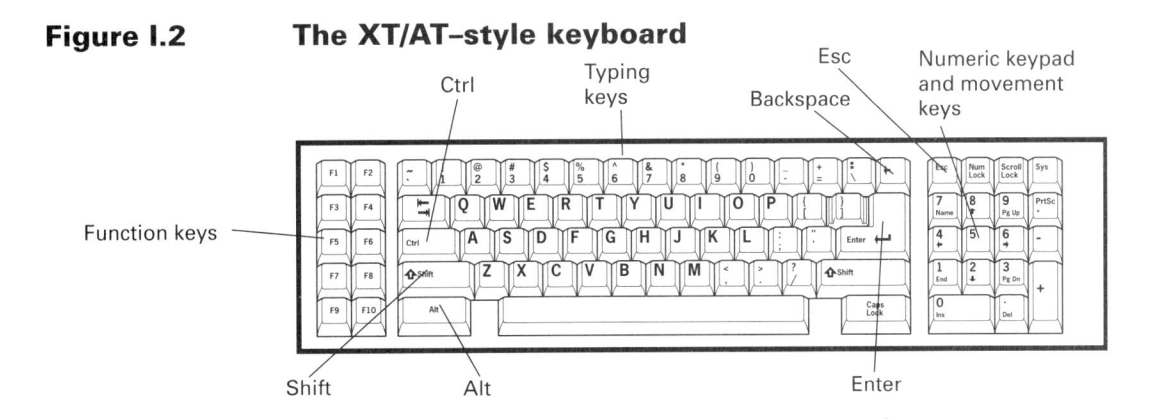

Figure I.3 **The PS/2-style Enhanced Keyboard**

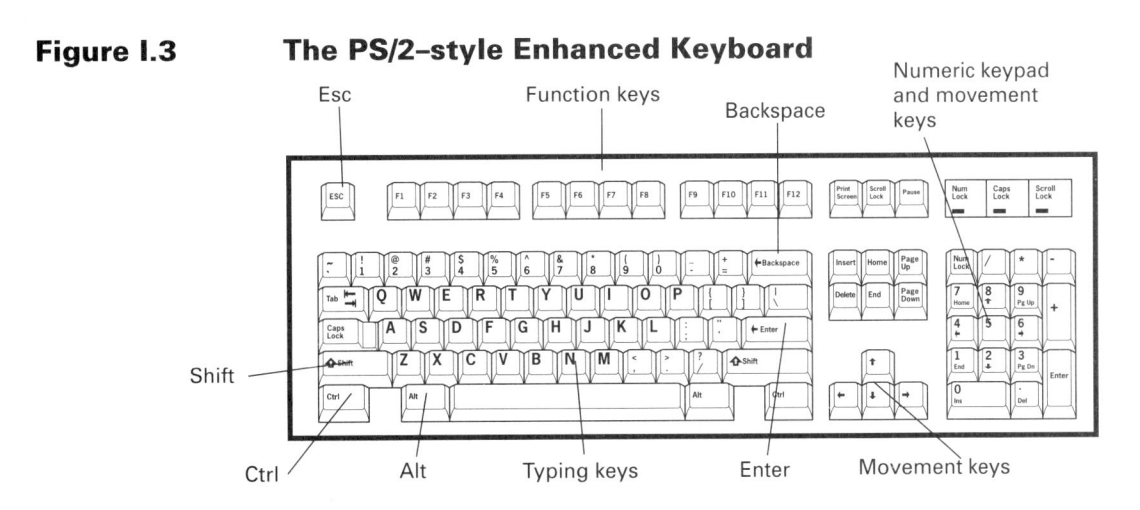

Throughout this book, we direct you to use a mouse, not a trackball or other pointing device. If you have a pointing device other than a mouse, you can use it to perform all the tasks that call for mouse techniques: pointing, clicking, dragging, and so on.

A PRINTER

Although you aren't absolutely required to have a printer to work through the activities, we strongly recommend it. A PostScript-type laser printer is ideal because that is the type of printer we used when preparing the activities and illustrations in this book. However, a non-PostScript laser or dot-matrix printer is acceptable.

To use your printer, you must first select it in Windows. If you have already printed successfully from Windows or any Windows accessory (for example, Windows Write or Windows Paintbrush), then your printer most likely will print from Ami Pro. If you have never printed from Windows or a Windows accessory, refer to your Windows documentation.

Even if you have no printer, select a PostScript printer in Windows, anyway. Then you'll be able to follow most of the steps in activities that involve printing. Either way, you'll learn in Chapter 1 how to view on your computer screen how a document will look when printed.

CONVENTIONS USED IN THIS BOOK

Certain conventions used in this book are designed to help you learn Ami Pro 3.0 easily and efficiently. Each chapter begins with a short introduction and ends with a summary that includes a quick-reference guide to the techniques introduced in the chapter. Main chapter topics (large, capitalized headings) and subtopics (headings preceded by a cube) explain Ami Pro features.

Hands-on activities enable you to practice using Ami Pro's features. In these activities, the menu choices, keystrokes, and anything we ask you to type are all presented in **boldface**. Here's an example from Chapter 2:

11. Click on **OK** to open the document.

Throughout the book, we've also used a **boldface** word to call your attention to important notes and tips, and we've used *italic* for new terms, for words we direct you to look at on screen, and for emphasis.

Activities in this book follow a cause-and-effect approach. Most steps tell you what to do (cause) and then what will happen (effect). In the Step 11 example above,

Cause: Click on **OK**.

Effect: The document opens.

A plus sign (+) is used with the Shift, Ctrl, and Alt keys to denote a multiple-key keystroke. For example, Ctrl+F10 means "Press and hold down the Ctrl key; then press the function key F10; and then release both."

To help you distinguish between steps presented for your general knowledge and steps you should carry out at your computer as you read, we have adopted the following system:

- A bulleted step, like this, is provided for your information and reference only.

1. A numbered step, like this, indicates one in a series of steps that you should carry out in sequence on your computer.

ABOUT THE ILLUSTRATIONS IN THIS BOOK

This book contains numerous illustrations, or *figures*. Most picture how your computer screen should look as you work through the activities.

When creating these figures, we ran Ami Pro 3.0 under Windows 3.1 using a VGA monitor and a PostScript laser printer. If you run Ami Pro under a different version of Windows, or use a different type of monitor, or select a non-PostScript laser printer, your screen may not *exactly* match the figures in this book. For the most part, however, Ami Pro will still run as described in the text.

Also, Ami Pro often displays the current date on the screen. Most likely, your current date will not match the date we have used throughout this book: October 10, 1994. When you are comparing your screen to figures that display dates in the book, your screen should display *your* current date.

CREATING YOUR WORK DIRECTORY

While using this book, you will be working with several Ami Pro document files that you'll copy from this book's Data Disk to your hard drive. To keep these files together on your hard drive, you need to create a *work directory*. (A hard drive functions like a big filing cabinet, holding an assortment of files; a directory functions like a hanging-file folder within that cabinet, storing a group of related files.)

Follow these steps to create your work directory and copy the files on the Data Disk into that directory:

1. Turn on your computer; after a moment, your *operating environment* loads automatically. If you are in Windows, please skip to step 2. If you are in DOS, please skip to step 4. If you are in a non-Windows, non-DOS operating environment (DOS Shell or GeoWorks, for example), exit to DOS, and then skip to step 4. (For help with exiting to DOS, consult your operating environment's documentation.)

2. Within Windows, locate the Program Manager, an on-screen window with the words *Program Manager* in its overhead title bar. If Program Manager is running as an *icon* (a small picture with the words *Program Manager* beneath it) instead of as a *window* (a

framed, large area on screen), use the mouse to *point*—that is, use the mouse to move the very tip of the on-screen *mouse pointer*—to the icon. Then *double-click*—that is, press the *left* mouse button twice in rapid succession—to open the icon into a window.

3. Move the mouse pointer to the word **File** in the upper-left corner of the Program Manager window. Click on **File** to open the File menu, and then click on **Exit Windows....** A *dialog box* entitled *Exit Windows* appears in the middle of the screen. Click the mouse pointer once on the **OK** button within this dialog box to exit from Windows to DOS. Then skip to step 8.

4. Your computer may prompt you for the current date; if not, skip to step 6. If the date displayed is incorrect, type today's date. Use the format *mm-dd-yy* or *mm/dd/yy* (for example, 11-30-93 or 11/30/93).

5. Press **Enter** to send the date to your computer.

6. Your computer may next prompt you for the current time; if not, skip to step 8. If the time displayed is incorrect, type the current time. Use the 24-hour format *hh:mm* (for example, 10:30 for 10:30 a.m. or 22:30 for 10:30 p.m.).

7. Press **Enter** to send the time to your computer.

8. The DOS prompt will appear on a line by itself

```
C:\>
```

(Your DOS prompt may look somewhat different.)

9. Type **dir**, and then press **Enter**. The contents of the current directory are displayed, followed by a final line reporting the number of free bytes on your hard disk. If you have 600,000 or more bytes free, skip to step 10. If you have fewer than 600,000 bytes free, you may not be able to create your work directory and perform all the hands-on activities in this book. Before you proceed, you'll need to delete enough files from your hard disk to bring the free-byte total up to 600,000. If you need help doing this, please refer to your DOS documentation. **Caution:** *Be sure to back up all important files before deleting them!*

10. Remove the Data Disk from the back of this book and insert it, label up, into the appropriately sized disk drive. Then, if necessary, close the drive door or latch.

Determine whether the disk is in drive A or drive B. On a system with a single floppy disk drive, the drive is generally designated as A. On a system with two floppy disk drives, the upper or left-hand drive is generally drive A, and the lower or right-hand drive is B.

11. Type **a:** if the Data Disk is in drive A, or type **b:** if the Data Disk is in drive B. Then press **Enter** to change the current drive to the Data Disk drive.

12. Type **install c: ami-work** (be sure to leave a space between **install** and **c:** and another space between **c:** and **ami-work**). Then press **Enter** to begin the installation.

(If you wish to create your work directory on a hard drive that is not designated as drive C, substitute that hard drive's letter for the **c** in this install command. For example, to install on a drive D hard drive, you would type *install d: ami-work*.)

13. If all is well, the message

```
Installation begun.
```

appears, followed by a message about copying files. When the procedure is complete, the message

```
Installation successful!
```

appears, followed by a line reporting the name of your work directory, for example,

```
c:\ami-work
```

If you get an error message indicating that the hard drive you specified does not exist, or that the directory name you specified already exists, repeat step 12, substituting a new hard drive letter or work directory name as appropriate. For example, you might type *install d: ami-work* or *install c: a-work*.

Note: Your work-directory name can be up to eight letters long. Do not use spaces, periods, or punctuation marks, and do not use the name *amipro*, as that name is normally used by the Ami Pro program itself.

Caution: If you use another work directory name, be aware that the activities in this book will all refer to your work directory as *C:\AMI-WORK*. You'll need to remember to substitute your chosen name for the name C:\AMI-WORK as you work through the book.

14. If you have not yet installed Ami Pro using the *Complete Ami Pro Install* option in the Install Choices dialog box, work through the activities in Appendix A, "Installation," before you begin Chapter 1.

BEFORE YOU START

The activities in each of the following chapters are designed to proceed sequentially. In many cases, you cannot perform an activity until you have performed one or more of the earlier activities. For this reason, we recommend that you allot enough time to work through an entire chapter in each session.

You are now ready to begin. Good learning… and *bon voyage*!

CHAPTER 1: AMI PRO BASICS

Introduction to Windows

Introduction to Ami Pro

The Basics of Entering Text

Saving a Document

Printing a Document

Closing a Document

Creating a New Document

Exiting Ami Pro

Welcome to Ami Pro 3.0 and the exciting world of word processing! In this first chapter, we'll lead you through one complete Ami Pro work session; you'll start the Ami Pro program, create and edit a document, save and print the document, create a new document, and, finally, exit Ami Pro. This, in a nutshell, is the procedure you'll use in your daily word processing work with Ami Pro.

2 • AMI PRO BASICS

When you're done working through this chapter, you will know how to

- Start Ami Pro
- Enter text
- Delete text
- Save and name a document
- Print and close a document
- Create a new document
- Exit Ami Pro

Note: Before you can continue any further with this chapter, you must have Ami Pro 3.0 and Windows (version 3.0 or higher) already installed on your computer. For directions on installing Ami Pro 3.0, see Appendix A; for directions on installing Windows, see your Windows documentation. Finally, you need to have created a work directory on your hard disk and copied the files from the enclosed Data Disk to this directory. If you have not already done this, please do so now; follow the directions in the "Creating Your Work Directory" section of this book's Introduction.

INTRODUCTION TO WINDOWS

Because Ami Pro is a *Windows application*—that is, a program designed to run in the Microsoft Windows environment—you must start Windows before you can start Ami Pro. (You can use the terms *application* and *program* interchangeably.)

Before you start learning about Ami Pro itself, let's take a few moments to learn more about Windows. If you are already somewhat familiar with Windows, you may want to skip ahead to "Introduction to Ami Pro," later in this chapter.

Windows is a program that provides a *graphical user interface*. This is a fancy way of saying that Windows gives your computer a new face—a graphical one—that makes Windows and Windows applications more intuitive and fun to use than many DOS programs.

Windows and Windows applications operate around a set of interactive *windows*—on-screen boxes of varying sizes through which information is passed between the user (you) and the computer. Instead of having to type complex commands at your keyboard, you can give your computer the same instructions simply by using a mouse (or the keyboard, if you prefer) to manipulate the windows and elements within those windows. This enables you to spend less time telling your computer *how* you would like to work, and more time actually working.

In addition to providing a graphical user interface, Windows provides other functions that are important to effective and efficient computer use:

- It enables you to run more than one application at a time on the same computer. (This is sometimes referred to as *multitasking*.) For example, you might play a game of Solitaire while you print a letter from Ami Pro.

- It manages your computer's memory and disk storage, thus enhancing your computer's performance and extending its capabilities.

- It provides a standard way to communicate with applications. Many Windows applications have the same commands for common tasks such as saving a file and printing. This means you do not have to learn a different set of commands for each application you use.

- It supports common window elements that help standardize the way your screen appears. As you'll soon see, Windows and Windows applications look similar.

These last two functions are the most important when learning Ami Pro and other Windows applications. Because Windows helps to standardize how applications operate, you can transfer many of the procedures that you use in one Windows application to another. For example, if you already use Excel or 1-2-3 for Windows, you already have a jump start on learning Ami Pro! In addition, because Windows applications look similar, you can concentrate more on your work and less on the screen's appearance.

STARTING WINDOWS

To start Windows, you must copy the Windows program from your hard disk into the computer's memory or *RAM* (random-access memory). Windows will remain in memory as long as you continue running it or any Windows application. When you exit Windows, it will remove itself from memory, thus freeing space for non-Windows programs to use. (Note that computer memory is a temporary data-storage space. When you exit Windows, the program clears itself from computer memory but remains installed on the hard drive, ready to copy again into computer memory when needed.)

Follow these steps to start Windows:

1. Turn on your computer; an operating environment should load automatically. If you are already in Windows, you may skip the rest of this activity. If you are in DOS, continue with step 2. If you are in another operating environment (DOS Shell or GeoWorks, for example), exit to DOS and continue with step 2. For help with exiting to DOS, see your operating environment's documentation.

2. Now your computer may prompt you for the current date (if it doesn't, skip to step 4). If the date is correct, skip to step 3. If the date is incorrect, type today's date. Use the format *mm-dd-yy* or *mm/dd/yy* (for example, 10-18-93 or 10/18/93).

3. Press the **Enter** key to send the date to your computer.

4. Your computer may now prompt you for the current time (if it doesn't, skip to step 6). If the time is correct, skip to step 5. If the time is incorrect, type the current time. Use the 24-hour format *hh:mm* (for example, 10:30 for 10:30 a.m. or 22:30 for 10:30 p.m.).

5. Press **Enter** to set the computer's internal clock.

6. Type **win** and then press **Enter** to start Windows.

7. Examine the screen. An hourglass may appear momentarily, indicating that the computer has not yet finished with the task of starting Windows. Once Windows is running, the hourglass disappears and you will see the *Program Manager window*. You can recognize this window by its *title bar*, located along the top of the window; it reads *Program Manager*. If you don't see a window entitled Program Manager, continue with step 8; otherwise, skip the rest of this activity.

8. Look for a small picture, or *icon*, with *Program Manager* beneath it. Use your mouse to move the tip of the on-screen *mouse pointer*, which appears as a left-pointing arrow, over the icon. Then, *double-click*—that is, press and release the left mouse button twice in rapid succession—to open the

icon into a window. If you do not double-click quickly enough, a *menu* may appear above the icon. If this happens, *click*—that is, press and release the left mouse button just once—on the word **Restore**. (From here on, when we say "click" or "double-click," we mean that you should use the *left* mouse button. If we want you to click or double-click with the right mouse button, we'll tell you that.)

THE PROGRAM MANAGER WINDOW

The Program Manager window serves as a command center, enabling you to start an application from within the window by double-clicking on the application's *program icon*. Because Windows is a *customizable* program, its screen appearance and overall setup upon startup can vary significantly from computer to computer. For this reason, we at PC Learning Labs cannot know exactly how your screen now appears. If your screen differs somewhat from Figure 1.1, don't worry. As long as the Program Manager window is open, you most likely will be able to start Ami Pro.

Figure 1.1 labels many of the elements of the Program Manager window. Table 1.1 defines the elements that are common to many windows, and Table 1.2 defines the elements that are specific to the Program Manager window. Your screen may contain some or all of these elements and may display elements not shown in Figure 1.1. Again, don't worry if your screen does not match the figure exactly. We're just familiarizing you with many of the window elements that you'll see when working in the Windows environment.

Table 1.1 **Common Window Elements**

Element	Location	Definition
Control menu box	Upper-left corner of a window	Controls the size and position of the window, and enables you to close the window.

Table 1.1 **Common Window Elements (Continued)**

Element	Location	Definition
Title bar	Across the top of a window	Displays the name of the window; at times, it may display additional information.
Maximize button	Upper-right corner of a window	Expands the window to its largest possible size; when the window is maximized, the button changes to a Restore button, which you can use to restore the window to its previous (unmaximized) size.
Minimize button	To the left of the Maximize or Restore button	Shrinks the window to an icon.
Menu bar	Below the title bar	Lists the window's *menu options* (*File*, *Options*, *Window*, and *Help* in the Program Manager window).

Table 1.2 **Window Elements Specific to the Program Manager**

Element	Location	Definition
Program group	Inside the Program Manager window	A window that holds a set of related program icons.
Program icon	Inside a program group window	Enables you to start a program.
Program group icon	Usually at the bottom of the Program Manager window	Opens into a program group window when double-clicked.

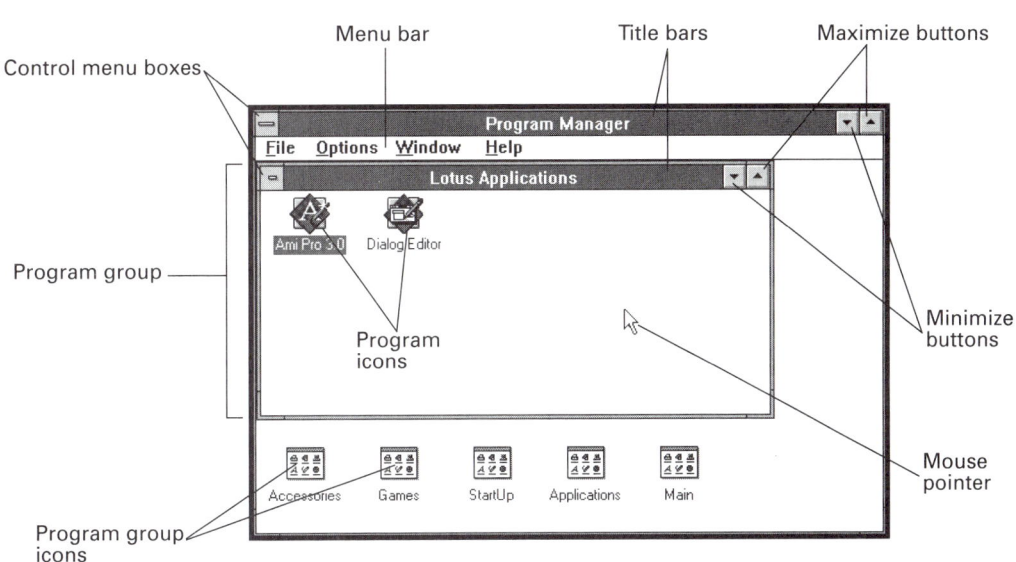

Figure 1.1   **The Program Manager window**

[Figure: The Program Manager window with labels pointing to: Control menu boxes, Menu bar, Title bars, Maximize buttons, Minimize buttons, Mouse pointer, Program icons, Program group, Program group icons. Menu items: File, Options, Window, Help. Window title: Lotus Applications. Icons: Ami Pro 3.0, Dialog Editor, Accessories, Games, StartUp, Applications, Main.]

INTRODUCTION TO AMI PRO

Now that you've learned a little about Windows, you are ready to get started in Ami Pro.

A word processor such as Ami Pro is an application that enables you to create, edit, print, and save documents for future retrieval and revision. You enter text into the computer using a keyboard. As you type, your computer displays your words on a screen, or *monitor*, and stores them in memory or on a disk instead of on paper.

One of the chief advantages of a word processor over a conventional typewriter is that a word processor enables you to make changes to a document without retyping the entire document. For example, you can create a letter in a word processor and then, after you are finished, go back and change margins, add sentences, delete words, move paragraphs, correct spelling errors, and so on. You can do all of this without retyping the original text.

STARTING AMI PRO

To start Ami Pro from the Program Manager window, you must locate the Ami Pro 3.0 program icon, and then double-click on it. The steps below will help you search for this icon. (We cannot know how your version of Windows is set up, so some of these instructions may not apply to you.)

1. In the Program Manager window, look for an icon entitled *Ami Pro 3.0* (refer to Figure 1.1 for the appearance of this icon). If you see this icon on your screen, skip ahead to step 4. If you cannot see the icon, continue with step 2.

2. Windows stores program icons in program groups. Within the Program Manager window, program groups can appear as program group icons (*Accessories, Games, StartUp, Applications,* and *Main* in Figure 1.1) or as windows (*Lotus Applications* in Figure 1.1). By default, Windows stores the Ami Pro 3.0 program icon in a program group called *Lotus Applications* (because Ami Pro is a product of the Lotus Development Corporation). If you see a program group icon with this title, double-click on the icon to open it into a window. If the window contains the Ami Pro 3.0 program icon, skip to step 4.

3. If you do not have a Lotus Applications program group icon, or if the Lotus Applications program group does not contain the Ami Pro 3.0 program icon, you will have to search for the icon in the other program groups. Start by opening program groups that are likely to hold the Ami Pro 3.0 program icon, such as *Applications* or *Windows Applications,* and then continue on to less-likely groups. Once you've found the icon, skip to step 4. If you cannot find the icon, there is a good chance that Ami Pro is not properly installed on your computer. In this case, refer to Appendix A for information on installing Ami Pro, and then return to step 1 of this activity.

4. Double-click on the **Ami Pro 3.0 program icon** to load Ami Pro into memory.

5. If this is the first time you've started Ami Pro after installing it, Ami Pro may display the message *Loading QuickStart Tutorial* followed by *Welcome to the Ami Pro QuickStart Tutorial*. This tutorial is designed to give you a quick overview of Ami Pro. Because you'll be using this book to learn Ami Pro in depth, click on **Exit Tutorial**. Your screen should now display a window entitled *Ami Pro - [Untitled]*.

INTRODUCTION TO AMI PRO • 9

SETTING AMI PRO'S DEFAULTS

Ami Pro, like Windows, is a user-customizable program. If you have already used Ami Pro after installing it on your computer, or if Ami Pro was installed on your computer previously, some of Ami Pro's basic settings, called *defaults*, may have been changed, and Ami Pro may behave in a manner that we at PC Learning Labs cannot anticipate. To help ensure that your version of Ami Pro will operate as described in this book, please perform the following steps.

Note: In order to walk you through these steps, we have to "jump the gun" and use some procedures without explaining their purpose. Please bear with us; you will learn more about these procedures later in this book.

1. In the menu bar near the top of your screen, click on the word **View**. (Take care to use the very tip of your mouse pointer when clicking. Otherwise, you may inadvertently click on one of the icons located directly below the menu bar.) The View menu opens. If your View menu *exactly* matches the one shown in Figure 1.2, skip to step 5.

Figure 1.2 **The View menu with appropriate settings**

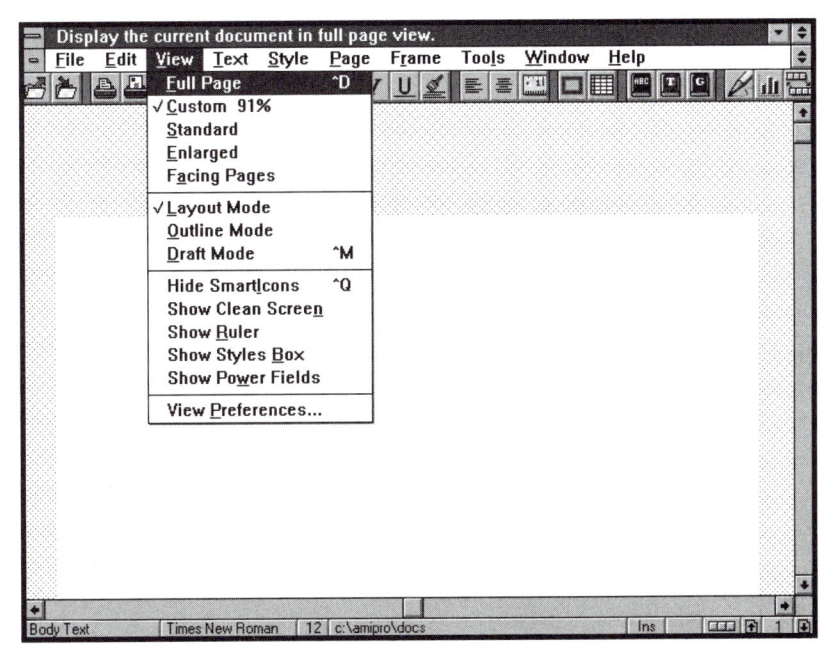

2. If there is a check mark next to *Custom*, skip to step 3. (If the number next to *Custom* is a number other than *91%,* don't worry; you'll learn how to change that in a moment.) If there is no check mark, click on **Custom**. The View menu closes. Click on **View** again to reopen the menu; a check mark now appears next to *Custom*.

3. If there is no check mark next to *Layout Mode,* click on **Layout Mode**. Then reopen the View menu (click on **View**).

4. The group of five *menu items* near the bottom of the View menu should read *Hide SmartIcons*, *Show Clean Screen*, *Show Ruler*, *Show Styles Box*, and *Show Power Fields*, as shown in Figure 1.2. If they do not, click on the appropriate menu item or items, reopening the View menu after each click, until the menu items match Figure 1.2. For example, if the first menu item in the group reads *Show SmartIcons,* you would click on that item to change the menu item to *Hide SmartIcons.*

5. With the View menu open, click on **View Preferences…** to open the View Preferences *dialog box*. Dialog boxes prompt you to enter information relating to the selected command (View, View Preferences in this case). You will work extensively with dialog boxes during the course of this book. Compare your dialog box to the one in Figure 1.3. If they exactly match, skip to step 8.

Figure 1.3 **The View Preferences dialog box with appropriate settings**

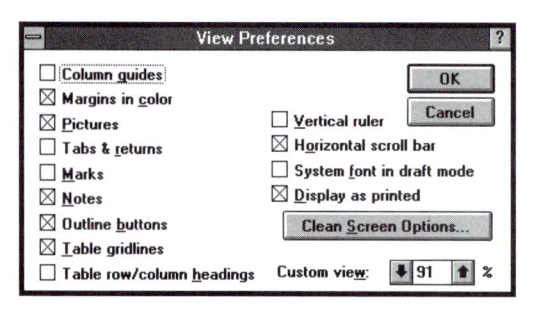

INTRODUCTION TO AMI PRO • 11

6. The View Preferences dialog box contains a number of options that are preceded by *check boxes*. For each option that does not match Figure 1.3, click inside the option's check box to add or remove an X as appropriate. The X means the option is turned on.

7. Observe the Custom View box. If it is not set to *91,* click on the box's **down increment arrow** (to the left of the box) or **up increment arrow** (to the right of the box) until the number is **91**.

8. Click on the **OK** button to close the View Preferences dialog box.

9. Open the **View** menu one more time. It should now exactly match the one shown in Figure 1.2. Click on **View** again to close the menu.

10. In the menu bar, click on **Tools** to open the Tools menu, and then click on **User Setup...** to open the User Setup dialog box. Compare your dialog box to the one shown in Figure 1.4. If the two match exactly (except for the information in the Name and Initials text boxes), skip to step 14.

Figure 1.4   **The User Setup dialog box with appropriate settings**

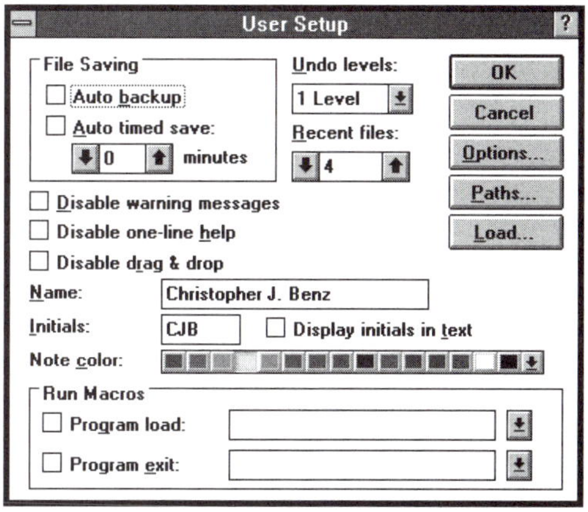

11. Observe the Undo Levels *drop-down list box*. If it is set to any option other than Off, skip to step 12. Otherwise, click on the box's **drop-down list arrow** (located to the right of the box) to open the box's *drop-down list*, and then click on **1 Level**.

12. Observe the Recent Files box. If it is not set to 4, use the box's **increment arrows** to change the number to **4**.

13. Observe the three check-box options *Disable Warning Messages, Disable One-Line Help,* and *Disable Drag & Drop*. If any of these options is checked, click in its check box to uncheck it.

14. Click on the **Load...** button to open the Load Defaults dialog box. If your dialog box exactly matches the one in Figure 1.5, click on **OK** to close the Load Defaults dialog box and return to the User Setup dialog box. Otherwise, use the skills you've already learned in this activity to change your current settings to match the figure, and then click on **OK**.

15. Click on **OK** one more time to close the User Setup dialog box.

Figure 1.5   **The Load Defaults dialog box with appropriate settings**

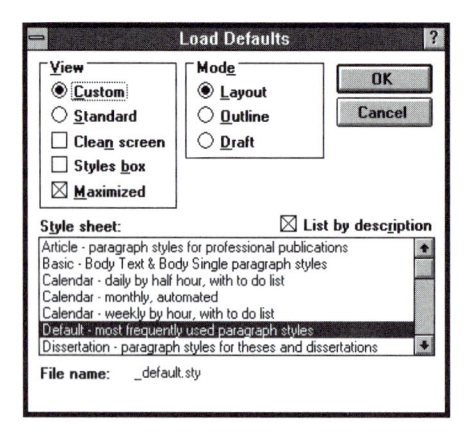

THE AMI PRO APPLICATION AND DOCUMENT WINDOWS

When you start Ami Pro, two windows appear on the screen, one within the other. The larger of these, called the *application window*, usually fills the entire screen; you use it to communicate with Ami Pro. The smaller window, called the *document window*, usually fits seamlessly within the application window; you use it to create and edit your Ami Pro documents.

Note that the two Ami Pro windows contain many of the elements that you've already seen in the Program Manager window: a title bar (it currently displays *Ami Pro - [Untitled]*); Control menu boxes (the one on top is for the application window, and the one below is for the document window); a Minimize box; and a menu bar.

Figure 1.6 illustrates many elements of the Ami Pro windows that you have not already seen; Table 1.3 defines these elements.

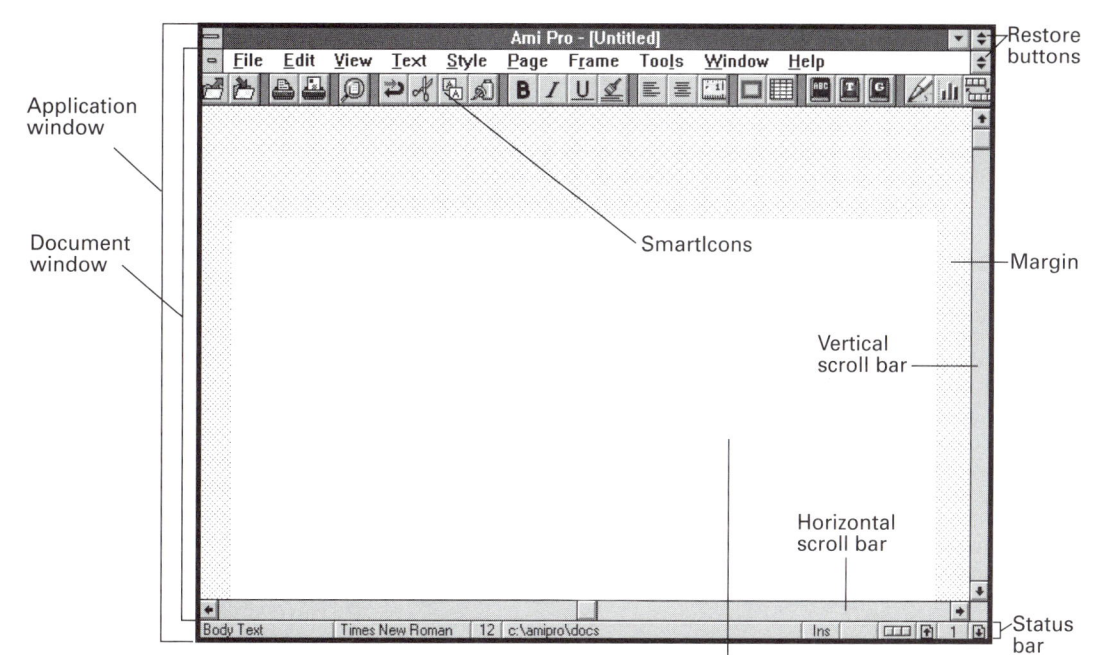

Figure 1.6   Ami Pro windows and window elements

Table 1.3 **Ami Pro Window Elements**

Term	Location	Definition
Application window	Usually fills entire screen	The larger of the two start-up windows; it provides an interface between you and Ami Pro.
Document window	Within the application window	The smaller of the two start-up windows; it holds the active Ami Pro document.
Restore buttons	Upper-right corner of screen	These control the size of the application window (upper button) and document window (lower button).
SmartIcons	Below menu bar	These provide quick access to some of Ami Pro's most frequently used commands.
Typing area	Inside document window	Provides an area for you to type text.
Margins	Around typing area	These represent the space between the typing area and the edge of the printed page.
Vertical and horizontal scroll bars	Along right side (vertical) and bottom (horizontal) of document window	Used to display various areas of a document.
Status bar	Along bottom of application window	Its buttons display a variety of information and enable you to perform various tasks; you'll learn more about these buttons throughout this book.

Let's take a closer look at some of these screen elements. (We will discuss the remaining elements in detail over the next few chapters.)

1. Click on the application window's **Control menu box** (the upper of the two Control menu boxes) to open the application's Control menu; *do not* double-click, as this will cause you to exit Ami Pro. Notice the Control menu items: *Restore*, *Move*, *Size*, *Minimize*, and so on. Click on the **Control menu box** again to close the menu.

2. Click on the document window's **Control menu box** (the lower of the two Control menu boxes). Observe that the Control menu items for the document window are similar to those for the application window. Click on the **Control menu box** again to close the menu.

3. Click on the application window's **Restore button** (the upper of the two Restore buttons). The application window shrinks (is *restored*) to a smaller size. Notice that the Restore button has now changed to a Maximize button; it displays a single up-pointing triangle rather than both up- and down-pointing triangles (see Figure 1.7).

4. Click on the application window's **Maximize button** to maximize the application window. The window once again fills the screen, and the Maximize button changes back to a Restore button.

5. Repeat steps 3 and 4, substituting the document window's Maximize and Restore buttons for the application window's Maximize and Restore buttons. Observe that when you click on the document window's Restore button, the button moves to the upper-right corner of the restored document window and becomes a Maximize button; this is the button you click on to maximize the document window (see Figure 1.7). Notice, also, that when you restore the document window, it gets its own title bar; when you maximize the document window, it shares the application window's title bar. (Leave both the application and document windows maximized for the remainder of this book.)

Figure 1.7   **Ami Pro's application and document windows, unmaximized**

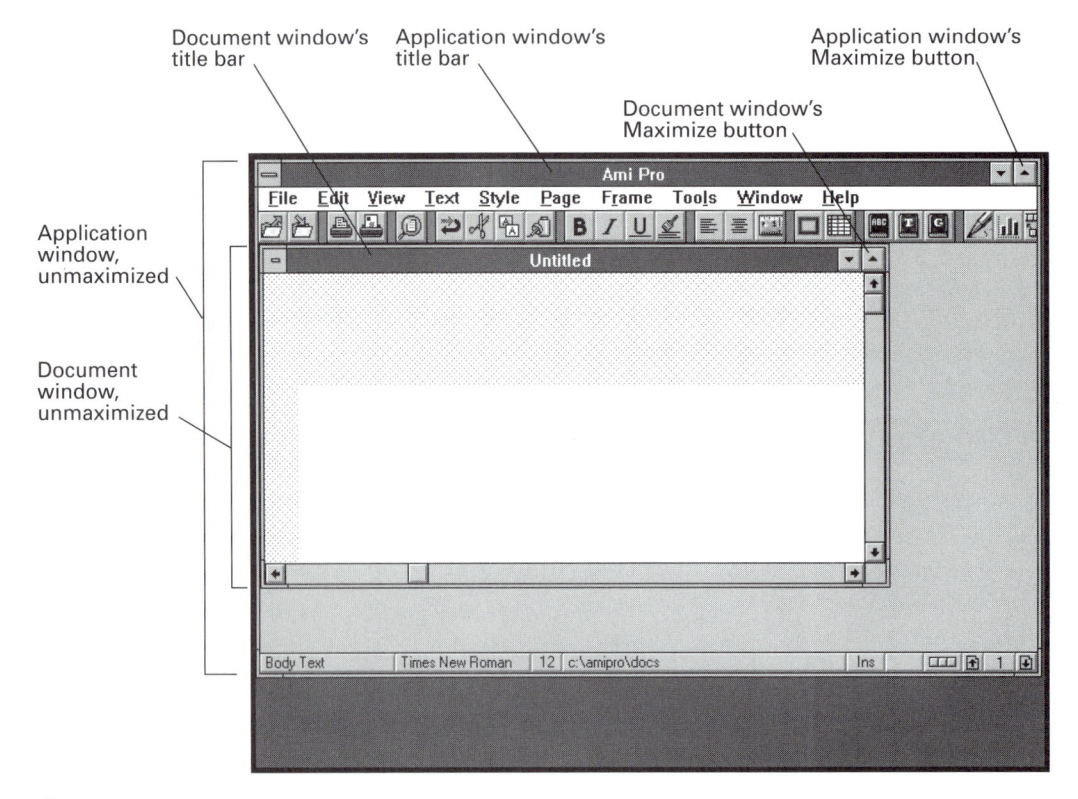

(Labels on figure: Document window's title bar; Application window's title bar; Document window's Maximize button; Application window's Maximize button; Application window, unmaximized; Document window, unmaximized)

ISSUING COMMANDS THROUGH THE MENU BAR

In order to perform your daily word processing tasks (such as saving a document, setting new margins, and so on), you must issue the appropriate Ami Pro commands. Because of Ami Pro's flexibility, you can issue commands through a variety of mouse and keyboard methods. However, the menu bar is the only method that enables you to issue *every* available Ami Pro command. For this reason, any time we teach you a new command, we'll show you how to issue the command through the menu bar. After you've learned the menu bar technique, we'll often show you alternate methods. (In addition, Appendix B provides a list of keyboard shortcuts for techniques covered in this book.)

INTRODUCTION TO AMI PRO • 17

You already learned the basics of issuing commands through the menu bar (in the previous section, "Setting Ami Pro's Defaults"). Let's practice using the menu bar now to explore Ami Pro's menus and to learn more about how they operate:

1. Move the tip of the mouse pointer to the **File** menu option, and then press and hold down the **left mouse button**. (Do not release this button until you're told to in step 4.) The File menu opens, displaying a set of file-related menu items: *New*, *Open*, *Close*, *Save*, *Save As...*, and so on.

2. Observe the text in the title bar. Ami Pro displays a *one-line Help message* describing the File menu option's function: *Display File menu items*.

3. Without releasing the button, *drag* the mouse pointer down to highlight **Save As**.... (You'll learn more about dragging in Chapter 3.) When you *highlight* an item in Ami Pro, the item is displayed in *reverse video*; that is, the words change from dark on light to light on dark. The title bar now displays a one-line Help message for the File, Save As... command.

4. Release the mouse button to open the Save As dialog box.

5. Click on the dialog box's **Cancel** button to close the dialog box. Whenever you inadvertently open a dialog box, you can click on Cancel to close the dialog box without affecting any settings.

6. Click on **Edit**. The Edit menu opens, displaying Ami Pro's editing commands. Note that, to open a menu, you can either press and hold the mouse button (as you did in steps 1 through 4), or press and release (click) the mouse button.

7. Observe that Ami Pro has dimmed several Edit commands (*Undo*, *Cut*, *Copy*, *Paste*, and so on). Ami Pro dims menu items to show that they are unavailable in the current context. For example, the Undo menu item is dimmed because you have not yet performed any actions that the Undo menu item can undo. (You'll learn about Undo in Chapter 3.)

8. Observe that an ellipsis (...) follows several Edit menu items (*Link Options...*, *Find & Replace...*, *Go To...*, and so on). Ami Pro adds an ellipsis to menu items that, when clicked on, open dialog boxes. To keep this book easy to read, from this point on we will no longer use the ellipsis when referring to these types of menu items. For example, we will ask you to

"Click on *Go To*," even though *Go To...* is how the item actually appears on your screen.

9. Click on **View** to open the View menu. Notice that the Edit menu closes automatically when you open the View menu.

PRACTICE YOUR SKILLS

1. Use the menu bar to examine the rest of Ami Pro's menus, being careful not to select any menu items.
2. Close any open menu.

THE BASICS OF ENTERING TEXT

Ami Pro is a WYSIWYG (What-You-See-Is-What-You-Get) word processor; the screen closely approximates how your document will look when you print it. Many computer users prefer WYSIWYG word processors because they eliminate the arcane codes and unpredictable page layouts that characterize non-WYSIWYG word processors. Ami Pro's WYSIWYG feature encourages you to work in a "visually intuitive" style, in which you treat the word processor as a computerized extension of a typewriter.

In the next several sections, we'll discuss the basics of entering text into an Ami Pro document.

THE TYPING AREA

When you start Ami Pro, a new document window automatically opens, providing you with a blank typing area. Ami Pro provides default settings for the margins, page size, line spacing, and several other document characteristics. Because of these default settings, you can begin to type immediately, without having to first specify any of these settings yourself.

As you type, you insert characters in front of a blinking vertical bar called the *insertion point*. To move the insertion point to a different location, you simply click the mouse pointer at the desired place in the text.

THE BASICS OF ENTERING TEXT • 19

Let's examine Ami Pro's typing area:

1. Observe the insertion point (see Figure 1.8). Its location determines where you will insert the next character you type. Note that the insertion point of a new, blank document appears in the upper-left corner (that is, at the beginning) of the typing area.

Figure 1.8 **The typing area with the insertion point and I-beam**

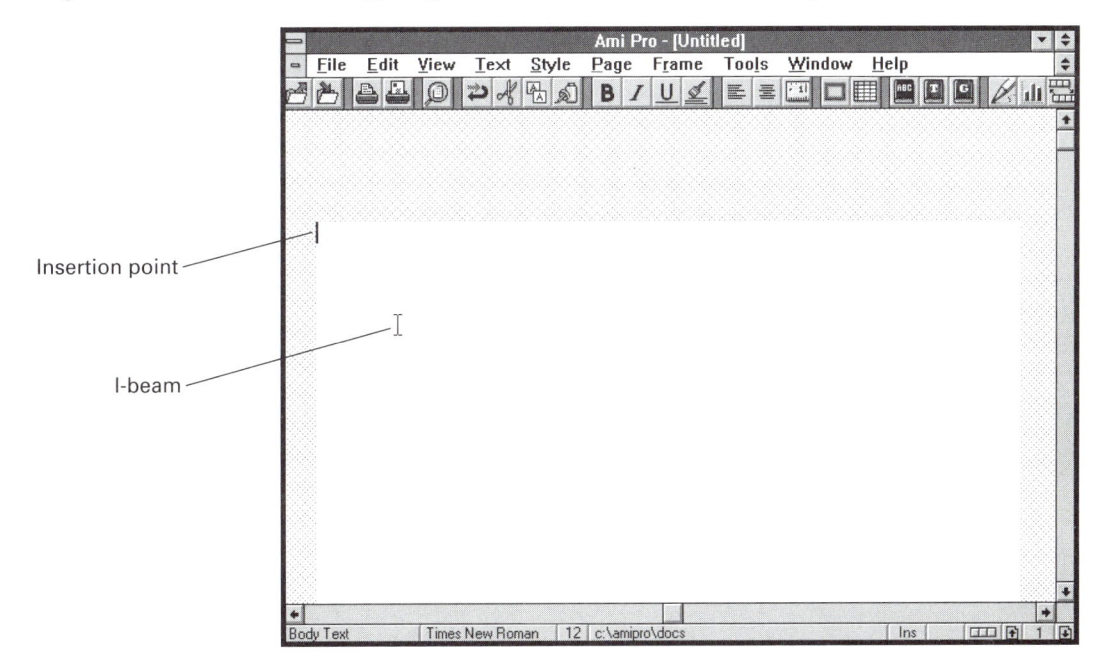

Insertion point

I-beam

2. Watch the mouse pointer as you move it around your screen. Whenever it is within the document window, the pointer changes to an *I-beam*. When you move it outside the document window, it turns back into a left-pointing arrow.

WORD WRAP AND THE ENTER KEY

The Enter key on your computer's keyboard works similarly to the Return key on a typewriter. There is an important difference, however: When using a typewriter, you need to press the Return key whenever you want to end a line; when you run out of room on a line in word processing, the last word in the line automatically drops to the beginning of the next line. This feature is called *word wrap*.

You do need, however, to use the Enter key to

- End a short line (one that does not extend to the right margin)
- End a paragraph
- Create a blank line

Let's type some text in the new document window and practice using the Enter key. (We will demonstrate word wrap later in this chapter under "Deleting Text with the Backspace Key.")

1. Type **Nancy Wright** to enter these characters at the insertion point, and then press **Enter** to end the line. Notice that the insertion point moves down and to the beginning of the next line.
2. Type **3325 Fillmore Avenue**, and then press **Enter**.
3. Type **North Hills, NY 14052**, and then press **Enter**.
4. Press **Enter** again to create a blank line.
5. Type **Dear Nancy:**, and then press **Enter** twice to end the line and create one blank line. Your screen should now match Figure 1.9.

USING TABS TO ALIGN TEXT

In word processing, *tabs* enable you to align text vertically. These two lines are properly aligned:

```
Line 1 ....
Line 2 ....
```

These two are not:

```
Line 1 ....
 Line 2 ....
```

Tabs are fixed horizontal positions within a line, and pressing the Tab key moves the insertion point to the next tab position to the right. By default, Ami Pro's tabs are set at ½" increments, so pressing Tab once moves the insertion point ½" to the right; pressing Tab again moves it another ½", for a total of 1" (½" + ½"); and so on.

THE BASICS OF ENTERING TEXT • 21

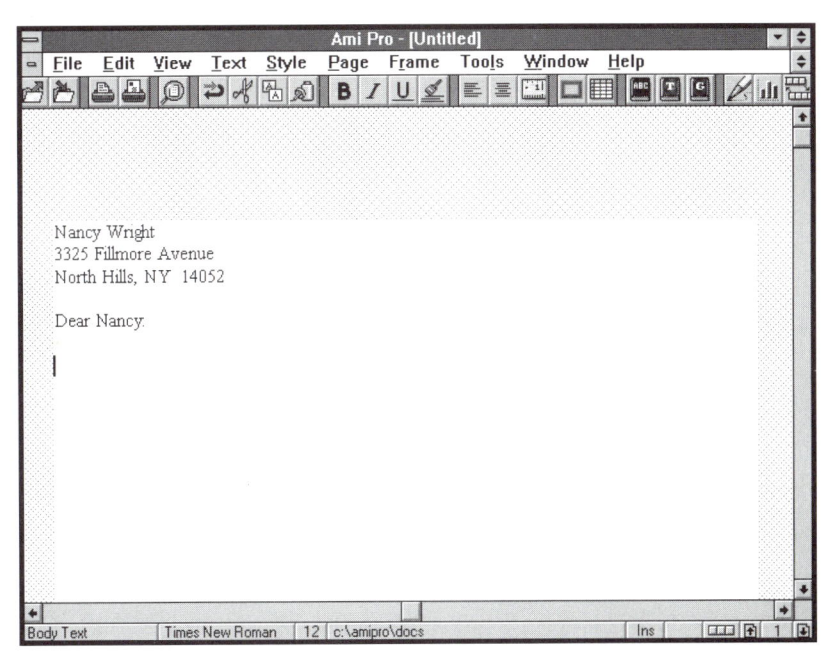

Figure 1.9 **Text typed in a document**

```
Ami Pro - [Untitled]
File  Edit  View  Text  Style  Page  Frame  Tools  Window  Help

Nancy Wright
3325 Fillmore Avenue
North Hills, NY  14052

Dear Nancy:
|

Body Text    Times New Roman   12  c:\amipro\docs            Ins          1
```

We created the properly aligned example shown just above by pressing Tab once at the beginning of each line. We created the improperly aligned example by using the Spacebar to insert blank spaces at the beginning of each line. When working in a WYSIWYG word processor, try not to align text using the Spacebar; it probably won't work.

DELETING TEXT WITH THE BACKSPACE KEY

You can use the Backspace key to delete text one character at a time. When you press Backspace, you delete the single character immediately to the left of the insertion point.

Let's experiment with Ami Pro's Tab, Backspace, and word-wrap features:

1. Press **Tab** to insert a *tab character* at the beginning of the line. This moves the insertion point to the first tab, ½" to the right. (Note that the tab character you have just inserted is invisible. You'll learn how to display it in the next activity.)

2. Press **Tab** again to insert a second tab character. This moves the insertion point to the second tab, 1" from the left margin.

3. Press **Backspace** to remove the second tab character.

4. Type **I have been happy with the service provided by Global Travel**. (Include the period.) Then, press the **Spacebar** to insert a space before the next sentence.

5. Type **I would like additional information**, and then examine the screen. Notice that the word *information* has automatically wrapped to the next line, even though you did not press Enter. This is an example of word wrap. (If you have not set up Windows and Ami Pro to use a PostScript printer, your text may wrap at a different word.)

6. Type **about your program.** (Include the period.) Then press **Enter** twice to end the paragraph and add one blank line to your document.

DISPLAYING NONPRINTING SYMBOLS

If you want, you can have Ami Pro display special symbols on the screen that show the places in the text where you press the Enter and Tab keys. These *nonprinting symbols* (so called because they do not appear on paper when you print the document) are often useful to see. This is particularly true when you are working with heavily formatted documents and need to keep track of your tabs, blank lines, and so on.

To control the display of Ami Pro's nonprinting symbols, you can use the View, View Preferences command. (You already used this command in the earlier section, "Setting Ami Pro's Defaults.")

Let's display some of the nonprinting symbols contained in your document so that you can see on screen where you have pressed the Enter and Tab keys:

1. Examine the first four lines of your document. The lines are short, not reaching the right margin, but there are no symbols marking the ends of these lines.

2. Examine the first line of the paragraph beginning *I have been*. The first word starts ½" in from the left margin, but you cannot see any symbol for the tab character that you inserted there.

THE BASICS OF ENTERING TEXT • 23

3. Choose **View, View Preferences** (that is, open the **View** menu, and then click on the **View Preferences** menu item) to open the View Preferences dialog box.

4. Examine the dialog box. The check boxes on the left side of this dialog box control which nonprinting symbols will display on screen and which ones will not.

5. Check **Tabs & Returns**, and then click on **OK**.

6. Observe your screen. Ami Pro now displays a *return symbol* (¶) at each point where you pressed Enter in the document. Where you pressed the Tab key, Ami Pro now displays a *tab symbol* (·····>) to represent the tab character you inserted (see Figure 1.10). Remember—these nonprinting symbols only appear on the screen; they will not appear on your printed document.

Figure 1.10   **The completed letter displaying tab and return symbols**

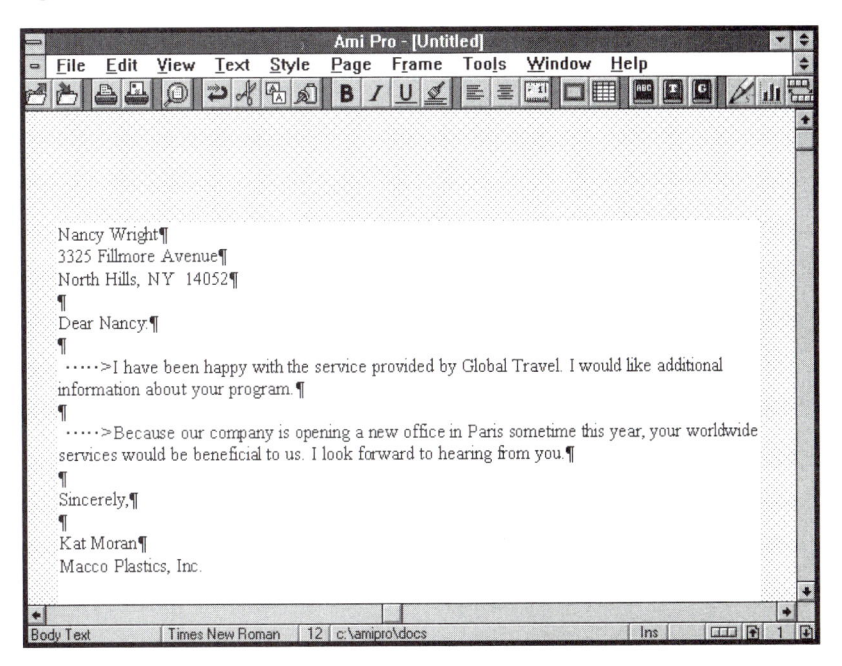

PRACTICE YOUR SKILLS

Complete your document as shown in Figure 1.10. Use **Backspace** to correct any typing mistakes you make.

SAVING A DOCUMENT

Before you save it, a document exists only in computer memory, a temporary storage area. For permanent storage, you must save the document to a permanent storage device, such as a hard or floppy disk. Ami Pro provides two commands you can use to save documents: File, Save As and File, Save.

THE FILE, SAVE AS COMMAND

There are three situations in which you should use the File, Save As command:

- When you are saving a document for the first time
- When you are saving a document with a new name
- When you are saving a document to a new location (on a different disk, for example)

Follow these steps when you want to save a document using the File, Save As command:

- Choose File, Save As to open the Save As dialog box.

- In the File Name *text box,* type a name for your document. (Because Ami Pro documents are a type of computer file, you use the File Name text box to name your Ami Pro documents.)

- If the appropriate disk drive is not already selected, use the Drives drop-down list box to select the drive onto which you want to save your document.

- If the appropriate disk-drive directory is not already selected, use the Directories list box to choose the *directory* or *subdirectory* into which you want to save your document. (Computer disks are arranged much like filing cabinets, with directories acting as hanging file folders that each hold a group of files. Subdirectories are a type of directory that act as file folders within file folders; they let you subdivide your files within a directory.)

- If desired, type a document description in the Document Description text box.
- Click on OK.

When you save a document, Ami Pro adds the .SAM *file name extension* to identify the file as an Ami Pro document file.

Note: Your hard disk and floppy disks can hold many types of files, such as .EXE program files, .WK3 spreadsheet files, .DBF database files, and so on. In order to help your computer understand which files belong to which programs, do not add file name extensions yourself; let Ami Pro do it for you automatically.

THE FILE, SAVE COMMAND

After you have saved a document once, you can use the File, Save command (instead of File, Save As) to save the document again with its current name and in its current location. File, Save simply updates the disk version of your document by replacing the last-saved version of the document with the version of the document that is currently stored in computer memory and displayed on your screen.

For example, let's say you have used File, Save As to save a business report to your reports directory as JAN-REPT, and then you go back and revise the report by adding an extra closing paragraph. If you then choose File, Save, the new report version (with the extra paragraph) will replace the last-saved version (no extra paragraph) on the disk.

Once you've used File, Save As to name and save a document, you should generally use File, Save for all subsequent updates of that document. However, if you later want to rename it or save it in a different location, you can use File, Save As.

Note: It's very important to save your active documents frequently. That way, if something happens to your computer's memory (for example, a power failure, which erases the contents of RAM), you will have a recent copy of your document safe on a disk. This precaution will keep retyping tasks to a minimum.

General rules for saving are as follows:

- Save at least once every 15 minutes.
- Save before printing.

- Save before using Ami Pro's spelling checker (which you'll learn about in Chapter 7).

NAMING A DOCUMENT

When you save a document for the first time, you must name it. These are the general guidelines for naming documents (or any file on an IBM-compatible computer, for that matter):

- A file name can contain from one to eight letters or numbers (not counting the .SAM file name extension, which Ami Pro supplies automatically).

- A file name can also contain some special characters, including hyphens and underscores, but you cannot use periods (.), slashes (/), square brackets ([and]), semicolons (;), equal signs (=), double quotation marks ("), backslashes (\), colons (:), vertical bars (|), and commas (,).

- A file name cannot contain spaces.

- A file name should be descriptive, so that you can remember the file's contents (for example, JAN-REPT rather than X117-A).

Let's save and name your document in the directory you created in the "Creating Your Work Directory" section of this book's Introduction. (If you named your work directory something other than C:\AMI-WORK, the following steps may not work exactly as described. You will need to substitute your own work directory's name for C:\AMI-WORK.)

1. Choose **File, Save As** to open the Save As dialog box.

2. Observe the File Name text box. It currently contains the highlighted, or *selected,* file name extension, *.SAM.*

3. Type **myfirst** to replace the selected text. (Letter case is not important when you are typing file names.)

4. Observe the Directory line directly beneath the File Name text box. By default, Ami Pro sets it to *c:\amipro\docs,* meaning that if you clicked on OK now, you would save your document on the C drive, in the DOCS subdirectory of the AMIPRO directory. (If your Directory line displays something other than *c:\amipro\docs,* don't worry; we'll get you set up properly in a moment.) Returning to our filing-cabinet analogy, C is the filing cabinet, AMIPRO is a hanging file folder within

that cabinet, and DOCS is a file folder within the AMIPRO hanging file folder.

5. Observe the Drives drop-down list box. It is set to the drive specified in the Directory line. (If you specified a different drive for your work directory, click on the drop-down list box's **drop-down list arrow** to open the list, and then select the appropriate drive letter. If the drive letter you want is not visible, use the **Up Arrow** and/or **Down Arrow keys** on your keyboard to select the appropriate drive, and then click again on the box's **drop-down list arrow** to close the drop-down list.)

6. Observe the Directories list box. It contains a single item, *[..]*, which represents the directory *above* the DOCS subdirectory. Double-click on [..] to move up to the AMIPRO directory. The list box now lists another *[..]*, plus the other subdirectories under the AMIPRO directory: *[drawsym]*, *[icons]*, *[macros]*, and *[styles]*.

7. Observe the Directory line. It confirms that you've moved up one level to the AMIPRO directory.

8. In the Directories list box, double-click on [..] to move up another directory level. The Directory line changes to *c:*, indicating that you are at the highest directory level of your C drive. (If you created your work directory on a drive other than C, double click on [..] until the Directory line shows no directories. For example, if you created your work directory on your D drive, double-click on [..] until your Directory line reads *d:*.) The Directory list box now lists every first-level directory on your selected disk.

9. In the Directories list box, double-click on **[ami-work]** to move down one level into your work directory.

10. Position the mouse pointer inside the Document Description text box (the pointer changes to an I-beam), and click once to place the insertion point. Then type **This is my first document**. (Document descriptions are optional when saving a document. In Chapter 2, however, you'll learn how they can be useful when retrieving saved documents.) Your dialog box should now resemble Figure 1.11.

11. Click on **OK** to save your document. Ami Pro closes the Save As dialog box.

28 • AMI PRO BASICS

Figure 1.11 **Saving a document for the first time**

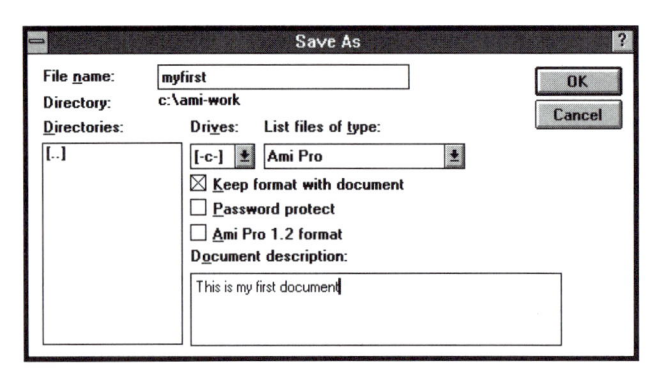

[Save As dialog box showing File name: myfirst, Directory: c:\ami-work, Drives: [-c-], List files of type: Ami Pro, Keep format with document checked, Password protect unchecked, Ami Pro 1.2 format unchecked, Document description: This is my first document]

12. Observe the title bar. It now displays your document's name, *MYFIRST.SAM*, rather than *Untitled*. (Notice that Ami Pro has added the .SAM file name extension automatically.)

PRINTING A DOCUMENT

Once you've completed and saved a document, you can then print it on paper. By default, Ami Pro is set up to print one copy of the entire active (current) document. You can also choose to print multiple copies, the current page only, a specific range of pages, just the even-numbered pages (2, 4, 6, and so on), or just the odd-numbered pages (1, 3, 5, and so on).

Follow these steps when you want to print one copy of the entire active document:

- Choose File, Print to open the Print dialog box.
- Click on OK.

Let's print your document:

1. Choose **File, Print** to open the Print dialog box shown in Figure 1.12. (Because Ami Pro uses your Windows default printer, your dialog box may not match Figure 1.12 exactly.)

2. Click on **OK**. (Or, if you do not have a printer, click on Cancel to close the dialog box without printing.) Compare your printout with Figure 1.13. Depending on the printer you are using, your printout may vary slightly from the one pictured.

Figure 1.12 **The Print dialog box**

Figure 1.13 **The printed document**

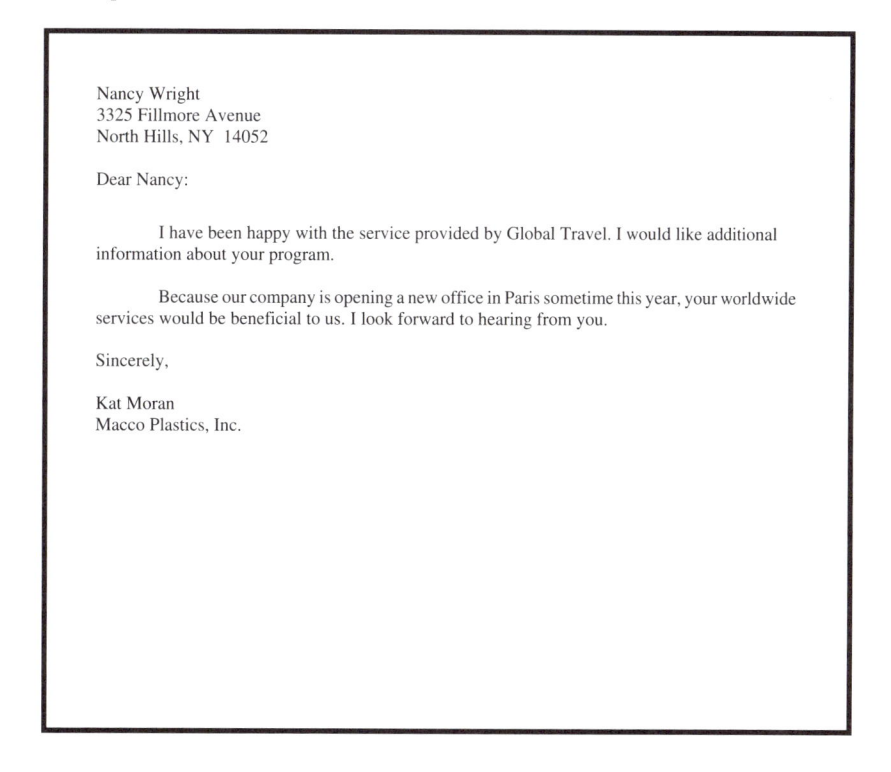

> Nancy Wright
> 3325 Fillmore Avenue
> North Hills, NY 14052
>
> Dear Nancy:
>
> I have been happy with the service provided by Global Travel. I would like additional information about your program.
>
> Because our company is opening a new office in Paris sometime this year, your worldwide services would be beneficial to us. I look forward to hearing from you.
>
> Sincerely,
>
> Kat Moran
> Macco Plastics, Inc.

3. If your document failed to print in step 2, refer to your printer and Windows documentation for information on setting up your printer properly. Do not attempt to issue the

File, Print command again; unless you are familiar with Windows, you may not be able to print any documents from Ami Pro until you exit and restart both Windows and Ami Pro.

CLOSING A DOCUMENT

When you're finished working with a document—that is, after you've completed, saved, and (if desired) printed it—you should close the document's window. To do this, you can either choose File, Close or double-click on the document window's Control menu box.

Let's close MYFIRST.SAM:

1. Choose **File, Close** to close the document window and remove the document from computer memory. (Remember, because you used File, Save earlier, a copy of the document is still stored safely in your work directory.)

2. Examine the screen. Ami Pro remains loaded, but no document window is open. The title bar displays only *Ami Pro*, the scroll bars have disappeared, and the status bar is almost completely blank.

CREATING A NEW DOCUMENT

Once you've completed a document and closed its document window, you're ready to create a new document. To do this, you need to:

- Choose File, New to open the New dialog box.
- Click on OK.

Let's practice these steps to create a new document:

1. Choose **File, New** to open the New dialog box.
2. Click on **OK**. Ami Pro opens a new, blank document window.
3. Type **This is my second document**.
4. Choose **File, Save As** to open the Save As dialog box.
5. In the File Name text box, type **mysecond** to name the document. Note that Ami Pro still displays your work directory on the Directory line; Ami Pro remembered it from the last time you saved a document.
6. Click on **OK**.

7. Double-click on your new document window's **Control menu box** (the lower of the two boxes in the upper-left corner of your screen) to close the document window. *Do not* double-click on the application window's Control menu box (the upper of the two boxes); this will cause you to exit Ami Pro.

EXITING AMI PRO

Your final step in every Ami Pro session is to exit Ami Pro. *Never turn off your computer before doing so,* as this could harm your computer and/or result in the loss of data. To properly exit Ami Pro and return to the Windows Program Manager, you can either choose File, Exit or double-click on the application window's Control menu box. As a safeguard, if you have not saved the latest version of an active document, Ami Pro will prompt you to do so before exiting.

Let's exit Ami Pro now. Simply choose **File, Exit**. The Ami Pro application window closes, revealing the Program Manager window once again.

SUMMARY

In this chapter, you learned the basics of the document creation-revision-saving-printing cycle, a procedure you'll use frequently in your daily word-processing work. You now know how to start Windows and Ami Pro; how to enter and delete text; how to save, name, print, and close a document; how to create a new document; and how to exit Ami Pro. Congratulations! You're well on your way to mastering Ami Pro.

Here's a quick reference guide to the Ami Pro features introduced in this chapter:

Desired Result	**How to Do It**
Start Windows	From DOS, type **win**; then press **Enter**.
Start Ami Pro	In Program Manager window, double-click on **Ami Pro 3.0 program icon**.

Desired Result	How to Do It
Maximize a window	Click on window's **Maximize button**.
Close a window	Double-click on window's **Control menu box**.
Restore a window	Click on window's **Restore button**.
Minimize a window	Click on window's **Minimize button**.
Choose a menu command	Click on a menu option to open that drop-down menu; then click on a menu item. Or press and hold the mouse button on a menu option, drag down to a menu item, and then release the mouse button.
End a paragraph or short line	Press **Enter**.
Create a blank line	Press **Enter**.
Insert a tab character	Press **Tab**.
Delete one character to the left of the insertion point	Press **Backspace**.
Display nonprinting symbols for tabs and returns	Choose **View, View Preferences**; check **Tabs & Returns**; then click on **OK**.
Save a new document, or save an existing document with a new name or in a new location	Choose **File, Save As**; type document name in File Name text box; select appropriate drive and directory (if necessary) in Drives drop-down list box and Directories list box; then click on **OK**.
Save a previously saved document with the same name and location	Choose **File, Save**.
Print the active document	Choose **File, Print**; then click on **OK**.

Desired Result	How to Do It
Close the active document window	Choose **File, Close**; or double-click on document window's **Control menu box**.
Create a new document	Choose **File, New**; then click on **OK**.
Exit Ami Pro	Choose **File, Exit**; or double-click on application window's **Control menu box**.

In the next chapter, we'll show you how to navigate through multiple-page Ami Pro documents. You'll learn how to open a document, change the default document path, scroll and move through a document, search for text, control document magnification, and obtain on-line Help.

A NOTE ON HOW TO PROCEED

If you wish to stop here, feel free to do so. If you wish to press onward, please proceed directly to the next chapter. Remember to allot enough time to work through an entire chapter at one sitting.

CHAPTER 2: NAVIGATING IN AMI PRO

Using File, Open to Open a Document

Understanding the Document Path

Scrolling through a Document

Moving through a Document

Using Edit, Find & Replace to Search for Text

Controlling Document Magnification

Obtaining On-Line Help

Saving a Modified Document

In Chapter 1, you learned how to start Windows and Ami Pro, how to enter text, and how to create, save, print, and close documents. Because the one-page documents you created in Chapter 1 were short enough to fit all at once on your screen, you didn't need to *navigate* in Ami Pro; in this chapter, however, you'll learn how to use the mouse and the keyboard to navigate through multiple-page documents that don't conveniently fit on one screen. It's essential for you to master these navigational techniques as early as possible in your Ami Pro career. The more comfortable you feel navigating through a document, the more you'll be able to concentrate on the contents of the document.

When you're done working through this chapter, you will know how to

- Open a document
- Set a default document path
- Use the mouse to scroll through a document
- Use the keyboard, menus, and status bar to move through a document
- Use the Edit, Find & Replace command to search for text
- Use the View menu to control document magnification
- Use Ami Pro's Help window to obtain on-line Help

USING FILE, OPEN TO OPEN A DOCUMENT

In Chapter 1 you learned how to create and save new documents. Here you'll learn how to open (*retrieve*) a saved document. This way, you'll be able to revise previously saved documents, and then save and print them again.

Follow these steps when you want to open a document:

- Choose File, Open to open the Open dialog box.
- If necessary, use the Drives drop-down list box and the Directories list box to select the appropriate disk drive and directory.
- In the Files list box, click on the desired document name and then click on OK, or simply double-click on the desired document name.

When you open a document, Ami Pro places a copy of the saved document in a document window on your screen. Because this is a *copy* of the saved document, and not the saved document itself, you can revise it to your heart's content without changing the original document stored on your disk.

Caution: If you save your revised document with the same name and in the same location as the original, you *do* change the original saved document. Whenever you want to preserve the original document, be sure to save the revised version with a new name and/or location.

Ami Pro also provides a convenient shortcut for opening a file: It keeps track of up to the last five documents (the last four, by default) that you opened, and places their names (preceded by a number) as menu items at the bottom of the File menu. To open one of these documents, you can open the File menu and then simply click on the desired document name.

Let's begin by opening a document, NAVIGATE.SAM, that is stored in your work directory:

1. Start Ami Pro. (For step-by-step instructions, refer back to "Starting Ami Pro" in Chapter 1.)

2. Choose **File, Open** to open the Open dialog box (see Figure 2.1).

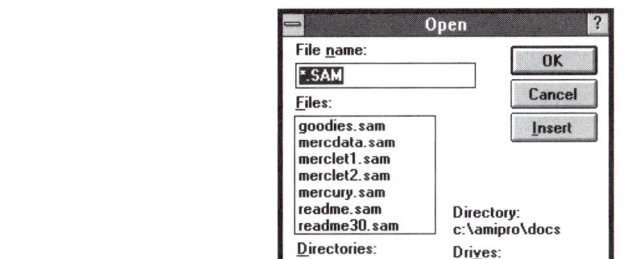

Figure 2.1   **The Open dialog box**

3. Observe the Directory line (located at the center-right of the dialog box). Because you exited Ami Pro at the end of Chapter 1 and have now restarted the program, Ami Pro no longer remembers your work directory. (If it has, skip to step 6.)

4. If necessary, use the Drives drop-down list box to select the drive containing your work directory.

5. In the Directories list box, double-click on **[..]** until the Directory line no longer displays any directory names. (For example, it should read *c:* or *d:*.) Then double-click on **[ami-work]** (or whatever name you gave your work directory).

6. Observe the Files list box. It now lists in alphabetical order every Ami Pro document stored in your work directory. Because there are too many documents to display at one time, *navigate.sam* is not visible.

7. Observe the vertical scroll bar on the right edge of the Files list box. It enables you to scroll down through the list of document names. Click on the scroll bar's **down scroll arrow** until *myfirst.sam*, *mysecond.sam*, and *navigate.sam* are visible. Notice that your work directory contains documents you created, such as myfirst.sam, as well as documents we supplied on this book's Data Disk, such as navigate.sam.

8. Click on **myfirst.sam**, and then observe the Description line (located near the bottom of the dialog box). It displays the document description you typed when saving this document. Document descriptions can help you determine the contents of documents *before* you open them.

9. Click on **navigate.sam**, and then observe the Description line. This document, too, contains a document description: *Document for Chapter 2*.

10. Observe the File Name text box. By clicking on *navigate.sam*, you automatically inserted the document's name in this text box.

11. Click on **OK** to open the document. A copy of the document appears in the active document window (see Figure 2.2). Notice that the title bar now reads *Ami Pro - [NAVIGATE.SAM]*.

12. Close NAVIGATE.SAM (choose **File, Close** or double-click on the document window's **Control menu box**).

Now let's try the shortcut method for opening this document:

1. Open the **File** menu, and then observe the bottom of the menu. It now lists the NAVIGATE.SAM document.

2. Click on **1 NAVIGATE.SAM** to reopen the document.

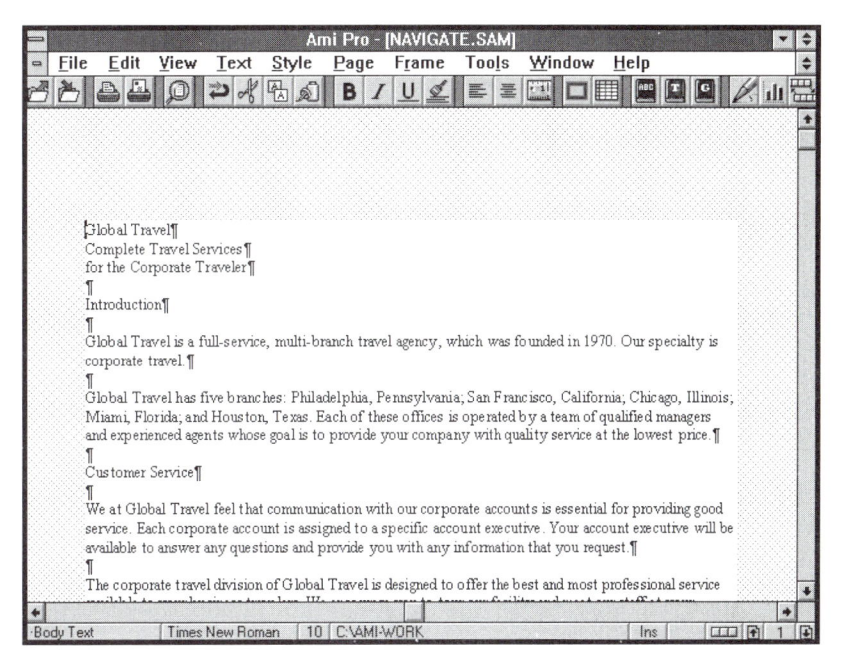

Figure 2.2   **The newly opened document, NAVIGATE.SAM**

UNDERSTANDING THE DOCUMENT PATH

Within a single session, Ami Pro by default remembers the last selected disk drive and directory for saving and opening files. Ami Pro calls this combination of drive and directory the *document path*; the document path determines the appropriate avenue for saving and opening documents.

As you saw in Chapter 1, when you establish a document path in the Save As dialog box, Ami Pro by default remembers the path for the next time you save a document. Because Ami Pro's Save As and Open dialog boxes are cooperative, once you set a document path in one of the dialog boxes, you automatically set it in the other. For example, if you use the Save As dialog box to save a document in your work directory, and then open the Open dialog box, Ami Pro will automatically list the files in that same directory.

However, whenever you exit and then restart Ami Pro, the program automatically resets the document path to the original directory (usually, C:\AMIPRO\DOCS). Having to change the document path every time you start Ami Pro can be time consuming. Luckily, Ami Pro offers a solution: the Default Paths dialog box.

CHANGING THE DEFAULT DOCUMENT PATH

By using Ami Pro's Default Paths dialog box, you can define a new default document path. That way, no matter how often you start and exit Ami Pro, it will automatically set itself to that directory for opening and saving files.

Follow these steps when you want to set a new default document path:

- Choose Tools, User Setup to open the User Setup dialog box.
- Click on the Paths button to open the Default Paths dialog box.
- In the Document text box, type the desired document path.
- Uncheck Use Working Directory if it is checked.
- Click on OK to close the Default Paths dialog box.
- Click on OK again to close the User Setup dialog box.

Let's set the document path to your working directory so that you will no longer have to designate it in the Save As or Open dialog boxes:

1. Choose **Tools, User Setup** to open the User Setup dialog box.
2. Click on **Paths** to open the Default Paths dialog box.
3. Examine the dialog box. It enables you to set default paths for documents and other Ami Pro-related files.
4. In the Document text box, type **c:\ami-work** (or whatever disk drive and directory name are appropriate).
5. Uncheck **Use Working Directory**. If this option is selected, Ami Pro will ignore the document path you typed in the Document text box (see Figure 2.3).
6. Click on **OK** to close the Default Paths dialog box, and then click on **OK** to close the User Setup dialog box.

Figure 2.3   **Setting the default document path**

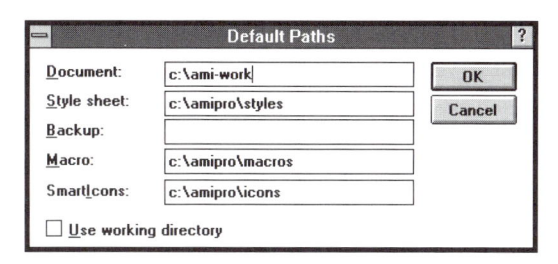

Default Paths	
Document:	c:\ami-work
Style sheet:	c:\amipro\styles
Backup:	
Macro:	c:\amipro\macros
SmartIcons:	c:\amipro\icons

☐ Use working directory

[OK] [Cancel]

USING THE DOCUMENT PATH BUTTON

Ami Pro's status bar contains a number of buttons that you can use to display information about Ami Pro and your current document.

Let's take a look at the *Document Path button*—the large button located in the center of the status bar. This button is a *toggle*; by clicking it, you can switch the display among three types of information:

- The current document path
- The current date and time
- The current position of the insertion point, including the current line, column, and page position (page position is the distance from the upper-left corner of the page)

Having an indicator of the current insertion-point position can be especially useful when you are navigating in a large document.

Let's work with the Document Path button for a moment, and then leave it in the insertion-point-position mode:

1. Observe the status bar's Document Path button. It displays the current document path.

2. Click once on the **Document Path button**. It now displays the current date and time (assuming your computer's internal clock is accurate).

3. Click on the **Document Path button** again. It now tells you the current position of your insertion point (see Figure 2.4). *Line 1* indicates the insertion point is in the document's first line of text; *Col 1* indicates the insertion point is in the document's first column, against the left margin; and *Pos: (1.25,1.00)* indicates the insertion point is 1¼" from the left edge of the page

42 • NAVIGATING IN AMI PRO

and 1" from the top of the page. (Because your insertion point is at the very beginning of the document, these position settings show that this document has a 1¼" left margin and a 1" top margin. You'll learn more about margins in Chapter 6.)

Figure 2.4 **Displaying the insertion point's position on the Document Path button**

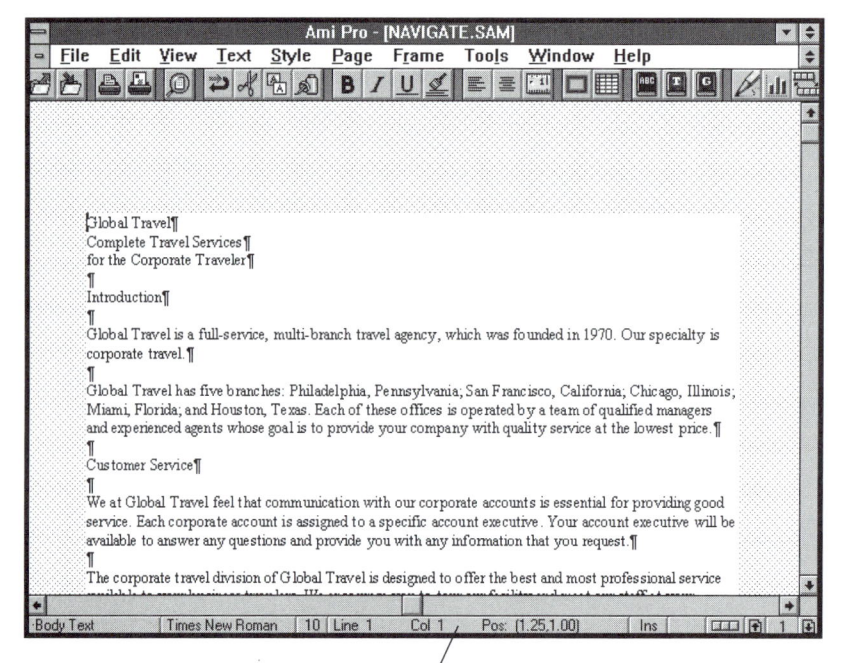

[Screenshot of Ami Pro - [NAVIGATE.SAM] window showing document text with Document Path button indicated at the bottom status bar displaying "Pos: (1.25,1.00)"]

Document Path button

4. Click on the **Document Path button** again. It now returns to displaying the document path. The Document Path button acts as a three-way toggle; by clicking on it three times, you cycle it through all three display modes.

5. Click on the **Document Path button** two more times so that it again displays the insertion point's position.

SCROLLING THROUGH A DOCUMENT

By default, an Ami Pro document window can display only about half of a standard business-size (8½" x 11") page at any one time. To view the other half of a page or other pages within the document, you can use the mouse together with the vertical and horizontal scroll bars to *scroll* through the document—that is, to display different areas of the document. The vertical scroll bar controls up/down scrolling; the horizontal scroll bar controls left/right scrolling.

Scrolling through a document changes the document display, but does not change the position of the insertion point. For example, if the insertion point is at the top of page 2 and you use the vertical scroll bar to scroll down to page 8, Ami Pro displays the contents of page 8 on the screen, but the insertion point remains at the top of page 2. If you then begin to type, your text is entered at the insertion point on page 2, not on page 8. In order to reposition the insertion point after scrolling, use the I-beam to click in the current document display.

When scrolling, you may find it useful to keep an eye on the Document Path button; this can help you determine the exact position of the insertion point, even when you can't see it. Figure 2.5 labels the Ami Pro scroll bars and their parts. Table 2.1 lists Ami Pro's vertical and horizontal scrolling options and how to perform them.

Table 2.1   **Scrolling Options**

To Scroll	Do This
Up or down one line at a time	Click on the **up** or **down scroll arrow**.
To the top, bottom, or middle of a document	Drag the **vertical scroll box** to the top, bottom, or middle of the vertical scroll bar.
Up or down a screen at a time	Click in the **vertical scroll bar** above or below the vertical scroll box.
Left or right a column at a time	Click on the **left** or **right scroll arrow**.

Table 2.1 **Scrolling Options (Continued)**

To Scroll	Do This
To the left edge, right edge, or middle of a document	Drag the **horizontal scroll box** to the left, right, or middle of the horizontal scroll bar.
Left or right a screen at a time	Click in the **horizontal scroll bar** to the left or right of the horizontal scroll box.

Figure 2.5 **The horizontal and vertical scroll bars**

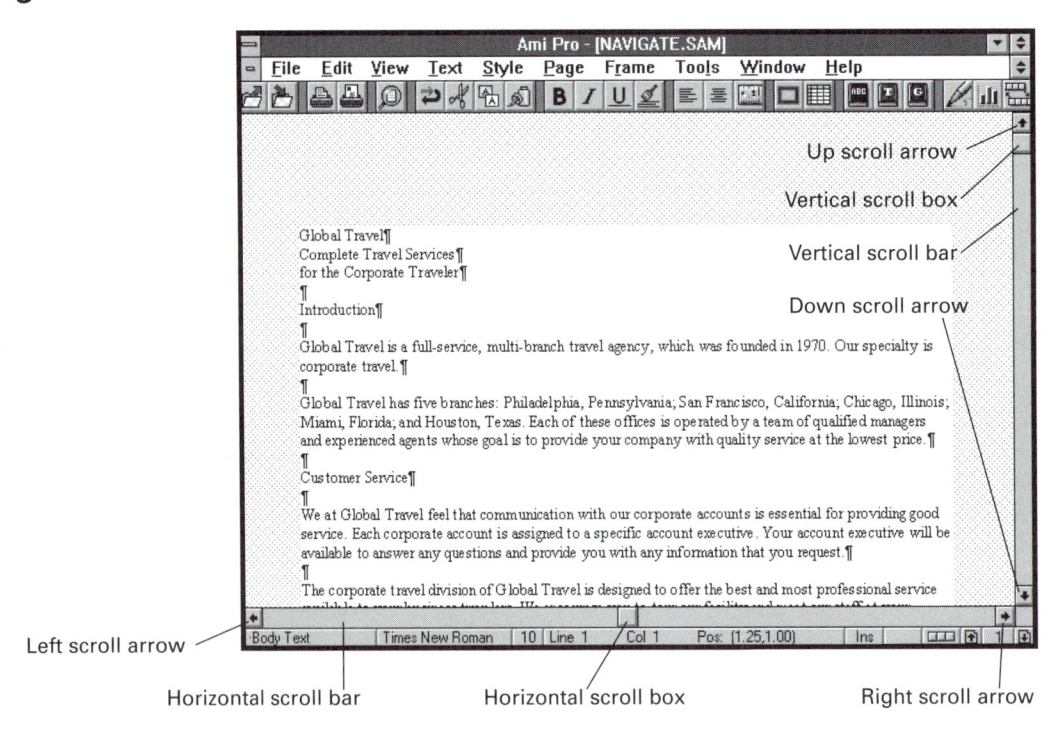

Let's practice using the mouse and scroll bars to scroll through the active document:

1. Click on the **down scroll arrow** several times to scroll down through the document one line at a time. Notice that the insertion point does not move.

2. Click on the **up scroll arrow** several times to scroll up through the document.

3. Drag the **vertical scroll box** to the bottom of the scroll bar to scroll to the bottom of the document (to the end of page 2).

4. Drag the **vertical scroll box** to the middle of the scroll bar to scroll to the middle of the document. (Because NAVIGATE-.SAM is a two-page document, you will see either the bottom of page 1 or the top of page 2.)

5. Drag the **vertical scroll box** to the top of the scroll bar to scroll to the top of the document. Notice that throughout all of your scrolling, the insertion point has remained at the top of the document.

6. Click in the **vertical scroll bar** below the vertical scroll box to scroll one screen length (about one-third of a page) down through the document.

7. Repeat step 6 as many times as necessary to scroll to the bottom of the document. Be careful! As you click, the vertical scroll box moves down within the scroll bar; you need to keep clicking *below* that box.

8. Click in the **vertical scroll bar** above the vertical scroll box to scroll one screen length up through the document.

9. Repeat step 8 as many times as necessary to scroll to the top of the document.

Next, take a moment to observe a common scrolling mistake. Let's say you want to type your initials at the end of the active document.

1. Drag the **vertical scroll box** to the bottom of the scroll bar to display the end of the document.

2. Type your initials. Observe that the text is inserted at the top of the document (where your insertion point is located), *not* at the end (where you had scrolled). Ami Pro has automatically repositioned the document to display the inserted text. To avoid making such a mistake, remember these two things: Text that you type is always inserted at the insertion point, and

the insertion point does not move automatically when you use the scroll bars.

3. Use **Backspace** to erase your initials.

4. Scroll back down to the end of the document and examine the Document Path button. It shows that the insertion point is still located at the top of the document.

5. Position the I-beam underneath the document's last word, *Travel*, and then click once. The insertion point now moves to the end of the document.

6. Look again at the Document Path button. It reflects the insertion point's new position.

MOVING THROUGH A DOCUMENT

As you have observed, when you *scroll* through a document, you change the document display but not the insertion point's position. Repositioning the insertion point when scrolling is a two-step process: You scroll, and then you click to position the insertion point.

Moving, on the other hand, is a one-step process: When you move through a document, you automatically change *both* the document display and the insertion point's position.

Generally, you should scroll when you just want to view various parts of a document, but you should move when you want to modify the document.

USING THE KEYBOARD TO MOVE THROUGH A DOCUMENT

Table 2.2 lists several keyboard techniques for moving through a document.

Table 2.2   **Keyboard Movement Techniques**

To Move	Press
Up one line	Up Arrow
Down one line	Down Arrow

Table 2.2   **Keyboard Movement Techniques (Continued)**

To Move	Press
Left one character	Left Arrow
Right one character	Right Arrow
To the beginning of a line	Home
To the end of a line	End
Up one screen	Page Up (or Pg Up)
Down one screen	Page Down (or Pg Dn)
Up one page	Ctrl+Page Up (or Ctrl+Pg Up)
Down one page	Ctrl+Page Down (or Ctrl+Pg Dn)
To the top of the document	Ctrl+Home
To the end of the document	Ctrl+End

Note: If you intend to use the Pg Up and Pg Dn keys on your numeric keypad, rather than the Page Up and Page Down keys, be sure that Num Lock is off. (For the remainder of this book, we will refer only to the Page Up and Page Down keys. If you would rather use the Pg Up and Pg Dn keys, feel free to do so.)

Now let's practice using the keyboard to move—rather than scroll—through the active document.

1. Press **Ctrl+Home** to move to the top of the document. Notice that the insertion point moves to the top along with the document display.

2. Press **Page Down** twice to move two screen lengths down through the document. The insertion point moves again.

3. Press **Page Up** twice to move two screen lengths up through the document. The insertion point returns to the top of the document.

4. Press **Ctrl+End** to move to the end of the document.

5. Press **Ctrl+Home** to return to the top of the document.

6. Press **Down Arrow** to move the insertion point down one line. Because you moved the insertion point within the current document display, Ami Pro did not need to change the display.

7. Press **Right Arrow** to move the insertion point between the *C* and the *o* in *Complete*.

8. Press **Up Arrow** to move the insertion point to the first line, between the *G* and the *l* in *Global*.

9. Press **Left Arrow** to move the insertion point to the left of *Global*. Notice that, unlike the Backspace key, the Left Arrow key moves the insertion point to the left without deleting text.

Let's repeat our initials-typing task, this time using the correct method:

1. Press **Ctrl+End** to move to the end of the document.

2. Type your initials. This time they are inserted at the end of the document.

3. Press **Ctrl+Home** to return to the top of the document.

USING EDIT, GO TO TO MOVE TO A PAGE

You can use the Edit, Go To command to move to the top of a specific page in the active document. This technique is particularly useful when you are moving through long, multiple-page documents.

Follow these steps when you want to move to the top of a page:

- Choose Edit, Go To to open the Go To dialog box.

- In the Page Number text box, type the desired page number.

- Click on the Go To ^H button (^H is an abbreviation for Ctrl+H, which is a keyboard shortcut for Edit, Go To).

Let's use the Edit, Go To command to move through the active document:

1. Look for the *Page Status button*, the second button from the right on the status bar. It currently displays a *1*.

2. Choose **Edit, Go To** to open the Go To dialog box (see Figure 2.6).

MOVING THROUGH A DOCUMENT • 49

Figure 2.6   **The Go To dialog box**

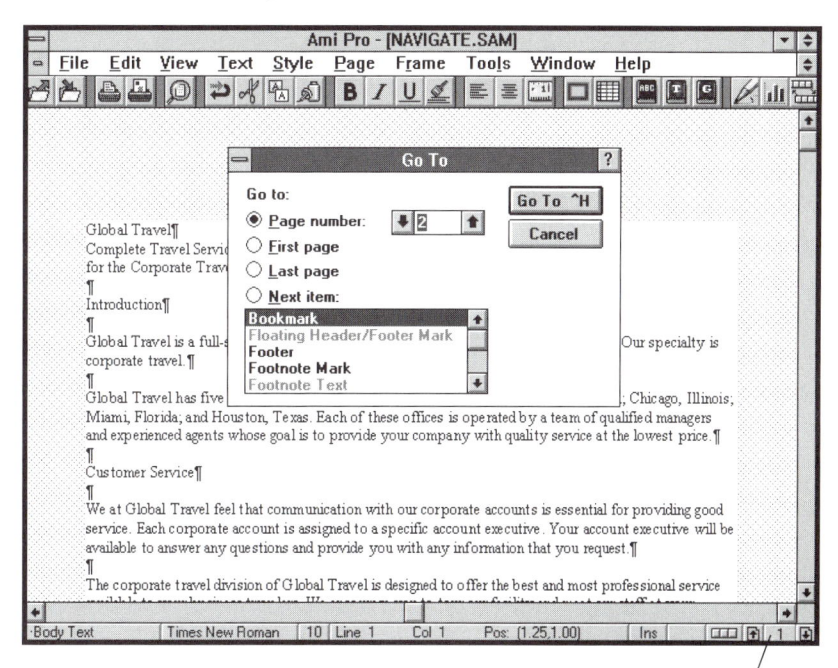

Page Status button

3. In the Page Number text box, type **2** (if necessary) to specify the destination page, and then click on **Go To ^H** to move both the document display and the insertion point to the top of page 2.

4. Observe the Page Status button. It now displays a *2*.

5. Choose **Edit, Go To**, type **1**, and then click on **Go To ^H** to move to the top of page 1.

USING THE STATUS BAR TO MOVE TO A PAGE

You can also use other buttons on the status bar to move to a different page: the Page Status button, along with the two *Page Arrow buttons* that flank the Page Status button at the right end of the status bar. The Page Status button opens the Go To dialog box; and the Page Arrow buttons move the insertion point to the top of the next or previous page, without opening the Go To dialog box.

Let's use the Page Status and Page Arrow buttons now:

1. Click on the **Page Status button** to open the Go To dialog box.
2. Type **2**, and then click on **Go To ^H** to move to the top of page 2.
3. Click on the **Up Page Arrow button** (located to the left of the Page Status button). The insertion point moves to the top of page 1 (see Figure 2.7).

Figure 2.7   **The Page Arrow buttons**

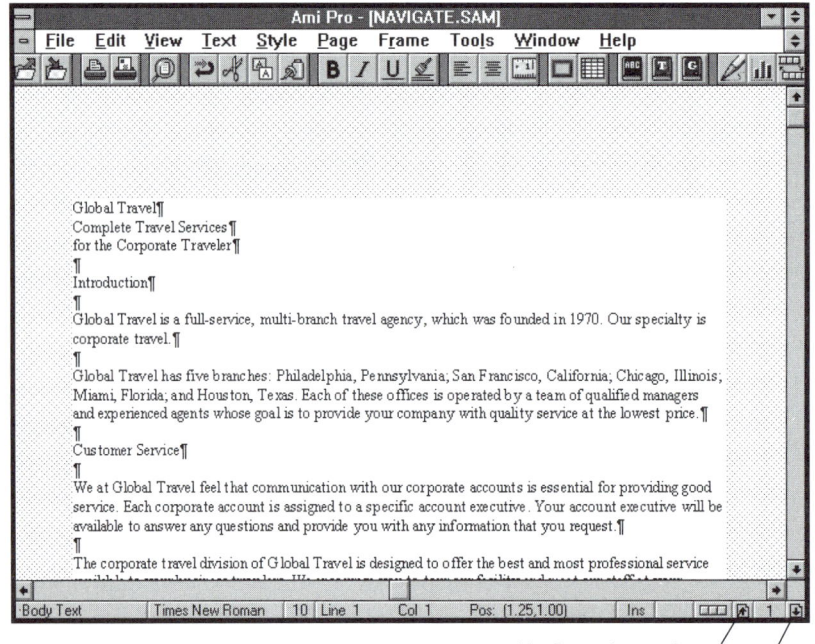

Up Page Arrow button
Down Page Arrow button

4. Click on the **Down Page Arrow button** (located to the right of the Page Status button). The insertion point moves to the top of page 2.

PRACTICE YOUR SKILLS

Use any of the insertion-point-movement techniques you've learned to perform the following steps:

1. Move the insertion point to the bottom of the document.
2. Move the insertion point to the top of page 2.
3. Move the insertion point to the top of the document.

USING EDIT, FIND & REPLACE TO SEARCH FOR TEXT

One of Ami Pro's most useful features is its ability to quickly locate a specific word or phrase in a document. You can use this feature to move rapidly to any desired document location. For example, you can move to the phrase *would like to establish*—even if you have no idea which page contains this phrase. To locate specific text, you use Ami Pro's Edit, Find & Replace command. (As you might expect, you can use the Edit, Find & Replace command to replace text as well as search for it. You'll learn how to use Edit, Find & Replace's replace functions in Chapter 3.)

Follow these steps when you use Edit, Find & Replace to search for text within a document:

- Place the insertion point where you wish to begin the search. By default, Ami Pro searches from the insertion point downward to the end of the document. To search an entire document, place the insertion point at the top of the document.

- Choose Edit, Find & Replace to open the Find & Replace dialog box.

- In the Find text box, type your *search text*—that is, the text that you want to find.

- Click on Find; Ami Pro will select (highlight) the first occurrence of your search text. If Ami Pro cannot find the text, it will close the dialog box and display a message briefly in the status bar.

- If you want to search your document beyond the first found occurrence, click on Find Next as many times as needed to search through the document. When you are ready, you can click on Cancel to cancel your search. When Ami Pro reaches the end

52 • NAVIGATING IN AMI PRO

of your document, it will close the dialog box and display a message briefly in the status bar indicating how many times it found your search text.

Edit, Find & Replace provides several find options to help you refine your text searches. These options are available by clicking on Options from within the Find & Replace dialog box. Some of these options are

- *Whole Word Only*, which instructs Ami Pro to find only whole words that match your search text. For example, Ami Pro could use the search text *rate* to find *rate* and *Rate*, but not *rates* or *operate*.

- *Exact Case*, which instructs Ami Pro to find only words that exactly match the case (capitalization) of your search text. For example, Ami Pro could use the search text *rate* to find *rate*, *rates*, and *operate*, but not *Rate*.

- *Exact Attributes*, which instructs Ami Pro to find your search text only when it has certain text attributes (you'll learn about text attributes in Chapter 4).

Let's experiment with the Edit, Find & Replace command:

1. Verify that the insertion point is at the top of the document (press **Ctrl+Home** if it isn't). This ensures that Ami Pro will search the entire document.

2. Choose **Edit, Find & Replace** to open the Find & Replace dialog box (see Figure 2.8).

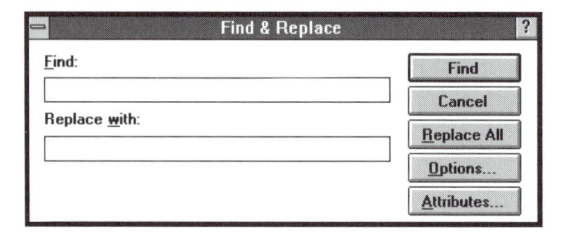

Figure 2.8   **The Find & Replace dialog box**

USING EDIT, FIND & REPLACE TO SEARCH FOR TEXT • 53

3. In the Find text box, type **vacation**. Be sure to type the word in all lowercase letters.

4. Click on **Options** to open the Find & Replace Options dialog box (see Figure 2.9).

Figure 2.9   **The Find & Replace Options dialog box with appropriate settings**

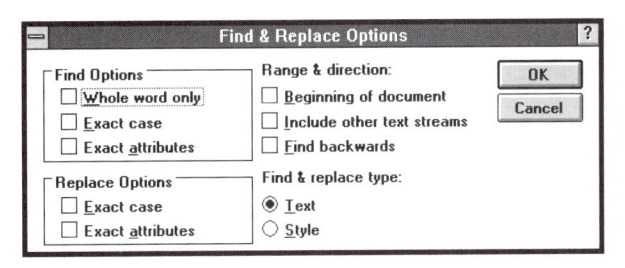

5. Examine the Find Options box. It contains three check boxes for controlling your searches: *Whole Word Only*, *Exact Case*, and *Exact Attributes*. (Notice also that the Replace Options box contains Exact Case and Exact Attributes check boxes. Do not try to use these options in this chapter; you'll learn about replace options in Chapter 8.)

6. In the Find Options box, verify that none of the options are checked. If they are, uncheck them.

7. Under Range & Direction, verify that no options are checked.

8. Under Find & Replace Type, verify that **Text** is selected. Your dialog box should now match Figure 2.9.

9. Click on **OK** to close the Find & Replace Options dialog box.

10. In the Find & Replace dialog box, click on **Find**. Ami Pro finds the word *Vacations* in the heading *Personal Vacations*.

11. Click on **Find Next** three times, pausing to examine each found word. Ami Pro finds *vacation*, *Vacation*, and *Vacation*.

12. Click on **Find Next** one more time. Because there are no more occurrences of your search text, Ami Pro closes the dialog box

and briefly displays the following message in the status bar: *Find/Replace Results: 4 found 0 replaced*.

Now let's refine our search by using the Whole Word Only and Exact Case options:

1. Move to the top of the document. (From here on, when we say "move," we mean that you should move both the document display and the insertion point.)

2. Choose **Edit, Find & Replace**. Notice that Ami Pro remembered your search text.

3. Click on **Options**, check **Whole Word Only**, and then click on **OK**.

4. Click on **Find**. Ami Pro finds *vacation*. Notice that because you checked Whole Word Only, Ami Pro skipped *Vacations* in the heading *Personal Vacations*.

5. Click on **Find Next** three times. Ami Pro finds *Vacation* twice, and then closes the dialog box.

6. Move the insertion point to the top of the document, and then choose **Edit, Find & Replace**. Click on **Options**, and check **Find Options Exact Case** (be sure to check the Exact Case option contained in the Find Options box, not in the Replace Options box). Then click on **OK**.

7. Click on **Find**. Once again, Ami Pro skips past *Vacations* to *vacation*.

8. Click on **Find Next**. Because you checked Exact Case, Ami Pro skips both occurrences of *Vacation* and closes the dialog box.

PRACTICE YOUR SKILLS

1. Move to the top of the document.

2. Open the Find & Replace dialog box, replace the word *vacation* with the word **news**, and then open the Find & Replace Options dialog box.

3. In the Find Options box, uncheck **Whole Word Only** and **Exact Case**, click on **OK**, and then search the entire document. There are three matches.

4. Return to the top of the document, open the Find & Replace and then the Find & Replace Options dialog boxes, check

Whole Word Only, and then repeat the search. There is one match.

5. Return to the top of the document, open the Find & Replace and the Find & Replace Options dialog boxes, uncheck **Whole Word Only**, check **Find Options Exact Case,** and then repeat the search. There are two matches.

CONTROLLING DOCUMENT MAGNIFICATION

You learned earlier in this chapter that Ami Pro normally shows you only about a half-page of text at one time in a document window. This is true because Ami Pro's default setting is to display documents in *Custom view*, which displays the document at 91% of its full size. However, Ami Pro also provides four other views—all available through the View menu—that enable you to control your document's magnification:

- *Full Page view* reduces the document's magnification so that you can see an entire page at once.

- *Standard view* displays the document at full size (100%).

- *Enlarged view* displays the document at double size (200%).

- *Facing Pages view* displays two entire document pages, side by side.

In addition, you can use the View, View Preferences command to customize the Custom view to any percentage from 10% to 400%.

Unlike some other WYSIWYG word processors, Ami Pro lets you edit your document in any view (except Facing Pages). Therefore, by using a variety of views you can view and edit your document at whatever size is most appropriate for the task at hand. For example, you can type text in the Standard or Custom views; check a page's overall layout in the Full Page or Facing Pages views; and study text and graphics close up in Enlarged view.

In addition to editing and viewing, you can use Ami Pro's various views as navigational tools, enabling you to quickly move the insertion point to the part of the page you wish to edit. Here is an example of this technique:

- Choose View, Full Page to view the entire page.

- Place the insertion point where you want to edit text.

- Choose View, Custom 91% to return to Ami Pro's default view. The document window will automatically reorient to the new position of the insertion point.

Let's try using some of Ami Pro's views as navigational tools to edit an entry in the tabbed table at the bottom of page 1 of NAVIGATE.SAM.

1. Move to the top of the document.
2. Choose **View, Full Page**. Ami Pro displays a miniature view of page 1, as shown in Figure 2.10.

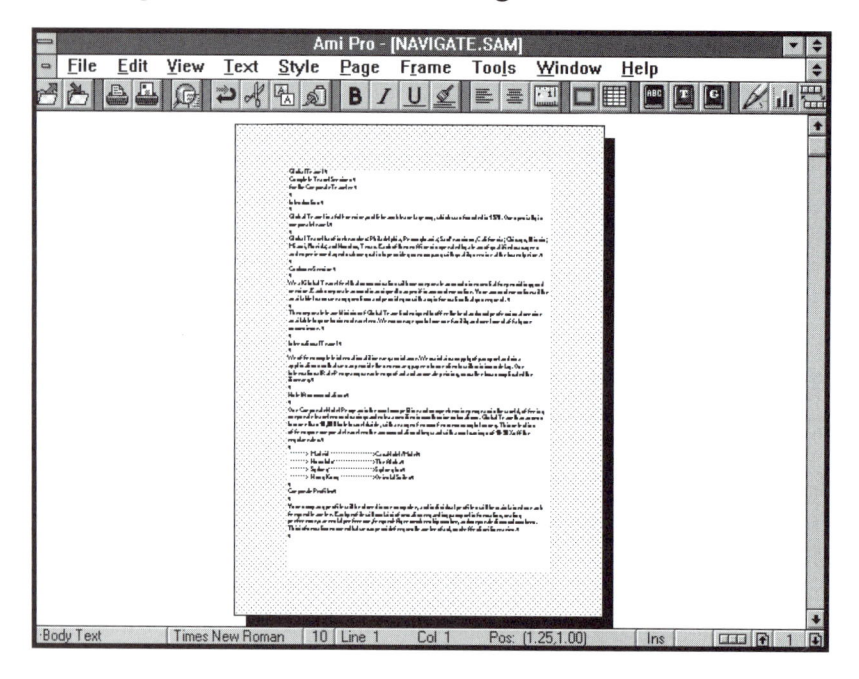

Figure 2.10 **Viewing a document in Full Page view**

3. Move the I-beam to the first line of the tabbed table near the bottom of page 1, and then click to position the insertion point. (Don't worry about perfect positioning. It's pretty difficult to place the insertion point just right in this view!)
4. Choose **View, Custom 91%** to return to 91% magnification.
5. Move the insertion point to the end of the first line in the tabbed table, and then use **Backspace** to delete **/Motel**.

6. Experiment with Ami Pro's Standard, Enlarged, and Facing Pages views. (**Tip:** To leave Facing Pages view, click on **Cancel** in the small Facing Pages dialog box.)

7. Return to the Custom 91% view.

OBTAINING ON-LINE HELP

In Chapter 1, you saw how Ami Pro sometimes uses the title bar to display one-line Help messages. Ami Pro offers another, much more extensive on-line Help system through its *Help window*. This Help window can provide you with "how-to" information on every aspect of the Ami Pro program.

The beauty of Help is its accessibility. No matter what you are doing in Ami Pro (choosing a command from the menu, editing a document, filling in a dialog box, and so on), Help is only a keystroke—or mouse click—away.

USING THE HELP TABLE OF CONTENTS

The Help window provides a table of contents that gives you an overview of available Help topics. Follow these steps when you want to use this Help table of contents:

- Choose Help, Contents to open the Help window and display the table of contents.

- To get Help for a specific topic, click on any underlined word or phrase in the index. Clicking on any solid-underlined word or phrase will jump you to a new Help screen; clicking on a dotted-underlined word or phrase will pop up a *definition window,* without leaving the current Help screen.

- To close the Ami Pro Help window, either double-click on the window's Control menu box or choose File, Exit.

Let's practice using the Help table of contents:

1. Choose **Help, Contents** to open the Help window and display the Help table of contents.

2. Maximize the Help window (click on the window's **Maximize button**).

3. Move the mouse pointer to the solid-underlined entry *Basics*. Notice that the mouse pointer changes to a *Help hand* (see Figure 2.11).

Figure 2.11 **Using the Help table of contents**

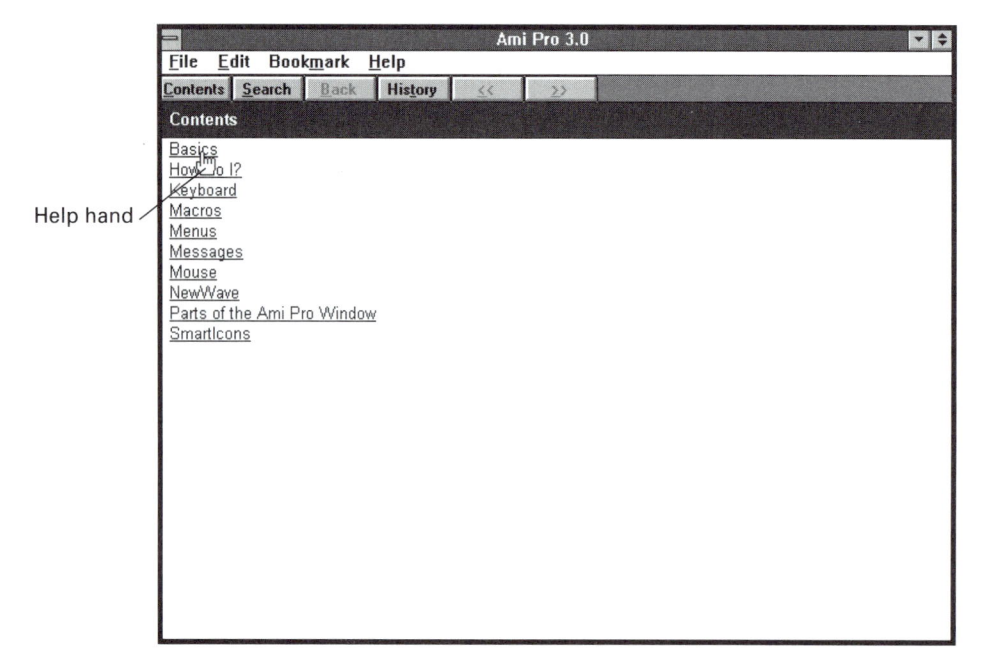

Help hand →

4. Use the Help hand to click on **Basics**. The Help window now displays basic information about Ami Pro.
5. Click on **Becoming Familiar With The Ami Pro Window**. The Help window now displays information about Ami Pro's windows. Notice that many words and phrases have a dotted underline.
6. Click on **Menu Bar**. Because Menu Bar has a dotted underline, Help pops up a definition window containing an illustration of the menu bar, rather than jumping to a new Help screen (see Figure 2.12).
7. Click on **Menu Bar** again to close the definition window.
8. Close the Help window (double-click on the window's **Control menu box** or choose **File, Exit**).

Figure 2.12 **Viewing a definition window**

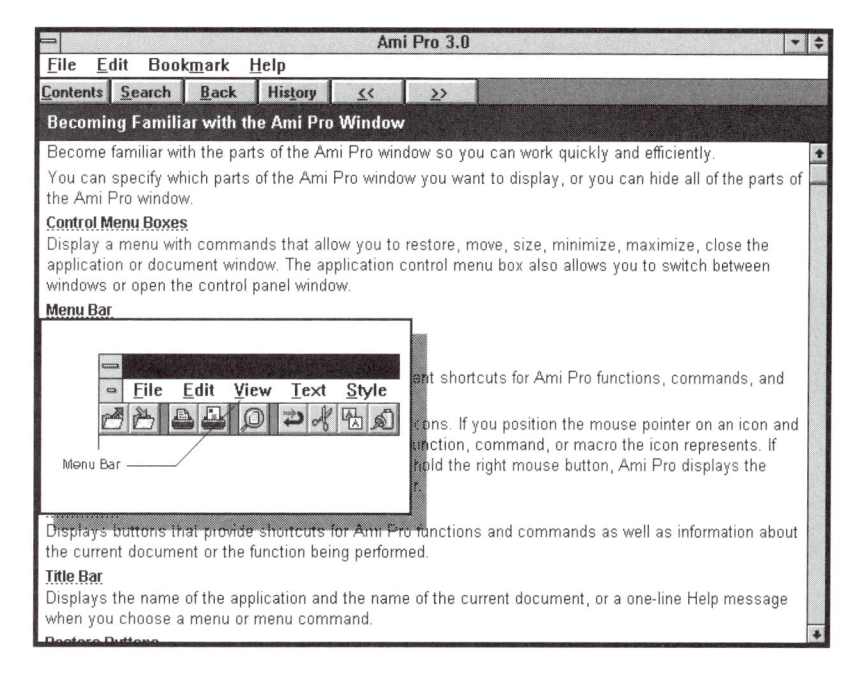

[Screenshot: Ami Pro 3.0 Help window showing "Becoming Familiar with the Ami Pro Window" topic with a pop-up definition window illustrating the Menu Bar]

OBTAINING CONTEXT-SENSITIVE HELP

In addition to the Help table of contents, Ami Pro offers you *context-sensitive Help*: information related to your current working context. For example, if a dialog box is open and you ask for context-sensitive Help, Help displays information about that particular dialog box. Used in this manner, Help can quickly provide information about specific dialog boxes, menu commands, or areas of the screen. This saves you the time and trouble of searching through a series of Help screens.

You can use any of the following methods to obtain context-sensitive Help:

- Press F1.

- From within any dialog box, click on the *Help icon*, located at the right end of the dialog box's title bar.

- Press Shift+F1; your mouse pointer will change to a *question mark*. Then use the question mark to make any menu choice or to click on a window element. (Ami Pro refers to this last type of context-sensitive Help as *point-and-shoot Help*.)

Let's use these three methods now to obtain context-sensitive Help:

1. Choose **Edit, Go To** to open the Go To dialog box.

2. Press **F1**. Ami Pro opens the Help window for the Edit, Go To command.

3. Close the Help window.

4. Observe the Go To dialog box. It displays a Help icon at the right end of its title bar (see Figure 2.13). Click on the **Help icon** to open once again the Help window for the Edit, Go To command.

Figure 2.13   Using a dialog box's Help icon

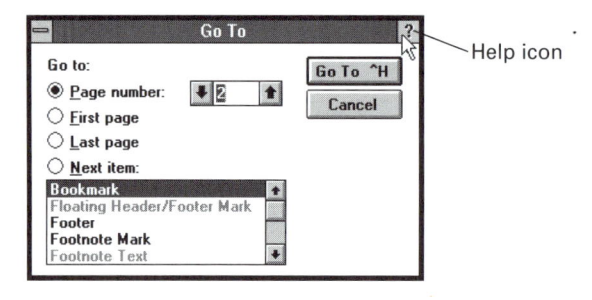

5. Close the Help window, and then click on **Cancel** to close the Go To dialog box.

6. Press **Shift+F1**. The mouse pointer changes to a question mark.

7. Use the tip of the question mark's arrowhead to choose **Edit, Find & Replace**. Rather than opening the Find & Replace dialog box, Ami Pro opens the Help window for the Edit, Find & Replace command.

8. Close the Help window, press **Shift+F1**, and then use the tip of the question mark's arrowhead to click on the status bar. Ami Pro opens the Help window for the status bar.

9. Close the Help window.

SAVING A MODIFIED DOCUMENT

Let's end this work session by using File, Save As to rename the active document and save it to your work directory. By using the File, Save As command, you preserve the original version of the document (NAVIGATE.SAM) along with your revised version. (If you were to instead use the File, Save command to save the active document, you would preserve the revision and overwrite the original.)

1. Choose **File, Save As** to open the Save As dialog box.
2. In the File Name text box, type **mynav** as the new document name.
3. Examine the Directory line to verify that your work directory is still selected, and then click on **OK**. Ami Pro saves your modified NAVIGATE.SAM document under the name MYNAV.SAM.
4. Close the document window.

PRACTICE YOUR SKILLS

You've learned a great deal about Ami Pro in these first two chapters. The following two activities enable you to apply this knowledge to practical word processing tasks. Please don't think of these activities as tests, but rather as opportunities to hone your Ami Pro skills. It is only through practice that you'll become more comfortable with the techniques you've learned.

After each activity step, a chapter reference (in parentheses) informs you of where we first introduced the relevant technique for that step.

In this first activity, you will create and edit the document shown in two different stages in Figures 2.14 and 2.15, to produce the final document shown in Figure 2.16.

1. Open a new document window. (Chapter 1)
2. Enter the text shown in Figure 2.14. (Chapter 1)
3. Use **Backspace** to edit the letter as shown in Figure 2.15. (Chapter 1) (Note that the replacement text in Figure 2.15—for instance, **Street** and **our**—is in boldface for emphasis only. Do not try to enter this text in boldface; you will learn about boldface formatting in Chapter 4.)
4. Save the document in your work directory as **myprac2a**. (Chapter 1)

Figure 2.14 **The first draft of the letter**

> Katherine Carlisle
> 1822 West 18th Avenue
> New York, NY 10021
>
> Dear Katherine:
>
> Thank you for accepting the invitation to the announcement press conference in June. Because your large orders, I have waived the $25.00 entrance fee.
>
> I look ahead to seeing you there!
>
> Yours truly,
>
> Kat Moran
> Conference Director

Figure 2.15 **Edits for the letter**

> Katherine Carlisle
> 1822 West 18th ~~Avenue~~ **Street**
> New York, NY 10021
>
> Dear Katherine:
>
> Thank you for accepting ~~the~~ **our** invitation to the **product-**announcement press conference in June. Because **of** your large orders, I have waived the ~~$25.00~~ entrance fee.
>
> I look ~~ahead~~ **forward** to seeing you there!
>
> ~~Yours truly,~~ **Sincerely,**
>
> Kat Moran
> Conference Director

5. Print your document, and then compare the results to Figure 2.16. (Chapter 1)

Figure 2.16   **The corrected letter**

```
Katherine Carlisle
1822 West 18th Street
New York, NY 10021

Dear Katherine:

        Thank you for accepting our invitation to the product-announcement press conference in
June. Because of your large orders, I have waived the entrance fee.

        I look forward to seeing you there!

Sincerely,


Kat Moran
Conference Director
```

6. Close the document window. (Chapter 1)

In this next activity, you will open, move through, and edit a saved document, to produce the final document shown in Figure 2.17.

1. Open **prac2b.sam**. (Chapter 2)
2. Move to the top of page 2, and then type **Auto Rentals**. (Chapter 2)
3. Move to the top of the document, and then type **Global Travel**. (Chapter 2)
4. Use **Edit, Find & Replace** to find the word *assistance*, and then close the Find & Replace dialog box. (Chapter 2)
5. Place the insertion point directly before *assistance*, and then type **itinerary** followed by a space. (Chapter 2)
6. Save the document as **myprac2b**. (Chapter 1)
7. Print the document, and then compare your letter with Figure 2.17. (Chapter 1)
8. Close the document window. (Chapter 1)

Figure 2.17   **The edited letter, MYPRAC2B.SAM**

Global Travel
Complete Travel Services

Introduction

Global Travel is a full-service, multi-branch travel agency, which was founded in 1970. Our specialty is corporate travel.

Global Travel has five branches: Philadelphia, Pennsylvania; San Francisco, California; Chicago, Illinois; Miami, Florida; and Houston, Texas. Each of these offices is operated by a team of qualified managers and experienced agents whose goal is to provide your company with quality service at the lowest price.

Customer Service

We at Global Travel feel that communication with our corporate accounts is essential for providing good service. Each corporate account is assigned to a specific account executive. Your account executive will be available to answer any questions and provide you with any information that you request.

The corporate travel division of Global Travel is designed to offer the best and most professional service available to your business travelers. We encourage you to tour our facility and meet our staff at your convenience.

Corporate Profiles

Your company profile will be stored in our computer, and individual profiles will be maintained on each frequent traveler. Each profile will contain information regarding passport information, seating preference, car rental preference, frequent-flyer membership number, and corporate discount numbers. This information ensures that we can provide frequent travelers, fast, cost-effective itineraries.

International Travel

We offer complete international itinerary assistance. We maintain a supply of passport and visa applications so that we can provide the necessary papers to our clients with minimum delay. Our International Rate Program guarantees you fast and accurate pricing, no matter how complicated the itinerary.

Worldwide Services

Global Travel's Reservation Center will handle all of your weekend and after-hour reservations and changes. The reservation center can be dialed toll-free 24 hours a day. The worldwide service emergency numbers will be clearly marked on your travel itineraries.

Discounts

Global Travel guarantees the lowest air fares available. Due to the volume of tickets that we issue, several of the large air carriers offer us special discounts that we can pass on to our clients.

Our quality-control specialists check each of your tickets to guarantee that your have received the lowest rate available. In addition, each ticket is checked to ensure that it includes seating assignments and boarding passes before it is delivered to you.

Figure 2.17   The edited letter, MYPRAC2B.SAM (Continued)

Auto Rentals

We guarantee the lowest prices on all car rentals. We will match the type of car with the information provided in the profile for each of your frequent travelers. Each car that is rented through Global Travel carries an extra $50,000 worth of liability insurance.

Hotel Accommodations

Our Corporate Hotel Program is the most competitive and comprehensive program in the world, offering corporate travelers cost savings and extra amenities in most business locations. Global Travel has access to more than 10,000 hotels worldwide, with a range of rooms from economy to luxury. This selection offers your corporate travelers the accommodations they want with a cost savings of 10-30% off the regular rates.

Additional Services

Global Travel also provides the following services for our corporate customers:

Newsletter

All clients receive our monthly newsletter that covers a variety of travel topics, including:

Travel costs—we will keep you informed about the competition among the large air carriers that will affect your travel costs.

Special fares—we will keep you apprised of the many unadvertised special airline fares that we offer.

Travel basics—our newsletter will provide you with suggestions to make your corporate travel safer and more enjoyable.

Telex

Telex service is available for international hotel confirmations.

Personal Vacations

Our corporate clients are invited to discuss their vacation and personal travel plans with an agent from Global Travel's Vacation Division. Our Vacation Division is skilled in both domestic and international travel.

Flight Insurance

We will supply all clients with $250,000 worth of flight insurance for every trip arranged through Global Travel.

Fax

Travel requests may be faxed to our office. Confirmed itineraries can be faxed to your office for immediate confirmation.

SUMMARY

In this chapter, you learned the basics of navigating in Ami Pro. You now know how to open a document, set a default document path, scroll and move through a document, search for text, control document magnification, and obtain on-line help.

Here's a quick reference guide to the Ami Pro features introduced in this chapter:

Desired Result	How to Do It
Open a document	Choose **File, Open**; select appropriate drive and directory (if necessary); click on document's name; then click on **OK** (or double-click on document's name).
Open a recently opened document	Open the **File** menu; then click on document's name.
Change default document path	Choose **Tools, User Setup**; click on **Paths**; type new path in Document text box; then click on **OK** twice.
Toggle Document Path button to display document path, current date and time, or insertion-point position	Click on **Document Path button**.
Scroll up or down one line	Click on **up** or **down scroll arrow**.
Scroll to the top, bottom, or middle of a document	Drag **vertical scroll box** to top, bottom, or middle of vertical scroll bar.
Scroll up or down one screen	Click in **vertical scroll bar** above or below vertical scroll box.
Scroll left or right one column	Click on **left** or **right scroll arrow**.
Scroll to left edge, right edge, or middle of a document	Drag **horizontal scroll box** to left, right, or middle of horizontal scroll bar.

Desired Result	How to Do It
Scroll to left or right one screen at a time	Click in **horizontal scroll bar** to left or right of horizontal scroll box.
Move up or down one line	Press **Up Arrow** or **Down Arrow**.
Move left or right one character	Press **Left Arrow** or **Right Arrow**.
Move to beginning or end of a line	Press **Home** or **End**.
Move up or down one screen	Press **Page Up** or **Page Down**.
Move up one page	Press **Ctrl+Page Up**; or click on **Up Page Arrow button**.
Move down one page	Press **Ctrl+Page Down**; or click on **Down Page Arrow button**.
Move to top of document	Press **Ctrl+Home**.
Move to end of document	Press **Ctrl+End**.
Move to top of specific page	Choose **Edit, Go To** or click on **Page Status button**; type page number; then click on **OK**.
Search for text	Place insertion point where you want to begin searching; choose **Edit, Find & Replace** and type search text; click on **Options** and select any desired search options; click on **OK**; then click on **Find** or **Find Next**.
Change a document's magnification	Open **View** menu, and then click on **Full Page, Custom, Standard, Enlarged,** or **Facing Pages**.
View the Help table of contents	Choose **Help, Contents**.
Jump to a new Help screen	In Help window, click on any **solid-underlined** word or phrase.

Desired Result	How to Do It
Open a definition window	In Help window, click on any **dotted-underlined** word or phrase.
Get context-sensitive Help	Press **F1**; or press **Shift+F1** and then make any menu choice or click on any window element; or click on a dialog box's **Help icon**.

In Chapter 3, you'll see how to edit text more efficiently than you can with just the Backspace key. You'll learn how to insert text; select text; delete and replace selected text; find and replace text; move and copy text; and reverse your most recent edits.

IF YOU'RE STOPPING HERE

If you need to take a break here, please exit Ami Pro. (For help with this, see "Exiting Ami Pro" in Chapter 1.) If you want to proceed directly to the next chapter, please do so now.

CHAPTER 3: EDITING TEXT

Basic Editing Techniques

More Techniques for Selecting Text

Using Edit, Find & Replace to Replace Found Text

Moving and Copying Text

Using Edit, Undo to Reverse Your Most Recent Operation

In Chapter 1, you learned the very basic way of editing text using your Backspace key. In this chapter, we'll introduce you to additional basic editing techniques, and then move on to some of Ami Pro's more advanced editing techniques. You'll learn methods for deleting text with your Delete key, for selecting text, and for deleting and replacing selected text. You'll also see how to use Edit, Find & Replace to find and replace text, and how to move and copy text. Finally, we'll show you how to use Ami Pro's Edit, Undo command to reverse your edits.

When you're done working through this chapter, you will know how to

- Delete text with the Delete key
- Select text
- Delete and replace selected text
- Use Edit, Find & Replace to replace found text
- Move and copy text
- Use the Edit, Undo command to reverse your last edit

BASIC EDITING TECHNIQUES

As you learned in Chapter 1, one of the best reasons for switching from a typewriter to a word processor is that the word processor makes your documents easier to edit. In the time it would take you to pencil in your desired changes to a typewritten document, you could incorporate those changes into a word-processed document and print out the new version.

In the next several sections, we'll discuss the basics of editing Ami Pro documents.

USING A SMARTICON TO OPEN A DOCUMENT

In Chapters 1 and 2, you learned two techniques for opening documents:

- For opening a document that you haven't opened recently, you can choose File, Open to display the Open dialog box. Within the dialog box, you then select a document location and name and click on OK (or simply double-click on the document's name).

- For a recently opened document, you can select the document's name from the bottom of the File menu.

You can also open a document by clicking on the leftmost Smart-Icon, the *Open An Existing File SmartIcon*, which displays an arrow pointing out of a file folder. (Remember from Chapter 1 that Smart-Icons are located directly below the menu bar.) This displays the

Open dialog box; from there, you can use the dialog box just as if you had chosen the File, Open command.

Generally, a SmartIcon's appearance provides an excellent clue to its function. For example, the Open An Existing File SmartIcon indicates something coming out of a file folder. However, you need not depend solely on a SmartIcon's appearance to determine its function. You can also point to the SmartIcon, and then press and hold the right (not the left) mouse button. When you do, Ami Pro will display the SmartIcon's name in the title bar.

If you are not running Ami Pro, please start it now. (For help, see "Starting Ami Pro" in Chapter 1.)

Let's work now with the Open An Existing File SmartIcon:

1. Point to the **Open An Existing File SmartIcon**, and then press and hold the *right* mouse button. The title bar displays the icon's name (see Figure 3.1).

2. Release the right mouse button.

3. Click (with the left mouse button) on the **Open An Existing File SmartIcon**. Ami Pro displays the Open dialog box.

4. In the Files list box, double-click on **editinga.sam** to open the document. (Or, click on **editinga.sam** and then click on **OK**.)

In Chapter 1, you learned that you can use your Backspace key to delete one character at a time to the left of the insertion point. Your Del or Delete key does just the opposite: It deletes one character to the *right* of the insertion point.

If you have a PS/2-style Enhanced keyboard, you have access to both a Del and a Delete key. The Del key is located on the numeric keypad; the Delete key is located on the auxiliary keypad to the left of the numeric keypad. Pressing either of these keys has the same effect on the text being deleted. If you intend to use the numeric keypad's Del key to perform your deletions, be sure that Num Lock is off. (Press the Num Lock key until the Num Lock light goes out.) If Num Lock is on, Del functions as a decimal-point key; when you press it, Ami Pro inserts a decimal point (.) instead of performing a deletion.

3. Click (with the left mouse button) on the **Open An Existing File SmartIcon**. Ami Pro displays the Open dialog box.

4. In the Files list box, double-click on **editinga.sam** to open the document. (Or, click on **editinga.sam** and then click on **OK**.)

DELETING TEXT WITH THE DELETE KEY

In Chapter 1, you learned that you can use your Backspace key to delete one character at a time to the left of the insertion point. Your Del or Delete key does just the opposite: It deletes one character to the *right* of the insertion point.

If you have a PS/2-style Enhanced keyboard, you have access to both a Del and a Delete key. The Del key is located on the numeric keypad; the Delete key is located on the auxiliary keypad to the left of the numeric keypad. Pressing either of these keys has the same effect on the text being deleted. If you intend to use the numeric keypad's Del key to perform your deletions, be sure that Num Lock is off. (Press the Num Lock key until the Num Lock light goes out.) If Num Lock is on, Del functions as a decimal-point key; when you press it, Ami Pro inserts a decimal point (.) instead of performing a deletion.

For the remainder of this book, we'll refer only to the Delete key. If you prefer to use—or only have access to—the Del key, feel free to use that key instead. Depending on your preference, as well as the location of your insertion point, you can use either the Backspace or the Delete key. Each one works equally well for deleting small amounts of text.

Let's practice deleting text with both the Backspace and Delete keys:

1. Examine EDITINGA.SAM. It is similar to the document you typed in Chapter 1, but needs some editing.

2. Examine Figures 3.2 and 3.3. Figure 3.2 shows edits for this document; Figure 3.3 shows the same document after those edits have been incorporated.

3. Use the I-beam to place the insertion point immediately to the right of the *e* in *Avenue* (located in the second line of the document).

Figure 3.2 Document edits

> Nancy Wright
> 3325 Fillmore ~~Avenue~~ **Circle**
> North Hills, NY 14052
>
> Dear ~~Janet~~ **Nancy**:
>
> I have been ~~happy~~ **very pleased** with the service provided by Global Travel. I would like additional information about your corporate travel program.
>
> Because ~~the~~ **our** company is opening a new office in Paris sometime this year, your worldwide services would be ~~most~~ beneficial to us. I look ~~ahead~~ **forward** to hearing from you**.**
>
> ~~Yours truly,~~ **Sincerely,**
>
> Kat Moran
> Macco Plastics, Inc.

Figure 3.3 The edited document

> Nancy Wright
> 3325 Fillmore Circle
> North Hills, NY 14052
>
> Dear Nancy:
>
> I have been very pleased with the service provided by Global Travel. I would like additional information about your corporate travel program.
>
> Because our company is opening a new office in Paris sometime this year, your worldwide services would be beneficial to us. I look forward to hearing from you.
>
> Sincerely,
>
> Kat Moran
> Macco Plastics, Inc.

4. Press **Backspace** six times to delete the six characters to the *left* of the insertion point.

5. Type **Circle**.

6. Place the insertion point immediately to the left of the *h* in *happy* (located in the first line of the paragraph beginning *I have been*).

7. Press **Delete** five times to delete the five characters to the *right* of the insertion point.

8. Type **very pleased**.

DELETING BLOCKS OF TEXT

Often, it is easier to work with a block of text rather than with single characters. For example, if you need to delete a paragraph, you probably will not want to delete each and every character individually (a multiple-step, tedious task); rather, you will want to delete the entire paragraph at once (a single-step, straightforward task).

In order to specify a block of text for deletion, you must first *select* it. One method of selecting is called *dragging* (you'll learn about other selection techniques later in this chapter). Follow these steps when you want to select text by dragging:

- Use the I-beam to point to the first (or final) character of the text you want to select.

- Press and hold the mouse button.

- Drag forward (or backward) across the text to the final (or first) character. As you drag, the selected text is displayed in reverse video.

- Release the mouse button.

You can select text from the first to the last character, or from the last to the first character. Both methods are equally effective; use whichever method you find is more comfortable.

Once you've selected a block of text, you can delete it by simply pressing Delete.

Let's select and delete a couple blocks of text:

1. Position the I-beam to the left of the *m* in *most* (located in the first sentence of the paragraph beginning *Because the company*).

2. Press and hold the mouse button; then, drag forward over the word **most** *and* the trailing space (the space that follows the *t* in *most*) to select the text and the space. As you drag, notice how the characters and the space appear in reverse video (see Figure 3.4). If you drag too far or not far enough, just keep the mouse button held down and continue moving the I-beam until you have highlighted exactly the text you want selected.

Figure 3.4   **Selected text**

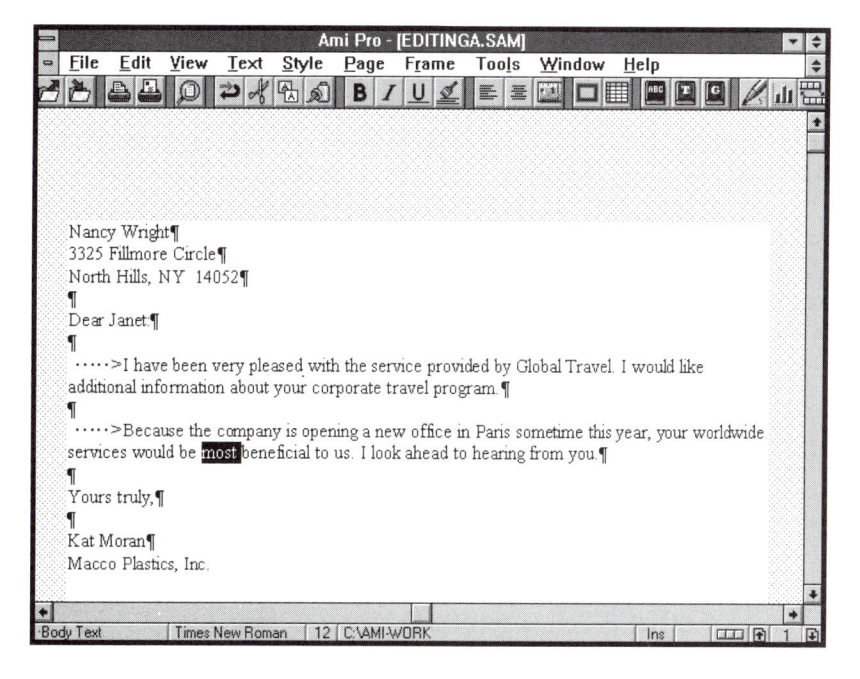

3. Release the mouse button.
4. Press **Delete** to delete the selected text and the space.

5. Position the I-beam before the *t* in *the* (in the phrase *Because the company*), and then drag to select **the**. This time, do *not* select the trailing space.

6. Press **Delete** to delete the selected text.

7. Type **our**.

REPLACING TEXT

To replace text, you can use the skills you've already learned to first select and delete the existing text and then insert new text in its place. For example, if you want to replace the standard letter closing, *Yours truly,* with *Sincerely,* you can select and delete *Yours truly* and then type *Sincerely* in its place. However, this three-step method is inefficient—particularly when you are replacing many blocks of text. Fortunately, Ami Pro provides a more convenient solution.

Here is a two-step method to replace existing text with new text:

- Select the existing text you want to replace.
- Type the new text.

As soon as you start typing your new text, Ami Pro automatically deletes your selected text. You do *not* have to press Delete.

Let's use this technique to replace some text:

1. In the salutation *Dear Janet:*, select **Janet** (but not the colon that follows).

2. Type **N**. Ami Pro automatically deletes your selected text and replaces it with *N*.

3. Type **ancy** to complete the word *Nancy*.

PRACTICE YOUR SKILLS

Use Figures 3.2 and 3.3 as guides for making the remaining edits to EDITINGA.SAM.

1. Use the Delete key to delete **ahead** (in the paragraph beginning *Because our company*), and then type **forward**.

2. Select **Yours truly** (in the closing), and then replace the selected text with **Sincerely**.

3. Compare your revised document with Figure 3.3.

4. Save the document as **myeditsa** (use the **File, Save As** command).

5. Close the document.

MORE TECHNIQUES FOR SELECTING TEXT

As you'll see throughout this book, selecting text is often a crucial first step to editing and formatting that text. For this reason, Ami Pro provides numerous text selection techniques besides dragging. Table 3.1 lists a variety of these techniques.

Don't be concerned about learning all of these techniques at once. Rather, be sure to learn some of the most basic methods (for example, dragging, selecting a word, and selecting a paragraph); then, as you become more familiar with Ami Pro, you can add new techniques to your repertoire. Before long, you'll find that you are using all of these techniques, or perhaps only a chosen few that work best for you.

Table 3.1   **Text Selection Techniques**

To Use This Technique	Follow These Steps
Drag	Use the I-beam to point at one end of the text you want to select, press and hold the mouse button, drag the I-beam to the other end of the text, and then release the mouse button.
Select a word	Point anywhere inside the word, and then double-click the mouse button. Ami Pro automatically selects the word's trailing space along with the word.

Table 3.1   **Text Selection Techniques (Continued)**

To Use This Technique	Follow These Steps
Select a sentence	Point anywhere inside the sentence, press and hold Ctrl, click the mouse button, and then release Ctrl. Ami Pro automatically selects, along with the sentence, its end punctuation (period, question mark, or exclamation point) and trailing space or spaces. (Ami Pro considers any text that ends with a period, question mark, or exclamation point to be a sentence.)
Select a paragraph	Point anywhere inside the paragraph, press and hold Ctrl, double-click the mouse button, and then release Ctrl. Ami Pro automatically selects the return that ends the paragraph, along with the paragraph. (Ami Pro considers any text between two returns to be a paragraph.)
Select multiple words, sentences, or paragraphs	Use the word, sentence, or paragraph selection technique to select a single word, sentence, or paragraph. Hold the mouse button down on the last click, and then drag.
Select using Shift and the mouse	Place the insertion point at one end of the text, press and hold Shift, click at the other end of the text you want to select, and then release Shift. Ami Pro automatically selects the text in between.
Select using Shift and the keyboard	Place the insertion point at one end of the text, press and hold Shift, use any keyboard movement technique (from Chapter 2) to move to the other end of the text, and then release Shift. Ami Pro automatically selects the text in between. (The "Select an entire document" method in this table is an example of this type of technique.)

Table 3.1   **Text Selection Techniques (Continued)**

To Use This Technique	Follow These Steps
Extend an existing selection	Press and hold Shift, click beyond the existing selection, and then release Shift.
Shorten an existing selection	Press and hold Shift, click inside the existing selection, and then release Shift.
Select an entire document	Place the insertion point at the top of the document and press Shift+Ctrl+End; or place the insertion point at the bottom of the document and press Shift+Ctrl+Home.
Deselect	Make another selection; or click the mouse button in the typing area anywhere outside the existing selection.

Let's open a document and practice the dragging technique first:

1. Open **editingb.sam**. Feel free to use either **File, Open** or the **Open An Existing File SmartIcon**.

2. Point to the left of the *C* in *Corporate* (located in the third line of the document).

3. Drag to the right to select **Corporate** and the trailing space, and then release the mouse button.

Now let's use the whole-word selection technique:

1. Use the I-beam to point to the word *five* in the first multiple-line paragraph of the document (the paragraph beginning *Global Travel has*).

2. Double-click to select the entire word **five**, including its trailing space. Notice that by selecting *five*, you automatically deselected *Corporate*.

Try selecting a sentence and a paragraph:

1. Point to the sentence beginning *Global Travel is a full-service* (in the document's second multiple-line paragraph).

82 • EDITING TEXT

    2. Press and hold **Ctrl**, click once, and then release **Ctrl**. Ami Pro selects the entire sentence, including the period and the trailing space (see Figure 3.5).

Figure 3.5   **Selecting a sentence**

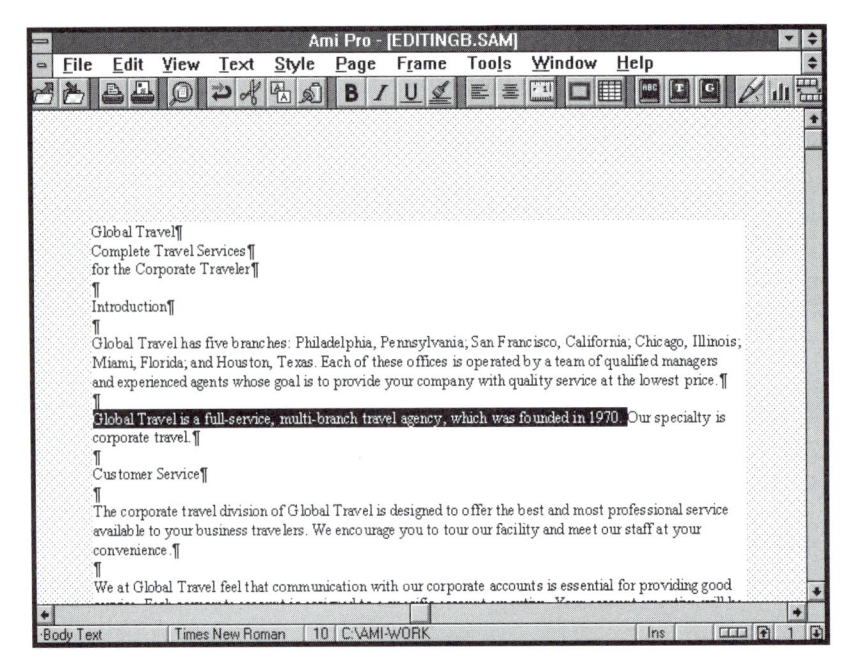

[Screenshot of Ami Pro - [EDITINGB.SAM] window showing a document with the sentence "Global Travel is a full-service, multi-branch travel agency, which was founded in 1970." highlighted.]

    3. Point to the document's first multiple-line paragraph.

    4. Press and hold **Ctrl**, double-click, and then release **Ctrl**. Ami Pro selects the entire paragraph, including the paragraph's ending return.

Now practice selecting multiple words and paragraphs:

    1. Point to *Global* (in the document's second multiple-line paragraph).

    2. Double-click to select **Global**, and hold the mouse button down on the second click.

    3. Observe the selection as you drag to the right. Ami Pro adds entire words at a time to the selection.

4. Release the mouse button.
5. Point to the document's first multiple-line paragraph.
6. Press and hold **Ctrl**, and then double-click, holding down the mouse button on the second click. Then release **Ctrl**.
7. Drag downward, observing the selection as you drag. Ami Pro adds entire paragraphs at a time to the selection.
8. Release the mouse button.
9. Click outside your selection to deselect the text.

Now use the Shift key to select a block of text, and then extend and shorten this selection:

1. Place the insertion point before the *C* in *Corporate* (in the document's third line).
2. Press and hold **Shift**, click in the space after *five* (in the document's first multiple-line paragraph), and then release **Shift**. Ami Pro selects all of the text from *Corporate* through *five*.
3. Point to the right of the *s* in *Texas* (in the next line down from *five*).
4. Press and hold **Shift**, click the mouse button, and then release **Shift**. Ami Pro extends the selection through to the end of *Texas* (see Figure 3.6).
5. Point to the left of the *P* in *Philadelphia* (one line up from *Texas*), press and hold **Shift**, click the mouse button, and then release **Shift**. Ami Pro shortens the selection.

Finally, select the entire document:

1. Move to the top of the document (press **Ctrl+Home**).
2. Press **Shift+Ctrl+End**. This combination of Shift with the keyboard movement technique Ctrl+End selects the entire document from beginning to end.
3. Click anywhere outside the selection to deselect the document.

PRACTICE YOUR SKILLS

1. Move to the top of the document.

Figure 3.6   **Extending a selection**

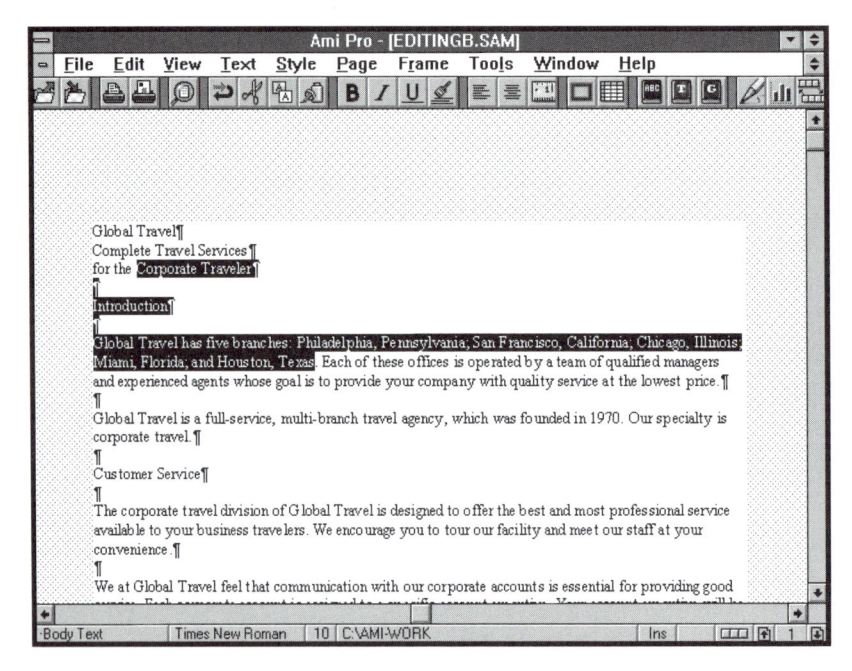

2. Use the dragging technique to select the first sentence of the paragraph beginning *Global Travel is a full-service*.

3. Deselect.

4. Select the same sentence as in step 2, this time using the mouse in conjunction with **Ctrl** to select the entire sentence without dragging. (For help, refer back to Table 3.1.)

5. Use the double-clicking technique to select each of the following words in the document's first multiple-line paragraph: **Global**, **Philadelphia**, **Texas**, **qualified**, and **price**. Notice that double-clicking selects a word's trailing space, but not trailing commas (as in *Philadelphia,*) or periods (as in *Texas.* and *price.*).

6. Use the multiple-paragraph selection technique to select the document's first four lines.

7. Extend the selection to include the first five lines.

8. Shorten the selection to include only the first two lines.

USING EDIT, FIND & REPLACE TO REPLACE FOUND TEXT

In Chapter 2, you learned how to use Edit, Find & Replace to search for text in a document. Here you'll learn how to use Edit, Find & Replace to search for text and then to replace that text with new text.

Edit, Find & Replace is one of Ami Pro's most powerful commands. Let's say you typed a 100-page document that made frequent reference to a woman named Gerta Sitauskus. Later, you found out that the correct spelling was Sitauskis. You could manually find each occurrence of Sitauskus and retype it—a tedious task, considering the length of the document. With Edit, Find & Replace, however, you could use Ami Pro to help you rapidly replace every occurrence of Sitauskus with Sitauskis.

Follow these steps when you want to use Edit, Find & Replace to replace found text in a document:

- Place the insertion point where you wish to begin the find-and-replace operation (remember from Chapter 2 that Edit, Find & Replace by default searches from the insertion point downward). To search an entire document, place the insertion point at the top of the document.
- Choose Edit, Find & Replace to open the Find & Replace dialog box.
- In the Find text box, type the *search text* (the text you want to find).
- In the Replace With text box, type the *replacement text* (the text you want to use instead of the search text).
- If necessary, click on Options to open the Find & Replace Options dialog box. Then select the appropriate find-and-replace options and click on OK.
- Click on Find; Ami Pro selects the first occurrence of your search text. (If you prefer to have Ami Pro automatically replace every occurrence, without asking you for confirmation, you can instead click on Replace All. However, this can be risky.)
- To replace the found text and then search again for the next occurrence, click on Replace & Find Next. To leave the found text unchanged and search for the next occurrence, click on Find Next. To replace all occurrences of the search text throughout the rest of the document, without verifying the replacements

(another risky choice), click on Replace Remaining. To stop the find-and-replace operation, click on Cancel.

- Repeat the previous step as many times as necessary until you have searched through the entire document, or cancel your search at any time by clicking on Cancel.

Once Ami Pro has searched the entire document, it automatically closes the Find & Replace dialog box.

Let's use the procedure described just above to find and replace some text:

1. In preparation for searching the entire document, move the insertion point to the top of the document.

2. Choose **Edit, Find & Replace** to open the Find & Replace dialog box. (If you haven't exited Ami Pro since Chapter 2, the Find text box might still contain your earlier search text.)

3. In the Find text box, type **20**. This is the text you will search for and replace.

4. Press **Tab** to move to the Replace With text box, and then type **50**. This is the text that will replace the search text (see Figure 3.7).

Figure 3.7 **Specifying search and replacement text**

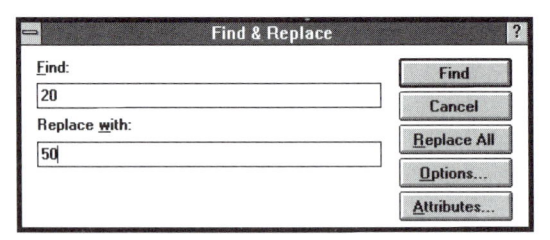

5. Click on **Options** to open the Find & Replace Options dialog box, and then observe the Replace Options box (on the left side of the dialog box). Just as you can tell Ami Pro to find text that meets certain conditions (Whole Word Only, Exact Case, Exact Attributes), so can you set conditions for the replacement text (Exact Case, Exact Attributes).

6. In both the Find Options and Replace Options boxes, uncheck any checked options, and then click on **OK**. (You'll learn how to use some of these options in Chapter 8.)

7. Click on **Find**. In the document window, Ami Pro selects the first occurrence of *20* (see Figure 3.8).

Figure 3.8 **Finding text for replacement**

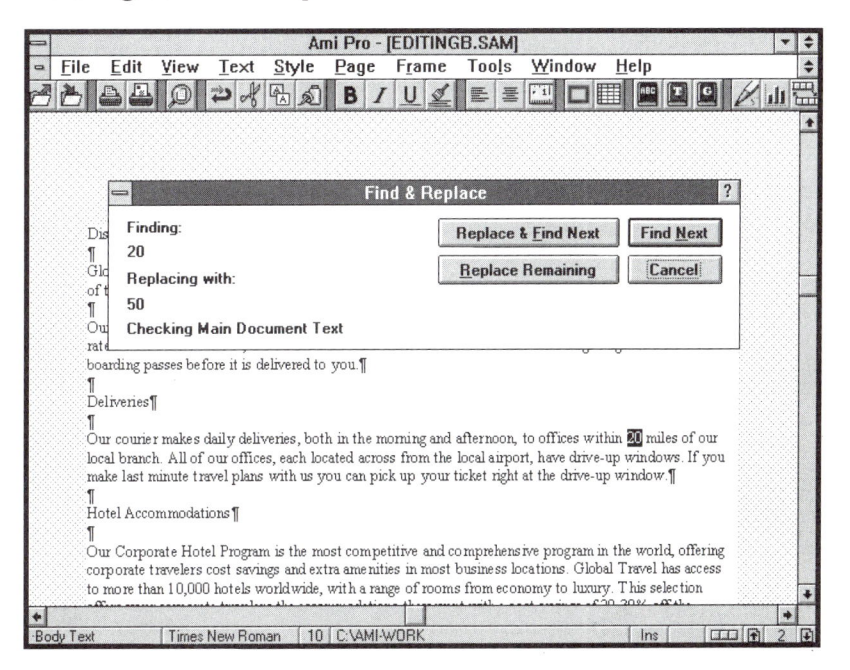

8. Click on **Replace & Find Next** to replace *20* with *50* and search for the next occurrence of *20*.

9. Examine the selected text in the document window. Replacing *20* with *50* here wouldn't make sense (50-30% off?). This shows why it's risky to use the Replace All or Replace Remaining buttons; Ami Pro would have changed this text blindly.

10. Click on **Find Next** to leave *20-30%* unchanged and search for the next occurrence of *20*.

88 • EDITING TEXT

11. Click on **Replace & Find Next** to replace *20* with *50* and search for the next occurrence of *20*. Because there are no more occurrences of *20*, Ami Pro closes the Find & Replace dialog box.

12. Save your revised document as **myeditsb**.

MOVING AND COPYING TEXT

Another of Ami Pro's powerful editing features is its ability to move and copy existing text. You can, for example, quickly and easily move entire paragraphs from the top of the fifth page of a business report to the bottom of the eleventh page, or copy a four-line address to several locations within the body of a letter.

One way to move and copy text is to use a combination of the *Edit, Cut*, the *Edit, Copy*, and the *Edit, Paste* commands. Ami Pro also provides three SmartIcons (described later) that you can use as replacements for those three Edit commands.

UNDERSTANDING THE WINDOWS CLIPBOARD

Windows provides a temporary storage area called the *Clipboard* that is useful for moving and copying text. When selected text is cut (removed) by using Edit, Cut or copied by using Edit, Copy, Ami Pro places a copy of that text on the Clipboard. When you paste by using Edit, Paste, Ami Pro inserts a copy of the Clipboard contents at the insertion point. Pasting does not empty the Clipboard. Barring computer problems (such as a power loss), entries remain on the Clipboard until you cut or copy another entry to it or until you exit from Windows.

MOVING TEXT

Follow these steps when you want to move text within a document:

- Select the text to be moved.

- Choose Edit, Cut or click on the *Cut To The Clipboard SmartIcon* (the seventh SmartIcon from the left, displaying a pair of scissors). This cuts the selected text from the document and places a copy on the Clipboard.

- Place the insertion point where you want to move the text.

MOVING AND COPYING TEXT • 89

- Choose Edit, Paste or click on the *Paste Clipboard Contents SmartIcon* (the ninth SmartIcon from the left, displaying a paste jar). This pastes the cut text at the insertion point.

Let's practice moving text from one location to another within a document:

1. Move to the top of the document.
2. Select both the paragraph beginning *Global Travel is a full-service* and the blank line that follows.
3. Choose **Edit, Cut** to remove the selected text from the document and place it on the Windows Clipboard.
4. Place the insertion point before the *G* in *Global Travel has five*.
5. Choose **Edit, Paste** to paste a copy of the Clipboard contents at the insertion point (see Figure 3.9).

Figure 3.9   **Page 1 of MYEDITSB.SAM, after moving text**

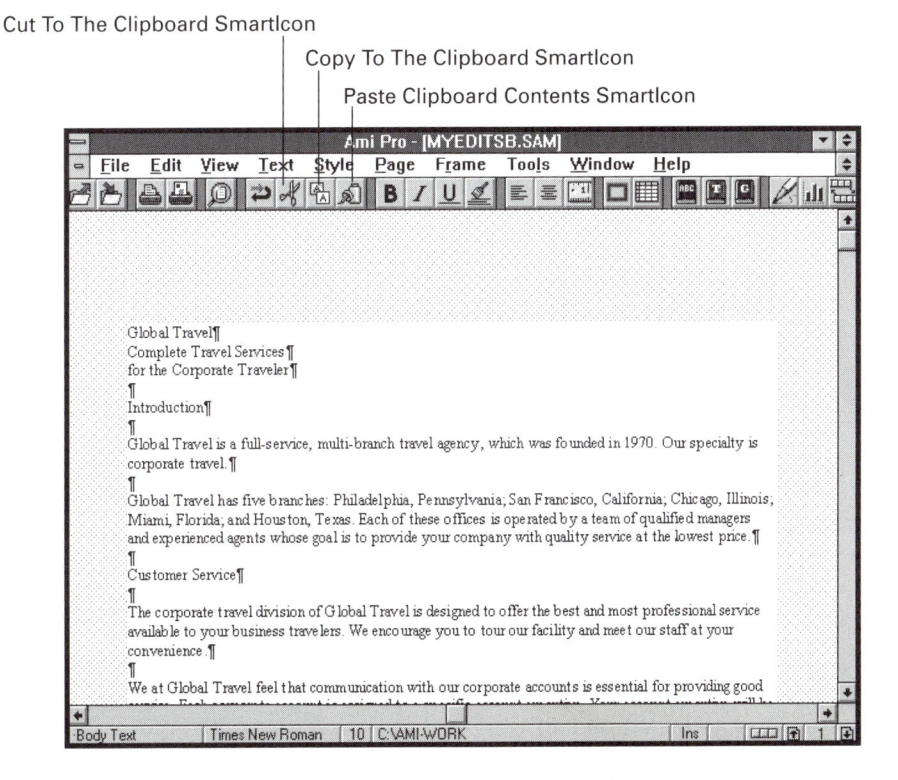

COPYING TEXT

Follow these steps when you want to copy text within a document:

- Select the text to be copied.
- Choose Edit, Copy or click on the *Copy To The Clipboard SmartIcon* (the eighth SmartIcon from the left, displaying two overlapping squares, each containing a capital *A*). This copies the selected text to the Clipboard.
- Place the insertion point where you want to copy the text.
- Choose Edit, Paste or click on the Paste Clipboard Contents SmartIcon to paste the Clipboard text at the insertion point.

Let's copy some text:

1. Select the first four lines of the document (the three-line page heading and the blank line following).

2. Choose **Edit, Copy** to place a copy of the selected text on the Clipboard. Notice that Ami Pro does not remove the selected text from the document, as it did when you chose Edit, Cut.

3. Move the insertion point to the top of page 2 (click on the **Down Page Arrow button**).

4. Choose **Edit, Paste** to paste a copy of the Clipboard contents at the insertion point (see Figure 3.10).

As you learned earlier, you can also use the Paste Clipboard Contents SmartIcon to paste text from the Clipboard.

Try this out:

1. Move the insertion point to the top of page 3.

2. Click on the **Paste Clipboard Contents SmartIcon**. (Because a copy of the text is still on the Clipboard from the last activity, you do not need to copy the text again before pasting.)

3. Choose **File, Save** to save your revised document. (Because you specified a document name and location earlier, you don't need to use File, Save As.)

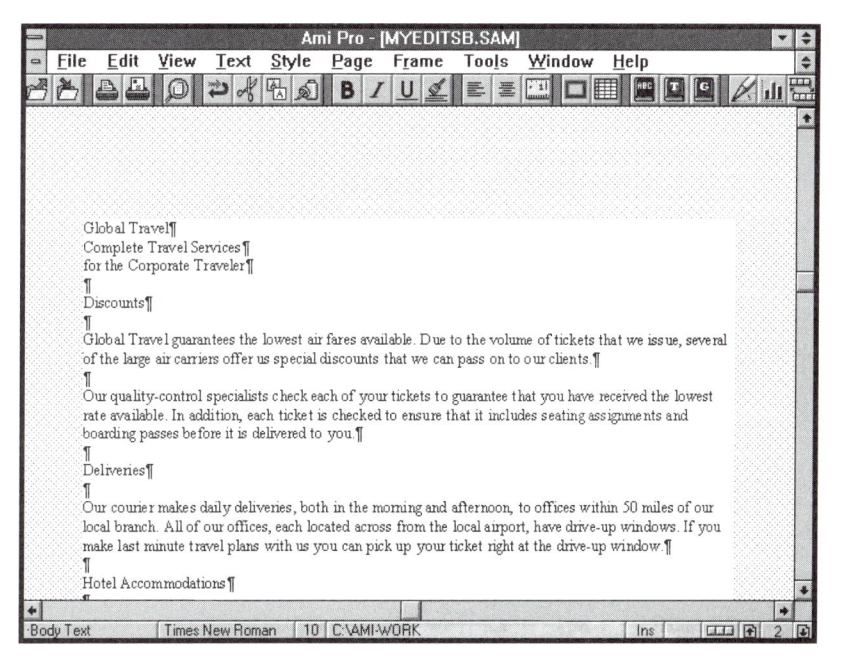

Figure 3.10   **Page 2 of MYEDITSB.SAM, after copying text**

USING EDIT, UNDO TO UNDO YOUR MOST RECENT OPERATION

Ami Pro provides an *Edit, Undo* command that enables you to reverse (undo) an operation you have just completed. You can set Edit, Undo to reverse just the most recent operation you performed (this is the default setting), or up to four operations (the four most recent ones). Since the default setting for Edit, Undo is to reverse only your last single operation, you should use Edit, Undo immediately after performing the operation.

As we said above, you *can* increase the number of Undo levels (by using the Tools, User Setup command). However, this can slow Ami Pro's operation considerably, and it might give you a false sense of security. Refer to your Ami Pro documentation for information on using the Tools, User Setup command.

Here are two methods for reversing an operation immediately after you've completed it: either choose Edit, Undo, or click on the *Undo Last Command Or Action SmartIcon* (the sixth SmartIcon from the left, displaying two arrows making a U-turn).

Let's delete a block of text from your document, and then use Edit, Undo to reverse the deletion:

1. Select the paragraph **Flight Insurance** (near the top of page 3).
2. Press **Delete** to delete the selected text. (When you use Delete rather than Edit, Cut or Edit, Copy, Ami Pro does *not* place the text on the Clipboard.)
3. Choose **Edit, Undo**. Ami Pro restores your deleted text.
4. Save your document.

Now let's use the Undo Last Command Or Action SmartIcon to reverse a potentially catastrophic text-replacement mistake:

1. Move the insertion point to the end of the document (press **Ctrl+End**) and press **Shift+Ctrl+Home** to select the entire document.
2. Type your first initial. Oops! All that's left in the document window is a single character!
3. Click on the **Undo Last Command Or Action SmartIcon**. Whew! Ami Pro restores the entire document.
4. To avoid deleting the entire document again, deselect it.
5. Save your document.
6. Close the document.

PRACTICE YOUR SKILLS

In this chapter, you have learned how to select, delete, and replace text; how to move and copy text; and how to undo edits. The following two Practice Your Skills activities give you the opportunity to practice some of these techniques. After each activity step, we've provided a chapter reference (in parentheses) to inform you of where we introduced the relevant technique for that step.

Follow these steps to produce the final document shown in Figure 3.11 from the original document PRAC3A.SAM:

1. Open **prac3a.sam**. (Chapter 2)
2. Replace all occurrences of *Mayco* with **Macco**. (Chapter 3)

Figure 3.11   **The completed document MYPRAC3A**

Macco Plastics Inc.
Quarterly Sales Report
First Quarter

1. Introduction

Congratulations to all of you! An initial review of the sales figures for the nation reveals a surge in sales in all of Macco's sales areas. Major new clients have been added and many new products are on the way.

As we expected when we entered the field, computer-related products, such as keyboard housings and protective carrying cases, are accounting for a major portion of this upswing.

2. Regional Updates

Midwestern Territory

After several years of falling sales due to the slump in the auto industry, Blair Williams and his folks have something to celebrate. The recent boom in auto manufacturing has led to renewed demand of Macco Products in Detroit.

Northeastern Territory

John Martinson and his group are doing a great job in Nashua. They have secured major contracts for a wide range of new and existing products. Much of this business is coming from Computer Equipment Corporation, a major client of Macco's.

Southern Territory

Mark Daley and his group have done a fine job of maintaining relations with Becker's Product Development Division in Boca Raton. They have been working closely with Becker to decrease manufacturing costs.

3. Computer Study

A companywide study will begin in March, under the direction of Cathy Donaldson and Bill Schuster in data processing, to determine how to most effectively implement automation in our firm. We will be making a large commitment to productivity gains via computerization sometime late this year.

Figure 3.11   **The completed document MYPRAC3A (Continued)**

> Macco Plastics Inc.
> Quarterly Sales Report
> First Quarter
>
> 4. Quarterly Meeting
>
> The quarterly meeting will take place in Memphis this time. You will find the agenda attached to this report.
>
> 5. Conclusion
>
> If the recovery continues at the current pace, this year should be a banner year for all of us at Macco. We want to thank all of you for the outstanding jobs you have done and, most important, for standing by Macco in hard times. Keep up the good work!
>
> John Smith
> Regional Coordinator
> Macco Plastics Inc.

3. Cut the document's second multiple-line paragraph (beginning with *Congratulations to all*) and the following blank line, and paste them before the document's first multiple-line paragraph (beginning with *As we expected*). (Chapter 3)

4. Copy the three-line heading and the following blank line on the top of page 1 to the top of page 2. (Chapter 3)

5. Save the document as **myprac3a**. (Chapter 1)

6. Print your document, and then compare it to Figure 3.11. (Chapter 1)

7. Close the document window. (Chapter 1)

Follow these steps to produce the final document shown in Figure 3.12, using the original document PRAC3B.SAM:

1. Open **prac3b.sam**. (Chapter 2)

2. Replace all occurrences of *Territory* with **Region**. (Chapter 3)

3. Cut the heading *3. Computer Study* and the remaining three paragraphs on page 1 (one multiple-line paragraph and two blank lines) and paste them before the heading *2. Regional Updates*. (Chapter 3)

4. Change *3. Computer Study* to **2. Computer Study**. (Chapter 3)

5. Change *2. Regional Updates* to **3. Regional Updates**. (Chapter 3)

6. Add your name as a fourth line to the three-line heading on the top of page 1. (Chapter 1)

7. Copy your name as a fourth line into the heading on the top of page 2. (Chapter 3)

8. Save the document as **myprac3b**. (Chapter 1)

9. Print your revised document and compare it to Figure 3.12. (Chapter 1)

10. Close the document. (Chapter 1)

Figure 3.12   **The completed document MYPRAC3B**

Macco Plastics Inc.
Quarterly Sales Report
First Quarter
(your name)

1. Introduction

Congratulations to all of you! An initial review of the sales figures for the nation reveals a surge in sales in all of Macco's sales regions. Major new clients have been added and many new products are on the way.

As we expected when we entered the field, computer-related products, such as keyboard housings and protective carrying cases, are accounting for a major portion of this upswing.

2. Computer Study

A companywide study will begin in March, under the direction of Cathy Donaldson and Bill Schuster in data processing, to determine how to most effectively implement automation in our firm. We will be making a large commitment to productivity gains via computerization sometime late this year.

3. Regional Updates

Midwestern Region

After several years of falling sales due to the slump in the auto industry, Blair Williams and his folks have something to celebrate. The recent boom in auto manufacturing has led to renewed demand of Macco Products in Detroit.

Northeastern Region

John Martinson and his group are doing a great job in Nashua. They have secured major contracts for a wide range of new and existing products. Much of this business is coming from Computer Equipment Corporation, a major client of Macco's.

Southern Region

Mark Daley and his group have done a fine job of maintaining relations with Becker's Product Development Division in Boca Raton. They have been working closely with Becker to decrease manufacturing costs.

Figure 3.12   **The completed document MYPRAC3B (Continued)**

Macco Plastics Inc.
Quarterly Sales Report
First Quarter
(your name)

4. Quarterly Meeting

The quarterly meeting will take place in Memphis this time. You will find the agenda attached to this report.

5. Conclusion

If the recovery continues at the current pace, this year should be a banner year for all of us at Macco. We want to thank all of you for the outstanding jobs you have done and, most important, for standing by Macco in hard times. Keep up the good work!

John Smith
Regional Coordinator
Macco Plastics Inc.

SUMMARY

In this chapter, you learned how to delete text with your Delete key, select text, delete and replace selected text, replace found text, move and copy text, and undo operations.

Here's a quick reference guide to the Ami Pro features introduced in this chapter:

Desired Result	How to Do It
Open a document with a SmartIcon	Click on **Open An Existing File SmartIcon**, select document location and name, and then click on **OK** (or double-click on document's name).
Display a SmartIcon's name in title bar	Point to SmartIcon; then press and hold right mouse button.
Delete a single character with Delete key	Place insertion point to left of character; then press **Delete**.
Select text by dragging	Point at one end of text, press and hold mouse button, drag I-beam to other end of text, and then release mouse button.
Select a word	Point inside word; then double-click.
Select a sentence	Hold down **Ctrl**, and click.
Select a paragraph	Hold down **Ctrl**, and double-click.
Select multiple words, sentences, or paragraphs	Use word, sentence, or paragraph selection technique to select single word, sentence, or paragraph, holding down mouse button on last click; then drag.
Select text using Shift and mouse	Place insertion point at one end of text, press and hold **Shift**, click at other end of text, and then release **Shift**.
Select text using Shift and keyboard	Place insertion point at one end of text, press and hold **Shift**, use any keyboard movement technique to move to other end of text, and then release **Shift**.

Desired Result	How to Do It
Extend an existing selection	While holding down **Shift**, click beyond existing selection.
Shorten an existing selection	While holding down **Shift**, click inside existing selection.
Select an existing document	Move to top of document and press **Shift+Ctrl+End**. Or move to end of document and then press **Shift+Ctrl+Home**.
Deselect text	Make another selection, or click outside existing selection.
Delete selected text	Press **Delete**.
Replace selected text	Type new text over the selection.
Find and replace text	Place insertion point where you want to start searching; choose **Edit, Find & Replace**; in Find text box, type your search text; in Replace With text box, type your replacement text; then click on **Find** or **Replace All**. For found text, click on either **Replace & Find Next** or **Replace Remaining**.
Move text	Select text; choose **Edit, Cut** or click on **Cut To Clipboard SmartIcon**; place insertion point where you want to move text; then choose **Edit, Paste** or click on **Paste Clipboard Contents SmartIcon**.
Copy text	Select text; choose **Edit, Copy** or click on **Copy To Clipboard SmartIcon**; place insertion point where you want to insert copy; then choose **Edit, Paste** or click on **Paste Clipboard Contents SmartIcon**.
Reverse last operation	Choose **Edit, Undo**; or click on **Undo Last Command Or Action SmartIcon**.

In Chapter 4, you'll learn the basics of text formatting—how to apply and remove text attributes (such as boldface and italic); how to change fonts; and how to use Ami Pro's Fast Format feature to copy and apply text formatting quickly.

IF YOU'RE STOPPING HERE

If you need to take a break here, please exit Ami Pro. If you want to proceed directly to the next chapter, please do so now.

CHAPTER 4: TEXT FORMATTING

Understanding Text Formatting

Applying Text Attributes

Changing Fonts

Using Fast Format to Copy Text Formatting

The way a document looks has a direct relationship to its overall effectiveness. The impact of a brilliantly written business report, for example, can be severely undermined by an inappropriate typeface, text that is too small to read comfortably, a dizzying barrage of italics or underlining, tables with columns that don't line up, an overly busy page layout, and so on.

We have devoted the next three chapters to controlling a document's appearance. We'll proceed logically: This chapter covers *text formatting*, which controls the appearance of Ami Pro's smallest appearance units: characters. Chapter 5 covers *text enhancements*, which control Ami Pro's intermediate units: paragraphs. And Chapter 6 covers *page layouts*, which control Ami Pro's largest units: pages.

When you're done working through this chapter, you will know how to

- Apply and remove text attributes
- Change fonts
- Use Ami Pro's *Fast Format* feature to copy text formatting

UNDERSTANDING TEXT FORMATTING

Text formatting controls a document's appearance at the character level. This means you can give every letter on a page a different look, if you'd like. (However, we don't advise it; too much text formatting can make a document hard to read and amateurish-looking.)

Ami Pro supports four types of text formatting:

- *Text attributes*. These include bold, italic, underline, and word underline—for example, **bold**, *italic*, underline, and word underline.

- *Fonts*. In Ami Pro a font consists of a *typeface* (the overall shape of characters), a *point size* (the overall height of characters), and a *color*. For example, the text you are reading is printed in a Univers 10-point black font: Univers is the typeface, 10-point is the point size, and black is the color.

- *Capitalization*, which includes uppercase, lowercase, initial caps, and small caps—for example, UPPERCASE, lowercase, Initial Caps, and SMALL CAPS.

- *Special Effects*, which include superscript, subscript, and strikethrough—for example, superscript, subscript, and ~~strikethrough~~ —as well as double underline and overstrike.

In this chapter, we'll show you how to apply and change two types of text formatting: text attributes and fonts. In general, you can apply the skills you learn here to controlling capitalization and special effects, as well.

APPLYING TEXT ATTRIBUTES

Text attributes help you to emphasize specific text. In this book, for example, we chose to use bold for certain headings, such as **Desired Result** and **How to Do It** (which appear in each chapter's Summary), and to italicize new terms, such as *text formatting*.

Ami Pro provides three methods for applying and removing text attributes: the Text menu, SmartIcons, and keyboard shortcuts. Here we'll show you how to apply text attributes with the Text menu and SmartIcons; for information on Ami Pro's keyboard shortcuts, see Appendix B.

USING THE TEXT MENU TO APPLY AND REMOVE TEXT ATTRIBUTES

Follow these steps when you want to use the Text menu to apply text attributes:

- Select the desired text.
- Open the Text menu.
- Click on your desired text attribute: Bold, Italic, Underline, or Word Underline.

Follow these steps when you want to use the Text menu to remove text attributes:

- Select the text that displays the text attribute you wish to remove.
- Open the Text menu.
- Click on the name of the text attribute you want to remove.

You can also remove *all* text attributes by choosing Text, Normal.

If you are not running Ami Pro, please start it now.

Let's begin by opening a new document and applying some text attributes:

1. Open **attribut.sam**.
2. Select **Introduction** (near the top of the document).
3. Choose **Text, Bold**.

4. Deselect **Introduction**, and then observe the text. (You can see text attributes better when the text is deselected.) *Introduction* is now displayed bolder (darker) than the surrounding text (see Figure 4.1).

Figure 4.1   **Bold text**

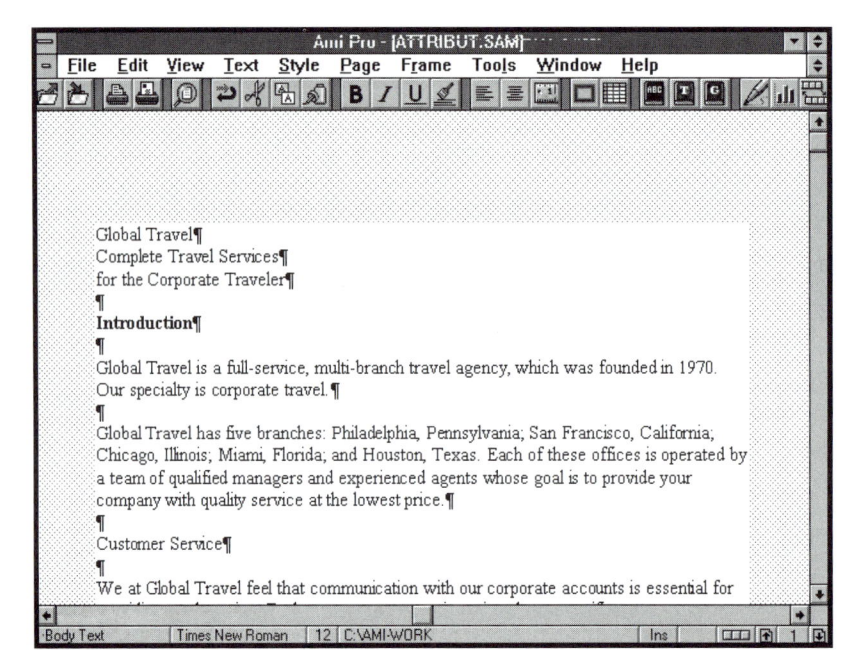

```
 ┌─────────────────────────────────────────────┐
 │              Ami Pro - [ATTRIBUT.SAM]       │
 │ File Edit View Text Style Page Frame Tools Window Help │
 │                                             │
 │  Global Travel¶                             │
 │  Complete Travel Services¶                  │
 │  for the Corporate Traveler¶                │
 │  ¶                                          │
 │  **Introduction**¶                          │
 │  ¶                                          │
 │  Global Travel is a full-service, multi-branch travel agency, which was founded in 1970. │
 │  Our specialty is corporate travel.¶        │
 │  ¶                                          │
 │  Global Travel has five branches: Philadelphia, Pennsylvania; San Francisco, California; │
 │  Chicago, Illinois; Miami, Florida; and Houston, Texas. Each of these offices is operated by │
 │  a team of qualified managers and experienced agents whose goal is to provide your │
 │  company with quality service at the lowest price.¶ │
 │  ¶                                          │
 │  Customer Service¶                          │
 │  ¶                                          │
 │  We at Global Travel feel that communication with our corporate accounts is essential for │
 │                                             │
 │ Body Text | Times New Roman | 12 | C:\AMI-WORK        Ins      1 │
 └─────────────────────────────────────────────┘
```

5. Select **Customer Service** (the next heading on page 1).
6. Choose **Text, Bold** to display *Customer Service* in boldface.

Now let's remove the text attribute that you just applied, and then restore it:

1. If it is not already selected, select **Customer Service**.
2. Open and observe the **Text** menu. A check mark is displayed next to the Bold menu item.
3. Click on **Bold**, and then observe your selected text. *Customer Service* is no longer in boldface.

4. Click on the **Undo Last Command Or Action SmartIcon** (or choose **Edit, Undo**) to restore the Bold text attribute.

Now let's use the Text menu to apply multiple text attributes:

1. Select **Global Travel** (the document's first line).

2. Choose **Text, Italic**. The selected text is now italicized.

3. Choose **Text, Underline**. The selected text is now italicized *and* underlined.

4. Deselect **Global Travel** in order to see the multiple text attributes more clearly (see Figure 4.2).

Figure 4.2   **Italicized and underlined text**

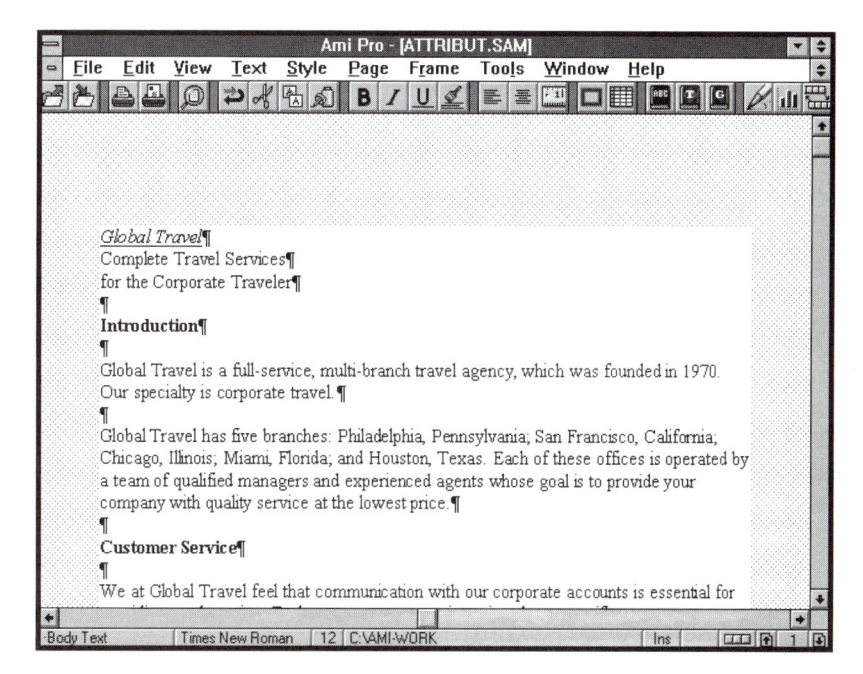

5. Select **Global Travel** again.

6. Choose **Text, Italic**.

7. Deselect, and observe the text. You have removed the italic, but not the underlining.

USING SMARTICONS TO APPLY AND REMOVE TEXT ATTRIBUTES

The following SmartIcons provide quick access to the Bold, Italic, and Underline text attributes:

- The *Bold Text SmartIcon* is the 10th SmartIcon from the left, displaying a boldface **B**.

- The *Italicize Text SmartIcon* is the 11th SmartIcon from the left, displaying an italicized *I*.

- The *Underline Text SmartIcon* is the 12th SmartIcon from the left, displaying an underlined U.

Follow these steps when you want to use a SmartIcon to apply a text attribute:

- Select the desired text.

- Click on the appropriate SmartIcon.

Follow these steps when you want to use a SmartIcon to remove a text attribute:

- Select the text that displays the text attribute you wish to remove.

- Click on the appropriate SmartIcon.

Let's practice using SmartIcons to apply text attributes:

1. Select the paragraph beginning *Global Travel has five branches* (while holding **Ctrl**, double-click on the paragraph).

2. Click on the **Bold Text SmartIcon** to apply the Bold text attribute to the entire paragraph.

3. Open and examine the **Text** menu. The Bold option is checked. Regardless of how you apply text attributes—by using SmartIcons or the Text menu—Ami Pro reflects the selected text's attributes on the Text menu.

4. Click on **Bold** to remove the Bold text attribute.

5. Click on the **Bold Text SmartIcon** again to reapply the Bold text attribute.

6. Click on the **Italicize Text SmartIcon** to italicize the text.

7. Click on the **Underline Text SmartIcon**. Your selected text now displays three text attributes: Bold, Italic, and Underline (see Figure 4.3).

Figure 4.3   **Selected text, with three text attributes applied**

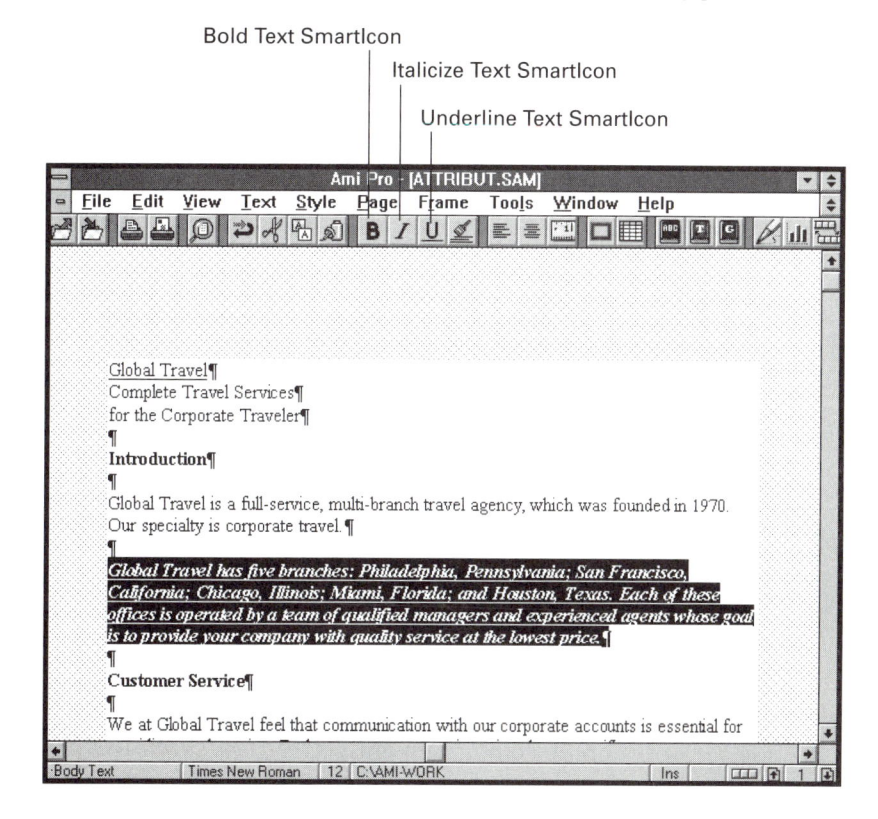

Bold Text SmartIcon
Italicize Text SmartIcon
Underline Text SmartIcon

Now let's use the Text, Normal command to remove *all* text attributes from your selected text:

1. If it is not already selected, select the paragraph beginning *Global Travel has five branches*.

2. Open and examine the **Text** menu. *Bold, Italic,* and *Underline* are all checked.

3. Click on **Normal** to remove all three of these text attributes from the selected text.

4. Open and examine the **Text** menu. All of the check marks are gone.

5. Close the **Text** menu.

PRACTICE YOUR SKILLS

1. Select the entire document, and then italicize all of the document's text.

2. Click on the **Undo Last Command Or Action SmartIcon** to reverse step 1.

3. Remove the underlining from the document's first line, *Global Travel*, and then apply the Bold and Italic attributes to it.

4. Move to the top of page 2.

5. Add Bold and Italic to the second page's first line, *Global Travel*.

6. Save your document as **myattrib**.

CHANGING FONTS

You can change the shape, size, and color of your selected text by changing the text's font. Some people use different fonts for various elements of their documents. For example, this book uses a small black Univers font for body text, and larger blue Tekton fonts for the chapter, section, and page headings.

A font's size, as suggested by the term *point size*, is measured in points. One point equals $1/72$ of an inch. The points measurement system makes it easier to refer to the relatively small size of fonts; thus, you can refer to a "10-point font" rather than a "$10/72$" font."

In Ami Pro, you can apply fonts through the Font dialog box or by using the status bar.

Note: The specific fonts that Ami Pro makes available for your use are dependent on your currently selected printer as well as how your version of Windows is set up. PostScript printers and Windows 3.1, for example, offer a large variety of fonts, whereas inexpensive dot-matrix printers and Windows 3.0 offer a much more limited selection. Throughout the rest of this book, we will ask you to apply fonts that are available automatically in Windows 3.1. If you are not using Windows 3.1, you might find that these fonts are not available. However, we will suggest alternative fonts that should be available to you.

CHANGING FONTS • 111

USING THE FONT DIALOG BOX TO CHANGE FONTS

Follow these steps when you want to use the Font dialog box to change fonts:

- Select the desired text.
- Choose Text, Font to open the Font dialog box.
- Select your desired typeface, point size, and/or color.
- Click on OK to close the Font dialog box.

Let's select some text and use the Font dialog box to change the font:

1. In the heading at the top of page 1, select the lines **Complete Travel Services** and **for the Corporate Traveler**.

2. Choose **Text, Font** to open the Font dialog box.

3. Compare your dialog box to Figure 4.4. (Because various computers have specific fonts available to them, your dialog box might differ somewhat from the figure.) You can use the available options to change the selected text's typeface, size, and color.

   Note: Because most printers can only print black text, we won't instruct you in this book to use any font colors other than black. If your printer supports color printing, or if you want to use various font colors strictly for on-screen purposes, you might want at some time to experiment with other font colors.

Figure 4.4 **The Font dialog box**

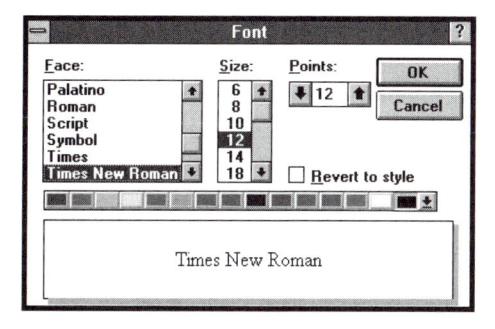

112 • TEXT FORMATTING

4. Observe the Face list box. It lists your available typefaces in alphabetical order, and indicates your selected text's current typeface, *Times New Roman* (or, perhaps, *Times* or *Tms Rmn*).

5. Notice that the sample box at the bottom of the dialog box shows how the currently selected typeface will appear.

6. Scroll up in the Face list box (if necessary), and select **Arial** (or, if Arial is not available, select **Helvetica** or **Helv**). The sample box now displays a sample of the newly selected typeface.

7. Observe the Size list box and the Points box. You can use either box to change your font's point size.

8. In the Size list box, click on **14** (or, if 14 is not available in the Size list box, use the Points box's increment arrows to change the number in that box to **14**). Note that when you change the number in the Size list box, the number in the Points box also changes.

9. Observe the sample box. It now displays a larger font.

10. Click on **OK** to apply your font changes to the selected text.

11. Deselect the text and compare your screen to Figure 4.5.

PRACTICE YOUR SKILLS

1. Select the document's first line, **Global Travel**.

2. Change the selected text's font to **Arial** (or **Helvetica** or **Helv**) **18**-point.

3. Save your document.

USING THE STATUS BAR TO CHANGE FONTS

In addition to the Font dialog box, you can also use the status bar's *Face button* and *Point Size button* to change fonts. (To change a font's color, however, you still must use the Font dialog box.) The Face button is the second button from the left on the status bar; the Point Size button is the third button from the left.

Follow these steps when you want to use the status bar buttons to change fonts:

- Select the desired text.

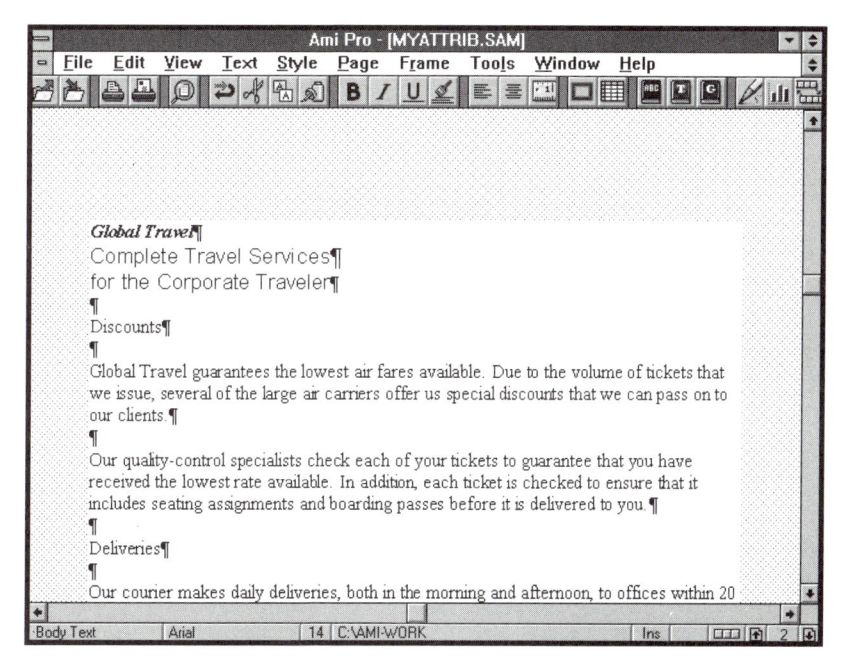

Figure 4.5   **Lines 2 and 3 of the heading, after changing the font**

- Click on the Face button and/or the Point Size button to open the list of available typefaces and/or point sizes.
- Select your desired typeface and/or point size.

Note: If you apply an unavailable typeface or point size to selected text, the typeface name and/or point size will be displayed in red (gray on a noncolor screen) on the Face button and/or the Point Size button. For the best printing results, you should then switch to an available typeface and/or point size. As you work through this book, however, don't worry about having unavailable typefaces or point sizes in your documents.

Let's use the status bar to change a typeface and point size:

1. Move to the top of page 2, and select the page's first line, **Global Travel**.
2. Observe the status bar's Face and Point Size buttons. They display *Times New Roman* and *12*, respectively—the typeface and point size of the currently selected text.

114 • TEXT FORMATTING

3. Click on the **Face button** to open the list of available typefaces (see Figure 4.6).

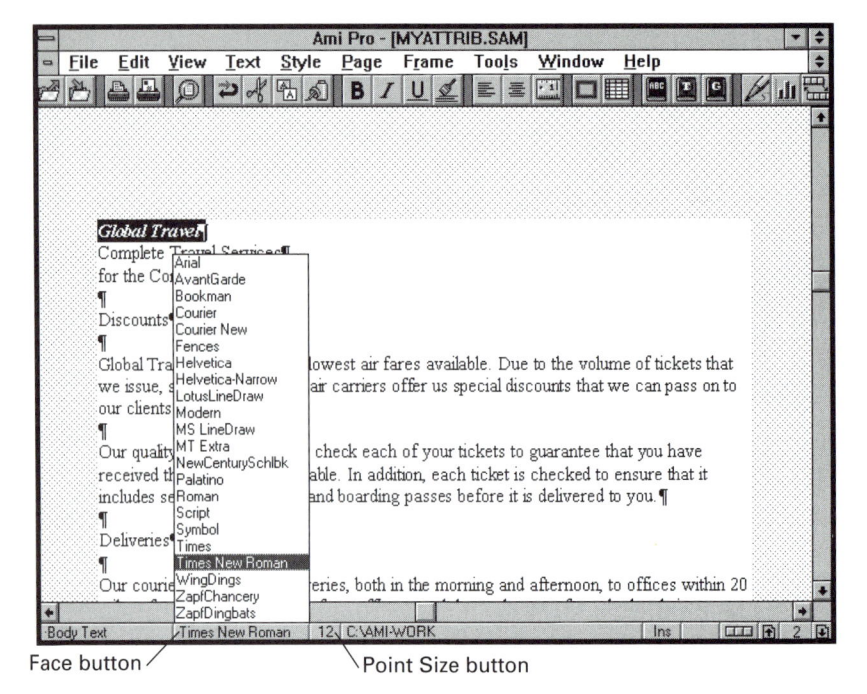

Figure 4.6   **Using the status bar's Face button**

Face button / Point Size button

4. From the list, select **Arial** (or **Helvetica** or **Helv**). Your selected text is displayed in the new typeface.

5. Click on the **Point Size button** to open the list of available point sizes, and then select **18** (or the closest available size). The selected text's point size increases.

PRACTICE YOUR SKILLS

1. Select the second and third lines on page 2, **Complete Travel Services** and **for the Corporate Traveler**.

2. Change the selected text's font to **Arial 14**-point (or the closest equivalent).

3. Save the document.

USING FAST FORMAT TO COPY TEXT FORMATTING

Once you have applied one or more text formats to some of your document's text, you can use Ami Pro's *Fast Format* feature to copy that formatting to other text. For example, if you've applied the Bold, Italic, Arial, and 18-point formats, you can use Fast Format to copy all four formats at once. This saves you the time and effort of applying each format individually for each text selection, and helps to ensure that you apply the formats consistently.

Follow these steps when you want to use Fast Format to copy text formatting:

- Drag to select the text that displays the text formatting you wish to copy.

- Choose Text, Fast Format or click on the *Toggle Fast Format SmartIcon* (the 13th SmartIcon from the left, displaying a paintbrush).

- If you selected an entire paragraph, Ami Pro will open the Fast Format dialog box. If it does, select Only Text Font And Attributes and click on OK; otherwise, go on to the next step.

- Your mouse pointer will change from an I-beam to a *Fast Format arrow*, which appears as an I-beam with a paintbrush attached. Use the Fast Format arrow to select the text to which you want to copy the text formatting. Ami Pro immediately will apply all of the copied text formats to the text you select.

- Repeat the previous step for all of the text to which you want to apply the same text formatting.

- When you're done copying text formats, choose Text, Fast Format or click on the Toggle Fast Format SmartIcon to exit the Fast Format mode.

As implied by the paintbrush on the Toggle Fast Format SmartIcon, you'll find that Fast Format works much like a paintbrush. You "dip" the paintbrush into text containing the text formatting you want, and then "paint" that formatting across other text.

Let's use Fast Format to copy text formatting:

1. Drag to select the first line on page 2, **Global Travel**.

2. Examine the selected text. It displays the Bold, Italic, Arial, and 18-point text formats.

116 • TEXT FORMATTING

3. Choose **Text, Fast Format**.

4. Ami Pro may now open the Fast Format dialog box to ask you if you want to *extract* ("dip into") the selected text's font and attributes, or its paragraph styles. If this box appears, select **Only Text Font And Attributes**, and then click on **OK**. (You'll learn about paragraph styles in Chapter 9.)

5. Observe your mouse pointer. It has changed to a Fast Format arrow.

6. Move to the top of page 3, and then select the page's first line, **Global Travel**. The text immediately changes to bold, italic, Arial, and 18-point (see Figure 4.7).

Figure 4.7   **Using Fast Format to apply text formatting**

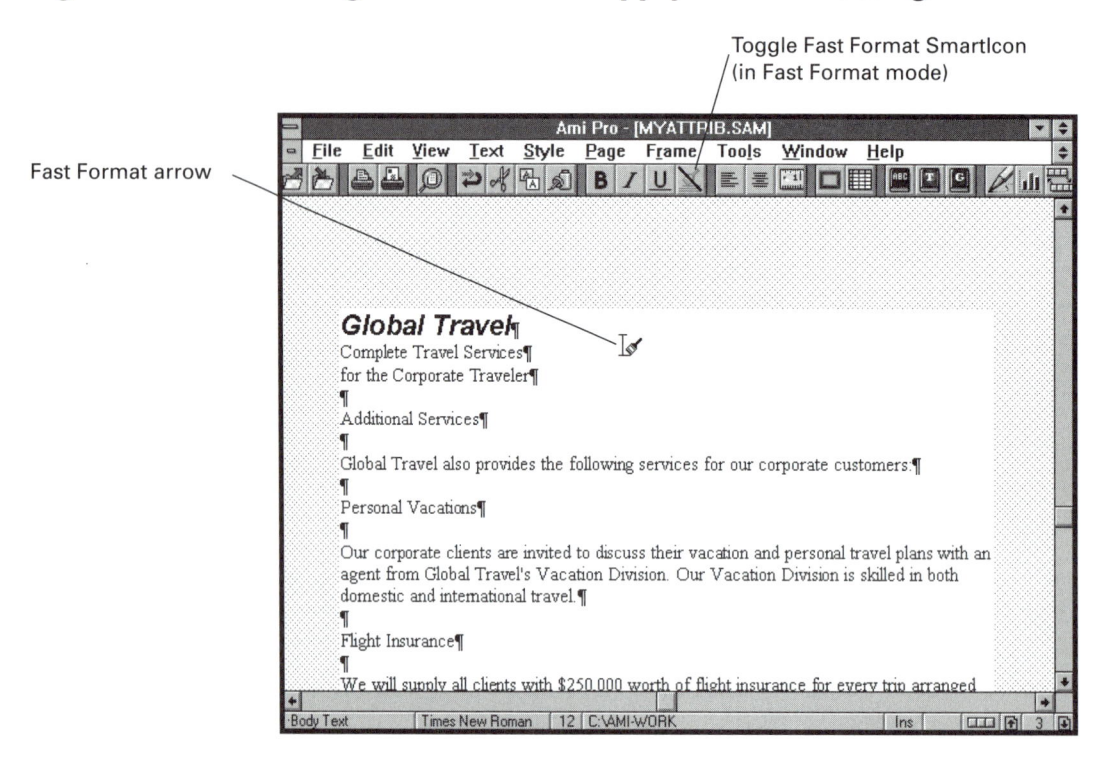

7. Choose **Text, Fast Format** again to exit Fast Format mode. Your mouse pointer changes back to an I-beam.

8. Return to the top of page 2, and then drag to select **Complete** in the page's second line, *Complete Travel Services*.

9. Click on the **Toggle Fast Format SmartIcon**. Because you did not select an entire paragraph this time, Ami Pro doesn't open the Fast Format dialog box.

10. Move to the top of page 3, and then select the page's second and third lines, **Complete Travel Services** and **for the Corporate Traveler**. The text changes to match the text formatting on page 2.

11. Click on the **Toggle Fast Format SmartIcon** to exit the Fast Format mode.

PRACTICE YOUR SKILLS

1. Move to the top of the document.

2. Use Fast Format to copy the text formatting of the word *Introduction* (the document's fifth line) to the following headings throughout the document: **International Travel**, **Corporate Profiles**, **Discounts**, **Deliveries**, **Auto Rentals**, **Hotel Accommodations**, **Additional Services**.

3. On page 3, add bold and italic formatting to the heading **Personal Vacations**.

4. Copy the same text formatting to the next two headings, **Flight Insurance** and **Telex**.

5. Save the document.

6. Print your document and compare it to Figure 4.8.

Figure 4.8 **MYATTRIB.SAM, after copying text formatting**

Global Travel
Complete Travel Services
for the Corporate Traveler

Introduction

Global Travel is a full-service, multi-branch travel agency, which was founded in 1970. Our specialty is corporate travel.

Global Travel has five branches: Philadelphia, Pennsylvania; San Francisco, California; Chicago, Illinois; Miami, Florida; and Houston, Texas. Each of these offices is operated by a team of qualified managers and experienced agents whose goal is to provide your company with quality service at the lowest price.

Customer Service

We at Global Travel feel that communication with our corporate accounts is essential for providing good service. Each corporate account is assigned to a specific account executive. Your account executive will be available to answer any questions and provide you with any information that you request.

The corporate travel division of Global Travel is designed to offer the best and most professional service available to your business travelers. We encourage you to tour our facility and meet our staff at your convenience.

International Travel

We offer complete international itinerary assistance. We maintain a supply of passport and visa applications so that we can provide the necessary papers to our clients with minimum delay. Our International Rate Program guarantees your fast and accurate pricing, no matter how complicated the itinerary.

Corporate Profiles

Your company profile will be stored in our computer, and individual profiles will be maintained on each frequent traveler. Each profile will contain information regarding passport information, seating preference, car rental preference, frequent-flyer membership number, and corporate discount numbers. This information ensures that we can provide frequent travelers, fast, cost-effective itineraries.

Figure 4.8   **MYATTRIB.SAM, after copying text formatting (Continued)**

Global Travel
Complete Travel Services
for the Corporate Traveler

Discounts

Global Travel guarantees the lowest air fares available. Due to the volume of tickets that we issue, several of the large air carriers offer us special discounts that we can pass on to our clients.

Our quality-control specialists check each of your tickets to guarantee that you have received the lowest rate available. In addition, each ticket is checked to ensure that it includes seating assignments and boarding passes before it is delivered to you.

Deliveries

Our courier makes daily deliveries, both in the morning and afternoon, to offices within 20 miles of our local branch. All of our offices, each located across from the local airport, have drive-up windows. If you make last minute travel plans with us you can pick up your ticket right at the drive-up window.

Auto Rentals

We guarantee the lowest prices on all car rentals. We will match the type of car with the information provided in the profile for each of your frequent travelers. Each car that is rented through Global Travel carries an extra $50,000 worth of liability insurance.

Hotel Accommodations

Our Corporate Hotel Program is the most competitive and comprehensive program in the world, offering corporate travelers cost savings and extra amenities in most business locations. Global Travel has access to more than 10,000 hotels worldwide, with a range of rooms from economy to luxury. This selection offers your corporate travelers the accommodations they want with a cost savings of 10-30% off the regular rates.

Figure 4.8   **MYATTRIB.SAM, after copying text formatting (Continued)**

Global Travel
Complete Travel Services
for the Corporate Traveler

Additional Services

Global Travel also provides the following services for our corporate customers:

Personal Vacations

Our corporate clients are invited to discuss their vacation and personal travel plans with an agent from Global Travel's Vacation Division. Our Vacation Division is skilled in both domestic and international travel.

Flight Insurance

We will supply all clients with $250,000 worth of flight insurance for every trip arranged through Global Travel.

Telex

Telex Service is available for international hotel confirmations.

SUMMARY

In this chapter, you have learned the basics of text formatting: how to apply and remove text attributes, how to change fonts, and how to use Fast Format to copy text formatting.

Here's a quick reference guide to the Ami Pro features introduced in this chapter:

Desired Result	How to Do It
Apply or remove the Bold text attribute	Select text; then choose **Text, Bold** or click on **Bold Text SmartIcon**.
Apply or remove the Italic text attribute	Select text; then choose **Text, Italic** or click on **Italicize Text SmartIcon**.
Apply or remove the Underline text attribute	Select text; then choose **Text, Underline** or click on **Underline Text SmartIcon**.
Remove all text attributes	Select text; then choose **Text, Normal**.
Change a typeface	Select text, choose **Text, Font**, select new typeface from Face list box, and then click on **OK**. Or select text, click on status bar's **Face button**, and then select new typeface.
Change a point size	Select text, choose **Text, Font**, select new point size from Size list box or specify new point size in Points box, and then click on **OK**. Or select text, click on status bar's **Point Size button**, and then select new point size.
Copy text formats using Fast Format	Drag to select text containing text formats you want to copy; choose **Text, Fast Format** or click on **Toggle Fast Format SmartIcon**. If Ami Pro opens Fast Format dialog box, select **Only Text Font And Attributes**, and then click on **OK**. Select every piece of text to which you want to copy the text formats. Then again choose **Text, Fast Format** or click on **Toggle Fast Format SmartIcon**.

In the next chapter, you will learn the basics of text enhancements. You'll see how to work with tabs and paragraph indents, create new lines within a paragraph, align paragraphs, and set line spacing.

IF YOU'RE STOPPING HERE

If you need to take a break here, please exit Ami Pro. If you want to proceed directly to the next chapter, please do so now.

CHAPTER 5: TEXT ENHANCEMENTS

Understanding the Current Ruler

Working with Tabs

Setting Indentions and Line Breaks

Changing Paragraph Alignment

Changing Line Spacing

In Chapter 4, you learned how to use text formatting to control the appearance of individual characters in your documents. In this chapter, you'll learn about *text enhancements*, which control Ami Pro's intermediate unit of appearance—the paragraph. You can control many important paragraph appearance features through text enhancements; text enhancements include tabs, indentions, paragraph alignment, and line spacing.

When you're done working through this chapter, you will know how to

- Display and hide the current ruler
- Clear, set, and change tabs
- Set indentions
- Create new lines within a paragraph
- Change paragraph alignment
- Change line spacing

UNDERSTANDING THE CURRENT RULER

To help you control tabs and indentions, Ami Pro supplies three different on-screen *rulers*. Ami Pro's rulers look like their physical counterparts, complete with tick marks that mark inches and fractions of inches. These three types of rulers are

- *Current rulers*, which can control text enhancements for single or selected paragraphs
- *Paragraph-style rulers*, which can control text enhancements for paragraph styles (You'll learn more about styles and paragraph-style rulers in Chapter 9.)
- *Page-layout rulers*, which can control text enhancements for *every* paragraph in a document

In this chapter, we'll work only with the current ruler. Many of the techniques you learn here, however, will apply to working with paragraph-style and page-layout rulers, as well.

As you work through this chapter, you'll find that the current ruler not only enables you to control your tabs and indentions, but also serves as a status indicator of those elements. In this way, the current ruler helps you understand, remove, and/or re-create existing text enhancements.

Ami Pro divides the current ruler into two halves: top and bottom. In this chapter, you'll use the top half to control tabs and indentions. In Chapter 6, you'll use the bottom half to control page layouts.

DISPLAYING THE CURRENT RULER

Ami Pro does not display the current ruler by default, but it is a simple matter to display it yourself. Use either of these two methods when you want to display the current ruler:

- Choose View, Show Ruler.
- Click on the *Show/Hide Ruler SmartIcon*, the 15th SmartIcon from the left, which displays one end of a ruler.

Bear in mind that when you have the current ruler displayed, you reduce the area in the document window available to you for viewing, typing, and editing text. Therefore, you might want to hide the current ruler once you are done working with it. Use one of these two methods when you want to hide the current ruler:

- Choose View, Hide Ruler.
- Click on the Show/Hide Ruler SmartIcon. (This SmartIcon acts as a toggle; click on it once to display the current ruler, click on it again to hide the current ruler.)

If you are not running Ami Pro, please start it now. Let's practice showing and hiding the current ruler:

1. Open **enhance.sam**. (You can choose to hide and display the current ruler only when a document window is open.)

2. Choose **View, Show Ruler**. Ami Pro displays the current ruler at the top of the document window, directly below the SmartIcons. Notice that by displaying the current ruler, you have reduced the available area in the document window for viewing, typing, and editing text (see Figure 5.1).

3. Choose **View, Hide Ruler**. Ami Pro hides the current ruler again, and increases your available typing area.

4. Now click on the **Show/Hide Ruler SmartIcon**. Once again, Ami Pro displays the current ruler.

5. Observe the current ruler. It looks like a physical ruler, complete with tick marks that divide the ruler into inches, and inches into 16ths of inches.

6. Examine the left end of the current ruler, and notice that the current ruler does not start at 0" at the left margin, but instead appears to extend past the left edge of the document window.

In fact, Ami Pro measures the current ruler's tick marks from the *left edge of the current page.*

Figure 5.1 **The current ruler**

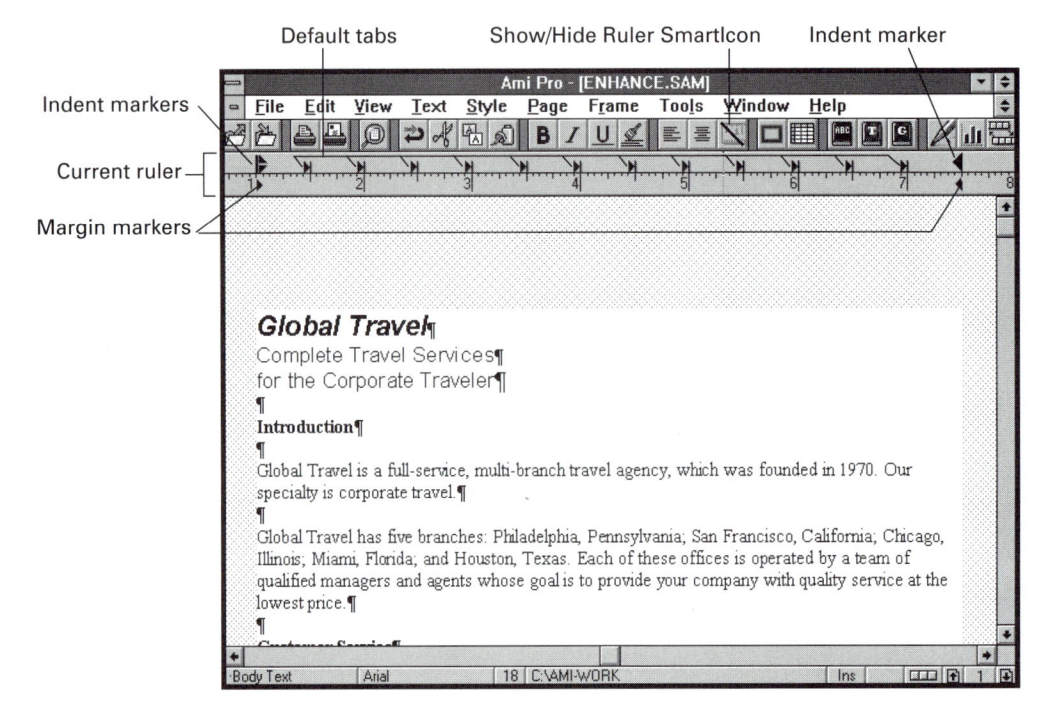

Labels on figure: Default tabs, Show/Hide Ruler SmartIcon, Indent marker, Indent markers, Current ruler, Margin markers

7. Compare the left margin with the current ruler. The left margin aligns with the current ruler's 1" mark, indicating that this document's left margin is 1" wide.

8. Compare the right margin with the current ruler. The right margin aligns with the current ruler's 7 1/2" mark, indicating that the document's right margin is 1" wide.

   (Calculating the right margin requires a bit of math. Because this document is set up for an 8 1/2"-by-11-inch piece of paper—the standard size for business paper and the default paper size for Ami Pro documents—you subtract the location of the right margin, 7 1/2", from the width of the paper, 8 1/2", to arrive at 1".)

9. Look at the top half of the current ruler. It contains the elements you will use for controlling text enhancements, including *default tabs* every half-inch and *indent markers* at the 1" and 7½" marks. (You'll learn how to use tabs and indent markers later in this chapter.)

10. Look at the bottom half of the current ruler. *Margin markers* are set even with the left and right margins, at the current ruler's 1" and 7½" marks. (You'll learn about margin markers in Chapter 6.)

Refer back to Figure 5.1 for the locations of the current ruler's default tabs, indent markers, and margin markers.

SELECTING PARAGRAPHS FOR TEXT ENHANCEMENTS

Before you apply or change text enhancements, you must first select the paragraph or paragraphs to be affected.

As you learned in the last chapter, when you select a paragraph for text formatting (text attributes and fonts), you must select every character in the paragraph. However, because text enhancements affect an entire paragraph at a time (for example, you can't single-space half a paragraph and double-space the other half), you do not have to select the *entire* paragraph when you select for text enhancements.

- To select a *single* paragraph for text enhancements, all you need to do is place the insertion point anywhere within the paragraph; you do not have to select any characters.

- To select *multiple* paragraphs for text enhancements, you only need to select a portion of each paragraph. (As with any multiple-paragraph selection technique, you can select only contiguous paragraphs—that is, paragraphs that immediately precede or follow one another.)

Throughout the rest of this book, we'll refer to these partial-paragraph selection techniques as *paragraph selection shortcuts*. If you feel more comfortable selecting entire paragraphs for text enhancements, please feel free to do so whenever we instruct you to use the paragraph selection shortcuts.

WORKING WITH TABS

You learned in Chapter 1 that you can use Ami Pro's default tabs to align text across the page. This type of alignment is particularly important in tabbed tables, where several categories of information must line up in precise columns. Ami Pro's default tabs, however, do not fit every purpose; sometimes, it's much better to set your own, *custom* tabs.

In this part of the chapter, you'll learn how to clear Ami Pro's default tabs, and how to set and change your own custom tabs.

TAB TYPES

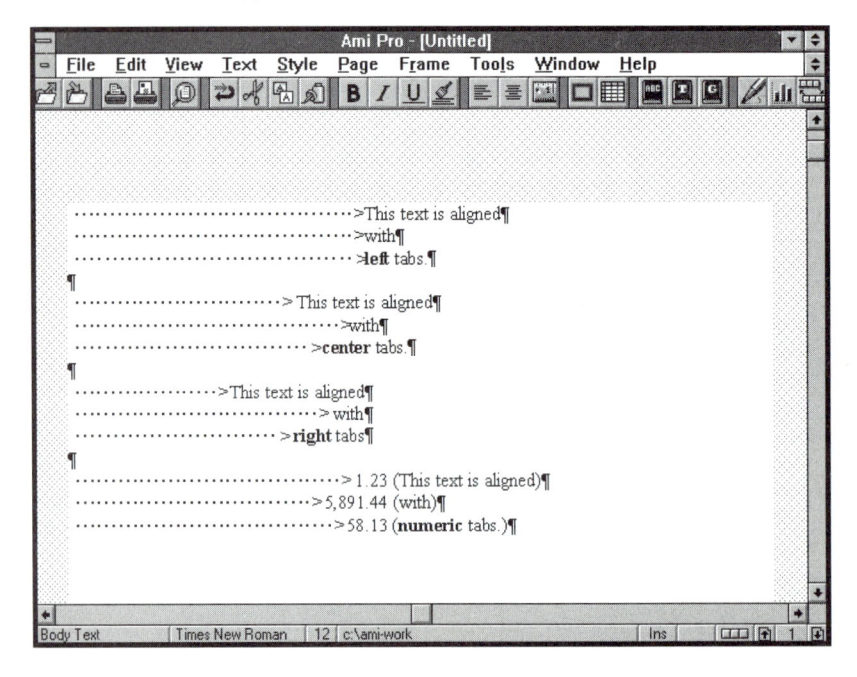

Ami Pro provides four types of tabs: left, center, right, and numeric. Ami Pro's default tabs are left tabs set at half-inch increments.

Figure 5.2 illustrates how the four different tab types align text; Table 5.1 defines each of the tab types.

Figure 5.2   **The four tab types**

WORKING WITH TABS • 131

Table 5.1 **The Four Types of Tabs**

Type	How Tab Affects Text
Left	The left edge of the text aligns against the tab, and then flows to the right.
Center	Text centers on the tab.
Right	The right edge of the text aligns against the tab, and then flows to the left.
Numeric	Text aligns on decimal points. (Numeric tabs are useful for aligning columns of numbers.)

SETTING CUSTOM TABS IN THE CURRENT RULER

For each tab character you want to have in each selected paragraph, you should set one and only one tab in the current ruler. (You set *tabs* in the current ruler; you insert *tab characters* in the typing area by pressing the Tab key.) For example, if you have two tab characters in each paragraph of a tabbed table, you should select those paragraphs and then set two tabs in the current ruler. These two tabs will then instruct each of the tab characters where to align the text in the tabbed table. If, on the other hand, you set too many or too few tabs, your text might not align properly.

Because Ami Pro's numerous default tabs often interfere with custom tabs, it's usually a good idea to clear the default tabs before setting your custom tabs.

Follow these steps when you want to clear Ami Pro's default tabs. **Note:** This procedure will also clear any custom tabs you have set.

- Select the paragraph(s) from which you want to clear tabs. You can select entire paragraphs, or use a paragraph selection shortcut.

- Click on the current ruler to activate and display the ruler's *tab bar*. (The current ruler is active whenever it displays the tab bar. The tab bar is an extension of the current ruler that helps you to set and control tabs.)

- Click on the tab bar's *Clear Tabs button.* (See Figure 5.3, which illustrates the tab bar.)

132 • TEXT ENHANCEMENTS

- Press Esc to deactivate the current ruler and close the tab bar, or you can leave the current ruler active and start setting your custom tabs. (You can also deactivate the current ruler by clicking anywhere in the typing area. However, this also deselects any selected text, which may not be what you want to happen.)

Figure 5.3   **The current ruler's tab bar**

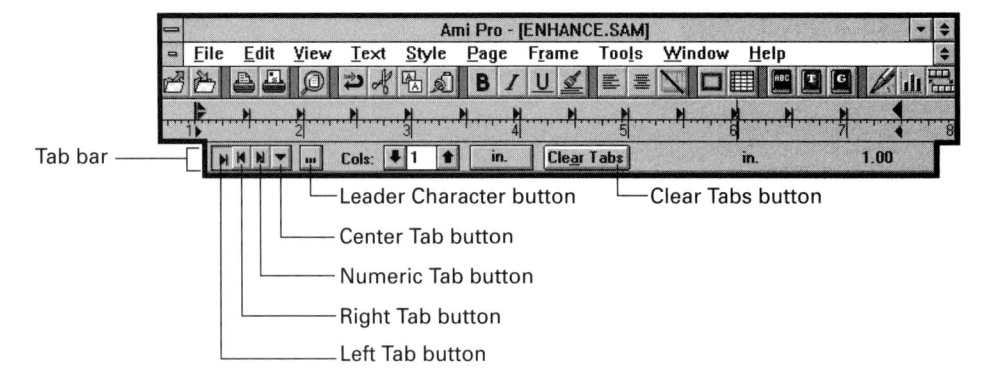

Tab bar
- Leader Character button
- Clear Tabs button
- Center Tab button
- Numeric Tab button
- Right Tab button
- Left Tab button

Follow these steps when you want to set custom tabs:

- Select the paragraph(s) for which you want to set custom tabs.
- Click on the current ruler to activate the ruler and display the tab bar.
- Select the desired tab type by clicking on the appropriate *tab button* in the tab bar.
- If desired, select the desired *tab leader* by clicking on the tab bar's *Leader Character button*. (For more information on the Leader Character button and tab leaders, use Ami Pro Help or refer to your Ami Pro documentation.)
- Point to the desired tab position in the top half of the current ruler (directly above the tick marks), and then click the mouse button.
- Repeat the previous three steps as necessary to set every tab that you want. You can set up to 22 tabs per paragraph.
- Press Esc to deactivate the current ruler.

Note: In Chapter 1, you saw the symbols for tab characters displayed on screen as ·····>. However, as you'll see in this chapter, Ami Pro expands or contracts the tab symbol to fill the available space. For example, when there's very little room between words, tab characters appear as >; when there's more room, they might look like ············>. Regardless of their length, each tab symbol represents a single tab character.

Let's begin our exploration of tabs by adding a line of text to an existing tabbed table:

1. Move to the top of page 2.

2. Scroll down and examine the tabbed table following the heading *Discounts*. The Paris and Sydney savings percentages (*20%* and *10%*) are misaligned.

3. Place the insertion point in the first blank line after the tabbed table.

4. Press **Tab** to move the insertion point to the first tab (½" to the right), and then type **Hong Kong**.

5. Press **Tab** again, and then type **25%**.

6. Press **Enter** to create a new blank line, and then compare your screen to Figure 5.4.

Now let's clear Ami Pro's default tabs, and then set some custom left tabs to fix the misalignment of the Paris and Sydney savings percentages:

1. Drag to select all the text from *Savings* (in the tabbed table's first line) down to and including *Hong* (in the last line). Even though you've only partially selected the first and last lines of the table, the paragraphs between are fully selected for applying text enhancements; this is the multiple-paragraph selection shortcut. Any text enhancements you make now will apply equally to all five lines.

2. Observe the current ruler. Ami Pro has set default tabs every ½".

3. Click once on the current ruler to activate the ruler and display its tab bar.

Figure 5.4   **Adding a line to a tabbed table**

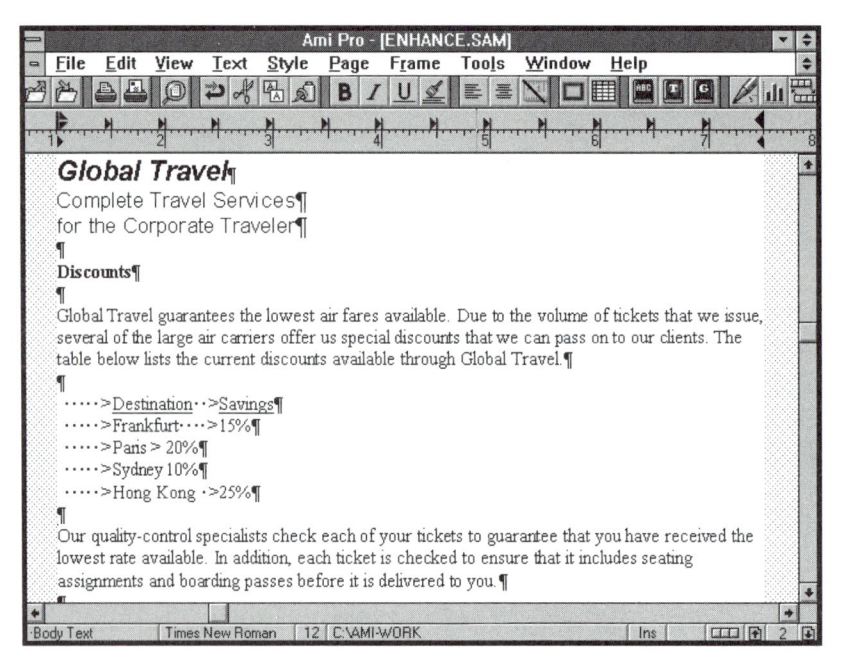

[Screenshot of Ami Pro window showing ENHANCE.SAM document with text:]

Global Travel
Complete Travel Services
for the Corporate Traveler

Discounts

Global Travel guarantees the lowest air fares available. Due to the volume of tickets that we issue, several of the large air carriers offer us special discounts that we can pass on to our clients. The table below lists the current discounts available through Global Travel.

>Destination >Savings
>Frankfurt >15%
>Paris > 20%
>Sydney 10%
>Hong Kong >25%

Our quality-control specialists check each of your tickets to guarantee that you have received the lowest rate available. In addition, each ticket is checked to ensure that it includes seating assignments and boarding passes before it is delivered to you.

4. Examine the left end of the tab bar. It contains four tab buttons. They are, from left to right, the Left Tab button, the Right Tab button, the Numeric Tab button, and the Center Tab button (refer back to Figure 5.3).

5. Look in the center of the tab bar. It contains a Clear Tabs button.

6. Click on **Clear Tabs**. Ami Pro removes all of the default tabs from the current ruler, and your tabbed table becomes completely misaligned. Notice how the tab characters stretch across the typing area; without tabs, the tab characters don't know where to stop (see Figure 5.5).

7. Verify that the tab bar's Left Tab button is selected. The currently selected tab button determines the alignment of the next tab that you set.

Figure 5.5   **The tabbed table, after clearing tabs**

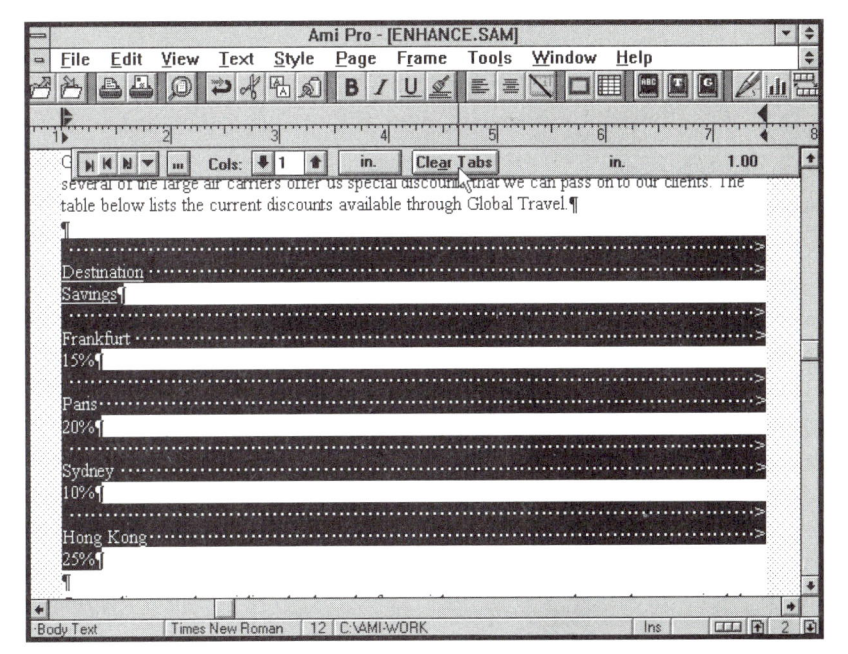

8. Point directly above the current ruler's 2" mark. Ami Pro displays a vertical line in the ruler to indicate the exact ruler position to which you are pointing.

9. Click the mouse button to set a left tab at 2". (Don't worry if the tab isn't *exactly* above the 2" mark. You'll learn how to adjust tab positions later in this chapter.)

10. Observe the tabbed table. The table's first column is now left-aligned under the current ruler's 2" mark, but long tab characters are pushing the second column's text onto the next line.

11. Click directly above the current ruler's 3 ½" mark to set another left tab. Ami Pro aligns the table's second column (see Figure 5.6).

12. Press **Esc** to deactivate the current ruler.

Figure 5.6   **The tabbed table, after setting two tabs**

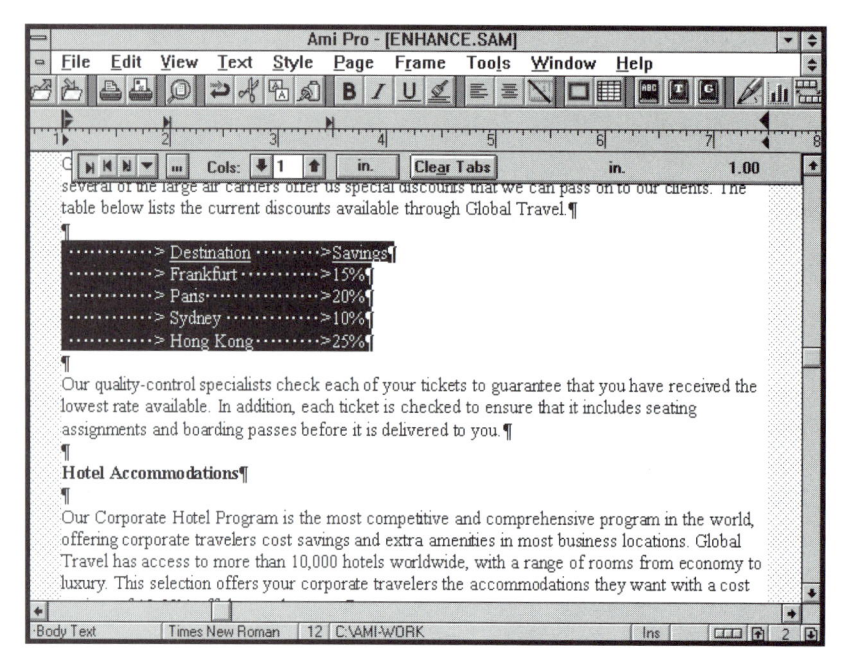

SETTING VARIOUS TYPES OF TABS

Now that you've had a chance to work with left tabs, let's set some other types of tabs:

1. Scroll down to the tabbed table following the heading *Hotel Accommodations*, near the bottom of page 2.

2. Use the multiple-paragraph selection shortcut to select the body (the lower four lines) of the tabbed table.

3. Activate the current ruler (click on it), and then click on **Clear Tabs** to clear the default tabs.

4. Click on the **Right Tab button** (the second tab button from the left) to make the next tab you set a right tab.

5. Click above the current ruler's 4½" mark to set a right tab at 4½". Notice that the on-screen marker for the right tab looks like the Right Tab button.

6. Look at your tabbed table. The right edges of the hotel names now align at 4½".

WORKING WITH TABS • 137

7. Click on the **Numeric Tab button** (the third tab button from the left) to make the next tab you set a numeric tab.

8. Set a numeric tab at 7" to align the numbers in the Daily Rate column by each number's decimal point. Notice that the marker for the numeric tab looks like the Numeric Tab button.

9. Deactivate the current ruler (press **Esc**).

PRACTICE YOUR SKILLS

1. Place the insertion point anywhere within the tabbed table's heading (the table's first line).

2. Clear the paragraph's default tabs.

3. Set a center tab at 3½" (use the **Center Tab button**, the fourth tab button from the left). Notice that the marker for the center tab looks like the Center Tab button.

4. Set a right tab at 6½". Notice that columns for the tabbed table's first line and remaining lines are misaligned (see Figure 5.7). We will fix this in the next activity.

5. Deactivate the current ruler.

MOVING CUSTOM TABS

Once you've set custom tabs, Ami Pro enables you to change their positions quickly and easily. Follow these steps when you want to move custom tabs:

- Select the desired paragraph(s).
- Activate the current ruler.
- Drag the custom tab to a new position.

Note: Even though you can drag to change the *position* of a custom tab (for example, from 2" to 3"), you cannot drag to change a custom tab's *type* (for example, from a left tab to a center tab). Instead, you must clear the existing tab, and then set a new tab with the desired tab type. You'll learn how to clear individual tabs next.

138 • TEXT ENHANCEMENTS

Figure 5.7   The Hotel Accommodations tabbed table, misaligned

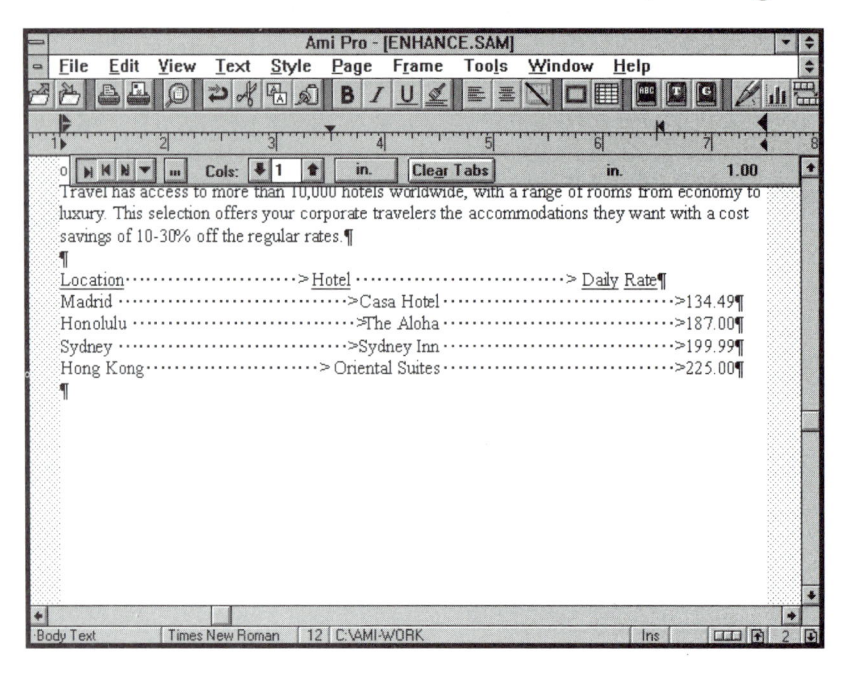

[Screenshot of Ami Pro window showing the misaligned tabbed table with Location, Hotel, and Daily Rate columns for Madrid/Casa Hotel/134.49, Honolulu/The Aloha/187.00, Sydney/Sydney Inn/199.99, and Hong Kong/Oriental Suites/225.00]

CLEARING INDIVIDUAL TABS

You've learned that you can clear *all* tabs, default and custom, by clicking on the Clear Tabs button. However, if you already have set up a number of custom tabs for a paragraph or paragraphs, you might wish to delete one or more *individual* tabs. Follow these steps when you want to clear individual tabs:

- Select the desired paragraph(s).
- Activate the current ruler.
- Drag the custom tab down into the typing area, and then release the mouse button.

Let's fix the Hotel Accommodations tabbed table's misalignment by changing and clearing individual tabs:

1. Select the body (the last four lines) of the tabbed table.

2. Activate the current ruler, and then drag the numeric tab at 7" over to 6¼", to adjust the position of all the table's numbers.

WORKING WITH TABS • 139

As you drag, notice that the right end of the tab bar indicates the tab's numerical position on the ruler as that position changes (see Figure 5.8).

Figure 5.8 **Moving a tab**

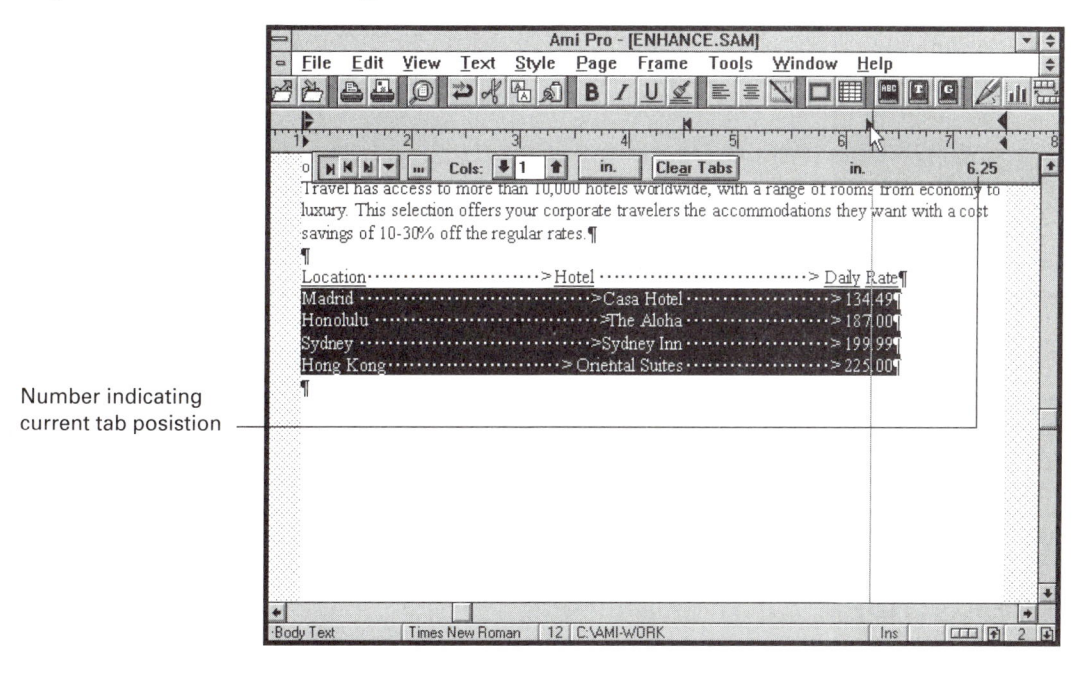

Number indicating current tab posistion

3. Place a center tab at 3½". Notice that this causes a severe misalignment, because there is now an unnecessary tab in the current ruler (the right tab at 4½"). This prevents the Daily Rate column from moving to its intended numeric tab location at 6¼".

4. Drag the unnecessary right tab at 4½" down off the current ruler into the typing area, and then release the mouse button to clear this tab. This corrects the tabbed table's misalignment problem.

5. Deactivate the current ruler.

6. Deselect the text, and then compare your screen to Figure 5.9.

7. Save your document as **myenhanc**.

Figure 5.9   **The Hotel Accommodations tabbed table, properly aligned**

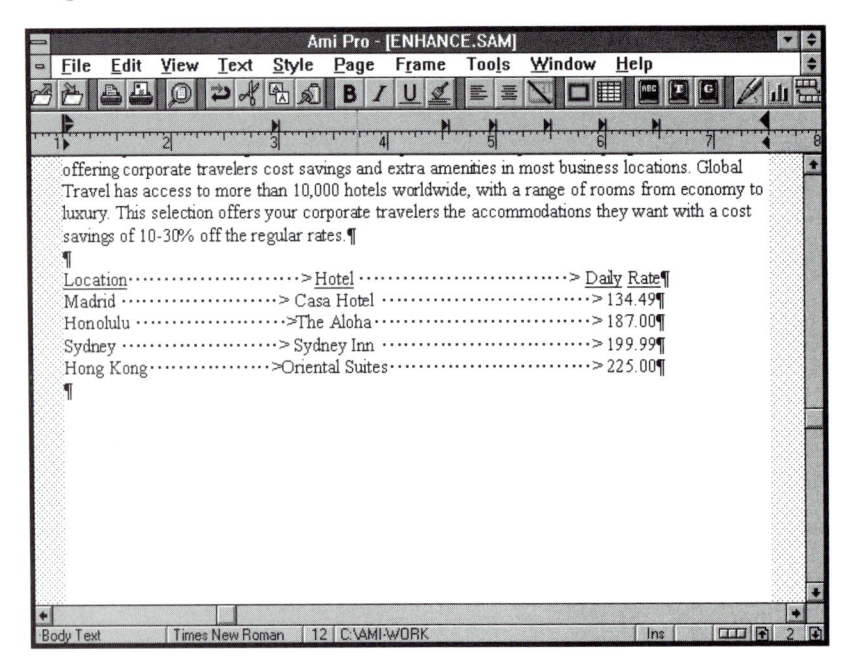

```
                    Ami Pro - [ENHANCE.SAM]
  File  Edit  View  Text  Style  Page  Frame  Tools  Window  Help
```

offering corporate travelers cost savings and extra amenities in most business locations. Global Travel has access to more than 10,000 hotels worldwide, with a range of rooms from economy to luxury. This selection offers your corporate travelers the accommodations they want with a cost savings of 10-30% off the regular rates.¶

Location	Hotel	Daily Rate
Madrid	Casa Hotel	134.49
Honolulu	The Aloha	187.00
Sydney	Sydney Inn	199.99
Hong Kong	Oriental Suites	225.00

SETTING INDENTIONS AND LINE BREAKS

Margins define the top, bottom, left, and right page-boundaries of an entire document. (You'll learn more about margins in Chapter 6.) *Indentions*, on the other hand, define the left and right boundaries for each paragraph within a document.

By default, Ami Pro sets a paragraph's left and right indentions equal to the document's left and right margins. By modifying indentions, however, you can set left and right paragraph boundaries that are different from the overall document's boundaries. Figure 5.10 illustrates the relationship between margins and indentions.

Ami Pro enables you to set indentions using either the current ruler's indent markers or the Indentions dialog box. Because the indent markers are more visually intuitive, we'll show you how to use the indent markers first. Then we'll proceed on to the Indention dialog box.

SETTING INDENTIONS AND LINE BREAKS • 141

Figure 5.10   Margins, indentions, and the current ruler's indent markers

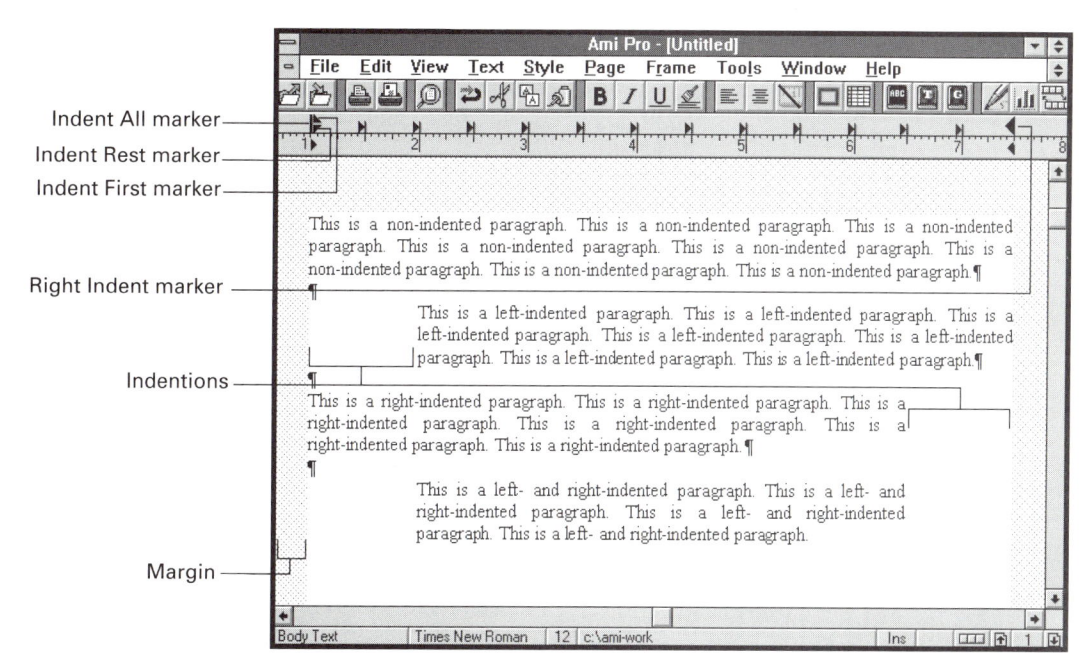

THE CURRENT RULER'S INDENT MARKERS

The current ruler contains four indent markers that you can use to control indentions. Table 5.2 defines the indent markers and their functions; refer back to Figure 5.10 for the location of these indent markers.

Table 5.2   **The Current Ruler's Indent Markers**

Indent Marker	What It Controls
Indent All	The left boundary for every line of the paragraph
Indent First	The left boundary for the first line of a paragraph
Indent Rest	The left boundary for every line in a paragraph except the first line
Right Indent	The right boundary for every line in a paragraph

SETTING INDENTIONS WITH THE CURRENT RULER

As it is for changing custom tabs, the procedure for setting indentions with the current ruler's indent markers is simply a matter of dragging. Follow these steps when you want to set indentions with the current ruler:

- Select the paragraph(s) you want to indent.

- Drag the appropriate indent marker(s) to new position(s) in the current ruler.

There are some limits on where and how you can drag indent markers:

- You can drag the Indent First, Indent Rest, and Right Indent markers independently; however, when you drag the Indent All marker, Ami Pro automatically moves the Indent First and Indent Rest markers along with it.

- You cannot drag the Indent First and Indent Rest markers to the left of the Indent All marker.

- You cannot drag any indent markers beyond the left and right margins.

Let's use the indent markers to set some indentions in MYENHANC.SAM:

1. Move to the top of page 3.

2. Scroll down, and then place the insertion point in the heading *Personal Vacations*. This heading is indented ½" from the left margin.

3. Observe the current ruler's indent markers, located at both ends of the current ruler's top half. At the left end, the Indent All marker (the vertical bar), the Indent First marker (the upper triangle), and the Indent Rest marker (the lower triangle) are all clustered at the 1½" mark, a half-inch in from the left margin. At the right end, the Right Indent marker (the single triangle) is at the 7" mark, a half-inch in from the right margin (see Figure 5.11).

SETTING INDENTIONS AND LINE BREAKS • 143

Figure 5.11 **Indent markers for a left- and right-indented paragraph**

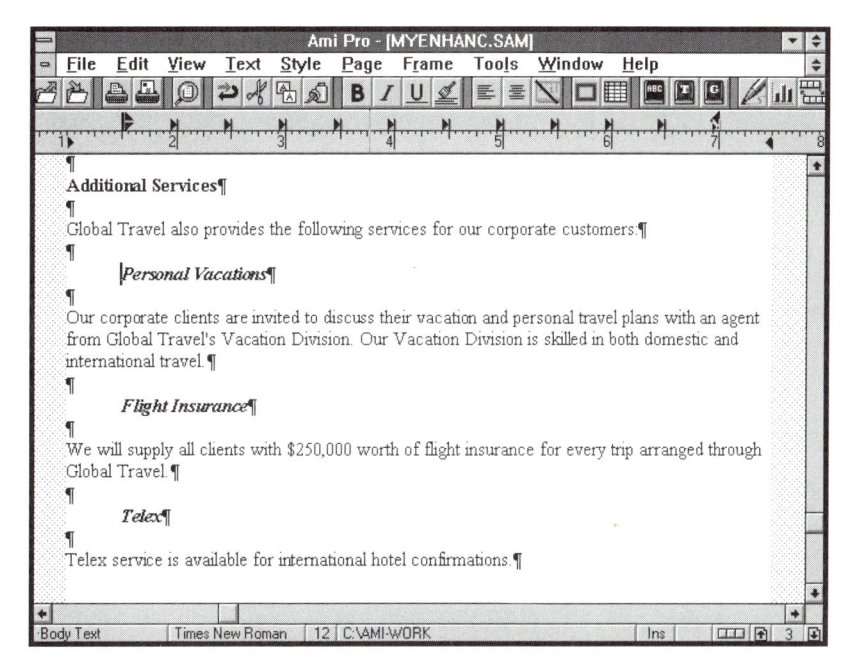

4. Place the insertion point in the paragraph beginning *Our corporate clients*. This paragraph is not indented. On the current ruler, you can see that the three indent markers at the left end are set even with the left margin at 1", and the Right Indent marker is set even with the right margin at 7½".

5. Drag the **Right Indent marker** to 7". (Align the indent marker's flat side with the current ruler's 7" mark. As you drag, notice that the right end of the tab bar displays the indent marker's exact numerical position.) This new right indention creates a different right-hand boundary for the selected paragraph.

6. Drag the **Indent All marker** to the 1½" mark to change the left-hand boundary of the selected paragraph. Notice that as you drag the Indent All marker, the Indent First and Indent Rest markers move along with it. (If you accidentally drag only the Indent First or only the Indent Rest marker, use **Edit, Undo** to reverse your change, and then try again.)

7. Deactivate the current ruler.

SETTING INDENTIONS USING THE INDENTION DIALOG BOX

If you are not fully comfortable with the mouse, you might prefer to set indentions using the Indention dialog box. This dialog box enables you to be very precise in setting indentions, even if your mousing skills are as yet only so-so. The disadvantage is that you cannot see the indentions you set until you close the Indention dialog box. Additionally, because using the dialog box is not visually intuitive, you might need to use some trial and error to find the settings that give you the results you want. A good compromise is to eyeball the indentions with the indent markers, and then set precise numbers in the Indention dialog box.

Follow these steps when you want to use the Indention dialog box to set indentions:

- Select the paragraph(s) you want to indent.
- Choose Text, Indention to open the Indention dialog box.
- Use any of the Indent boxes to set the desired indentions.
- Click on OK to close the dialog box.

The numbers you set in the Indention dialog box define the distance of the indentation from the left or right margin, *not* the location on the current ruler. As examples, in a document with 1" left and right margins, to set a one-inch left indention you would type 1, *not* 2, in the Indent All box; to set a one-inch right indention, you would type 1, *not* 6.5, in the Indent From Right box.

Let's use the Indention dialog box to set some indentions:

1. Verify that the insertion point is still in the paragraph beginning *Our corporate clients*, and then open and examine the **Text** menu. Because you have set indentions for the current paragraph, *Indention* is checked.

2. Click on **Indention** to open the Indention dialog box. Observe that both the Indent All and Indent From Right boxes are set to *0.50* (one-half inch), as shown in Figure 5.12. If they are not, type **.5** in each of the boxes now.

3. Click on **OK** to close the dialog box.

SETTING INDENTIONS AND LINE BREAKS • 145

Figure 5.12   **The Indention dialog box**

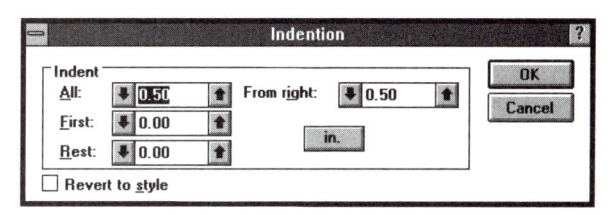

4. Place the insertion point in the paragraph beginning *We will supply all clients* (the next multiple-line paragraph on page 3).

5. Choose **Text, Indention**.

6. In the Indent All box, type **.5**.

7. Press **Tab** three times to move to the Indent From Right box, and then type **.5**.

8. Click on **OK** to close the dialog box, and then examine the current paragraph. It is now indented one-half inch from both sides, just like the previous paragraph.

9. Observe the current ruler. All four indent markers reflect the indentions you set in the Indention dialog box.

PRACTICE YOUR SKILLS

1. Scroll down, if necessary, and then place the insertion point in the paragraph beginning *Telex service is available*.

2. Use either the indent markers or the Indention dialog box to indent the paragraph one-half inch in from both the left and right margins.

3. If you used the indent markers in step 2, deactivate the current ruler.

4. Compare your screen to Figure 5.13.

146 • TEXT ENHANCEMENTS

Figure 5.13   **MYENHANC.SAM, after indenting three paragraphs**

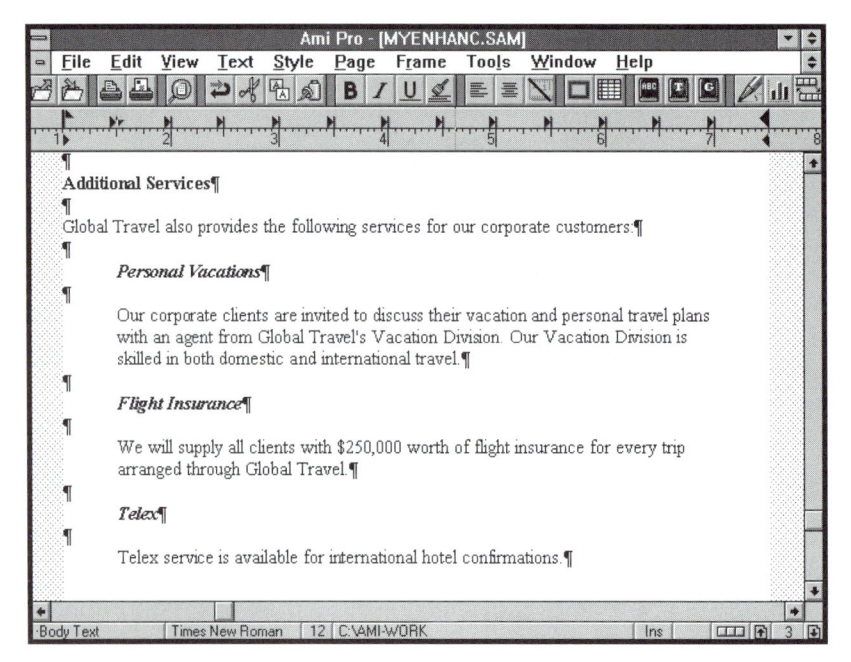

SETTING HANGING INDENTS

Paragraphs with *hanging indents* are paragraphs where the first line is left-indented less than all of its subsequent lines. In effect, the first line *hangs* to the left over the rest of the lines. People commonly use hanging indents for bulleted or numbered lists, like the lists throughout this book.

As with all indentions in Ami Pro, you can create hanging indents using either the current ruler's indent markers and/or the Indention dialog box.

Follow these steps when you want to set a hanging indent with the current ruler:

- Select the paragraph(s) for which you want to set a hanging indent.

- Drag the Indent Rest marker so that it is farther from the left margin than the Indent First marker.

Follow these steps when you want to set a hanging indent using the Indention dialog box:

- Select the paragraph(s) for which you want to set a hanging indent.
- Choose Text, Indention to open the Indention dialog box.
- In the Indent Rest box, set a number that is higher than the number in the Indent First box.
- Click on OK.

Let's set a hanging indent with the current ruler:

1. Scroll up to the heading *Newsletter* (near the top of page 3).
2. Place the insertion point in the paragraph beginning *1. Travel Costs*.
3. Drag the **Indent Rest marker** (the lower of the two triangles on the current ruler's left end) to 1½". Be careful to drag *only* the Indent Rest marker! If you inadvertently drag the other indent markers, choose **Edit, Undo**, and then try again.
4. Observe your hanging indent. The second line of the paragraph is indented one-half inch, and the first line remains unindented at the left margin (see Figure 5.14).

Now let's use the Indention dialog box to set a hanging indent:

1. Verify that the insertion point is still in the paragraph beginning *1. Travel Costs*.
2. Choose **Text, Indention**, and then observe the Indention dialog box. The Indent Rest box is set to *0.50*, but all of the other Indent boxes are set to *0.00*. (If they are not, adjust them now.)
3. Click on **OK** to close the dialog box.
4. Place the insertion point in the paragraph beginning *2. Special Fares*, and then choose **Text, Indention**.
5. Press **Tab** twice to move to the Indent Rest box, type **.5**, and then click on **OK**. The current paragraph's hanging indent now matches the hanging indent above it.

Figure 5.14   **A paragraph with a hanging indent**

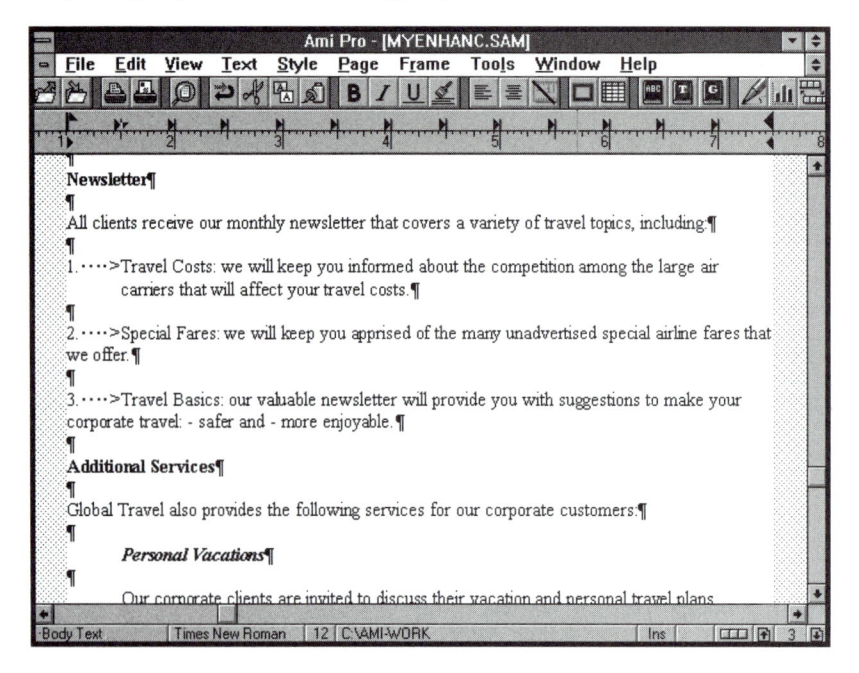

PRACTICE YOUR SKILLS

1. Place the insertion point in the paragraph beginning *3. Travel Basics*.
2. Use either the current ruler or the Indention dialog box to set a half-inch hanging indent.
3. If you used the current ruler in step 2, deactivate the ruler.
4. Compare your screen to Figure 5.15.

USING CTRL+ENTER TO CREATE A NEW LINE

You learned in Chapter 1 that when you press Enter to begin a new line, you also create a new paragraph. (Remember—in Ami Pro, a paragraph is any amount of text between two returns.) To save you some formatting effort, Ami Pro automatically carries down into your new paragraph any text enhancements that you set in the previous paragraph. For example, if you apply a one-inch left indent to a paragraph, and then press Enter anywhere within that paragraph in order to create a new paragraph, your new paragraph will also have a one-inch left indent.

SETTING INDENTIONS AND LINE BREAKS • 149

Figure 5.15   **MYENHANC.SAM, after creating three paragraphs with hanging indents**

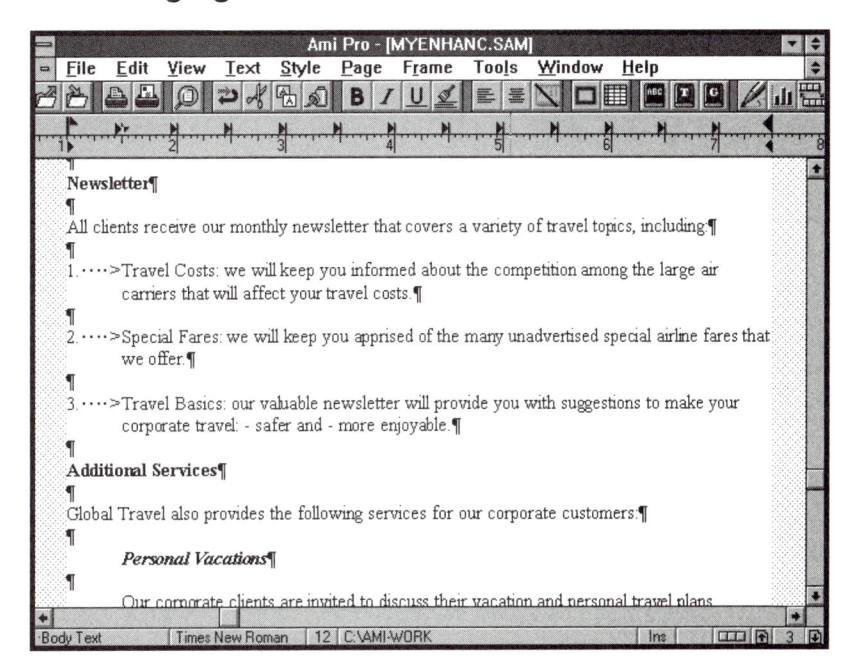

This carrying down of text enhancements is convenient for many paragraphs, but may not work well for maintaining hanging indents. For example, let's say you want to insert a new line in the middle of a list that is within a hanging-indent paragraph. When you press Enter after adding the list item, you lose your hanging indent. Why? It's because you've created a new hanging-indent paragraph, and the first line of that new paragraph aligns itself with the Indent First marker, rather than with the Indent Rest marker.

To remedy this situation, Ami Pro lets you use Ctrl+Enter to insert a *hard return.* A hard return creates a new line *without* creating a new paragraph. In this way, the new line, not being a new paragraph, aligns with the Indent Rest marker and maintains the hanging indent.

Follow these steps when you want to create a new line within a paragraph without creating a new paragraph:

- Place the insertion point at the place where you want to end the current line and create a new line.

150 • TEXT ENHANCEMENTS

- Press Ctrl+Enter to insert a *hard return*.

Let's see how Ctrl+Enter works to maintain a hanging indent:

1. In the paragraph beginning *3. Travel Basics*, place the insertion point immediately to the left of the hyphen (-) in *- safer and*.

2. Press **Enter** to create a new paragraph. Ami Pro moves all the text that is to the right of the insertion point onto the next line. Because you've created a new paragraph, the first (and in this case, the only) line loses the hanging indent and moves back flush with the left margin.

3. Press **Backspace** to delete the return you just inserted and bring the text back up to its original position.

4. Now press **Ctrl+Enter** to enter a hard return and create a new line without creating a new paragraph. You maintain your hanging indent (see Figure 5.16). Pressing Ctrl+Enter ends the line with a hard return instead of with a regular return. Unlike regular returns, you cannot view symbols for hard returns on screen.

Figure 5.16   **Maintaining a hanging indent**

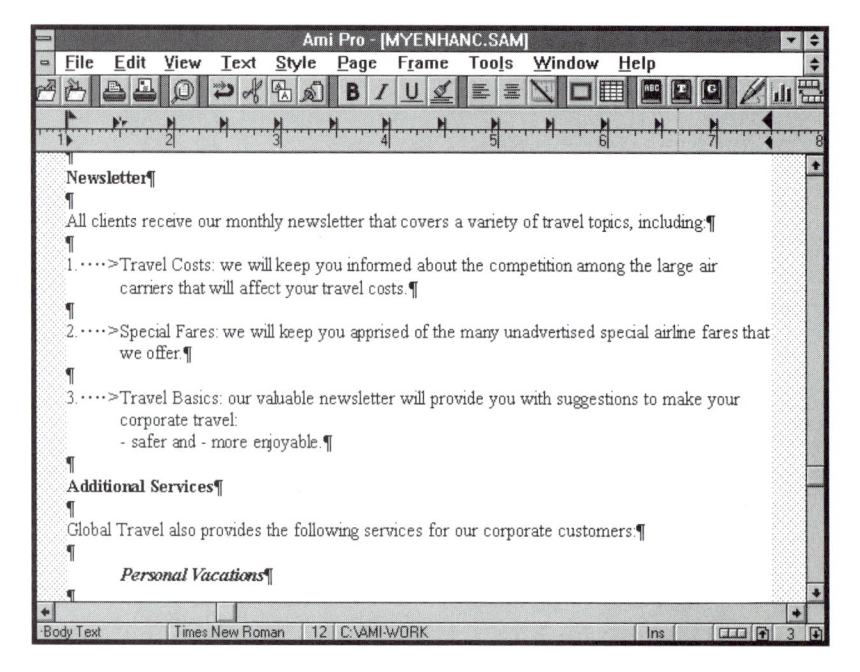

5. Press **Ctrl+Enter** again to create a blank line while still maintaining the hanging indent.

6. Place the insertion point to the left of the second hyphen in the same paragraph, before - *more enjoyable*.

7. Press **Ctrl+Enter** twice to create two new lines while maintaining the hanging indent.

CHANGING PARAGRAPH ALIGNMENT

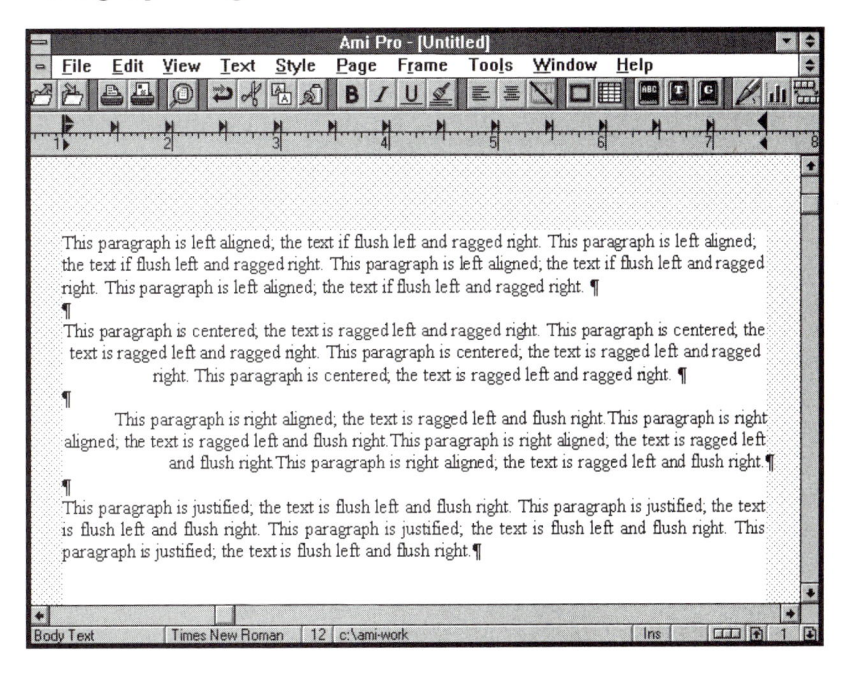

Paragraph alignment determines how Ami Pro positions a paragraph between the left and right indents. Ami Pro provides four options for paragraph alignment. Figure 5.17 illustrates how the various paragraph alignments appear on your computer screen; Table 5.3 defines each paragraph alignment option.

Figure 5.17   **Paragraph alignment**

Table 5.3   **Paragraph Alignment Options**

Alignment Option	How It Affects Text
Left	Lines of text are *flush left* (aligned evenly along the left indent) and *ragged right* (aligned unevenly near the right indent). This is Ami Pro's default paragraph alignment setting.
Center	Lines of text are centered between the left and right indents; both the left and right sides of a centered paragraph are ragged.
Right	Lines of text are *flush right* (aligned evenly along the right indent) and *ragged left* (aligned unevenly near the left indent).
Justify	Lines of text are both flush left and flush right; Ami Pro adjusts the spacing between words so that each line stretches from the left indent to the right indent. On the last line of a paragraph, Ami Pro usually does not attempt to justify; it leaves the line flush left.

The Text menu enables you to select any of the four paragraph alignment options. Follow these steps when you want to use the Text menu to align paragraphs:

- Select the paragraph(s) you wish to align.

- Choose Text, Alignment to open the Text, Alignment *submenu*. (A submenu is displayed as a menu extension off to the side of the open menu.)

- Click on any of the submenu's four alignment options: Left, Center, Right, or Justify.

To left-align or center paragraphs, you can also use SmartIcons. Follow these steps when you want to use a SmartIcon to left-align or center paragraphs:

- Select the paragraph(s) you wish to align.

- Click on the *Left Align Selected Text SmartIcon* (the 13th SmartIcon from the left, displaying left-aligned lines) or the *Center*

CHANGING PARAGRAPH ALIGNMENT • 153

Selected Text SmartIcon (the 14th SmartIcon from the left, displaying centered lines).

Let's use both the Text menu and the two SmartIcons to center some paragraphs:

1. Move to the top of the document, placing the insertion point in the document's first line, *Global Travel.*

2. Choose **Text, Alignment**. A submenu opens to display Ami Pro's paragraph alignment options (see Figure 5.18).

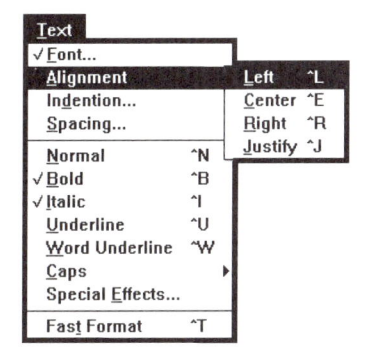

Figure 5.18   **The Text, Alignment submenu**

3. Click on **Center** to center the current paragraph between the left and right indents.

4. Select lines 2 and 3 of the heading.

5. Click on the **Center Selected Text SmartIcon** to center both paragraphs.

6. Deselect, and then compare your screen with Figure 5.19.

Now let's try out the other paragraph alignments:

1. Place the insertion point in the paragraph beginning *Global Travel has five branches* (the second multiple-line paragraph on page 1).

2. Look at the last word in each line of the selected paragraph. Because the paragraph is left aligned, text is ragged right and does not always reach the right indent before wrapping to the next line.

154 • TEXT ENHANCEMENTS

Figure 5.19   **Centered paragraphs**

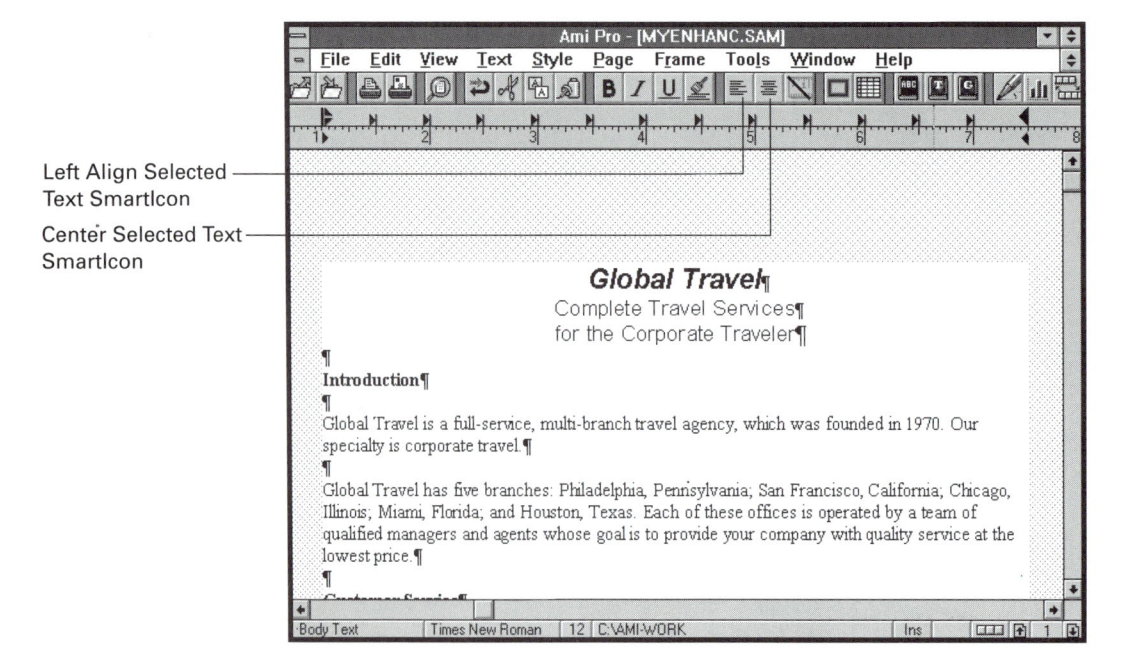

Left Align Selected Text SmartIcon

Center Selected Text SmartIcon

3. Choose **Text, Alignment**, and then select **Justify**.

4. Look again at the last word in each line. Ami Pro has increased the spacing between words in the current paragraph to fill each line (except the last one) so that the text is even with both the left and right indents (flush left and flush right).

5. Choose **Text, Alignment**, **Right** (that is, choose **Text, Alignment**, and then select **Right**), and then observe your document. Text in the current paragraph is now aligned only with the Right Indent marker; the left edge of the paragraph is now ragged.

6. Click on the **Left Align Selected Text SmartIcon** to return the paragraph to its original left alignment.

PRACTICE YOUR SKILLS

1. Use the **Text** menu to center all three lines of the heading on the top of page 2.

2. Use the **Center Selected Text SmartIcon** to center the three-line heading on the top of page 3.
3. Save the document.

CHANGING LINE SPACING

Line spacing (also known as *leading*) is the vertical distance between lines of text. Too little line spacing makes text difficult to read, and too much line spacing can waste paper by making documents unnecessarily long. Ami Pro provides four line-spacing options:

- *Single*, Ami Pro's default, which single-spaces lines of text
- *1 1/2,* which increases the line spacing 50% over single spacing
- *Double*, which increases the line spacing to twice the amount of single spacing.
- *Custom*, which enables you to set any line spacing you want if none of the other three line-spacing options are suitable

Note: The first three line-spacing options above—Single, 1 1/2, and Double—provide spacing that is *relative to* the point size of the largest character in a line; that is, the larger the font, the greater the line spacing, and vice versa. (You might have noticed in Chapter 4 that when you increased the point size of selected text, Ami Pro automatically increased the line spacing for that text.) When you use the Custom option, on the other hand, Ami Pro uses an *exact and unchanging* value for line spacing, regardless of the text's point size. For this reason, it's a good idea to avoid using Custom line spacing unless you absolutely need it.

Follow these steps when you want to change line spacing in a document:

- Select the paragraph(s) for which you want to change line spacing.
- Choose Text, Spacing to open the Spacing dialog box.
- Select the desired line-spacing option.
- Click on OK.

156 • TEXT ENHANCEMENTS

Let's use the above procedure to change the line spacing for every paragraph in MYENHANC.SAM:

1. Select the entire document. (Move to the top of the document, and then press **Shift+Ctrl+End**.)

2. Choose **Text, Spacing** to open the Spacing dialog box (see Figure 5.20).

Figure 5.20   **The Spacing dialog box**

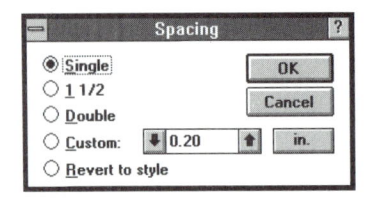

3. Select **1 1/2**, and then click on **OK**.

4. Move to the top of the document, and then observe the text. The line spacing has increased from 1 to 1½ lines (see Figure 5.21).

5. Select the entire document again.

6. Choose **Text, Spacing**, select **Double**, and then click on **OK**.

7. Return to the top of the document and examine the text. The entire document is now double-spaced.

8. Select the entire document one more time.

9. Choose **Text, Spacing**, select **Single** (if necessary), and then click on **OK**. The document returns to single spacing.

10. Deselect to avoid inadvertently deleting the entire document.

Up to now, you've always saved the changes you made to your active document before closing it. However, you can also close a document *without* saving the changes. This might be helpful should you open a document and make too many mistakes for the Edit, Undo command to reverse. By closing the document without saving changes, you effectively reverse any changes you made since the last time you saved the document.

Figure 5.21   **1 ½ line spacing**

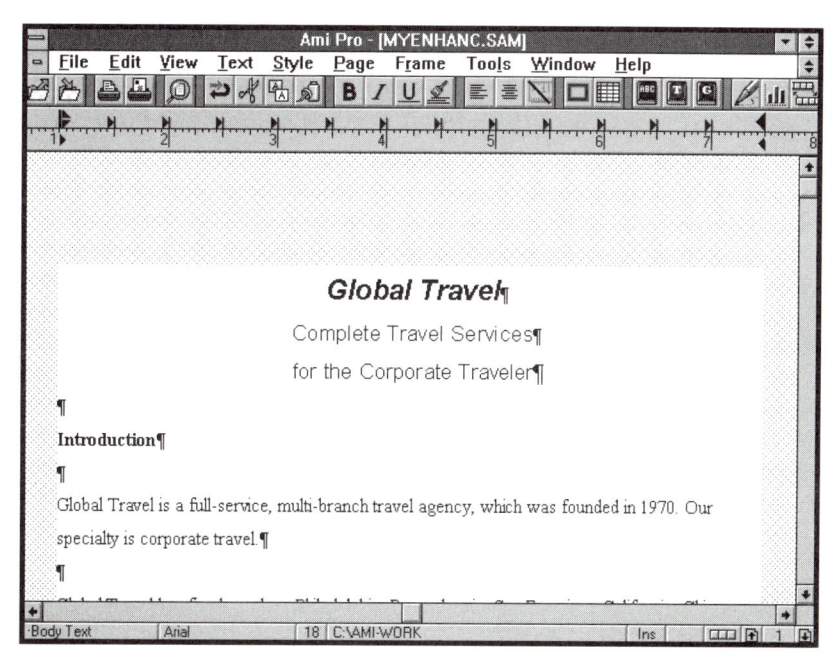

Let's see how to close a document without saving changes:

1. Choose **File, Close**. Ami Pro prompts:

   MYENHANC.SAM has changed. Save changes?

2. Click on **No** to close the document without saving your latest changes. (Don't worry; it's safe to do this now because all you have done since the last time you saved is increase the document's line spacing and then return it to single spacing.)

PRACTICE YOUR SKILLS

In Chapters 4 and 5, you have learned how to use text formatting to control character appearance, and how to use text enhancements to control paragraph appearance. The following two "Practice Your Skills" activities give you the opportunity to practice some of these techniques. After each activity step, we've provided a chapter reference (in parentheses) to inform you of where we introduced the relevant technique for that step.

Follow these steps to produce the final document shown in Figure 5.22 from the original document PRAC5A.SAM:

1. Open **prac5a.sam**. (Chapter 2)

2. Select the entire document, and then remove all text attributes. (Chapters 3 and 4) (**Hint**: Use the **Text, Normal** command.)

3. Change the following headings to boldface. (Chapter 4)

   ```
   1. Introduction
   2. Computer Study
   3. Regional Updates
   4. Quarterly Meeting
   5. Conclusion
   ```

4. Change the font of the three-line heading on the top of page 2 to **Arial 14-point** (or the closest available equivalent). (Chapter 4)

5. Use Fast Format to copy the text formatting you applied in step 4 to the three-line heading on the top of page 1. (Chapter 4)

6. Scroll to the bottom of page 1. (Chapter 2)

7. For the 11 paragraphs (including blank lines) under the heading *3. Regional Updates*—beginning with *Midwestern Region* and ending with *manufacturing costs*—set left and right indents of one-half inch. (Chapter 5)

8. Center the three-line headings on the top of pages 1 and 2. (Chapter 5)

9. Save the document as **myprac5a**. (Chapter 2)

10. Print the document, and then compare it to Figure 5.22. (Chapter 1)

11. Close the document. (Chapter 1)

Figure 5.22 **The completed document MYPRAC5A**

> Macco Plastics Inc.
> Quarterly Sales Report
> First Quarter
>
> **1. Introduction**
>
> Congratulations to all of you! An initial review of the sales figures for the nation reveals a surge in sales in all of Macco's sales regions. Major new clients have been added and many new products are on the way.
>
> As we expected when we entered the field, computer-related products, such as keyboard housings and protective carrying cases, are accounting for a major portion of this upswing.
>
> **2. Computer Study**
>
> A companywide study will begin in March, under the direction of Cathy Donaldson and Bill Schuster in data processing, to determine how to most effectively implement automation in our firm. We will be making a large commitment to productivity gains via computerization sometime late this year.
>
> **3. Regional Updates**
>
> > Midwestern Region
> >
> > After several years of falling sales due to the slump in the auto industry, Blair Williams and his folks have something to celebrate. The recent boom in auto manufacturing has led to renewed demand of Macco Products in Detroit.
> >
> > Northeastern Region
> >
> > John Martinson and his group are doing a great job in Nashua. They have secured major contracts for a wide range of new and existing products. Much of this business is coming from Computer Equipment Corporation, a major client of Macco's.
> >
> > Southern Region
> >
> > Mark Daley and his group have done a fine job of maintaining relations with Becker's Product Development Division in Boca Raton. They have been working closely with Becker to decrease manufacturing costs.

Figure 5.22   **The completed document MYPRAC5A (Continued)**

Macco Plastics Inc.
Quarterly Sales Report
First Quarter

4. Quarterly Meeting

The quarterly meeting will take place in Memphis this time. You will find the agenda attached to this report.

5. Conclusion

The following items will be discussed at the next managers' meeting:

A.   Marketing and sales strategies for the introduction of the new System 400 and System 500 product lines.

B.   Current available positions resulting from the early retirement program and normal attrition of personnel.

C.   Development of the new expense form to facilitate the prompt payment of - travel reimbursements - other out-of-pocket expenses and - commissions.

If the recovery continues at the current pace, this year should be a banner year for all of us at Macco. We want to thank all of you for the outstanding jobs you have done and, most important, for standing by Macco in hard times. Keep up the good work!

John Smith
Regional Coordinator
Macco Plastics Inc.

PRACTICE YOUR SKILLS • 161

Follow these steps to produce the final document shown in Figure 5.23 from the original document PRAC5B.SAM:

1. Open **prac5b.sam**. (Chapter 2)

2. Italicize the first line on page 1, *Macco Plastics Inc.*, and then change the point size to **24**. (Chapter 4)

3. Use Fast Format to copy the text formatting you applied in step 2 to the first line on page 2. (Chapter 4)

4. Underline the following subheadings (near the bottom of page 1). (Chapter 4)

    ```
    Midwestern Region
    Northeastern Region
    Southern Region
    ```

5. Add a left tab at 1½" for the paragraph that begins *B. Current available positions* (near the top of page 2). (Chapter 5)

6. Set half-inch hanging indents for the five paragraphs (including blank lines) from the paragraph beginning with *A. Marketing and sales* through the paragraph ending *and - commissions.* (Chapter 5)

7. In the paragraph beginning *C. Development of the*, maintain the paragraph's hanging indent while creating three new lines for the following text. (Chapter 5)

    ```
    - travel reimbursements
    - other out-of-pocket expenses and
    - commissions
    ```

8. Save the document as **myprac5b**. (Chapter 1)

9. Print the document and compare it to Figure 5.23. (Chapter 1)

10. Close the document. (Chapter 1)

Figure 5.23   **The completed document MYPRAC5B**

Macco Plastics Inc.
Quarterly Sales Report
First Quarter

1. Introduction

Congratulations to all of you! An initial review of the sales figures for the nation reveals a surge in sales in all of Macco's sales regions. Major new clients have been added and many new products are on the way.

As we expected when we entered the field, computer-related products, such as keyboard housings and protective carrying cases, are accounting for a major portion of this upswing.

2. Computer Study

A companywide study will begin in March, under the direction of Cathy Donaldson and Bill Schuster in data processing, to determine how to most effectively implement automation in our firm. We will be making a large commitment to productivity gains via computerization sometime late this year.

3. Regional Updates

Midwestern Region

After several years of falling sales due to the slump in the auto industry, Blair Williams and his folks have something to celebrate. The recent boom in auto manufacturing has led to renewed demand of Macco Products in Detroit.

Northeastern Region

John Martinson and his group are doing a great job in Nashua. They have secured major contracts for a wide range of new and existing products. Much of this business is coming from Computer Equipment Corporation, a major client of Macco's.

Southern Region

Mark Daley and his group have done a fine job of maintaining relations with Becker's Product Development Division in Boca Raton. They have been working closely with Becker to decrease manufacturing costs.

Figure 5.23   **The completed document MYPRAC5B (Continued)**

Macco Plastics Inc.
Quarterly Sales Report
First Quarter

4. Quarterly Meeting

The quarterly meeting will take place in Memphis this time. You will find the agenda attached to this report.

5. Conclusion

The following items will be discussed at the next managers' meeting:

A.   Marketing and sales strategies for the introduction of the new System 400 and System 500 product lines.

B.   Current available positions resulting from the early retirement program and normal attrition of personnel.

C.   Development of the new expense form to facilitate the prompt payment of
- travel reimbursements
- other out-of-pocket expenses and
- commissions.

If the recovery continues at the current pace, this year should be a banner year for all of us at Macco. We want to thank all of you for the outstanding jobs you have done and, most important, for standing by Macco in hard times. Keep up the good work!

John Smith
Regional Coordinator
Macco Plastics Inc.

SUMMARY

In this chapter, you learned how to use text enhancements. You learned how to display and hide the current ruler; how to clear, set, and change tabs; how to set indentions; how to create new lines without creating new paragraphs; how to align paragraphs; and how to change line spacing.

Here's a quick reference guide to the Ami Pro features introduced in this chapter:

Desired Result	How to Do It
Display current ruler	Choose **View, Show Ruler**, or click on **Show/Hide Ruler SmartIcon**.
Hide current ruler	Choose **View, Hide Ruler**, or click on **Show/Hide Ruler SmartIcon**.
Select single paragraph for text enhancements	Place insertion point anywhere in paragraph.
Select multiple paragraphs for text enhancements	Select at least portions of each paragraph.
Activate current ruler	Click on current ruler.
Deactivate current ruler	Press **Esc**.
Set a custom tab	Select paragraph(s); activate current ruler; select tab type and/or tab leader (if necessary); click at desired tab position in top half of current ruler; then deactivate current ruler.
Clear all tabs	Select paragraph(s); activate current ruler; click on **Clear Tabs**; then deactivate current ruler.
Clear a single tab	Select paragraph(s); activate current ruler; drag tab down into typing area; then deactivate ruler.

SUMMARY • 165

Desired Result	How to Do It
Move a tab	Select paragraph(s); activate current ruler; drag tab to new position; then deactivate current ruler.
Set indentions using current ruler	Select paragraph(s); activate current ruler; drag appropriate indent marker(s) to new position(s); then deactivate current ruler.
Set indentions using Indention dialog box	Select paragraph(s); choose **Text, Indention**; type desired indention value(s); then click on **OK**.
Set hanging indent using current ruler	Select paragraph(s); activate current ruler; drag **Indent Rest marker** to right of Indent First marker; then deactivate current ruler.
Set hanging indent using Indention dialog box	Select paragraph(s); choose **Text, Indention**; set Indent Rest value higher than Indent First value; then click on **OK**.
Create a new line without creating a new paragraph	Press **Ctrl+Enter**.
Change paragraph alignment using menu	Select paragraph(s); choose **Text, Alignment**; then click on desired alignment option.
Left-align paragraph(s) using SmartIcon	Select paragraph(s); then click on **Left Align Selected Text SmartIcon**.
Center paragraph(s) using SmartIcon	Select paragraph(s); then click on **Center Selected Text SmartIcon**.
Change line spacing	Select paragraph(s); choose **Text, Spacing**; select line spacing option; then click on **OK**.
Close document without saving changes	Choose **File, Close**; then click on **No**.

In the next chapter, you will learn about page layouts. You'll see how to work with headers and footers, add today's date, add page numbers, change margins, manually paginate a document, and control your document printing.

IF YOU'RE STOPPING HERE

If you need to take a break here, please exit Ami Pro. If you want to proceed directly to the next chapter, please do so now.

CHAPTER 6: PAGE LAYOUTS

Creating Headers and Footers

Changing Document Margins

Paginating a Document

Controlling the Printing of Your Documents

In Chapters 4 and 5, you learned how to control document appearance at the character level with text formatting and at the paragraph level with text enhancements. In this chapter, we'll introduce you to *page layouts*, which control a document's appearance at the page level. Page layouts include headers and footers, margins, and page breaks.

When you're done working through this chapter, you will know how to

- Create and edit headers and footers
- Add today's date and page numbers to a footer
- Change margins
- Use manual page breaks to paginate a document
- Control document printing

CREATING HEADERS AND FOOTERS

A *header* is text that prints at the top of every page in a document; a *footer* is text that prints at the bottom of every page. People commonly use headers and footers to repeatedly print information such as a document's title and/or author name, the current date, page numbers, and so on. Any time you want certain text to appear on every page, you'll probably find that a header or footer is the best tool for the job.

Ami Pro offers you two types of headers and footers: *fixed* and *floating*. Fixed headers and footers enable you to print the same header and footer throughout a document, with options for omitting them from the document's first page, and for alternating them on the document's left and right pages. (For instance, this book uses left and right alternating headers; the header text on the left-hand pages is different from that on the right-hand pages.) Floating headers and footers are even more flexible; they enable you to change the headers and footers throughout a document. For example, you can have one header print on pages 1 through 10, and another header on pages 11 through 20.

Because most people only need the basic features of fixed headers and footers, we will not cover the more advanced floating headers and footers in this chapter. For more information on creating and using floating headers and footers, refer to your Ami Pro documentation.

Note: For easier reading, we will refer to fixed headers and footers in this chapter simply as headers and footers.

Ami Pro provides two ways to create headers and footers: through the Page, Header/Footer command, or by clicking in the document's top and bottom margins.

CREATING HEADERS AND FOOTERS • 171

Follow these steps when you want to create a header or footer using the Page, Header/Footer command:

- Choose Page, Header/Footer to open the Headers & Footers dialog box.
- Select Header or Footer, and then click on OK. Ami Pro places the insertion point in the current page's top margin (for the header) or bottom margin (for the footer).
- Type your header or footer text.
- Press Esc or click inside the typing area to move the insertion point out of the header or footer.

Follow these steps when you want to create a header or footer by clicking:

- Click in any page's top or bottom margin to place the insertion point.
- Type your header or footer text.
- Press Esc or click inside the typing area to move out of the header or footer.

CREATING A HEADER

If you are not running Ami Pro, please start it now. Let's open a document and use the Page, Header/Footer command to create a header:

1. Open **layout.sam**.
2. Choose **Page, Header/Footer** to open the Headers & Footers dialog box (see Figure 6.1).

Figure 6.1 **The Headers & Footers dialog box**

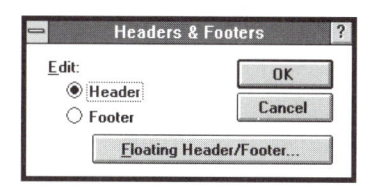

3. Verify that **Header** is selected, and then click on **OK**. Ami Pro places the insertion point in the top margin.

4. Type **Global Travel**, press **Tab** twice, and then type **Travel Services** (see Figure 6.2).

Figure 6.2   **Adding a header**

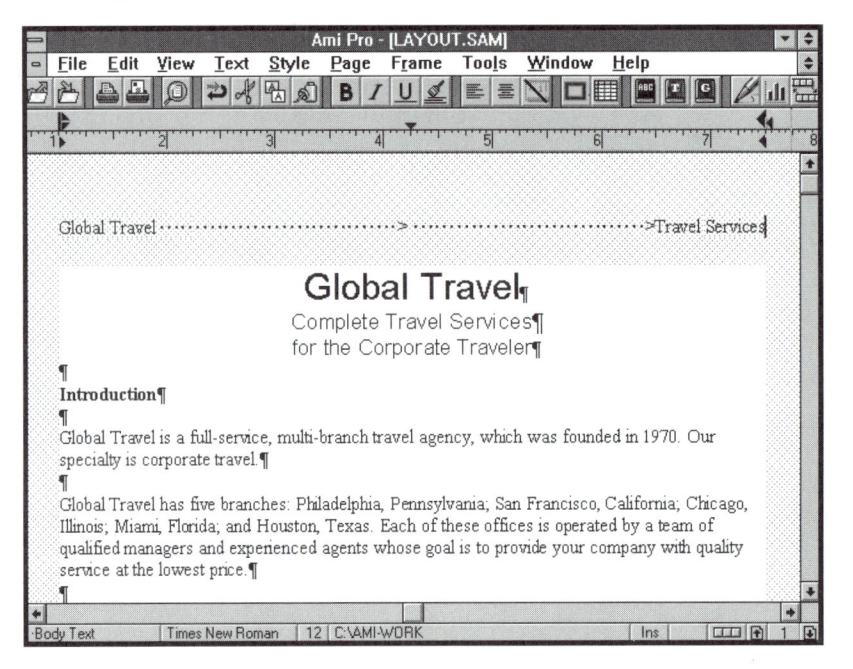

[Screenshot of Ami Pro - [LAYOUT.SAM] window showing a document with the header "Global Travel" on the left and "Travel Services" on the right. The document body shows "Global Travel" as a title, "Complete Travel Services / for the Corporate Traveler", followed by an Introduction section with text: "Global Travel is a full-service, multi-branch travel agency, which was founded in 1970. Our specialty is corporate travel." and "Global Travel has five branches: Philadelphia, Pennsylvania; San Francisco, California; Chicago, Illinois; Miami, Florida; and Houston, Texas. Each of these offices is operated by a team of qualified managers and experienced agents whose goal is to provide your company with quality service at the lowest price."]

5. Observe the header text. Notice that *Travel Services* is flush right. Now examine the ruler. For headers and footers, Ami Pro automatically sets a center tab halfway between the left and right margins (at 4 $\frac{1}{4}$" in this case) and a right tab flush right. Using these preset tabs helps you to quickly and easily center your header text and/or align it with the right margin.

6. Click inside the typing area, scroll to the top of page 2, and then examine the top margin there. By adding a header to page 1, you automatically added a header to every page in the document.

7. Save your document as **mylayout**.

CREATING A FOOTER

Now let's create a footer by clicking:

1. Scroll up to the bottom of page 1 until you can see the page's bottom margin.

2. Click in the bottom margin to place the insertion point in the page's footer.

3. Type your name.

ADDING A DATE

If you want to date- or time-stamp your document, headers and footers are often the ideal place to do so. Ami Pro provides five options for inserting dates and times:

- *Today's Date*, which always displays and prints the day when you inserted the date
- *System Date*, which displays and prints your computer system's current date
- *System Time*, which displays and prints your computer system's current time
- *Date Of Last Revision*, which displays and prints the date you last edited the document
- *Date Created*, which displays the date you first created the document

For each date option, Ami Pro also offers 21 different *date styles*. Here are four examples of date styles for the same date:

> October 10, 1994
>
> 10 October, 1994
>
> 10/10/94
>
> OCTOBER 10 1994

Follow these steps when you want to insert a date or time:

- Place the insertion point where you want to insert the date or time.

- Choose Edit, Insert, Date/Time to open the Insert Date/Time dialog box.

- Select the desired date/time option.
- If you selected one of the date options, pick a date style.
- Click on OK. Ami Pro inserts the appropriate date or time at the insertion point.

Note: For Ami Pro to insert the correct dates and times, your computer's internal clock must be set correctly. Whenever you insert a date or time, double-check to make sure that Ami Pro inserts the correct information. If it doesn't, refer to your DOS or Windows documentation for information on resetting your computer's clock.

Let's insert today's date in the footer:

1. Verify that the insertion point is still in the footer.
2. Press **Tab** to center the insertion point.
3. Choose **Edit**, **Insert,** and select **Date/Time** to open the Insert Date/Time dialog box, shown in Figure 6.3. (The date listed in *your* dialog box should reflect *your* computer's current date. Therefore, your dialog box will probably differ somewhat from Figure 6.3.)

Figure 6.3   **The Insert Date/Time dialog box**

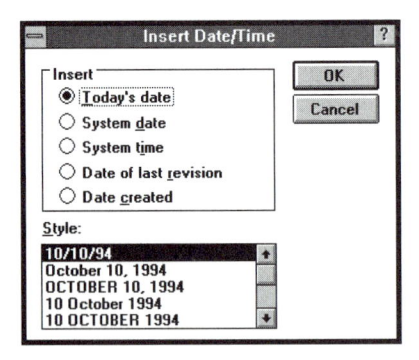

4. Notice the options available in the dialog box's Insert box. You can insert today's date, the system date, the system time, the date you last revised the document, or the date you first created the document.

5. Observe the Style list box. It provides a list of different date styles.

6. If necessary, select **Insert Today's Date** and choose the first option in the Styles list box. Then click on **OK**. Your footer now displays today's date.

ADDING PAGE NUMBERS

Like dates, page numbers are useful elements to include in headers and footers, particularly if the document is longer than a couple of pages. When page numbers are placed in a header or footer, Ami Pro will automatically provide the correct number on each page.

Follow these steps when you want to insert page numbers:

- Place the insertion point where you want to insert the page number. If you want page numbers to appear on every page, place the insertion point in either the header or footer.

- Choose Page, Page Numbering to open the Page Numbering dialog box.

- If desired, choose a *number style* from the Style drop-down list box. Ami Pro offers arabic numerals (1, 2, 3), uppercase roman numerals (I, II, III), lowercase roman numerals (i, ii, iii), uppercase letters (A, B, C), or lowercase letters (a, b, c).

- If you want *leading text* before your page numbers (for example, if you want your first page number to read *Page 1*, rather than just *1*), type that text in the Leading Text text box. Be sure to include a space at the end of your leading text, so that your page numbers don't display as *Page1*, *Page2*, and so on.

- Click on OK.

By default, Ami Pro starts page numbering on your document's first page, and starts with the number 1 (or I, i, A, or a, as appropriate). If you want your page numbers to start on a page other than the first one, or if you want to start with a page number other than 1, you can override the defaults for the Start On Page and Start With Number options in the Page Numbering dialog box.

Let's add page numbers to your document, using Ami Pro's defaults:

1. Verify that the insertion point is still in the footer.

2. Press **Tab** to move the insertion point to the right margin.

3. Choose **Page, Page Numbering**, and then observe the Page Numbering dialog box. Ami Pro is set by default to number your pages with arabic numerals, to start the page numbers on page 1, and to use 1 as the first page number (see Figure 6.4).

Figure 6.4   **The Page Numbering dialog box**

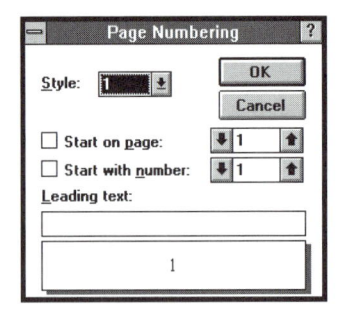

4. Place the insertion point in the Leading Text text box, type **Page**, and then press **Spacebar**. This provides leading text for your page numbers.

5. Click on **OK** to insert your leading text, *Page*, and the current page number, *1*, in the footer (see Figure 6.5).

6. Scroll down to the bottom of page 2, and look at the footer there. Ami Pro displays the correct page number, *2*.

EDITING HEADERS AND FOOTERS

Once you've created headers and footers, you can edit them as you would any other text. By default, Ami Pro will incorporate any edits you make in one header or footer into every one of the document's headers or footers.

If you wish to completely remove a header or footer from the entire document, select the header or footer text, and then press Delete.

Let's edit your header now by adding a word:

1. Scroll down to the top of page 3.

Figure 6.5 **The completed footer**

[Screenshot of Ami Pro window titled "Ami Pro - [MYLAYOUT.SAM]" showing document text:]

International Rate Program guarantees you fast and accurate pricing, no matter how complicated the itinerary.

Corporate Profiles

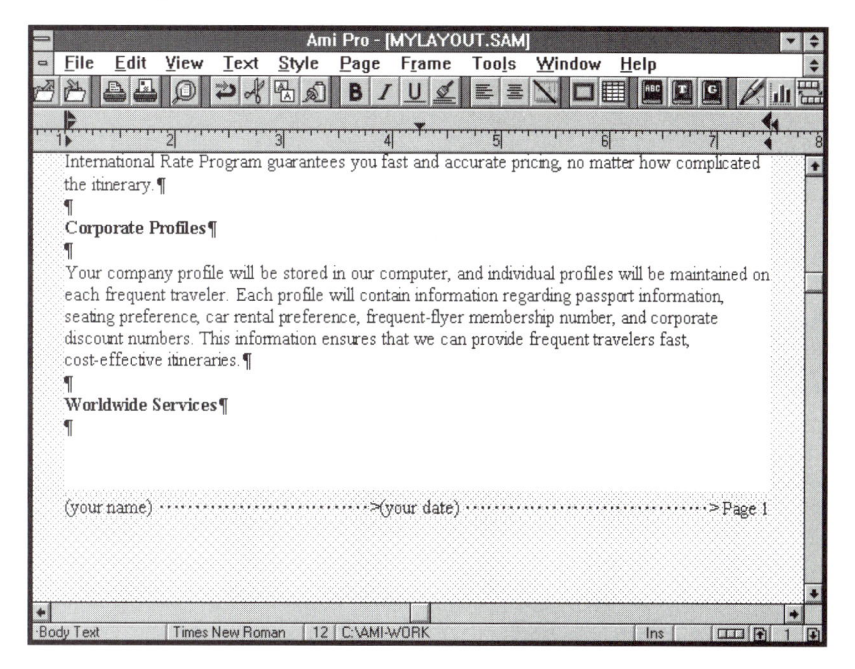

Your company profile will be stored in our computer, and individual profiles will be maintained on each frequent traveler. Each profile will contain information regarding passport information, seating preference, car rental preference, frequent-flyer membership number, and corporate discount numbers. This information ensures that we can provide frequent travelers fast, cost-effective itineraries.

Worldwide Services

(your name) ·············>(your date) ·············>Page 1

2. Place the insertion point in the header, immediately before the *T* in *Travel Services*.

3. Type **Complete**, and then press **Spacebar** (see Figure 6.6).

4. Scroll up and observe the headers on pages 1 and 2. Ami Pro has incorporated on both pages the header edit you made on page 3.

CHANGING DOCUMENT MARGINS

As you learned in Chapter 1, Ami Pro displays each page's margins as a colored or shaded area around the document window's typing area. Document margins provide space between your document's text and the page's physical edge.

Generally, each document margin should be 1 to 1½" wide. Wider margins waste paper, and narrower margins can make documents look busy and difficult to read. By default, Ami Pro sets all document margins to 1".

178 • PAGE LAYOUTS

Figure 6.6 **Editing a header**

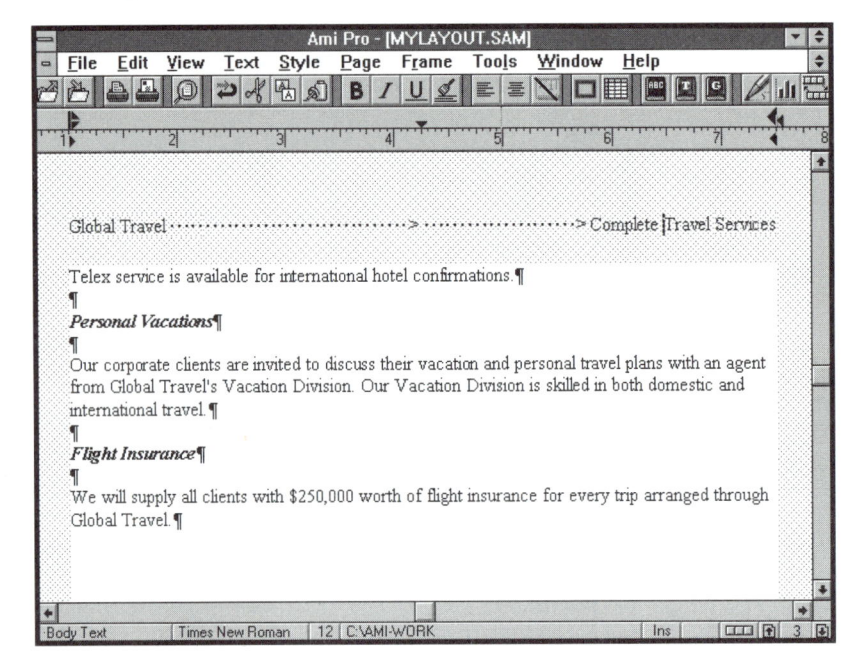

In Ami Pro, you can change any document margin through the Modify Page Layout dialog box. You can also use the current ruler to change the left and right document margins. Because document margins work at the page level, it usually does not matter on which page you change the margins; by default, Ami Pro changes document margins for entire documents, not for single pages.

Note: Although Ami Pro allows you to set every document margin to 0", most printers cannot print to every edge of the page. Many laser printers can only print to within ½" of every edge; many dot-matrix printers can print all the way over to the left and right edges, but can only print to within 1" of the top and bottom edges. Before attempting to set document margins to less than 1", check your printer's documentation.

CHANGING DOCUMENT MARGINS THROUGH THE MODIFY PAGE LAYOUT DIALOG BOX

Follow these steps when you want to change document margins using the Modify Page Layout dialog box:

- Choose Page, Modify Page Layout, or click in the left or right margin with the *right* mouse button, to open the Modify Page Layout dialog box.
- Verify that Modify Margins & Columns is selected.
- Verify that Pages All is selected. (Ami Pro allows you to set different document margins for left and right pages. To change document margins equally for *every* page, Pages All must be selected.)
- Use the dialog box's Margins Left, Margins Right, Margins Top, and/or Margins Bottom boxes to specify the desired margin widths.
- Click on OK.

Let's use the Modify Page Layout dialog box to change your document's left margin:

1. Move to the top of the document (if necessary), and examine the document's left and right margins. The left margin is set at 1"; the right margin is set at 7 1/2" (one inch from the right edge of the 8 1/2-by-11-inch page).

2. Observe the ruler's margin markers: the two triangles located in the *bottom* half of the ruler. The markers are even with the left and right margins.

3. Choose **Page, Modify Page Layout** to open the Modify Page Layout dialog box (see Figure 6.7). This dialog box enables you to control a number of page layout settings, including margins and columns. (You'll learn about columns in Chapter 12.)

4. On the left side of the dialog box, verify that Modify Margins & Columns and Pages All are selected. If they are not, select them now.

5. Observe the four Margins boxes: Left, Right, Top, and Bottom. They are each set to *1.00* (1").

180 • PAGE LAYOUTS

Figure 6.7   **The Modify Page Layout dialog box**

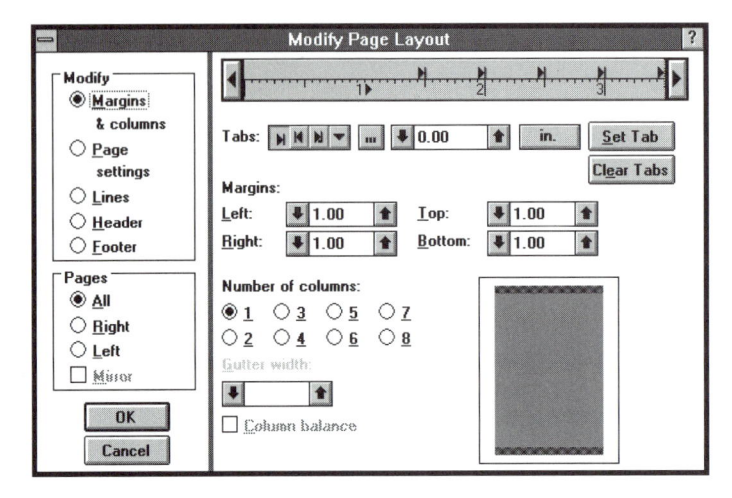

6. Double-click in the Margins Left box to select it, and then type **1.25** to increase the left margin by ¼".

7. Click on **OK** to close the dialog box.

8. Examine your document. The left margin has increased to 1 ¼". Also, the ruler's left margin marker has moved to the ruler's 1 ¼" mark (see Figure 6.8).

CHANGING DOCUMENT MARGINS THROUGH THE CURRENT RULER

As you saw in the last activity, there is a direct relationship between the left and right document margins and the current ruler's margin markers. You can use the margin markers as you used the indent markers in Chapter 5.

Follow these steps when you want to use the margin markers to change your document's left and/or right margins:

- Place the insertion point anywhere inside the typing area.
- Drag the Left and/or Right Margin marker to the desired position.
- Deactivate the current ruler.

Figure 6.8 **MYLAYOUT.SAM, with a 1 ¼" left margin**

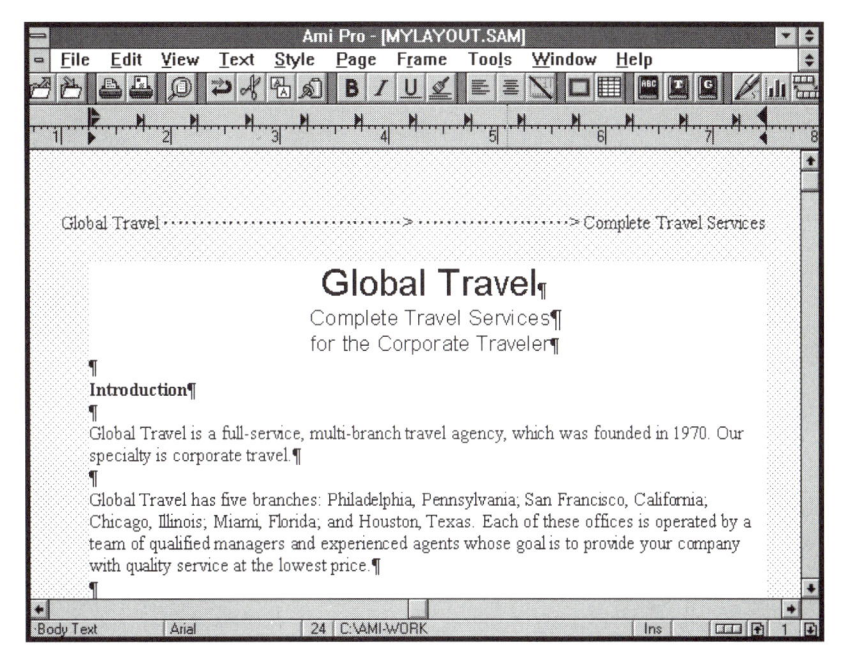

Let's use the Right Margin marker to change your document's Right Margin:

1. Drag the ruler's **Right Margin marker** from 7 ½" to 7 ¼". As you drag, notice that Ami Pro displays a line along the right side of the document window, even with the margin marker (see Figure 6.9).

2. Look at the right margin. It has moved to the 7 ¼" mark, 1 ¼" from the page's right edge.

3. Deactivate the current ruler.

4. Point to the document's left or right margin, and then click on the *right* mouse button to open the Modify Page Layout dialog box.

5. In the Margins Right box, notice that the setting has increased to *1.25*, indicating that the left margin is 1 ¼" from the page's right edge. (If the Margins Right box isn't set to exactly 1.25, double-click inside the box, and then type **1.25**.)

Figure 6.9   **Dragging the Right Margin marker**

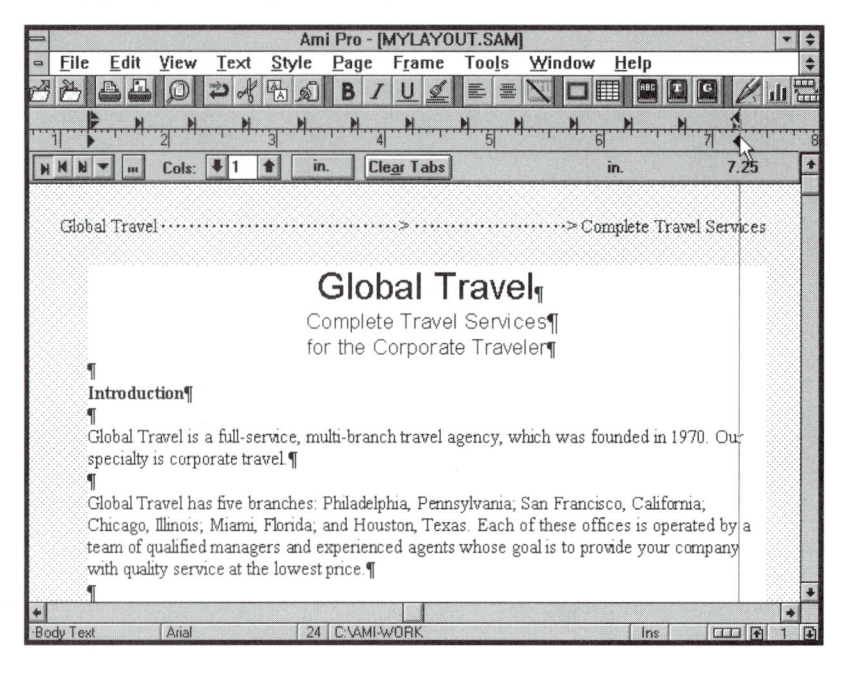

6. Click on **OK** to close the dialog box.

7. Scroll down through the document's four pages. Notice that Ami Pro has applied your margin changes to the entire document, not just on the page where you made the changes.

CHANGING HEADER AND FOOTER MARGINS

In Ami Pro, header and footer margins are independent of document margins. Therefore, if you change a document's margins, you often will have to change the header and footer's margins, as well. As with document margins, you can change header and footer margins through the Modify Page Layout dialog box, or by using the current ruler's margin markers.

Follow these steps when you want to change a header or footer's margins using the Modify Page Layout dialog box:

- Choose Page, Modify Page Layout.

- Select Modify Header or Modify Footer.

- Unless you want separate header or footer margins for right and left pages, verify that Pages All is selected.
- Use the Margins boxes to set the desired margin widths. Before you decrease a header or footer's top or bottom margins, be sure that your printer can print that close to the top or bottom of the page.
- Click on OK.

Follow these steps when you want to use the current ruler to change a header or footer's left and/or right margins:

- Place the insertion point in the header or footer.
- Drag the left and/or right margin marker to the desired location.
- Deactivate the ruler.

Let's take a look at the header and footer margins, and then use the Modify Page Layout dialog box to change the footer's left and right margins:

1. Move to the top of the document, and look at the header. It extends ¼" past the document's left and right margins.

2. Scroll to the bottom of page 1, and look at the footer. The footer, too, extends beyond the document's left and right margins. In Ami Pro, header and footer margins are independent of document margins. Therefore, by increasing the document margins by ¼" each, you caused the headers and footers to be too wide.

3. Place the insertion point in the footer, and then observe the ruler. The footer's margin markers are set at 1" and 7 ½".

4. Open the Modify Page Layout dialog box (choose **Page, Modify Page Layout**, or click in the document's left or right margin with the right mouse button).

5. Observe the Modify box in the dialog box's upper-left corner. Because Modify Margins & Columns is selected, the right side of the dialog box displays options for modifying the *document's* margins and columns. Select **Modify Footer**. The right side of the dialog box now shows settings for the document's footers.

6. Observe the Margins Left and Margins Right boxes. They are each set to *1.00*.

7. Double-click in the Margins Left box, and type **1.25**. Press **Tab** to move to the Margins Right box, type **1.25**, and then click on **OK**.

8. Examine the footer. Its margins are now even with the document's margins (see Figure 6.10). Notice that the ruler's margin markers also reflect this.

Figure 6.10 **The footer, with margins equal to the document's margins**

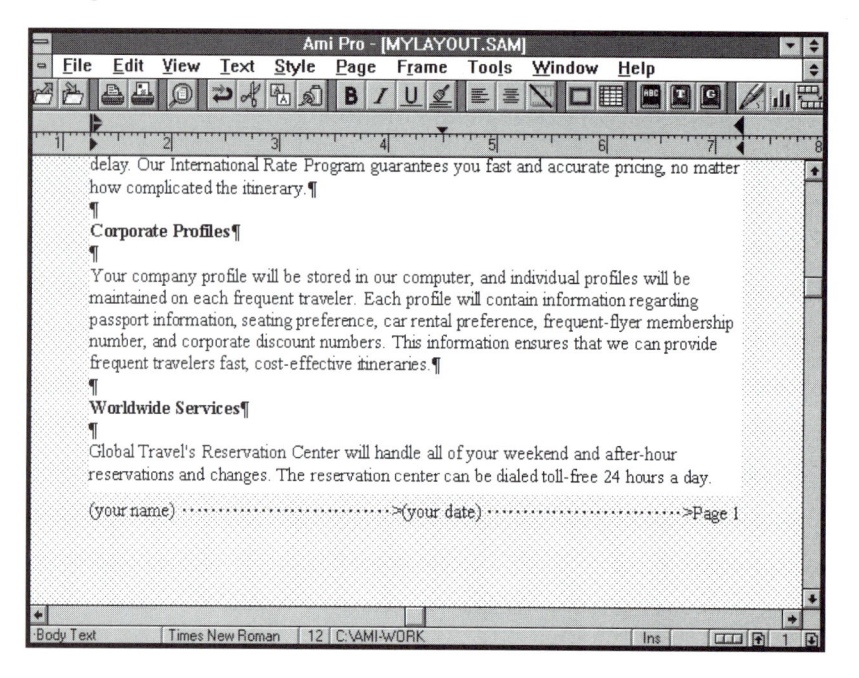

Now let's change the header's margins by using the ruler's margin markers:

1. Scroll down to the top of page 2, and then place the insertion point in the page's header.

2. Drag the **Left Margin marker** to 1 1/4", and then drag the **Right Margin marker** to 7 1/4". The header's margins now match the document's margins.

PAGINATING A DOCUMENT • 185

3. Deactivate the ruler.

4. Move to the top of the document, and then scroll down through all four pages. The document, header, and footer margins are the same for every page.

PAGINATING A DOCUMENT

Pagination is the process of separating a document's text into separate pages. The separations between pages are called *page breaks*.

Ami Pro provides two types of page breaks:

- *Automatic page breaks* are page breaks that Ami Pro inserts automatically whenever a page runs out of room for text. Whenever you add or delete text, increase or decrease the size of text, change margins or indentions, or perform any action that creates more or less room for text on a page, Ami Pro automatically repaginates your document, inserting or removing automatic page breaks as necessary.

- *Manual* (or *hard*) *page breaks* are page breaks that you insert wherever you want them. If you perform any action that creates more or less room for text on a page, you might need to manually add or remove these page breaks yourself.

Generally, you should use manual page breaks only when Ami Pro's automatic page breaks do not produce the desired result. Otherwise, let Ami Pro do the work of paginating your documents. Also, it's best to avoid inserting manual page breaks until you finish editing the document. If you don't, you might have to manually repaginate the document later.

VIEWING PAGE LAYOUTS IN FULL PAGE VIEW

As you saw in Chapter 2, you can use Ami Pro's Full Page view to view entire pages of a document at a time. Full Page view can be very useful for examining each page's overall appearance on screen. For instance, you can use Full Page view to see if your margins should be wider or narrower, or to find out where you need to add or remove manual page breaks.

In addition to choosing View, Full Page (as we showed you in Chapter 1), you can switch to Full Page View by clicking on the *Toggle Full Page/Layout View SmartIcon*. This SmartIcon is the fifth SmartIcon from the left; it displays a magnifying glass. To return to your previous view, just click on the Toggle Full Page/Layout View SmartIcon again.

Let's use Full Page view to view your document's current pagination:

1. Return to the top of the document.

2. Click on the **Toggle Full Page/Layout View SmartIcon** (or choose **View, Full Page**) to switch to Full Page view. Ami Pro displays a miniature of page 1 (see Figure 6.11).

3. Click on the **down scroll arrow** to display page 2. In Full Page view, each click on the down scroll arrow scrolls the document down one full page.

Figure 6.11   **Page 1 of MYLAYOUT.SAM, in Full Page view**

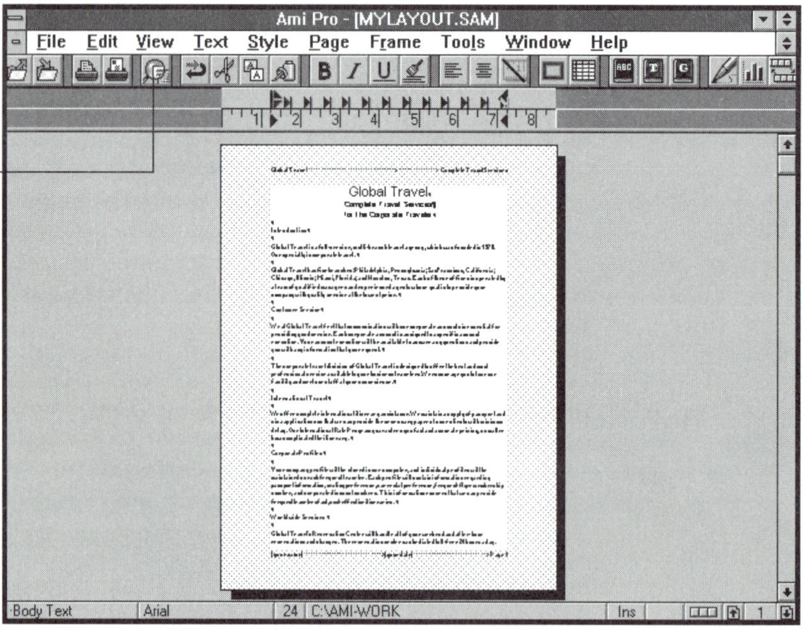

4. Scroll down to page 3. Notice that the text on page 3 fills less than half the page.

5. Scroll down to page 4. There is some text on page 4, even though there is plenty of room for that text on page 3. We'll fix this problem shortly.

INSERTING MANUAL PAGE BREAKS

Follow these steps when you want to insert a manual page break:

- Place the insertion point immediately to the left of the first character that you want to appear on the new page.
- Choose Page, Breaks to open the Breaks dialog box.
- Select Insert Page Break (if necessary), and then click on OK.

You cannot view automatic page breaks on screen, but you *can* view the symbols for manual page breaks. Follow these steps when you want to examine manual page breaks:

- Choose View, View Preferences to open the View Preferences dialog box.
- Check the Marks option.
- Click on OK.

Note: As with the Tabs & Returns option you checked in Chapter 1, Ami Pro remembers, from session to session, any option you set in the View Preferences dialog box. Therefore, once you've set Ami Pro to display manual page breaks, Ami Pro will continue to display these symbols until you uncheck the Marks option.

Let's observe automatic page breaks in action, and then insert a manual page break:

1. Click on the **Toggle Full Page/Layout View SmartIcon** (or choose **View, Custom 91%**) to return to Custom view.

2. Move to the bottom of page 1, and then select the entire paragraph beginning *Your company profile* (under the heading *Corporate Profiles*).

3. Observe the text on the bottom of page 1 as you press **Del etc**. Because deleting the paragraph creates empty space on page 1, Ami Pro automatically moves some text from page 2 up to page 1.

4. Click on the **Undo Last Command Or Action SmartIcon** (or choose **Edit, Undo**) to restore the deleted paragraph. Ami Pro automatically pushes some text back down to page 2.

5. Scroll down to the top of page 2, and look at the first sentence on the page. It is part of a paragraph that starts on page 1.

6. Scroll back up to the bottom of page 1, and place the insertion point before the *W* in the heading *Worldwide Services*.

7. Choose **Page, Breaks** to open the Breaks dialog box (see Figure 6.12). This dialog box enables you to insert and remove page breaks and column breaks. (You'll learn about column breaks in Chapter 12.)

Figure 6.12 **The Breaks dialog box**

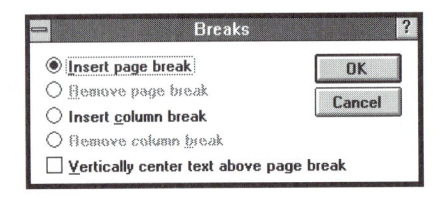

8. Verify that **Insert Page Break** is selected, and then click on **OK** to insert a manual page break. *Worldwide Services* and the remaining text on page 1 move to the top of page 2.

9. Scroll up to the bottom of page 1. Notice that the manual page break you just inserted is not visible.

10. Choose **View, View Preferences** to open the View Preferences dialog box.

11. Check **Marks**, and then click on **OK**. Ami Pro now displays a symbol where you inserted the manual page break (see Figure 6.13). Like the symbols for tabs and returns, manual page break symbols only appear on screen; they do not print.

Figure 6.13 **Viewing a manual page break symbol**

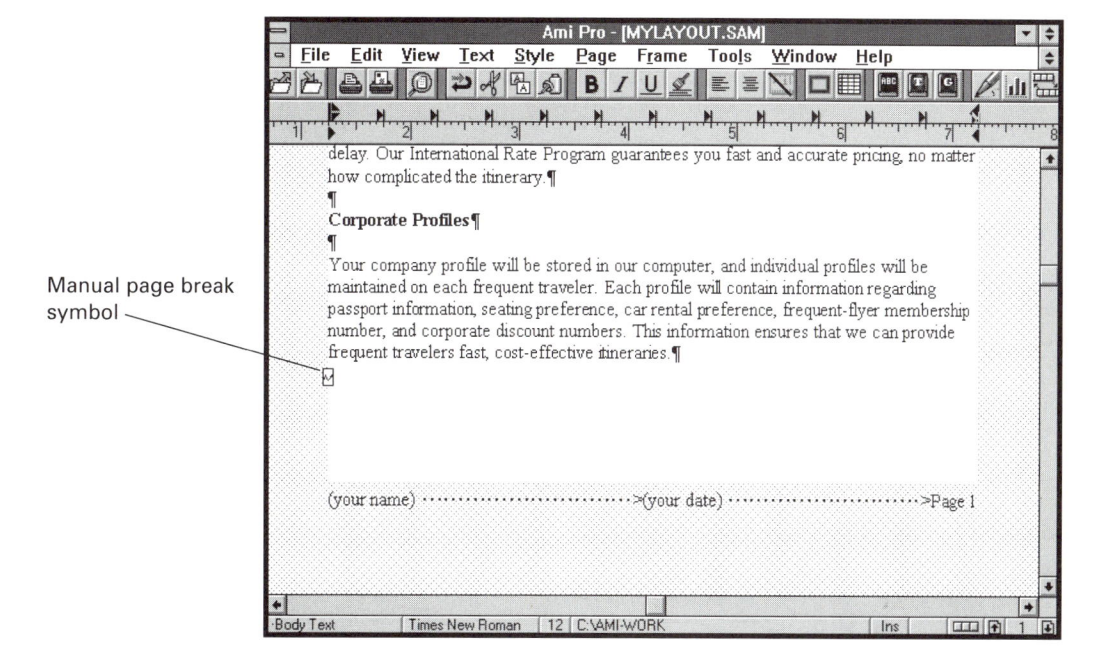

Manual page break symbol

PRACTICE YOUR SKILLS

1. Move to the bottom of page 2.
2. Insert a manual page break before the *A* in the heading *Additional Services*.
3. Save the document.

REMOVING A MANUAL PAGE BREAK

As we said earlier, one drawback of manual page breaks is that you sometimes have to remove them and insert new ones as you work in a document. Follow these steps when you want to remove a manual page break:

- Place the insertion point anywhere on the page that contains the break.
- Choose Page, Breaks.

- Select Remove Page Break.
- Click on OK.

Let's remove a manual page break now:

1. Switch to Full Page view (click on the **Toggle Full Page/Layout View SmartIcon**), and then observe page 3. Notice that the text extends only about halfway down the page.

2. Scroll to page 4. You can see that the text on this page could easily fit on page 3.

3. Return to Custom view (click on the **Toggle Full Page/Layout View SmartIcon** or choose **View, Custom 91%**), and then move up to the end of the document text on page 3. The text on page 3 ends prematurely because of the manual page break here.

4. Verify that the insertion point is on page 3, choose **Page, Breaks**, select **Remove Page Break**, and then click on **OK**. The text on page 4 moves up onto page 3.

Now that you've finished paginating, let's hide the manual page breaks:

1. Choose **View, View Preferences**.
2. Uncheck **Marks**, and then click on **OK**.

CONTROLLING THE PRINTING OF YOUR DOCUMENTS

Several times in this book, you've used the Print dialog box to print your entire active document. Let's revisit this dialog box and learn how to use it to more specifically control your document printing. As we said way back in Chapter 1, in addition to printing a single copy of your entire document, options in the Print dialog box enable you to print multiple copies, the current page only, a specific range of pages, even-numbered pages only, and/or odd-numbered pages only.

Tip: Because it is often faster and cheaper to make large numbers of multiple copies with a photocopy machine, we suggest that you avoid using Ami Pro to print multiple copies of a document.

As with many other commands, Ami Pro provides a SmartIcon for opening the Print dialog box: the *Print SmartIcon*. The Print SmartIcon is the third SmartIcon from the left; it displays a printer.

CONTROLLING THE PRINTING OF YOUR DOCUMENTS • 191

Let's work with both the Print SmartIcon and the Print dialog box to print different pages of the current document:

1. Move to the top of the document.

2. Click on the **Print SmartIcon** to open the Print dialog box.

3. Observe the settings under Page Range. The current selection is Page Range All, the Page Range From box is set to *1*, and the Page Range To box is set to *9999*. With these settings, Ami Pro will print one copy of the entire document, regardless of how many pages it contains.

4. Select **Page Range Current Page**, and then observe the Page Range From and Page Range To boxes. As shown in Figure 6.14, each has changed to *1*, indicating that Ami Pro will now only print page 1—the current page. (**Note:** Because Ami Pro uses the Windows default printer, your dialog box might not exactly match Figure 6.14.)

Figure 6.14   **Setting Ami Pro to print the document's current page**

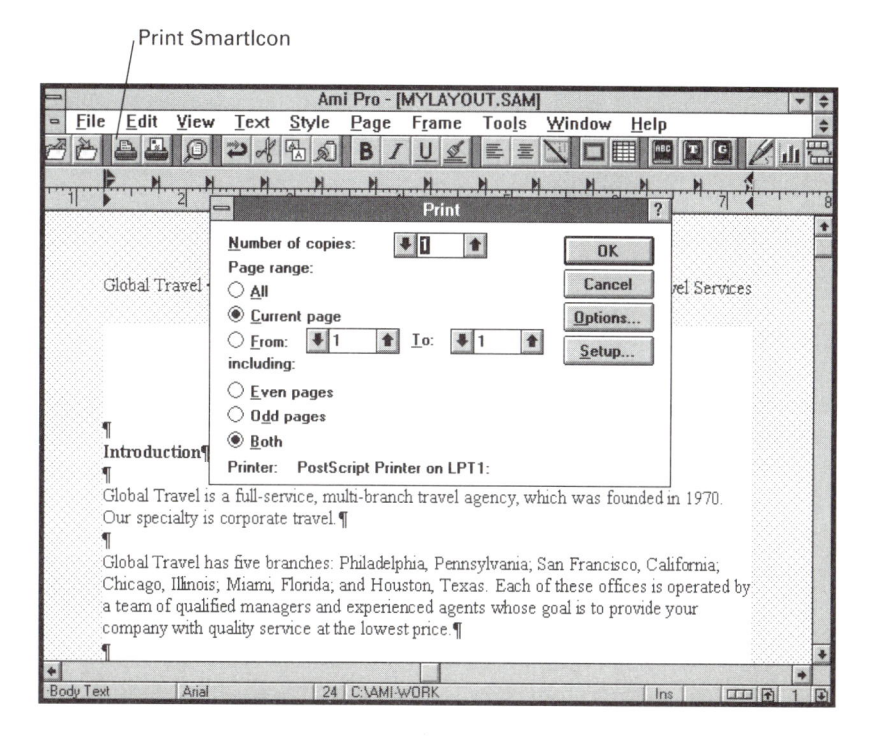

5. Click on **OK** to print page 1.

6. After page 1 has finished printing, reopen the Print dialog box (click on the **Print SmartIcon** or choose **File, Print**). Notice that Page Range Current Page is still selected. Until you close this document, Ami Pro will remember your most recent Page Range setting.

7. Select **Page Range From**, double-click in the Page Range From box, and type **2**. Press **Tab** to move to the Page Range To box, and type **3**. You've now set Ami Pro to print pages 2 and 3.

8. Click on **OK** to print pages 2 and 3 of MYLAYOUT.SAM.

9. Save and close your document.

SUMMARY

In this chapter, you learned the basics of page layouts, including how to create and edit headers and footers, add today's date, add page numbers, change margins, and control document printing.

Congratulations on completing your foundation of skills for controlling document appearances! You now know how to format your documents at the character, paragraph, and page levels, using text formatting, text enhancements, and page layouts. These skills will enable you to create professional-looking documents.

Here's a quick reference guide to the Ami Pro features introduced in this chapter:

Desired Result	How to Do It
Create a fixed header or footer	Choose **Page, Header/Footer** and select **Header** or **Footer** (if necessary); click on **OK**; then type header or footer text. Or click in top or bottom margin, and type header or footer text.
Edit a header or footer	Use any text-editing techniques.
Delete a fixed header or footer	Select header or footer text; then press **Delete**.

SUMMARY • 193

Desired Result	How to Do It
Add today's date	Choose **Edit**, **Insert**, **Date/Time**; select **Insert Today's Date** (if necessary); then click on **OK**.
Add page numbers	Choose **Page**, **Page Numbering**; choose a number style and type leading text (if desired); then click on **OK**.
Open Modify Page Layout dialog box	Choose **Page**, **Modify Page Layout**; or click in left or right margin with right mouse button.
Change document margins with Modify Page Layout dialog box	Open Modify Page Layout dialog box; verify that **Modify Margins & Columns** and **Pages All** are selected; set new values in Margins boxes; then click on **OK**.
Change margins with current ruler	Place insertion point in typing area; activate current ruler; drag **Left** and/or **Right Margin marker** to new position(s); then deactivate current ruler.
Change header or footer margins	Open Modify Page Layout dialog box; select **Modify Header** or **Modify Footer**; set new values in Margins boxes; then click on **OK**. Or place insertion point in header or footer; activate current ruler; drag **Left** and/or **Right Margin marker** to new position(s); then deactivate current ruler.
Switch to/from Full Page view with SmartIcon	Click on **Toggle Full Page/Layout View SmartIcon**.
Insert manual page break	Place insertion point at desired location; choose **Page, Breaks**; select **Insert Page Break** (if necessary); then click on **OK**.
Remove manual page break	Place insertion point on page ending with manual page break; choose **Page, Breaks**; select **Remove Page Break**; then click on **OK**.
Display manual page break symbols	Choose **View, View Preferences**; check **Marks**; then click on **OK**.

Desired Result	How to Do It
Hide manual page break symbols	Choose **View, View Preferences**; uncheck **Marks**; then click on **OK**.
Open Print dialog box with SmartIcon	Click on **Print SmartIcon**.
Print current page	Open Print dialog box; select **Page Range Current Page**; then click on **OK**.
Print a range of pages	Open Print dialog box; select **Page Range From**; type first page number in range in **Page Range From** box and last page number in range in **Page Range To** box; then click on **OK**.

In the next chapter, we'll explore ways in which Ami Pro can help you improve your writing. You'll learn how to check your spelling; how to use Ami Pro's on-line thesaurus to find alternative words; and how to check the grammar, style, mechanics, and readability of your documents.

IF YOU'RE STOPPING HERE

If you need to take a break here, please exit Ami Pro. If you want to proceed to the next chapter, please do so now.

CHAPTER 7: PROOFING YOUR DOCUMENTS

Checking Spelling

Finding and Placing Synonyms with Thesaurus

Checking Grammar, Style, and Mechanics

Misspellings and grammatical errors can severely undermine the credibility of your documents. In this chapter, we'll introduce you to tools that help you to *proof* (check) your documents for repeated words and for potential spelling, grammar, style, and mechanical errors (such as incorrect punctuation). Wording is also a critical factor in determining the effectiveness of a document; using inappropriate words can alienate or confuse your readers. We'll explore Ami Pro's on-line thesaurus to see how easy it is to find and use synonyms for existing words in your documents.

When you're done working through this chapter, you will know how to

- Check for spelling errors and repeated words
- Use the on-line thesaurus to find and place synonyms
- Check for grammar, style, and mechanical errors

CHECKING SPELLING

Ami Pro provides a spelling checker, called *Spell Check*, that you can use to check the spelling in your documents. Ami Pro checks each word in a document against the words in Ami Pro's own 115,000-word dictionary, and highlights the words it does not recognize, including words with irregular capitalization (such as *tHe*). Ami Pro also checks for repeated words (such as *the the*).

Note: Do not depend solely on Spell Check or any of Ami Pro's proofing tools for document correctness. Although spell-checkers, on-line thesauruses, and grammar-checkers are valuable tools, they are no substitute for a human proofreader. For best results, use Ami Pro to proof your documents on line to catch obvious errors, and then have someone proofread the document for you.

STARTING SPELL CHECK

Ami Pro provides these two methods for starting Spell Check:

- Choose Tools, Spell Check.
- Click on the *Spell Check SmartIcon*, the 19th SmartIcon from the left, displaying a book with the letters *ABC*.

Before you use either of the foregoing methods, you must tell Ami Pro what part of the document you want to spell-check. You can select text before starting, and Ami Pro will check only the selected text. Or you can just move the insertion point to an appropriate spot, and Ami Pro will check every word in the current *text stream*, from the insertion point downward, and then continue on to check lower-priority text streams.

Ami Pro divides documents into a variety of text streams, including *main document text*, headers, and footers. Main document text— that is, text you type in the typing area—is the highest-priority text stream. If the insertion point is somewhere in main document text when you start Spell Check, Ami Pro can check the entire document (because all other text streams are of a lower priority). Otherwise, Ami Pro might be able to check only the current text stream. For example, fixed headers and footers are the lowest-priority text streams; if you start Spell Check while the insertion point is in a fixed header or footer, Ami Pro will only be able to check headers and footers.

Follow these steps when you want to start Spell Check:

- Select the text you want to spell-check, or place the insertion point in the appropriate location in the document. If you want to spell-check your entire document, place the insertion point anywhere in main document text.

- Choose Tools, Spell Check or click on the Spell Check SmartIcon.

- If you did not make a text selection in the first step, Ami Pro opens a Spell Check dialog box where you can specify some Spell Check options. (If you *did* select text, Ami Pro starts Spell Check immediately, preventing you from specifying any options. In that case, skip the rest of this procedure.)

    If you placed the insertion point in main document text in the first step, the Spell Check dialog box will provide two check-box options—Check From Beginning Of Document and Include Other Text Streams—to help you designate which parts of your document to spell-check. (Otherwise, Ami Pro will dim these two options.) If you want to check all of the main document text, regardless of where in that text you placed the insertion point, check Check From Beginning Of Document; otherwise, Ami Pro will only check from the insertion point forward. If you want to check every lower-priority text stream, check Include Other Text Streams.

- Click on OK.

Note: The Spell Check dialog box also contains Options, Language Options, and Edit Dictionary buttons for further customizing Spell Check. See your Ami Pro documentation for more information on using these buttons.

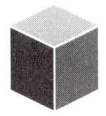

USING SPELL CHECK

Once you've started Spell Check, Ami Pro starts checking for words that it does not recognize and for repeated words. When it finds an unrecognized word, Ami Pro places that word in the Spell Check dialog box's Replace With text box, and often provides in the Alternatives list box a list of words with spellings that are similar to your unrecognized word. For example, if you typed *ther*, Ami Pro might suggest *the*, *there*, and *their* as alternatives.

To correct a word if it is an error, or to skip past the word if it is correct, use one of the following methods:

- If the word is correct, click on Skip to skip the current word and have Ami Pro continue checking. To skip every occurrence of that unrecognized word throughout the document, click on Skip All. To add the word to Ami Pro's dictionary so that Ami Pro *will* recognize the word next time you check spelling, click on Add To Dictionary.

    Note: For Ami Pro to use the words that you add to the dictionary for later spelling checks of all your documents, you must check Include User Dictionary Alternatives in the Spell Check Options dialog box. (To open the Spell Check Options dialog box, deselect any selected document text, open the Spell Check dialog box, and then click on Options.)

- If the word is incorrect and Ami Pro has listed the correct word in the Alternatives list box, select the alternative word and then click on Replace, or simply double-click on the alternative word. To replace every occurrence of the unrecognized word throughout the document with the alternative word, select the alternative word and then click on Replace All.

- If the word is incorrect and Ami Pro does *not* list a correct alternative, type the correct word in the Replace With text box, and then click on Replace. To replace every occurrence of the incorrect word with the word you type, click on Replace All.

- If the word is the second occurrence of two repeated words, Ami Pro opens an Ami Pro dialog box explaining that it found a word that is spelled exactly the same as the one before; click on OK to close this dialog box. If you want to keep both the repeated words (for example, if you are writing about the island of Bora Bora), click on Skip or Skip All. If you want to delete the second word, press Delete to delete the word and its leading space from the Replace With text box, and then click on Replace. This effectively deletes the second word by replacing it with nothing.

Once Ami Pro finishes spell-checking all designated text, it closes the Spell Check dialog box automatically.

If you are not running Ami Pro, please start it now. Let's begin our work in this chapter by opening a document and spell-checking some selected text:

1. Open **proof.sam**.

2. Select the three-line heading at the top of page 1 (from *Global* through *Traveler*).

3. Choose **Tools, Spell Check** to start spell-checking the selected text.

4. Examine the document. Ami Pro has selected the first word it doesn't recognize, *Travle* (see Figure 7.1).

Figure 7.1 **Spell-checking selected text**

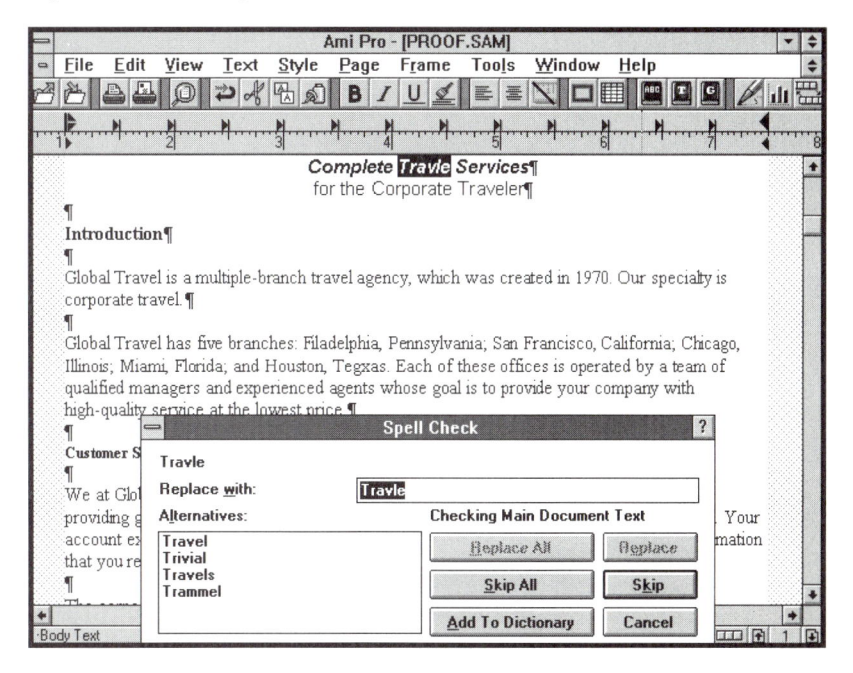

5. Observe the Spell Check dialog box. Ami Pro has placed *Travle* in the dialog box's Replace With text box. In the Alternatives list box, Ami Pro lists some correctly spelled alternatives (*Travel*, *Trivial*, and so on).

6. Observe the Replace All and Replace buttons. They are dimmed because you haven't yet selected an alternative word.

7. In the Alternatives list box, select **Travel**. The Replace All and Replace buttons are now available.

8. Click on **Replace** to replace *Travle* with *Travel*, and to instruct Ami Pro to continue spell-checking. Because it recognizes all the rest of the selected words, Ami Pro closes the Spell Check dialog box and deselects the text.

Now let's spell-check the entire document:

1. Click on the **Spell Check SmartIcon** to open the Spell Check dialog box. Because you have selected no text this time, Ami Pro provides you with some Spell Check options before it starts spell-checking. You can choose to check spelling from the beginning of the document, or in other text streams (in headers and footers, for example).

2. Check both **Check From Beginning Of Document** and **Include Other Text Streams** (if necessary). By checking these two options, you guarantee that Ami Pro will spell-check the entire document, regardless of the insertion point's position (see Figure 7.2).

3. Click on **OK** to start spell-checking the document. Ami Pro places the first word it doesn't recognize, *multiple-branch*, in the Replace With text box. (Ami Pro often doesn't recognize hyphenated compound words.)

4. Click on **Skip** to leave *multiple-branch* unchanged. Ami Pro continues checking the document, finds *Filadelphia*, and lists *Philadelphia* as an alternative.

5. In the Alternatives list box, double-click on **Philadelphia** (or select **Philadelphia** and then click on **Replace**) to replace *Filadelphia*. Ami Pro continues checking and finds *Tegxas*, but this time lists no alternative words.

6. In the Replace With text box, type **Texas**, and then click on **Replace** to replace *Tegxas* in the document. Ami Pro continues

CHECKING SPELLING • 203

checking and finds another hyphenated compound word that it doesn't recognize: *high-quality*.

Figure 7.2 **Setting some Spell Check options**

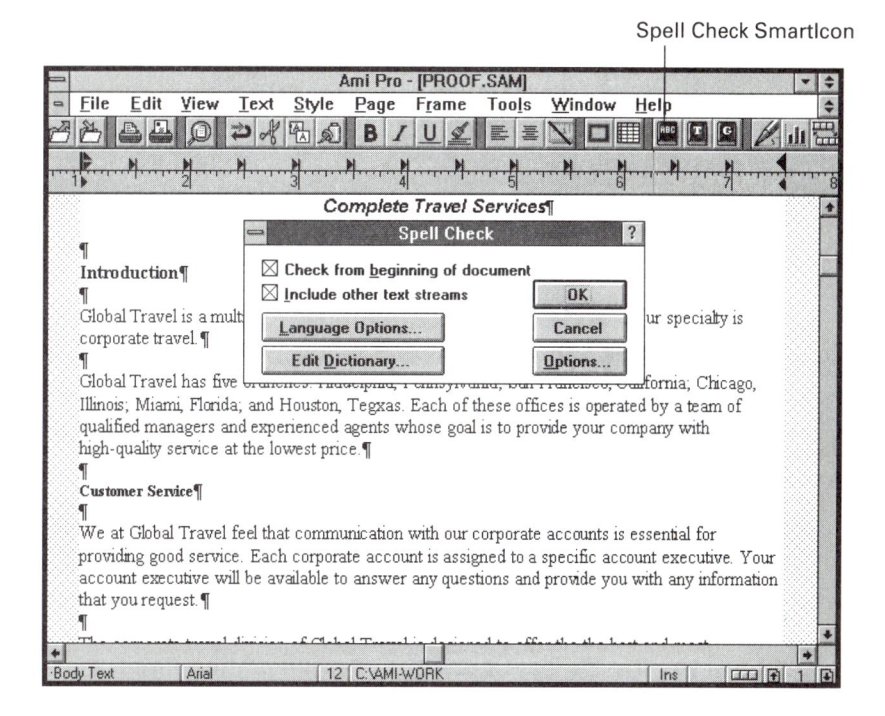

[Figure 7.2: Screenshot of Ami Pro with Spell Check dialog box, showing "Check from beginning of document" and "Include other text streams" checkboxes, with Language Options, Edit Dictionary, OK, Cancel, and Options buttons. Spell Check SmartIcon is labeled.]

7. Click on **Skip** to leave *high-quality* unchanged. Ami Pro continues checking and then opens an Ami Pro dialog box that prompts:

    ```
    The word immediately before this one was spelled exactly the same.
    ```

8. Click on **OK** to close the Ami Pro dialog box, and then observe the Spell Check dialog box and the document window. Ami Pro has found the repeated words *the the* and has placed the second occurrence of *the*, along with its leading space, in the Replace With text box (see Figure 7.3).

9. Press **Delete** to delete *the* from the Replace With text box, and then click on **Replace** to remove the second occurrence of *the* and its leading space from the document. Ami Pro continues

checking and finds the word *Complet* in the header. (If Include Other Text Streams had not been checked back in step 2, Ami Pro would have ignored this spelling error.)

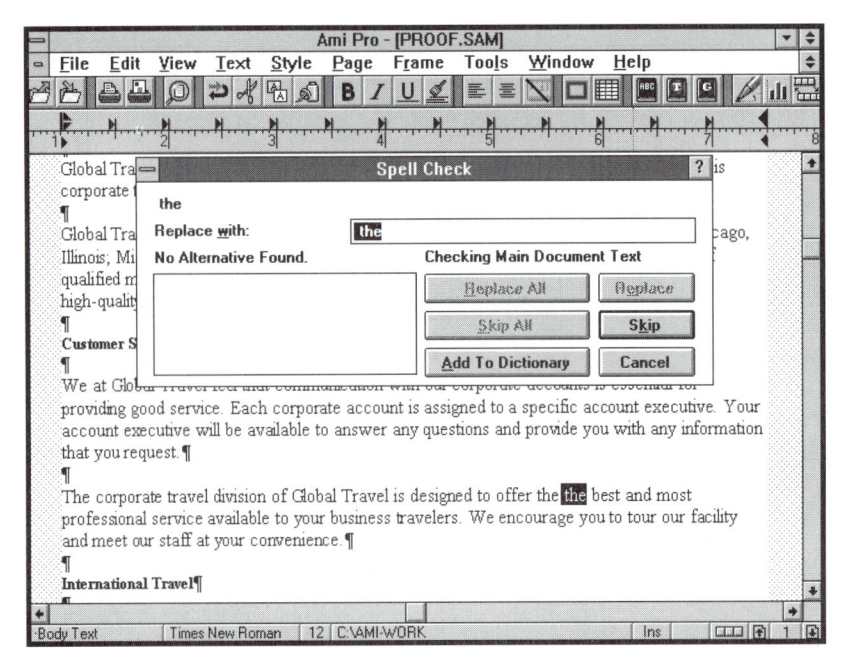

Figure 7.3 Finding repeated words

10. In the Alternatives list box, double-click on **Complete** to replace *Complet*. Ami Pro continues checking, but because it finds no more repeated words or possible spelling errors, it closes the Spell Check dialog box.

11. Save the document as **myproof**.

FINDING AND PLACING SYNONYMS WITH THESAURUS

Thesaurus—Ami Pro's 1,400,000-word, on-line thesaurus—helps you to look up *synonyms* for words that you've typed in your document. Synonyms are words with similar meanings. For example, if you typed the word *created*, Thesaurus would suggest alternatives such as *founded*, *constituted*, and *established*.

Although you should never use a word from a thesaurus—on-line or otherwise—that you don't recognize, Ami Pro's Thesaurus feature can greatly enhance the quality of the writing in your documents by providing you with just the right word when you have trouble thinking of it by yourself. Using Thesaurus, Ami Pro not only can look up synonyms, but can help you replace your original word with a synonym.

Follow these steps when you want to use Thesaurus to look up a synonym and replace your original word:

- Select or place the insertion point in the word you wish to replace.
- Choose Tools, Thesaurus or click on the *Thesaurus SmartIcon*—the 20th SmartIcon from the left, displaying a book with the letter *T*—to open the Thesaurus dialog box.
- If the Synonyms list box does not list the exact word you want, click on any of the words in the Meaning Variations list box, or click on a word in the Synonyms list box and then click on Lookup. Ami Pro will list the synonyms for the word you just selected. (To return to the previous list of synonyms after clicking on Lookup, click on Previous.)
- Once you find the synonym you want, select it, and then click on Replace. In the document window behind the dialog box, Ami Pro replaces your original word with the selected synonym.
- Click on Cancel to close the Thesaurus dialog box.

Let's practice using Thesaurus to find and place a synonym:

1. Scroll to the top of the document (if necessary), and then place the insertion point anywhere in the word *created* (located in the paragraph beginning *Global Travel is a multiple-branch*).

2. Choose **Tools, Thesaurus** (or click on the **Thesaurus SmartIcon**) to open the Thesaurus dialog box and display a list of synonyms for *created* (see Figure 7.4).

3. Observe the dialog box's Meaning box. It displays the definition for the word selected in the Meaning Variations list box: *founded*.

Figure 7.4   **Finding synonyms with Thesaurus**

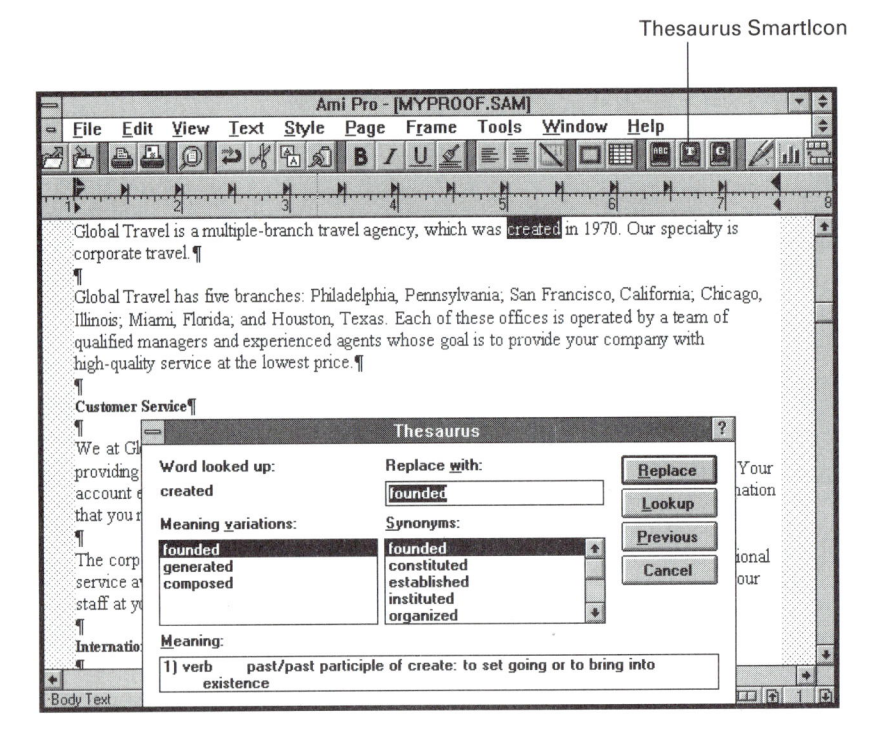

4. In the Synonyms list box, verify that **founded** is selected, and then click on **Replace**.

5. Click on **Cancel** to close the Thesaurus dialog box, and then observe the document window. Ami Pro has replaced *created* with *founded*.

CHECKING GRAMMAR, STYLE, AND MECHANICS

Ami Pro's grammar-checker, *Grammar Check*, helps you to identify and correct sentences in your document that contain grammatical and mechanical errors, and that exhibit a weak writing style.

Note: Explaining the ins and outs of proper grammar, style, and mechanics is beyond the scope of this book. For books on writing well, consult your local librarian.

STARTING GRAMMAR CHECK

To start Grammar Check:

- Select the text you wish to check, or place the insertion point in the appropriate document location. (To determine which parts of a document Ami Pro can grammar-check, Grammar Check follows the same guidelines as Spell Check. For example, if you want to grammar-check the entire document, place the insertion point in the main document text so that Ami Pro can check all text streams.)

- Choose Tools, Grammar Check or click on the *Grammar Check SmartIcon*—the 21st SmartIcon from the left, displaying a book with the letter *G*—to open the Grammar Check dialog box.

- If desired, use the dialog box's Use Grammar And Style Set drop-down list box to select the appropriate *grammar and style set* for checking your document. Because various kinds of writing tend to follow their own sets of grammar and style rules, Ami Pro provides seven grammar and style sets: *Business Writing*, *All Rules*, *Legal Writing*, *Fiction Writing*, *Academic Writing*, *Formal Writing*, and *Casual Writing*.

    (If none of these suits your purposes, you can use the Options button to modify an existing grammar and style set, or to create your own set. See your Ami Pro documentation for information on editing and creating grammar and style sets.)

- If desired, check or uncheck any of the options in the Preferences box: Show Readability Statistics, Show Explanations, Check From Beginning Of Document, Include Other Text Streams, and Check In Draft Mode. (You'll learn about many of these options shortly.)

- Click on OK.

USING GRAMMAR CHECK

Once you've started Grammar Check, Ami Pro begins checking your document. When Ami Pro finds a sentence that does not follow all the rules in the current grammar and style set, the Grammar Checker dialog box appears, with suggestions for correcting the error displayed in the Suggestions list box. The sentence and any replacement options, if available, appear in the list box labeled either *Sentence* or *Replacement Options*. (When the current selection

208 • PROOFING YOUR DOCUMENTS

in that list box is your original sentence, you will see a Sentence list box. When the current selection is a replacement for your original sentence, you will see a Replacement Options list box.) If Show Explanations was checked when you started Grammar Check, the Suggestions list box also explains the error Ami Pro has found.

Each time Ami Pro finds what it considers a "problem" sentence, you can use one of the following methods to ignore Ami Pro's suggestion or to correct the sentence:

- To skip the current rule for the sentence, click on Skip. If there are any more errors in the sentence, Ami Pro will point out those errors next. Otherwise, Ami Pro continues on to the rest of the document.

- To skip the current rule during the remainder of the Grammar Check session, click on Skip Rule.

- To skip the current sentence, regardless of other errors in the sentence, click on Next Sentence.

- If you wish to correct the sentence, and Ami Pro lists an appropriate replacement sentence in the Sentence/Replacement Options list box, select the replacement sentence, and then click on Replace.

- If you wish to correct the sentence but Ami Pro does not list an appropriate replacement sentence, click in the document window, correct your sentence manually, and then click on Resume in the dialog box to restart Grammar Check.

READABILITY STATISTICS

If Show Readability Statistics was checked when you started Grammar Check, Ami Pro will open a Readability Statistics dialog box when the program has finished grammar-checking. This dialog box provides document statistics such as the total number of words, sentences, and paragraphs, and provides readability statistics based on four scales: Gunning's Fog Index, Flesch-Kincaid Score, Flesch Reading Ease Score, and Flesch Reading Ease Grade Level. These measurements indicate the relative reading ease of your document. For more information on interpreting these measurements, see your Ami Pro documentation.

Once you've finished viewing the Readability Statistics dialog box, click on Close.

Note: The Readability Statistics dialog box shows statistics only for the portion of the document that you most recently checked. If you used Grammar Check on only a portion of the document, this dialog box will not accurately reflect the entire document's totals, averages, percentages, and readability statistics.

Let's use the grammar checker to check MYPROOF.SAM for grammar, style, and mechanics:

1. Move the insertion point to the top of the document. (Press **Ctrl+Home**.)

2. Choose **Tools, Grammar Check** (or click on the **Grammar Check SmartIcon**), and then examine the Grammar Check dialog box. Ami Pro is set by default to use the Business Writing grammar and style set, to show readability statistics after checking grammar and style, and to show explanations for each grammar or style rule that it thinks you have broken (see Figure 7.5).

Figure 7.5   Viewing some Grammar Check options

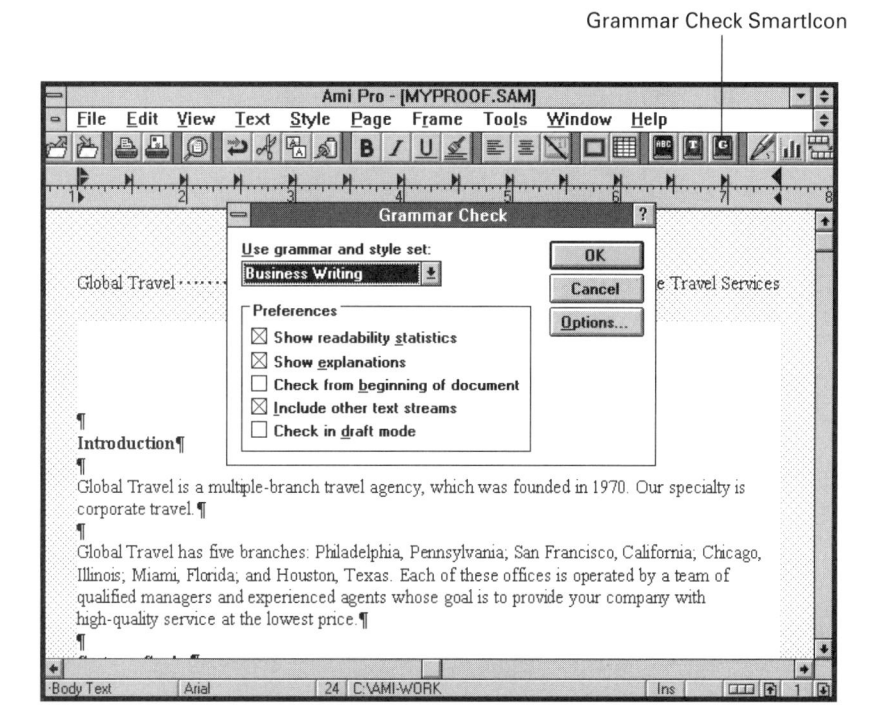

3. Click on **OK** to accept the defaults and to instruct Ami Pro to start checking for potential grammar and style errors. Because the insertion point is already at the top of the document, you do not have to check *Check From Beginning Of Document*. (See your Ami Pro documentation for more information about using the *Check In Draft Mode* option.)

4. Observe the Grammar Checker dialog box. Ami Pro finds *was founded*, and informs you in the Suggestions list box that this verb group may be in the passive voice. (In the Business Writing grammar and style set, Ami Pro considers passive-voice verb groups to be grammatical errors.) Because Show Explanations was checked when you started Grammar Check, the dialog box also explains the passive-voice rule in the Suggestions list box (see Figure 7.6).

5. Let's say we disagree; we find passive-voice verbs appropriate in this instance. Click on **Skip** to leave the sentence unchanged. Ami Pro continues checking and finds *is operated*, another passive-voice verb.

Figure 7.6   **Finding a sentence with a passive-voice verb group**

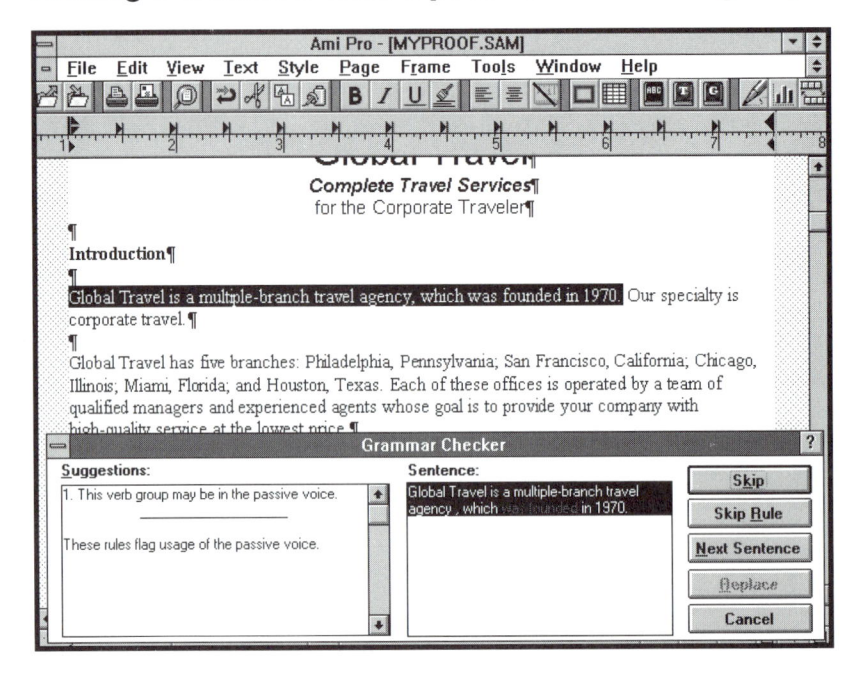

CHECKING GRAMMAR, STYLE, AND MECHANICS • 211

6. Clearly, Ami Pro is going to point out every passive-voice verb group that it finds. Let's stop it from doing this for now. Click on **Skip Rule** to ignore all passive-voice verb groups for the remainder of this grammar check. Ami Pro continues checking and finds *You're* in the sentence beginning *You're company profile*. Notice that the Sentence list box has become a Replacement Options list box, and suggests changing *You're* to *Your*.

7. This time, we'll take Ami Pro's advice. Click on **Replace** to accept the suggested correction and change *You're* to *Your*. Ami Pro continues checking and finds *right* in the phrase *right at the pickup window*. In the Suggestions list box, Ami Pro explains that *right* and *rite* are *homonyms* (words that sound alike), and asks you to double-check that *right* is the correct word in this context. (It is.)

8. Click on **Skip** to leave the sentence unchanged. Ami Pro continues checking and finds *access*, which sounds like *excess*. Apparently, as with passive-voice verb groups earlier, Ami Pro is going to be insistent about checking homonyms.

9. Click on **Skip Rule** to leave the sentence unchanged and to instruct Ami Pro to ignore homonyms for the remainder of this grammar check. Ami Pro continues checking, but because it finds no more potential grammar or style errors, it closes the Grammar Check dialog box and opens the Readability Statistics dialog box (see Figure 7.7).

Figure 7.7   **Readability statistics**

Document Statistics			
Totals:		**Averages:**	
Words	533	Words per sentence	17.2
Sentences	31	Sentences per Paragraph	1.3
Paragraphs	24		
Syllables	904	**Percentages:**	
3-syllable words	89	Passive sentences	35%

Readability Statistics			
Gunning's Fog Index:	12.5	Flesch Reading Ease Score:	42.6
Flesch-Kincaid Score:	10.7	Flesch Reading Ease Grade Level:	14.1

212 • PROOFING YOUR DOCUMENTS

10. Observe the Readability Statistics dialog box. In addition to the readability statistics at the bottom, Ami Pro lists some document statistics, including the total number of words, sentences, and paragraphs. For the readability statistics, Ami Pro has graded the document according to four readability measurements: Gunning's Fog Index, Flesch-Kincaid Score, Flesch Reading Ease Score, and Flesch Reading Ease Grade Level.

11. Press **F1** or click on the dialog box's **Help icon** to open a Help window that explains each of the readability measurements (see Figure 7.8).

Figure 7.8   **Viewing the Help window on readability statistics**

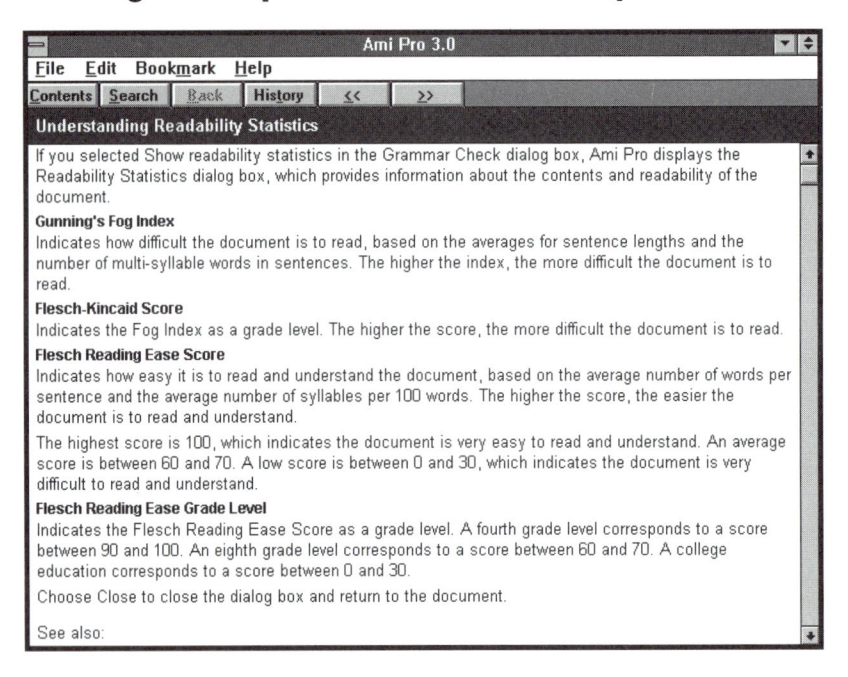

```
┌─────────────────────────────── Ami Pro 3.0 ───────────────────────────┬─┐
│ File  Edit  Bookmark  Help                                            │ │
│ Contents │ Search │ Back │ History │  <<  │  >>  │                    │
│ Understanding Readability Statistics                                   │
│ If you selected Show readability statistics in the Grammar Check dialog box, Ami Pro displays the
│ Readability Statistics dialog box, which provides information about the contents and readability of the
│ document.
│ Gunning's Fog Index
│ Indicates how difficult the document is to read, based on the averages for sentence lengths and the
│ number of multi-syllable words in sentences. The higher the index, the more difficult the document is to
│ read.
│ Flesch-Kincaid Score
│ Indicates the Fog Index as a grade level. The higher the score, the more difficult the document is to read.
│ Flesch Reading Ease Score
│ Indicates how easy it is to read and understand the document, based on the average number of words per
│ sentence and the average number of syllables per 100 words. The higher the score, the easier the
│ document is to read and understand.
│ The highest score is 100, which indicates the document is very easy to read and understand. An average
│ score is between 60 and 70. A low score is between 0 and 30, which indicates the document is very
│ difficult to read and understand.
│ Flesch Reading Ease Grade Level
│ Indicates the Flesch Reading Ease Score as a grade level. A fourth grade level corresponds to a score
│ between 90 and 100. An eighth grade level corresponds to a score between 60 and 70. A college
│ education corresponds to a score between 0 and 30.
│ Choose Close to close the dialog box and return to the document.
│ See also:
└────────────────────────────────────────────────────────────────────────┘
```

12. Close the Help window, and then click on **Close** to close the Readability Statistics dialog box.

13. Save and close the document.

SUMMARY

In this chapter, you learned how to proof your documents: You used Spell Check to check for spelling errors and repeated words, and Grammar Check to check grammar, style, mechanics, and overall readability. You also learned how to use Ami Pro's Thesaurus to find and place synonyms.

Here's a quick reference guide to the Ami Pro features introduced in this chapter:

Desired Result	How to Do It
Spell-check selected text	Select text; choose **Tools**, **Spell Check** or click on **Spell Check SmartIcon**; then follow Spell Check dialog box prompts.
Spell-check an entire document	Place insertion point in main document text; choose **Tools**, **Spell Check** or click on **Spell Check SmartIcon**; check **Check From Beginning Of Document** and **Include Other Text Streams** (if necessary); then click on **OK** and follow Spell Check dialog box prompts.
Use Thesaurus to find and place a synonym	Select or place insertion point in existing word; choose **Tools**, **Thesaurus** or click on **Thesaurus SmartIcon**; select desired synonym in Synonyms list box; then click on **Replace**.
Grammar-check entire document	Place insertion point in main document text; choose **Tools**, **Grammar Check** or click on **Grammar Check SmartIcon**; select grammar and style set (if desired); check **Check From Beginning Of Document** and **Include Other Text Streams** (if necessary); check other options (if desired); click on **OK**; and then follow Grammar Check dialog box prompts.

In the next chapter, you will explore some advanced editing and formatting techniques. You will learn how to copy and move text without using the Clipboard; copy text between documents; add bullets;

and find and replace text attributes. You will also learn how to gain access to and customize all of Ami Pro's over 150 SmartIcons.

IF YOU'RE STOPPING HERE

If you need to take a break here, please exit Ami Pro. If you want to proceed directly to the next chapter, please do so now.

CHAPTER 8: ADVANCED EDITING AND FORMATTING TECHNIQUES

Copying and Moving Text with Drag & Drop

Copying Text between Documents

Adding Bullets

Finding and Replacing Text Attributes

Customizing SmartIcons and SmartIcon Sets

Back in Chapters 3 and 4, you learned basic techniques for moving and copying text, for finding and replacing text, and for applying and removing text formats. Throughout this book so far, you've also learned how to use many of Ami Pro's SmartIcons to help you perform common tasks such as opening and printing documents. Here in this chapter, you will build on these fundamental "survival skills." You will learn some advanced methods for editing and formatting text, as well as how to go beyond the 24 default SmartIcons you've seen so far and access the rest of Ami Pro's over 150 available SmartIcons.

When you're done working through this chapter, you will know how to

- Move and copy text using Drag & Drop
- Copy text from one document to another
- Add bullets to your documents
- Find and replace text attributes
- Access and customize all of Ami Pro's SmartIcons

COPYING AND MOVING TEXT WITH DRAG & DROP

In Chapter 3, you saw how to copy and move text by using Edit commands and SmartIcons to cut, copy, and paste to and from the Windows Clipboard. You learned to follow these four steps when you want to move or copy text:

- Select the text.
- Cut or copy the text (using an Edit command or a SmartIcon).
- Position the insertion point.
- Paste the text (using an Edit command or a SmartIcon).

Ami Pro also provides an even more convenient and shorter three-step method for moving and copying text, called *Drag & Drop*. With Drag & Drop, you simply drag the selected text to a new location without using any Edit commands or SmartIcons.

Follow these three steps when you want to move text with Drag & Drop:

- Select the text you want to move.
- Position the I-beam over the selected text, press and hold the mouse button, and then start dragging. When you do, Ami Pro changes the mouse pointer to a *move arrow* (a left-pointing arrow with a pair of scissors attached) and displays a colored insertion point near the move arrow (the color of the insertion point depends on your Windows color setup).
- Drag the move arrow until the colored insertion point is where you want to move the text, and then release the mouse button. Ami Pro moves your selected text to the new location.

COPYING AND MOVING TEXT WITH DRAG & DROP • 219

The procedure to copy text with Drag & Drop is almost identical to moving; you only need to add the Ctrl key. Follow these three steps when you want to copy text with Drag & Drop:

- Select the text you want to copy.

- Position the I-beam over the selected text, press and hold Ctrl, press and hold the mouse button, start dragging, and then release Ctrl. When you start dragging, Ami Pro changes the mouse pointer to a *copy arrow* (a left-pointing arrow attached to two capital *A*'s in boxes) and displays a colored insertion point near the copy arrow.

- Drag the copy arrow until the colored insertion point is where you want to copy the text, and then release the mouse button. Ami Pro copies your selected text to the new location, leaving your original in place.

When you use Drag & Drop, Ami Pro does *not* use the Windows Clipboard. This can be an advantage when you have text on the Clipboard that you want to preserve. However, this means that if you want to copy some text to multiple locations, you cannot simply copy once and then paste repeatedly (as you did with the three-line page heading in Chapter 3). In such cases, you should use Edit commands and/or SmartIcons, rather than Drag & Drop, to copy and paste the text.

Note: If you find that you inadvertently move text with Drag & Drop, you can disable the feature through the Tools, User Setup command. For the remainder of this chapter, however, please leave Drag & Drop enabled.

If you are not running Ami Pro, please start it now. Now let's practice moving text using Drag & Drop:

1. Open **advanced.sam**.

2. Scroll down a few lines until you can see the headings *Customer Service*, *Introduction*, and *International Travel*.

3. Let's say *Introduction* and the five paragraphs below it should be above *Customer Service*. Select the six paragraphs from *Introduction* through to the blank line just above *International Travel*.

4. Position the I-beam over the selected text, press and hold the mouse button, and then start dragging. As you drag, notice

that the mouse pointer becomes a move arrow, with a colored insertion point nearby (see Figure 8.1).

Figure 8.1 **Moving text with Drag & Drop**

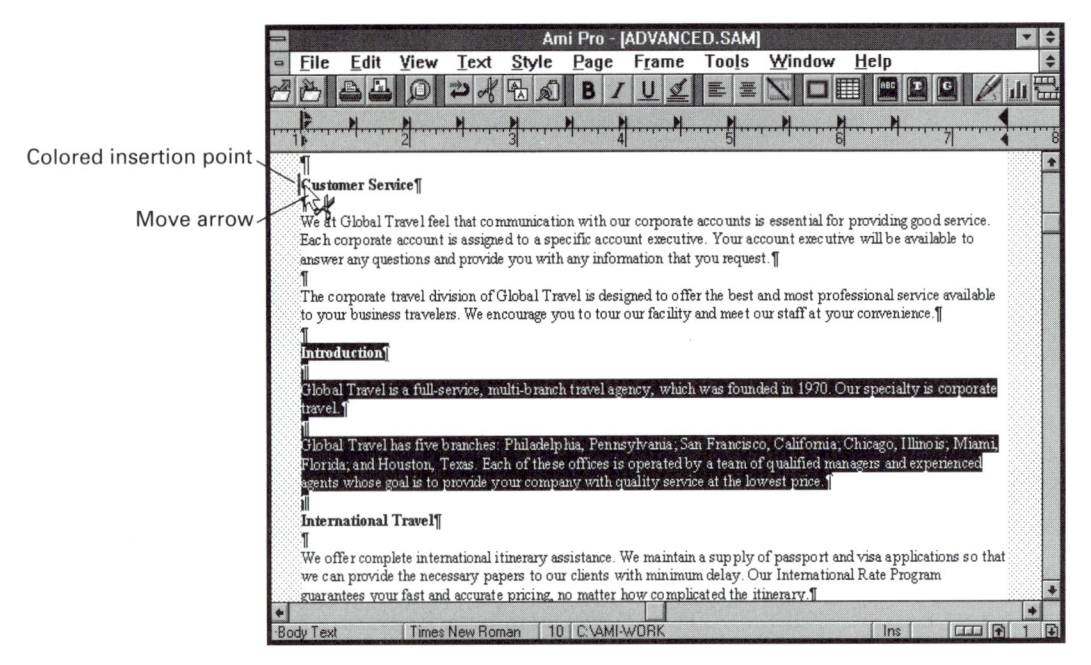

Colored insertion point

Move arrow

5. Drag the colored insertion point up, to the position immediately before the *C* in *Customer Service*, and then release the mouse button. Ami Pro moves the selected text up and places it above *Customer Service*.

Now let's copy some text with Drag & Drop:

1. Scroll up (if necessary), and then select the two-line heading and the following blank line at the top of page 1.

2. Position the I-beam over the selected text, press and hold **Ctrl**, and then start dragging. This time, the mouse pointer changes to a copy arrow (see Figure 8.2).

3. Release **Ctrl**, and then drag down to the top of page 2 until the colored insertion point is immediately before the *D* in the heading *Deliveries*.

Figure 8.2   **Copying text with Drag & Drop**

Copy arrow —

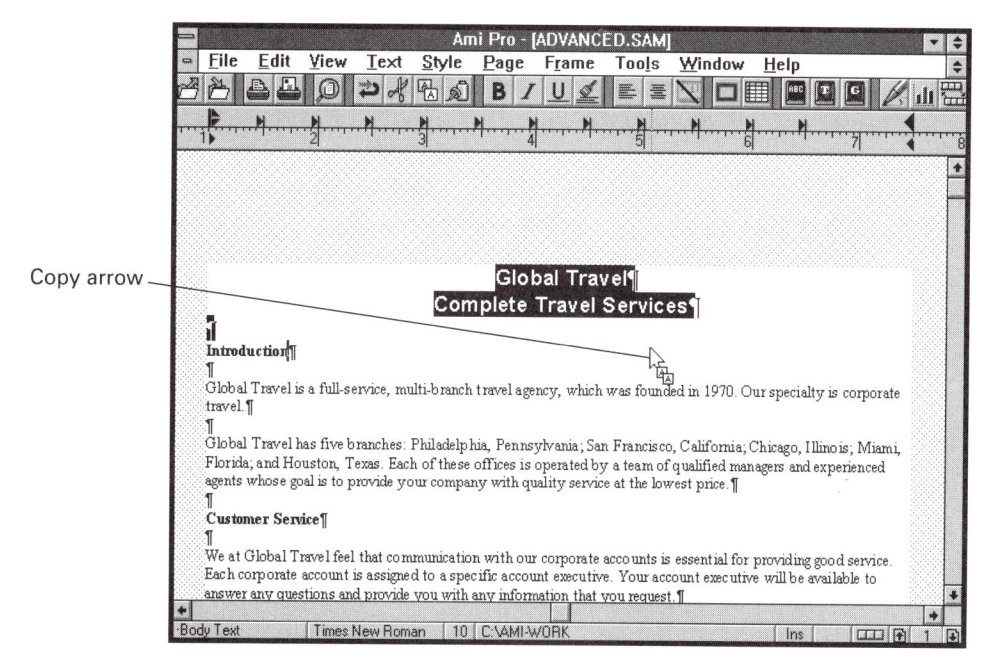

4. Release the mouse button. Ami Pro places a copy of the selected text at the top of page 2.

5. Return to and observe the top of page 1. Ami Pro has left the original text in place.

6. Save the document as **myadvanc**.

COPYING TEXT BETWEEN DOCUMENTS

Whenever you open a document, Ami Pro places the document in its own document window. Throughout this book so far, you have opened and worked with only one document and document window at a time. In Ami Pro, you can also create or open a second document, without closing the first one. Ami Pro will open a second document window on top of the first document window so that both documents are open at the same time. The second document window then becomes the active document window; any document-specific commands you issue (such as saving and printing) will affect only that second document. You can open up to nine document windows, but only one document window can be active at a time.

Opening multiple documents is useful for copying or moving text from one document to another, or for comparing the contents of two documents.

To help you manage multiple document windows, Ami Pro lists the name of each open document window (preceded by a number) in the Window menu. To activate an inactive document window, open the Window menu, and then click on the document window's name.

Note: You can also use the Window, Tile and the Window, Cascade commands to view more than one document window at a time. For more information on these commands, see your Ami Pro documentation.

Ami Pro offers many ways to move and copy text from one document to another. One of the most convenient methods is to open both documents and then use the Clipboard. Follow these steps when you want to copy text from one document to another:

- Open the document to which you want to copy text (the *target* document).

- Without closing the target document, open the document that contains the text you want to copy (the *source* document). The title bar will change to display the source document's name.

- In the source document, select the text you want to copy; then choose Edit, Copy, or click on the Copy To The Clipboard SmartIcon.

- Open the Window menu, and then click on the name of your first document (the target document). Ami Pro activates the target document window, moving it in front of the source document window, and changes the title bar to display the target document's name.

- In the target document, place the insertion point where you want to paste the copied text.

- Choose Edit, Paste or click on the Paste Clipboard Contents SmartIcon.

When you finish working with the source document, you can close it by first activating its document window, and then choosing File,

Close or double-clicking on the document window's Control menu box. Or, if you need to, you can leave the document open as long as you are in Ami Pro. When you exit Ami Pro, the document window will close along with any other open document windows.

Note: Although you can open up to nine documents at a time, you might find that this makes your computer run more slowly. If this is a problem, close some document windows.

Let's open a second document, XTRATEXT.SAM, without closing MYADVANC.SAM, and then copy text between the two documents:

1. Choose **File, Open** or click on the **Open An Existing File SmartIcon** to display the Open dialog box.

2. Scroll to the bottom of the Files list box, and then double-click on **xtratext.sam**. Ami Pro opens a document window for XTRATEXT.SAM on top of the MYADVANC.SAM document window.

3. Examine XTRATEXT.SAM. It consists of a multiple-line paragraph and a blank line.

4. Select the entire document (press **Shift+Ctrl+End**), and then choose **Edit, Copy** or click on the **Copy To The Clipboard SmartIcon**.

5. Open and examine the **Window** menu. It lists both open documents, MYADVANC.SAM and XTRATEXT.SAM. Because XTRATEXT.SAM is the active document window, Ami Pro has checked 2 XTRATEXT.SAM (see Figure 8.3).

6. Select **1 MYADVANC.SAM** to activate the MYADVANC.SAM document window.

7. In the MYADVANC.SAM document window, scroll to the top of page 2, and then place the insertion point immediately to the left of the *H* in the heading *Hotel Accommodations*.

8. Choose **Edit, Paste** or click on the **Paste Clipboard Contents SmartIcon**. Ami Pro inserts the selected paragraph and blank line from XTRATEXT.SAM at the insertion point.

9. Save MYADVANC.SAM.

10. Choose **Window, 2 XTRATEXT.SAM** to activate the XTRATEXT.SAM document window.

224 • ADVANCED EDITING AND FORMATTING TECHNIQUES

Figure 8.3 **The Window menu, listing two open document windows**

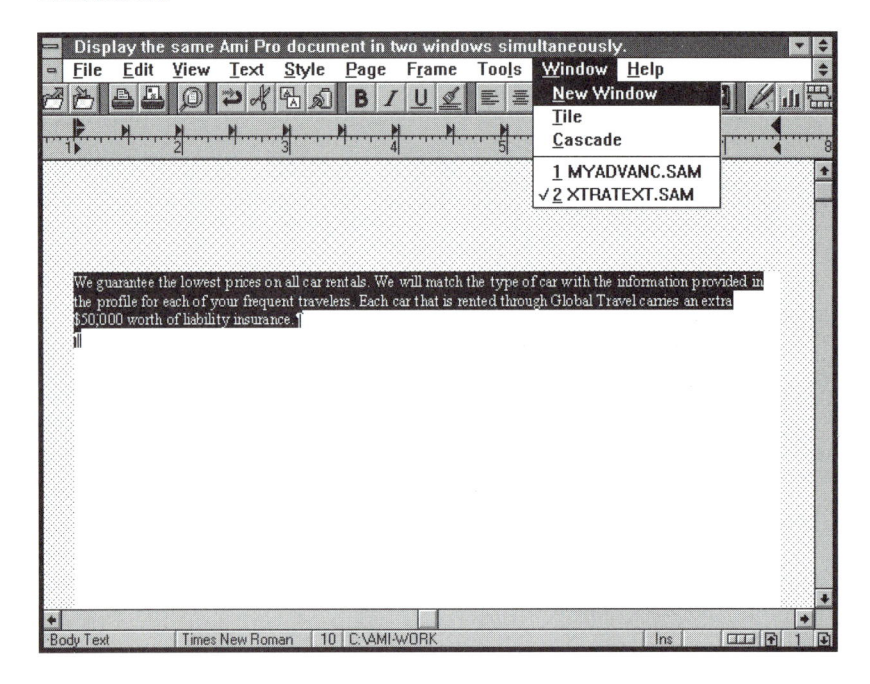

11. Choose **File, Close** or double-click on the XTRATEXT.SAM document window's **Control menu box** to close XTRATEXT.SAM. MYADVANC.SAM again becomes the active document window.

ADDING BULLETS

If you've used a typewriter before moving to Ami Pro, you might have noticed that your computer keyboard is very similar to a typewriter keyboard. The computer keyboard probably has many more buttons, but both keyboards contain many of the same types of keys: letters, numbers, punctuation marks, and some symbols (such as @, #, and $). One of the limitations of both typewriter and computer keyboards, however, is that neither contains any good symbols for *bullets* (for example, •). Bullets are useful for organizing and drawing attention to certain text, as we have done in the *bulleted lists* throughout this book.

Ami Pro provides 17 different *bullet styles*, from solid dots (•) to check boxes (❑) to arrows (➤). You can insert a bullet anywhere in your document. For bulleted lists, you should insert bullets at the beginning of each paragraph's first line, and then set hanging indents for the paragraphs. (In the activities of this chapter, you'll use documents that already contain hanging indents. All you'll need to do is insert a bullet, and then a tab character to separate the bullet from the rest of the paragraph.)

Once they're inserted, you can delete bullets as you would any other text.

Follow these steps when you want to insert a bullet:

- Place the insertion point where you want to insert the bullet.
- Choose Edit, Insert, Bullet to open the Insert Bullet dialog box, containing Ami Pro's 17 available bullet styles.
- In the Bullets box, select the desired bullet style, and then click on OK.

Let's insert some bullets in order to complete a bulleted list:

1. Scroll down on page 2 until the subheading *Newsletter* appears near the top of the document window.
2. Place the insertion point immediately before the *T* in *Travel costs* (located beneath the *Newsletter* subheading).
3. Choose **Edit, Insert, Bullet**, and then observe the Insert Bullet dialog box. It provides 17 different bullet styles (see Figure 8.4).

Figure 8.4   **The Insert Bullet dialog box**

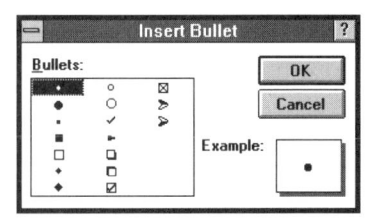

4. In the Bullets box, select the second bullet from the top of the leftmost row (the large, solid dot), and then click on **OK**. Ami Pro inserts the bullet at the insertion point.

5. Press **Tab** to align *Travel costs* with the second line of the paragraph.

PRACTICE YOUR SKILLS

1. Insert a large, solid-dot bullet *and* a tab character for each of the two paragraphs beginning *Special fares* and *Travel basics*.

2. Compare your screen to Figure 8.5.

3. Save the document.

Figure 8.5   **Bulleted paragraphs**

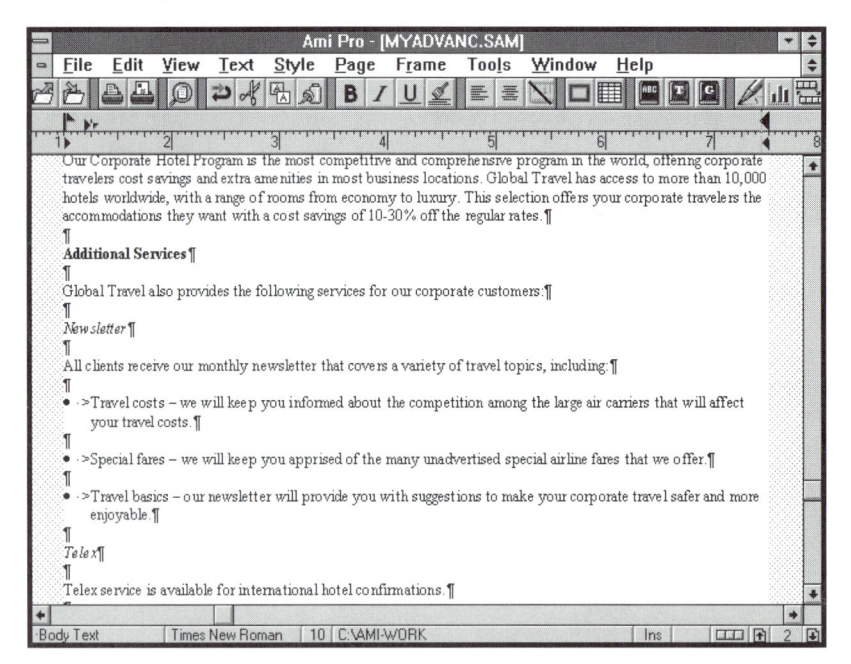

FINDING AND REPLACING TEXT ATTRIBUTES

In Chapter 3, you learned how to find and replace text; in Chapter 4, you learned how to apply text attributes to selected text. In this section, you'll see how to combine these two skills, using Edit, Find & Replace to find text with certain text attributes and then replace it with text that has other text attributes. For example, you can find every underlined occurrence of your company's old name, and then replace it with your company's new name in boldface.

If you want to change just the text attributes and not the text itself, you can do that, too. For example, you can find every occurrence of your own name when it is italicized, and replace each occurrence with the same name but without text attributes.

Using Find & Replace is a quick and convenient way to add and remove text attributes throughout long documents.

Follow these steps when you want to find and replace text attributes:

- Place the insertion point where you wish to begin the find-and-replace operation. (Remember from Chapters 2 and 3 that Edit, Find & Replace by default searches from the insertion point downward.) To search an entire document, place the insertion point at the top of the document.

- Choose Edit, Find & Replace to open the Find & Replace dialog box.

- In the Find text box, type your search text.

- In the Replace With text box, type your replacement text. To change only text attributes, just type the same text you typed in the Find text box.

- Click on Attributes to open the Find & Replace Attributes dialog box.

- In the Find Attributes box, check attributes for your search text.

- In the Replace Attributes box, check the new attributes you want your replacement text to have.

- Click on OK to return to the Find & Replace dialog box, and then click on Options to open the Find & Replace Options dialog box.

- If you want Ami Pro to use the exact attributes you specified in the Find & Replace Attributes dialog box's Find Attributes box, check Find Options Exact Attributes. Otherwise, Ami Pro will find every occurrence of your search text—regardless of exact attributes. (For example, it will find text that is boldface and italic, even if you specified only boldface.)

- If you want Ami Pro to use the exact attributes you specified in the Find & Replace Attributes dialog box's Replace Attributes box, check Replace Options Exact Attributes. Otherwise, Ami Pro will *add* the attributes of any text it finds, rather than *replacing* the existing attributes.

- Select any other appropriate options in the Find & Replace Options dialog box (refer back to Chapters 3 and 4 and to your Ami Pro documentation for more information on these options), and then click on OK.

- Click on Find or Replace All to start the find-and-replace operation, and then use the skills you learned in Chapter 3 to complete the find-and-replace operation.

Let's use Edit, Find & Replace to find every occurrence of *Global Travel* with no text attributes, and replace each with *Global Travel* in boldface:

1. Move to the top of the document (press **Ctrl+Home**).

2. Choose **Edit, Find & Replace** to open the Find & Replace dialog box. Type **Global Travel** in both the Find and Replace With text boxes.

3. Click on **Attributes**, and then observe the Find & Replace Attributes dialog box. This dialog box enables you to specify attributes for search text and for replacement text. Every time you use the Edit, Find & Replace command, Ami Pro checks Normal in both boxes by default.

4. Check **Replace Attributes Bold** (notice that Ami Pro automatically unchecks *Replace Attributes Normal*), and then observe the dialog box. Ami Pro is now set to find every occurrence of *Global Travel* with no text attributes, and to replace each occurrence with attribute *Global Travel* in boldface (see Figure 8.6).

Figure 8.6   **The Find & Replace Attributes dialog box**

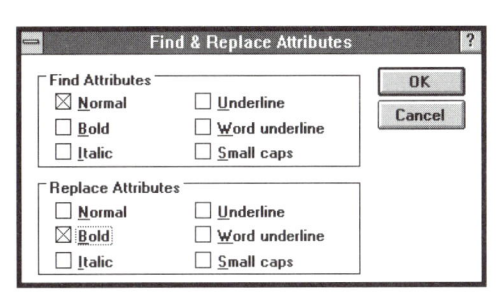

```
┌─ Find & Replace Attributes ───────────────┐
│  ┌─Find Attributes──────────────┐  ┌────┐ │
│  │ ☒ Normal    ☐ Underline      │  │ OK │ │
│  │ ☐ Bold      ☐ Word underline │  └────┘ │
│  │ ☐ Italic    ☐ Small caps     │ ┌──────┐│
│  └──────────────────────────────┘ │Cancel││
│  ┌─Replace Attributes───────────┐ └──────┘│
│  │ ☐ Normal    ☐ Underline      │         │
│  │ ☒ Bold      ☐ Word underline │         │
│  │ ☐ Italic    ☐ Small caps     │         │
│  └──────────────────────────────┘         │
└───────────────────────────────────────────┘
```

5. Click on **OK** to return to the Find & Replace dialog box.

6. Click on **Options** to open the Find & Replace Options dialog box, and then check **Find Options Exact Attributes** and **Replace Options Exact Attributes**. Now, Ami Pro will find only text that has no attributes, and it will apply only the Bold attribute to that text.

7. Click on **OK** to return to the Find & Replace dialog box, and then click on **Find** to start searching for the first occurrence of *Global Travel* with no text attributes. Ami Pro skips past the boldface *Global Travel* in the two-line heading on the top of page 1, and selects the no-attribute *Global Travel* under the heading *Introduction*.

8. Click on **Replace & Find Next**. Ami Pro replaces the no-attribute *Global Travel* with a boldface *Global Travel*, and then selects the next no-attribute *Global Travel* (see Figure 8.7).

PRACTICE YOUR SKILLS

1. Continue the find-and-replace operation until you have replaced each *Global Travel* without attributes in MYADVANC-.SAM with a boldface *Global Travel*.

2. Save your document.

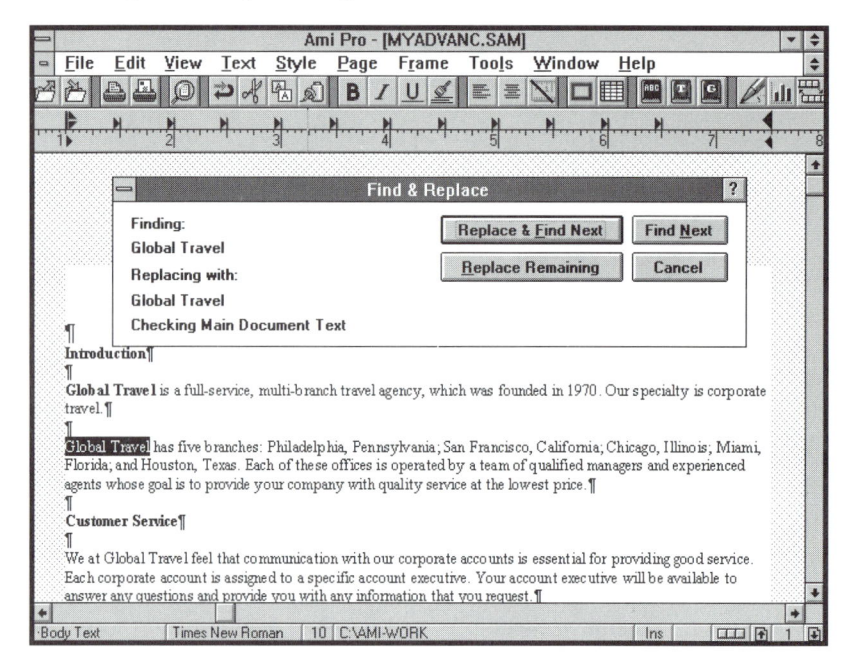

Figure 8.7 **Finding and replacing text attributes**

CUSTOMIZING SMARTICONS AND SMARTICON SETS

At this point, you've used most of the 24 default SmartIcons that Ami Pro displays across the top of the document window. Ami Pro also provides over 125 additional SmartIcons that can help you perform a wide variety of tasks, from creating new documents to starting other Windows applications from within Ami Pro. There's even a SmartIcon that starts an Ami Pro game called Mind Blaster!

Ami Pro's SmartIcons are almost completely customizable. If you don't like the current set of SmartIcons, or if you want to display the SmartIcons in a different position on the screen, or if you want to change the order within a set of SmartIcons, or if you want to add some SmartIcons to a set and remove some others, you can. Ami Pro even enables you to change the appearance of individual SmartIcons, and to build your own SmartIcons from scratch!

In the next few sections, you'll learn a number of techniques for customizing Ami Pro's SmartIcons. For information on customizing SmartIcons beyond the methods covered here, refer to your Ami Pro documentation.

Note: Ami Pro remembers SmartIcon customizations from session to session. For safety's sake, the steps in this chapter show you how to customize SmartIcons, but in the end leave every SmartIcon in its original position. If you share your computer with other Ami Pro users, be sure to discuss with them any SmartIcon customizations you perform on your own. Otherwise, the next time someone tries to click on a favorite SmartIcon, it might have mysteriously disappeared.

SWITCHING SMARTICON SETS

Because Ami Pro has so many SmartIcons, it would be impractical to display them all on screen at the same time; there might not be any room to type! Instead, Ami Pro provides eight sets of SmartIcons (called *SmartIcon sets*), each designed for a different purpose. So far, you've only seen Ami Pro's Default SmartIcon set, which is a general-purpose assortment. Other SmartIcon sets are geared to more specific purposes, such as editing documents, working with long documents, and proofing documents.

Anytime you have a document window open, you can instruct Ami Pro to display a particular SmartIcon set. For example, if you are editing a document, you might want to use Ami Pro's Editing SmartIcon set rather than the Default SmartIcon set.

Use any of these three methods when you want to switch to another SmartIcon set:

- Click on the *SmartIcon button* (the fourth button from the right on the status bar, displaying a horizontal row of three blank buttons) to open a list of available SmartIcon sets, and then select the set you want to use.

- Click on the *Next Icon Set SmartIcon*, often the rightmost SmartIcon in any SmartIcon set, displaying two horizontal rows of blank buttons and two arrows.

- Choose Tools, SmartIcons to open the SmartIcons dialog box, and open the unlabeled drop-down list at the top-center of the dialog box (we'll call it the *Current Set drop-down list box*).

- Select the desired SmartIcon set, and then click on OK.

When you switch to a new SmartIcon set, Ami Pro displays the new set immediately. To explore the SmartIcons you don't recognize, remember the trick from Chapter 3 for viewing SmartIcon names: Point to the SmartIcon, and then press and hold the *right* mouse button; Ami Pro will display the SmartIcon's name in the title bar.

Let's use the SmartIcons button and the Next Icon Set SmartIcon to explore Ami Pro's other SmartIcon sets:

1. Observe the SmartIcons located at the top of the document window. They enable you to perform a very general variety of tasks, from opening and saving documents to running Spell Check and Grammar Check.

2. Click on the status bar's **SmartIcons button** to open a list of Ami Pro's eight available SmartIcon sets: *Default*, *Editing*, *Graphics*, *Long Documents*, *Macro Goodies*, *Proofing*, *Tables*, and *Working Together*. (The list also contains a *Hide SmartIcons* choice for removing SmartIcons from the screen altogether.) *Default* is selected because Ami Pro is currently displaying the Default SmartIcon set (see Figure 8.8).

3. In the list of SmartIcon sets, select **Editing**, and then observe the new set of SmartIcons that appears at the top of the document window (see Figure 8.9).

Figure 8.8   Displaying a list of SmartIcon sets

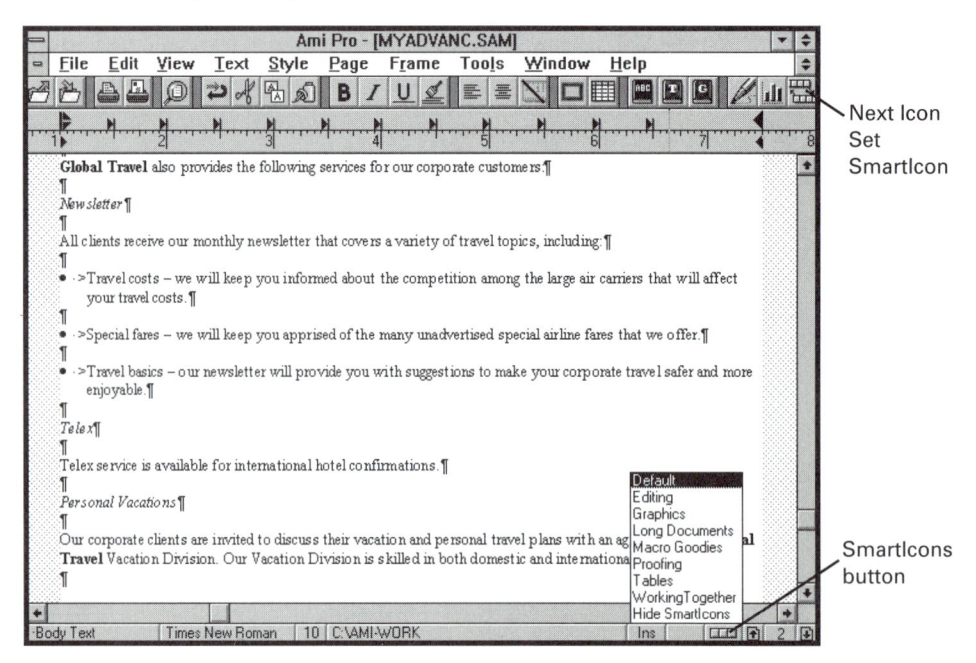

Figure 8.9   **The Editing SmartIcon set**

4. Use your *right* mouse button to click on each of the new SmartIcons and view their names in the title bar. These new SmartIcons can help you when you're editing documents.

5. Click on the **Next Icon Set SmartIcon**. Ami Pro switches to the next SmartIcon set, but gives no indication of which set it is.

6. Click on the status bar's **SmartIcons button**, and observe the displayed list. Now you can see that Ami Pro is showing the Graphics SmartIcon set, the next set down in the list from Editing.

7. Click on the **SmartIcons button** again to close the displayed list, and then use the *right* mouse button to view the names of the Graphics SmartIcons.

PRACTICE YOUR SKILLS

1. Use the **SmartIcons button** and/or the **Next Icon Set SmartIcon** to view Ami Pro's other SmartIcon sets. For each set, use the *right* mouse button to view the name of each SmartIcon.

2. Switch back to the Default SmartIcon set.

POSITIONING SMARTICON SETS

Besides choosing the SmartIcon set that Ami Pro displays, you can also determine the *position* of SmartIcon sets. You can position SmartIcon sets at the top, bottom, left, or right edge of the document window. If none of these positions is exactly right for you, you can also place the current SmartIcon set in its own *floating window*, a window that you can drag to any part of your screen.

Follow these steps when you want to change the position of the current SmartIcon set:

- Choose Tools, SmartIcons to open the SmartIcons dialog box.

- Open the Position drop-down list box.

- Select Floating, Left, Top, Right, or Bottom.
- Click on OK to close the dialog box.
- Once you designate a floating SmartIcon set, you can reposition it by pressing and holding on any SmartIcon, dragging to a new location, and then releasing the mouse button.

Note: When you position SmartIcons at the left or right edge of the document window, you might find that Ami Pro displays fewer SmartIcons. Because the document window is wider than it is high, Ami Pro consequently has less room to display SmartIcons. If this is a problem, position the SmartIcon set somewhere else on the screen, or move your most important SmartIcons to the top (or left) of the SmartIcon set. (You'll learn how to move SmartIcons within a set in the next section.)

Let's try some different positions for the current SmartIcon set:

1. Choose **Tools, SmartIcons**, and then observe the SmartIcons dialog box (see Figure 8.10). This dialog box enables you to add any available SmartIcon to any SmartIcon set, to reorder SmartIcons within a set, to control the screen position of SmartIcon sets, to edit the appearance of SmartIcons, to save and delete SmartIcon sets, and to control the display size of SmartIcons.

Figure 8.10   **The SmartIcons dialog box**

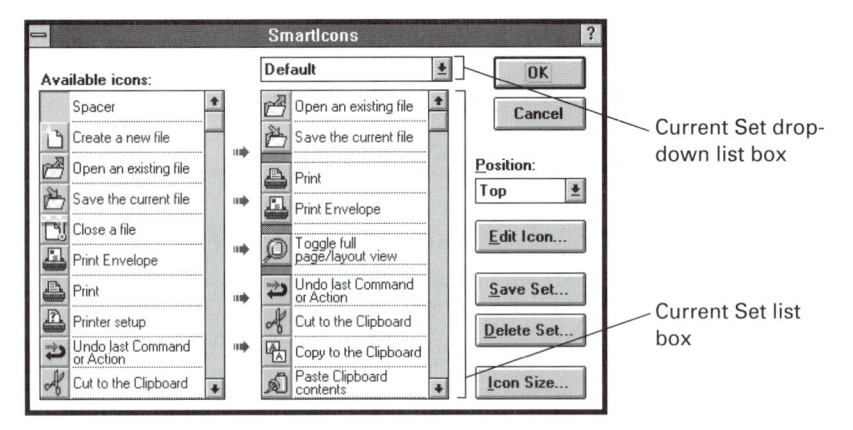

CUSTOMIZING SMARTICONS AND SMARTICON SETS • 235

2. Look at the Position drop-down list box, located on the right side of the dialog box. By default, Ami Pro positions SmartIcons at the top of the document window.

3. Click on the Position drop-down list box's **drop-down list arrow**, and then observe the displayed list. You can position a SmartIcon set at any edge of the document window, or you can choose *Floating* to position a SmartIcon set anywhere on the screen.

4. Select **Bottom**, and then click on **OK** to close the dialog box. Ami Pro places the current SmartIcon set at the bottom of the document window, between the horizontal scroll bar and the status bar (see Figure 8.11).

Figure 8.11 **Positioning SmartIcons at the bottom of the document window**

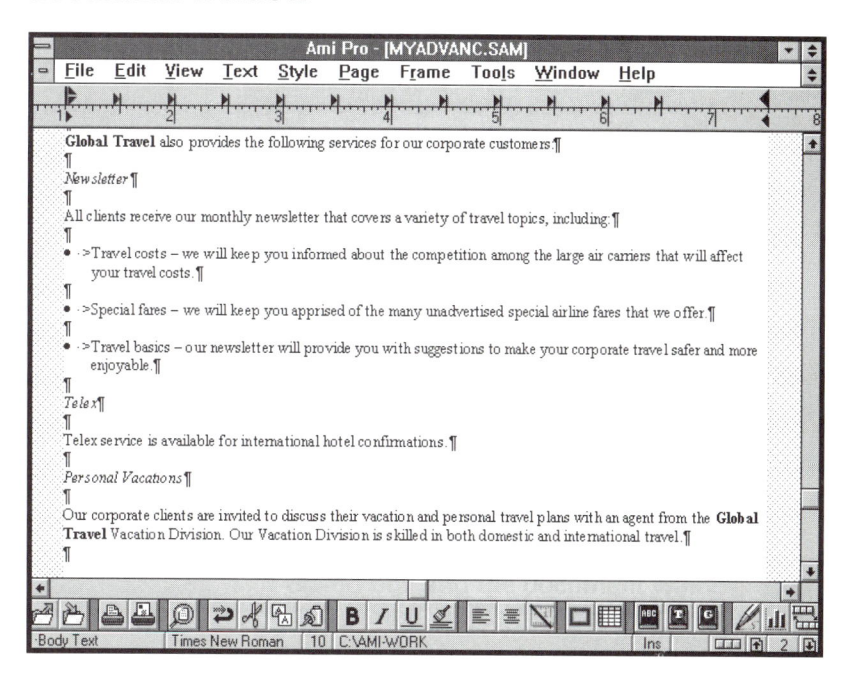

5. Choose **Tools, SmartIcons**, select **Left** from the Position drop-down list box, and then click on **OK**. Ami Pro now moves the SmartIcon set to the left edge of the document window. Notice that because your document window is wider than it is high,

Ami Pro has less room for the SmartIcons, and shows only part of the set.

6. Choose **Tools, SmartIcons**, select **Floating** from the Position drop-down list box, and then click on **OK**. Ami Pro now places the SmartIcon set in its own window.

7. Press and hold the mouse button on any of the SmartIcons, drag the outline of the floating SmartIcon set toward the bottom of your screen (see Figure 8.12), and then release the mouse button. The floating SmartIcon set moves to this new location.

Figure 8.12   **Dragging a floating SmartIcon set**

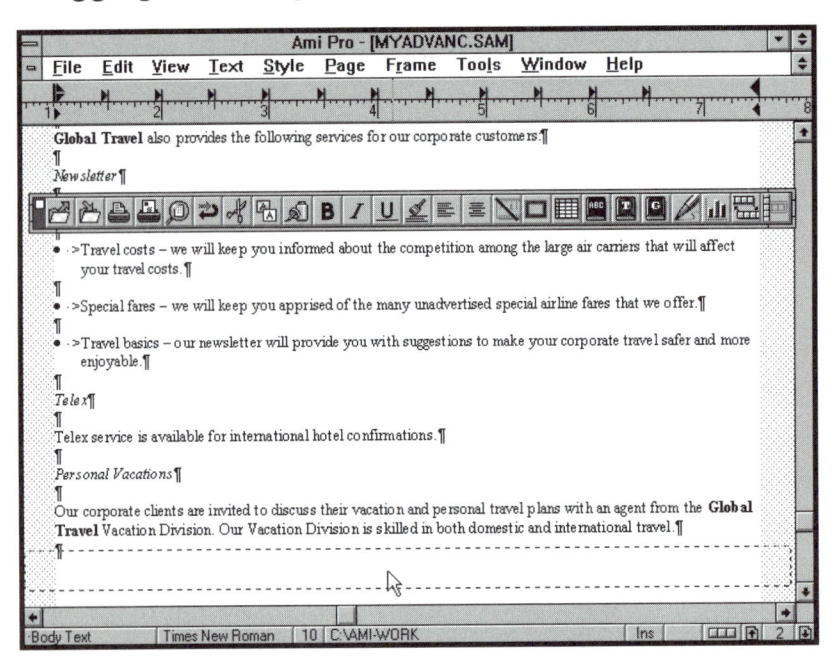

8. Choose **Tools, SmartIcons**, select **Top** from the Position drop-down list box, and then click on **OK** to return the Default SmartIcon set to its original position at the top of the document window.

CHANGING THE ORDER OF SMARTICONS WITHIN A SET

Besides controlling the position of a SmartIcon set, you can also determine the order of SmartIcons *within* a set. For example, if you find it more comfortable to click in the left half of the SmartIcon set, you can move all of your favorite SmartIcons to that side.

You can change the order of SmartIcons within a set directly on screen, or through the SmartIcons dialog box.

Follow these steps when you want to reposition a SmartIcon on screen:

- Point to the SmartIcon you want to move.
- Press and hold Ctrl, drag the SmartIcon to another position in the SmartIcon set, and then release Ctrl. (Generally, if you drop the SmartIcon you're moving on top of another SmartIcon, the SmartIcon you're moving will land to the left of the other SmartIcon.)

Note: Be careful to drop a SmartIcon only when it is over the SmartIcon set. Otherwise, Ami Pro will move the SmartIcon to the end of the current set, and you might not be able to see it. If this happens, you'll need to use the following procedure to find the SmartIcon at the bottom of the SmartIcons dialog box's Current Set list box and then drag the SmartIcon to the desired location.

Follow these steps when you want to reposition a SmartIcon using the SmartIcons dialog box:

- Choose Tools, SmartIcons.
- If necessary, use the Current Set drop-down list box at the top-center of the dialog box (refer back to Figure 8.10 for the location of this drop-down list box) to select the SmartIcon set within which you want to reposition the SmartIcon.
- In the unlabeled list box in the center of the dialog box (we'll call it the *Current Set list box*), find the SmartIcon you wish to reposition (scroll to it, if necessary), and then drag it to a new location within the list box.
- Click on OK.

Tip: When repositioning SmartIcons, you can visually group them as Ami Pro does by positioning *spacer icons* between related groups of SmartIcons. Spacer icons appear as dark gray rectangles between SmartIcons (see Figure 8.13). For example, Ami Pro groups together the Spell Check, Thesaurus, and Grammar Check SmartIcons by placing spacer icons on each side of the group. To group SmartIcons yourself, simply position related SmartIcons between existing spacer icons. If the current SmartIcon set does not contain enough spacer icons, use the procedure outlined later in this chapter to add spacer icons to the set as you would add any SmartIcon.

Figure 8.13 **Moving the Show/Hide Ruler SmartIcon on screen**

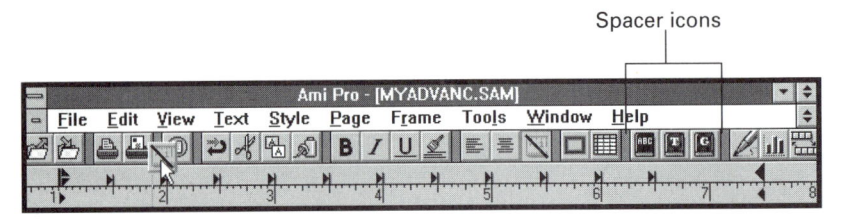

Let's use both repositioning methods to move the Show/Hide Ruler SmartIcon from the right to the left side of the Default SmartIcon set:

1. Find the Show/Hide Ruler SmartIcon. It is grouped in the right half of the Default SmartIcon set, with the Left Align Selected Text and Center Selected Text SmartIcons. Perhaps it would make more sense to group the Show/Hide Ruler SmartIcon with the Toggle Full Page/Layout View SmartIcon, in the left half of the SmartIcon set.

2. Press **Ctrl**, drag the **Show/Hide Ruler SmartIcon** onto the Toggle Full Page/Layout View SmartIcon (see Figure 8.13), and then release **Ctrl** to move the Show/Hide Ruler SmartIcon to the immediate left of the Toggle Full Page/Layout View SmartIcon. (If the Show/Hide Ruler SmartIcon lands in the wrong place, try this step again.)

3. Choose **Tools, SmartIcons**, and then examine the Current Set list box (the unlabeled list box in the center of the dialog box). It lists, in top-to-bottom order, the SmartIcons that now appear left to right in the Default SmartIcon set. Notice that the list box reflects the Show/Hide Ruler SmartIcon move you just made.

4. In the Current Set list box, drag the **Show/Hide Ruler SmartIcon** from above to immediately below the Toggle Full Page/Layout View SmartIcon (see Figure 8.14). (You might have to repeat this step a couple of times to get the Show/Hide Ruler SmartIcon in the right place.)

Figure 8.14 **Moving the Show/Hide Ruler SmartIcon in the Current Set list box**

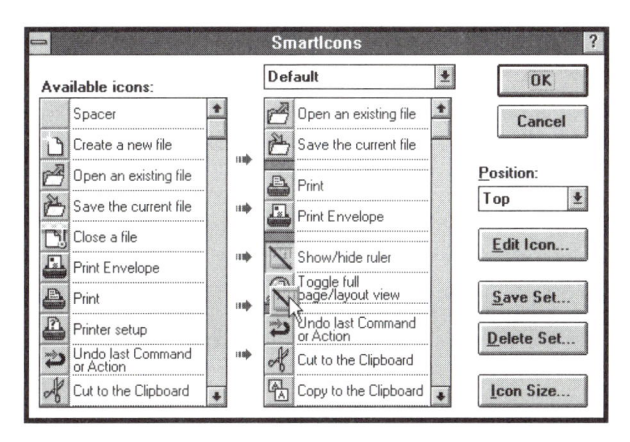

5. Click on **OK**, and then observe the Default SmartIcon set. The Show/Hide Ruler SmartIcon now appears to the *right* of the Toggle Full Page/Layout View SmartIcon.

REMOVING A SMARTICON FROM A SET

As you've learned, Ami Pro has over 150 SmartIcons, but usually displays only 24 at a time. For this reason, you might want to remove some SmartIcons that you never use, and replace them with SmartIcons that are handier for you. In this section, you'll learn how to remove a SmartIcon; in the next section, you'll learn how to add one back.

Remember—for safety's sake we want every SmartIcon to end up in the same position as when we started this chapter. Therefore, in the next activities we'll be removing and adding the same SmartIcon, the Show/Hide Ruler SmartIcon. You can, however, add or remove *any* available SmartIcon to or from *any* SmartIcon set, regardless of whether the SmartIcon was an original part of the set. Just be sure

240 • ADVANCED EDITING AND FORMATTING TECHNIQUES

to discuss any additions or removals with other Ami Pro users who share your computer.

Follow these steps when you want to remove a SmartIcon from a SmartIcon set:

- Choose Tools, SmartIcons.

- If necessary, use the Current Set drop-down list box to select the set from which you want to remove a SmartIcon.

- In the Current Set list box, find the SmartIcon you wish to remove (scroll to it, if necessary), and then drag the SmartIcon to anywhere outside the list box.

- Click on OK.

Note: When you remove a SmartIcon, you might find that Ami Pro displays an additional SmartIcon at one end of the current SmartIcon set. This is because many of Ami Pro's SmartIcon sets contain more SmartIcons than can fit across the screen. By removing a SmartIcon, you've simply made room for another one that did not fit before.

Let's remove the Show/Hide Ruler SmartIcon from the Default SmartIcon set:

1. Choose **Tools, SmartIcons**, and then drag the **Show/Hide Ruler SmartIcon** from the Current Set list box to anywhere else on the screen. Ami Pro removes the SmartIcon from the Current Set list box.

2. Click on **OK** to close the dialog box, and then observe the Default SmartIcon set. Ami Pro no longer displays the Show/Hide Ruler SmartIcon. However, there is now room for another SmartIcon (the Floating/Fixed SmartIcons SmartIcon), which Ami Pro displays at the right end of the Default SmartIcon set (see Figure 8.15).

Figure 8.15 **The Default SmartIcon set after removing the Show/Hide Ruler SmartIcon**

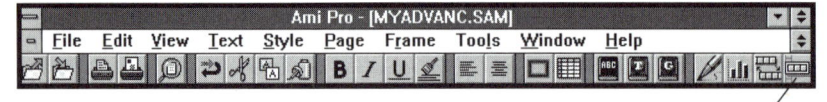

Floating/Fixed SmartIcons SmartIcon

ADDING A SMARTICON TO A SET

As you might expect, adding a SmartIcon to a set is almost exactly the reverse of removing a SmartIcon. Instead of dragging the SmartIcon *out* of the Current Set list box, you drag a SmartIcon *into* the Current Set list box.

Follow these steps when you want to add a SmartIcon to a set:

- Choose Tools, SmartIcons.
- If necessary, use the Current Set drop-down list box to select the set to which you want to add a SmartIcon.
- If necessary, scroll down in the Current Set list box until you can see the position where you'd like to place the new SmartIcon.
- In the Available SmartIcons list box, find the SmartIcon you wish to add (scroll to it, if necessary), and then drag the SmartIcon to the desired position in the Current Set list box. Keep trying, if you need to, until you have the new SmartIcon positioned just right within the Current Set list box.
- Click on OK.

Now let's add the Show/Hide Ruler SmartIcon back into the Default SmartIcon set. To make sure the set is returned to its original state, we'll put the SmartIcon back in its position to the right of the Center Selected Text SmartIcon:

1. Choose **Tools, SmartIcons**, and then scroll down in the Current Set list box until you can see the space immediately below the Center Selected Text SmartIcon.

2. Scroll all the way down through the Available Icons list box, which lists every one of Ami Pro's over 150 available SmartIcons.

3. Scroll back up through the Available Icons list box until you find the Show/Hide Ruler SmartIcon. (It's the 45th SmartIcon from the top, about one-quarter of the way down through the list.)

4. Drag the **Show/Hide Ruler SmartIcon** from the Available Icons list box to the Current Set list box, immediately below the Center Selected Text SmartIcon (see Figure 8.16). (If you don't get the positioning right the first time, just keep trying.)

5. Click on **OK**, and then observe the Default SmartIcon set. The Show/Hide Ruler SmartIcon is back in its original position. Notice that there's no longer room for the Floating/Fixed SmartIcons SmartIcon at the right end of the Default SmartIcon set.

Figure 8.16   **Adding the Show/Hide Ruler SmartIcon to the Default SmartIcon set**

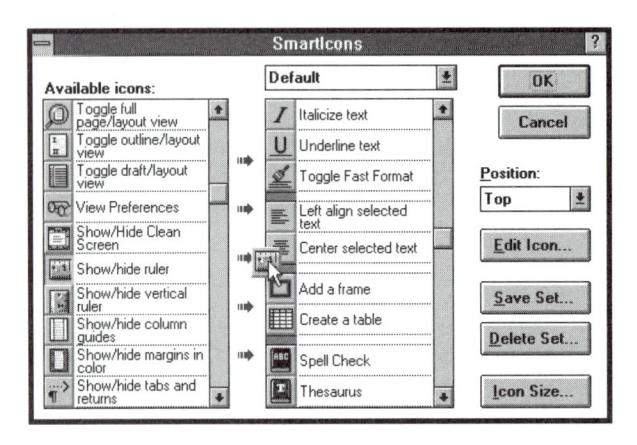

6. Close **MYADVANC.SAM**. If Ami Pro prompts you to save changes, click on **Yes**.

SUMMARY

In this chapter, you learned a number of advanced editing and formatting techniques. You learned how to move and copy text with Drag & Drop, copy text between documents, add bullets, find and replace text attributes, and customize SmartIcons.

Here is a quick reference guide to the Ami Pro features introduced in this chapter:

Desired Result	How to Do It
Move text with Drag & Drop	Select text you want to move; position I-beam over selected text; then drag colored insertion point to new location.
Copy text with Drag & Drop	Select text you want to copy; position I-beam over selected text; press **Ctrl** and drag colored insertion point to new location; then release Ctrl.
Open multiple document windows	Open a document window without closing the one currently open.

Desired Result	How to Do It
Switch between open document windows	Open Window menu, and then select name of desired document window.
Copy text between documents	Open target document; open source document; select text and copy it to Clipboard; switch to target document window and place insertion point where you want to paste text; paste text from Clipboard.
Add bullets	Place insertion point where you want to add bullet; choose **Edit**, **Insert**, **Bullet** and select desired bullet style; then click on **OK**.
Find and replace exact text attributes	Choose **Edit**, **Find & Replace**; type search text in Find text box; type replacement text in Replace With text box; click on **Options** and check desired find attributes and/or replace attributes; click on **OK**; click on **Options**; check **Find Options Exact Attributes** and/or **Replace Options Exact Attributes** (if necessary); click on **OK**; click on **Find** or **Replace All**; then follow Find & Replace dialog box prompts.
Switch to another SmartIcon set	Click on **SmartIcons button** and select desired SmartIcon set. Or click on **Next Icon Set SmartIcon** until Ami Pro displays desired set. Or choose **Tools**, **SmartIcons**, select set from Current Set drop-down list box, and then click on **OK**.
Change position of SmartIcon set	Choose **Tools**, **SmartIcons**; select desired position from Position drop-down list box; then click on **OK**.
Move floating SmartIcon set	Press and hold mouse button on any SmartIcon in set, drag, and then release mouse button.

Desired Result	How to Do It
Reposition SmartIcon within set	Press and hold **Ctrl**, drag SmartIcon to new position within set, and release **Ctrl**. Or choose **Tools**, **SmartIcons**, drag SmartIcon to new position within Current Set list box, and then click on **OK**.
Remove SmartIcon from set	Choose **Tools**, **SmartIcons**; drag SmartIcon out of Current Set list box; then click on **OK**.
Add SmartIcon to set	Choose **Tools**, **SmartIcon**; drag SmartIcon from Available Icons list box to desired position in Current Set list box; then click on **OK**.

In the next chapter, you will learn how to use paragraph styles to format and reformat your documents quickly and easily.

IF YOU'RE STOPPING HERE

If you need to take a break here, please exit Ami Pro. If you want to proceed directly to the next chapter, please do so now.

CHAPTER 9: PARAGRAPH STYLES AND STYLE SHEETS

Understanding Paragraph Styles

Assigning Styles

Modifying Styles

Creating Styles

Understanding Style Sheets

By applying and modifying text formatting, text enhancements, and page layouts, you've been able to control many aspects of your document's appearance. In this chapter, you'll learn how to use paragraph styles and style sheets to very quickly and easily create, format, and reformat a wide variety of documents to the desired appearance. You'll also see how paragraph styles and style sheets promote consistency among similar types of documents.

When you're done working through this chapter, you'll know

- About paragraph styles
- How to assign paragraph styles
- How to modify paragraph styles
- How to create paragraph styles
- About style sheets
- How to select and use a style sheet

UNDERSTANDING PARAGRAPH STYLES

Paragraph styles are named sets of paragraph-appearance instructions that help you to format paragraphs quickly and easily. (**Note:** To make this book easier to read, from now on we'll generally refer to paragraph styles as simply *styles*.)

Whenever you create a document, Ami Pro provides a number of built-in styles for your use. Styles are helpful because most paragraphs within a document fall into a particular category; for example, many paragraphs are either headings, subheadings, body text, headers, or footers. With styles, you don't have to select and modify the appearance of paragraphs on a paragraph-by-paragraph basis; instead, you can assign an appropriate style to each paragraph. For instance, rather than individually formatting every heading paragraph as Arial 12-point, italic and centered, you can just tell Ami Pro that certain paragraphs are heading paragraphs. Then, by controlling the heading style itself, you can directly control the appearance of every paragraph in your document that you have assigned that style.

Styles incorporate a number of the following *style elements* (including many of the appearance elements you've already learned about):

- Fonts, text attributes, capitalization, and special effects
- Tabs and indentions
- Paragraph alignment
- *Spacing* (the amount of vertical space between lines and paragraphs) and *text tightness* (the amount of horizontal space between letters)

- Page breaks
- Leading bullets, numbers, and text
- Horizontal lines (also know as *rules*) above and below paragraphs
- Numeric formatting
- Hyphenation

Because there are so many style elements, we can't cover all of them in single chapter, but we'll show you all the necessary basics of using styles. In later chapters, we'll show you some additional style elements when appropriate. For information on style elements not covered in this book, see your Ami Pro documentation.

ASSIGNING STYLES

Paragraph styles, as the term suggests, work at the paragraph level—that is (as with text enhancements), you can assign styles only to entire paragraphs at a time, not just to selected text. For this reason, you can use the same paragraph selection shortcuts you learned for applying text enhancements (in Chapter 5) to select paragraphs for assigning styles. Here's a recap of the shortcuts:

- To select a single paragraph for assigning a style, place the insertion point or current selection anywhere within that paragraph.
- To select multiple paragraphs for assigning a style, select at least part of each paragraph.

If you prefer, you can instead select entire paragraphs before assigning styles; the methods above are just convenient shortcuts.

Once you've selected a paragraph or paragraphs, you can use any one of four tools to assign a style:

- The *Style Status button*, the leftmost button on the status bar
- Function keys (F2, F3, F4, and so on)
- The *Styles box*, which you can display as a floating window on screen
- Fast Format

In this chapter, you'll learn how to use the Style Status button and the function keys to assign styles. For more information on assigning styles with the Styles box and Fast Format, see your Ami Pro documentation.

ASSIGNING STYLES WITH THE STYLE STATUS BUTTON

Follow these steps when you want to assign a style using the Style Status button:

- Select the appropriate paragraph or paragraphs.
- Click on the Style Status button to display a list of available styles.
- From the list, select the desired style.

Like many of the status bar's other buttons, the Style Status button works as a status indicator: It displays the name of the style currently assigned to the paragraph that contains the insertion point or current selection. (Throughout this book, you might have noticed that the Style Status button has always read *Body Text*, the style that Ami Pro by default assigns to all paragraphs.)

If you are not running Ami Pro, please start it now. Let's use the Style Status button to assign some styles:

1. Open **styles.sam**.
2. Place the insertion point in the heading *Introduction* (near the top of page 1).
3. Observe the Style Status button. Ami Pro by default assigns the Body Text style to all paragraphs.
4. Click on the **Style Status button** to open a list of available styles (see Figure 9.1).
5. Select **F4 Bullet** from the styles list, and then look at *Introduction*. Ami Pro has added a small bullet to the beginning of the paragraph, and has indented the rest of the paragraph ½".
6. Observe the Style Status button. It confirms that you've successfully assigned the Bullet style.
7. Click on the **Style Status button**, and then select **F6 Number List** to assign the Number List style to *Introduction*. Ami Pro replaces the bullet with the number *1*, and indents the entire paragraph another ½".

ASSIGNING STYLES • 251

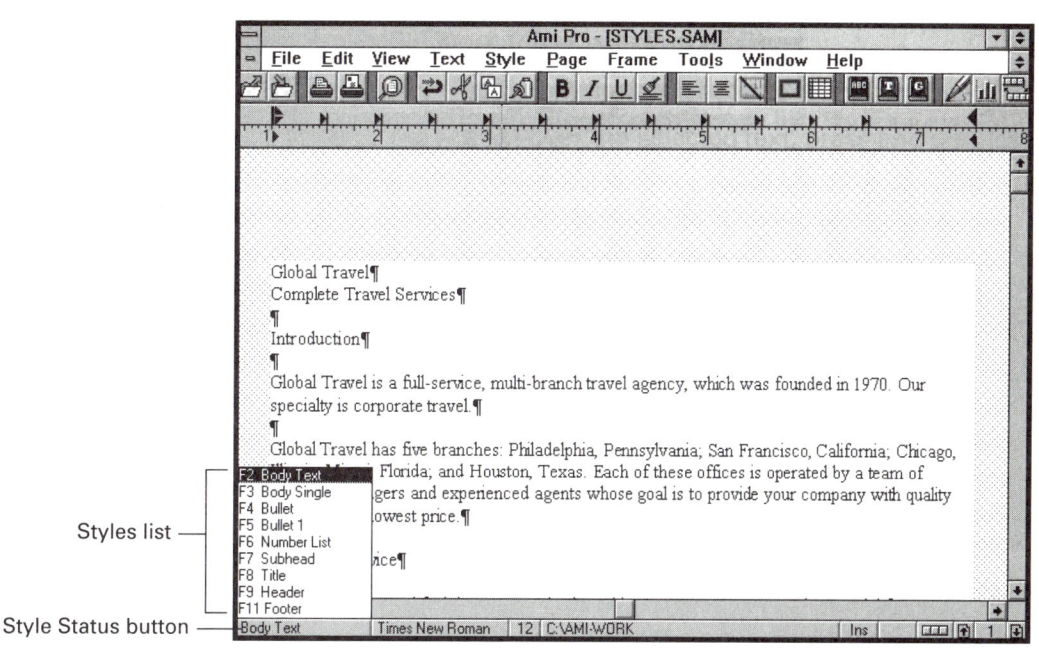

Figure 9.1	**Viewing the Style Status button's styles list**

Styles list
Style Status button

8. Assign the **Subhead** style to *Introduction* (click on the **Style Status button**, and then select **F7 Subhead**). Ami Pro removes the number *1*, removes the indent, and applies the Bold and Italic text attributes.

9. Select the two-line heading at the top of the document, **Global Travel** and **Complete Travel Services**, and then assign the **Title** style. Ami Pro changes the characters in both paragraphs from Times New Roman 12-point to Arial 18-point boldface, and centers the paragraphs (see Figure 9.2).

PRACTICE YOUR SKILLS

In the following steps, use the Style Status button to assign styles:

1. Assign the **Subhead** style to the remaining headings on page 1:

```
Customer Service
International Travel
Corporate Profiles
```

Figure 9.2 **STYLES.SAM, with styles assigned**

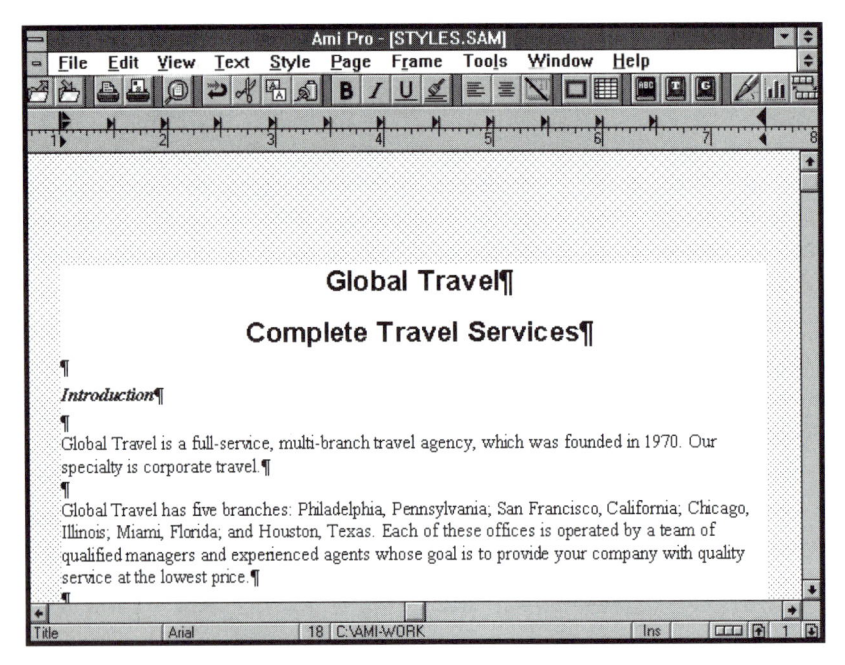

2. Assign the **Title** style to the two-line heading on the top of page 2.
3. Save the document as **mystyles**.

ASSIGNING STYLES WITH FUNCTION KEYS

You may have noticed by now that the Style Status button's styles list displays function key names to the left of every available style. Once you've learned which function key Ami Pro has assigned to each style, you can use those function keys to assign the styles quickly.

Follow these steps when you want to use a function key to assign a style:

- Select the appropriate paragraph or paragraphs.
- Press the function key assigned to the desired style.

Note: Because Windows uses the F1 and F10 function keys as standard keys for other purposes, Ami Pro does not assign those keys to styles.

Let's use some function keys to assign styles:

1. Place the insertion point in the heading *Worldwide Services* (located near the top of page 2).

2. Click on the **Style Status button**, and then observe the styles list. Ami Pro displays the name of a function key before each style (*F2*, *F3*, and so on). Notice that *F6* is the function key for *Number List*, and *F7* is for *Subhead*.

3. Click again on the **Style Status button** to close the styles list, and then press **F7**. Ami Pro assigns the Subhead style to *Worldwide Services*.

4. Scroll down to page 3 until you can see the two headings *Newsletter* and *Telex*.

5. Under the heading *Newsletter*, select the three paragraphs that begin with *Travel costs*, *Special fares*, and *Travel basics*.

6. Press **F6** to assign the Number List style, and then examine the selected paragraphs. Ami Pro numbers them sequentially, as shown in Figure 9.3.

PRACTICE YOUR SKILLS

In the following steps, use function keys to assign styles:

1. Scroll to the top of page 2, and then assign the **Subhead** style to the following heading paragraphs located on pages 2 and 3:

   ```
   Discounts
   Deliveries
   Auto Rentals
   Hotel Accommodations
   Additional Services
   ```

2. Assign the **Title** style to the two-line heading on the top of page 3. (**Hint:** Use the **F8** function key.)

3. Save your document.

Figure 9.3 **MYSTYLES.SAM, after assigning the Number List style**

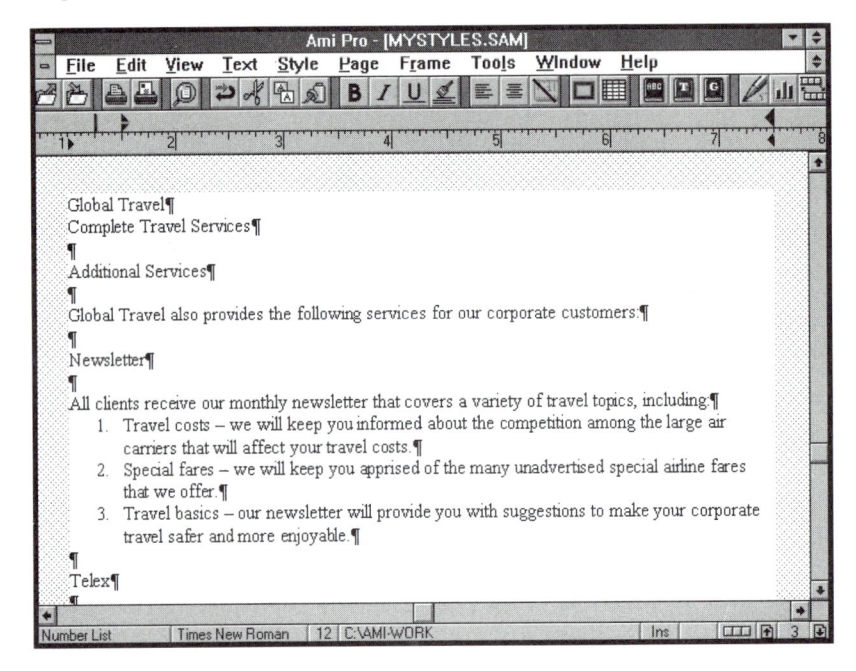

[Screenshot of Ami Pro window displaying MYSTYLES.SAM document with the following text:

Global Travel¶
Complete Travel Services¶
¶
Additional Services¶
¶
Global Travel also provides the following services for our corporate customers:¶
¶
Newsletter¶
¶
All clients receive our monthly newsletter that covers a variety of travel topics, including:¶
   1. Travel costs – we will keep you informed about the competition among the large air carriers that will affect your travel costs.¶
   2. Special fares – we will keep you apprised of the many unadvertised special airline fares that we offer.¶
   3. Travel basics – our newsletter will provide you with suggestions to make your corporate travel safer and more enjoyable.¶
¶
Telex¶

Status bar: Number List | Times New Roman | 12 | C:\AMI-WORK | Ins | 3]

MODIFYING STYLES

Although Ami Pro provides an assortment of styles for various paragraph types, there's no guarantee that those styles will contain exactly the style elements that you want. For example, Ami Pro defines the Subhead style as Times New Roman 12-point boldface and italic, but you might want your headings to appear as Arial 14-point boldface. For this reason, Ami Pro provides the Modify Style dialog box.

When you modify a style, you start to see more of the potential power of Ami Pro's styles capability. By modifying a single style, you can automatically change the appearance of every one of a document's paragraphs that has that style assigned. Without styles, you would have to reformat each of those paragraphs manually.

The Modify Style dialog box serves as a "one-stop shopping" control center for modifying styles. From within this single dialog box, you can control every element of every available style.

Follow these steps when you want to modify a style:

- Choose Style, Modify Style or click the right mouse button anywhere in the main document text.

- In the Style drop-down list box, select (if necessary) the style that you want to modify. (When you open the Modify Style dialog box, the style that is assigned to the current paragraph is selected by Ami Pro in this drop-down list box.)

- On the left side of the dialog box, select the appropriate Modify option: Font, Alignment, Spacing, Breaks, Bullets & Numbers, Lines, Table Format, or Hyphenation. The option you select determines which style element options Ami Pro displays on the right side of the dialog box (except for Hyphenation, which is a simple on-off check box). For example, if you choose Modify Alignment, Ami Pro will display style element options for paragraph alignment, tabs, and indentions.

- Select the desired style element options.

- If desired, select another Modify option, and choose from the style element options that are displayed on the dialog box's right side. Repeat this step as necessary until you have selected all the desired style elements.

- Click on OK to save your changes and close the dialog box. If you'd like to modify another style, click on Save or Save As to save your changes without closing the dialog box; then return to the second step of this procedure.

Whenever you modify an Ami Pro style from its original settings, Ami Pro displays a small dot (·) before the style's name, to remind you that you've modified the style. (For more information on the significance of this dot, see your Ami Pro documentation.)

Note: By default, style modifications affect only the current document.

MODIFYING A STYLE'S TEXT-FORMATTING ELEMENTS

You learned in Chapter 4 how to use the Text menu and SmartIcons to apply and remove text formatting (such as fonts and text attributes) on a character-by-character basis. When you modify the text-formatting elements of a style, however, Ami Pro will apply those modifications to entire paragraphs at a time.

Let's modify some text-formatting elements of the Subhead style, and see how it affects paragraphs with that style assigned:

1. Return to the top of the document, and then examine the heading *Introduction*. It displays both the Bold and Italic text attributes.

2. Place the insertion point in *Introduction*, choose **Style, Modify Style**, and then observe the Modify Style dialog box. This dialog box enables you to view and control all the elements that comprise a style (see Figure 9.4).

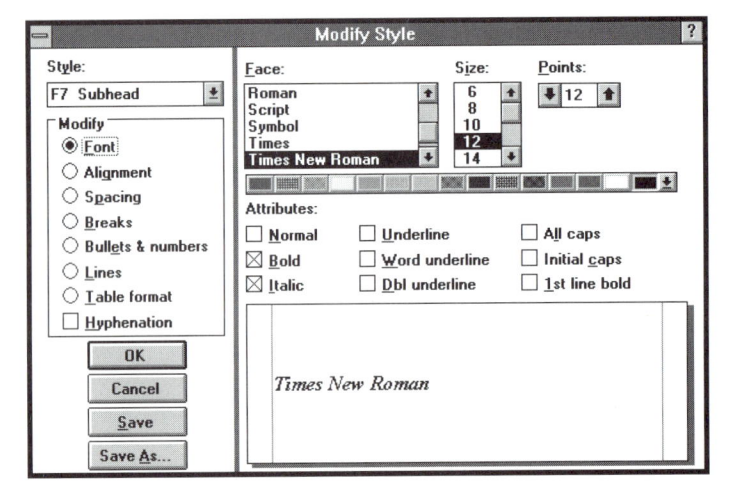

Figure 9.4 **The Modify Style dialog box**

3. On the left side of the dialog box, verify that **F7 Subhead** (the style assigned to *Introduction*) is selected in the Style drop-down list box, and that **Modify Font** is selected. (If they are not, select them now.)

4. Examine the options on the right side of the dialog box. Because *F7 Subhead* and *Modify Font* are selected on the left side, Ami Pro displays all the Subhead style's font elements: Times New Roman, 12, black (notice the black button selected at the right end of the color bar), Bold, and Italic.

5. Uncheck **Italic**, and then click on **OK** to close the dialog box.

6. Observe *Introduction*. It no longer has the Italic text attribute.

7. Observe the Style Status button. Because you modified the style, Ami Pro now displays a dot before *Subhead* (see Figure 9.5).

Figure 9.5   **MYSTYLES.SAM, after modifying the Subhead style**

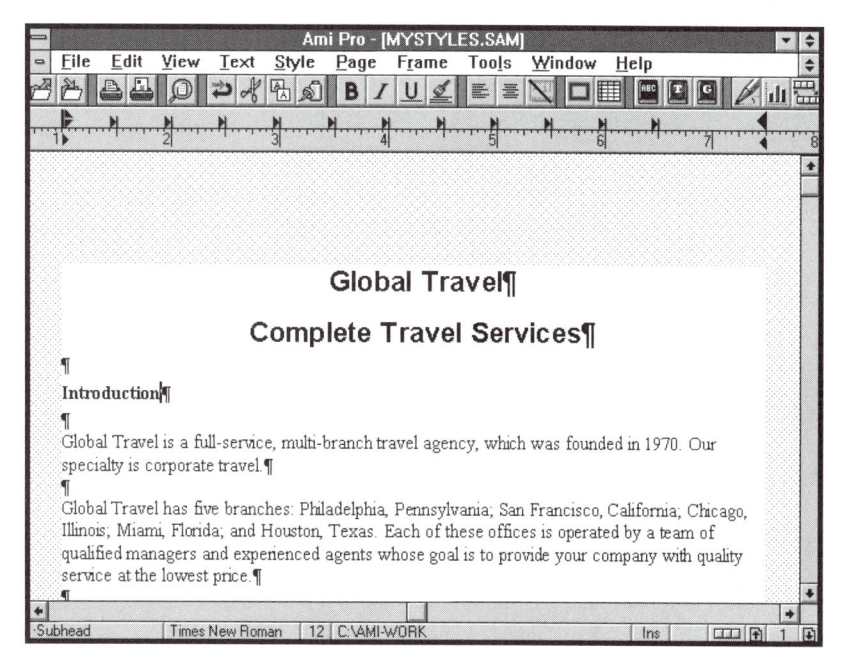

8. Scroll down through the document and observe all the other headings with the Subhead style. By modifying the Subhead style, you have automatically removed the Italic text attribute from every heading assigned that style.

PRACTICE YOUR SKILLS

1. Change the Subhead style's typeface to **Arial**.
2. Scroll through the document to verify that you successfully changed the typeface for every heading with the Subhead style.
3. Save MYSTYLES.SAM.

MODIFYING A STYLE'S SPACING ELEMENTS

As you work in the Modify Style dialog box, you'll find that Ami Pro offers many paragraph appearance options that you can't access outside of styles. One of these options is *paragraph spacing*, which enables you to add space automatically above and/or below paragraphs. You might use paragraph spacing, for example, to add some space before every heading in a document; that way you won't have to keep pressing the Enter key to insert blank lines manually.

Note: Be careful not to confuse *line spacing* with *paragraph spacing*. As you learned in Chapter 5, line spacing determines the vertical distance between lines of text *within* a paragraph. Paragraph spacing, on the other hand, determines the *additional* amount of vertical space *between* paragraphs.

Follow these steps when you want to add or remove space above or below paragraphs that are assigned a particular style:

- Open the Modify Style dialog box.
- Select (if necessary) the style you want to modify from the Style drop-down list box.
- Select Modify Spacing.
- Use the Paragraph Spacing Above and/or Paragraph Spacing Below boxes to specify the desired amount of space in inches.
- Click on OK.

Because Ami Pro's Title style incorporates paragraph spacing that is not appropriate for MYSTYLES.SAM, let's modify the style and change the paragraph spacing to 0":

1. Move to the top of page 1 (press **Ctrl+Home**), and then observe the page's two-line heading. There is too much space between the heading's two lines.

2. Position the I-beam over any main document text and click the *right* mouse button to open the Modify Style dialog box.

3. On the left side of the dialog box, verify that **F8 Title** is selected in the Style drop-down list box. (If it is not, select it now.)

4. Examine the dialog box. Because *F8 Title* is selected, Ami Pro now displays the elements of the Title style.

MODIFYING STYLES • 259

5. Select **Modify Spacing** to display the Title style's spacing elements. Line Spacing is set to *Single*, and Text Tightness is set to *Normal (100%)*. (See Figure 9.6.)

Figure 9.6 **Viewing the Title style's spacing elements**

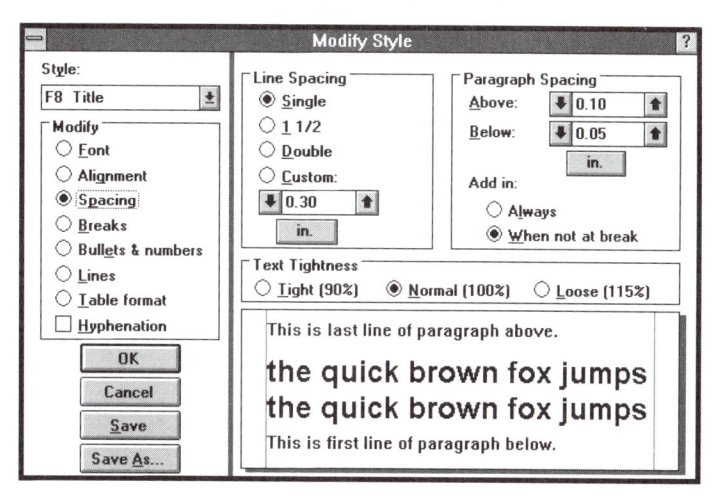

6. Observe the Paragraph Spacing box. Ami Pro defines the Title style as having .10" above each paragraph and .05" below each paragraph. These are the style elements that are causing the wide gap between the page heading's two lines.

7. Click on the **down increment arrow** for the Paragraph Spacing Above box until the box's number changes to *0.00*; then do the same for the Paragraph Spacing Below box. As you click, notice that the sample box in the dialog box's bottom-right corner shows how your changes will affect paragraphs with the Title style.

8. Click on **OK**, and then observe page 1's two-line heading. The two lines are now closer together (see Figure 9.7).

9. Scroll to the top of pages 2 and 3 to verify that the two-line headings there have also changed.

Figure 9.7   **MYSTYLES.SAM, after modifying the Title style**

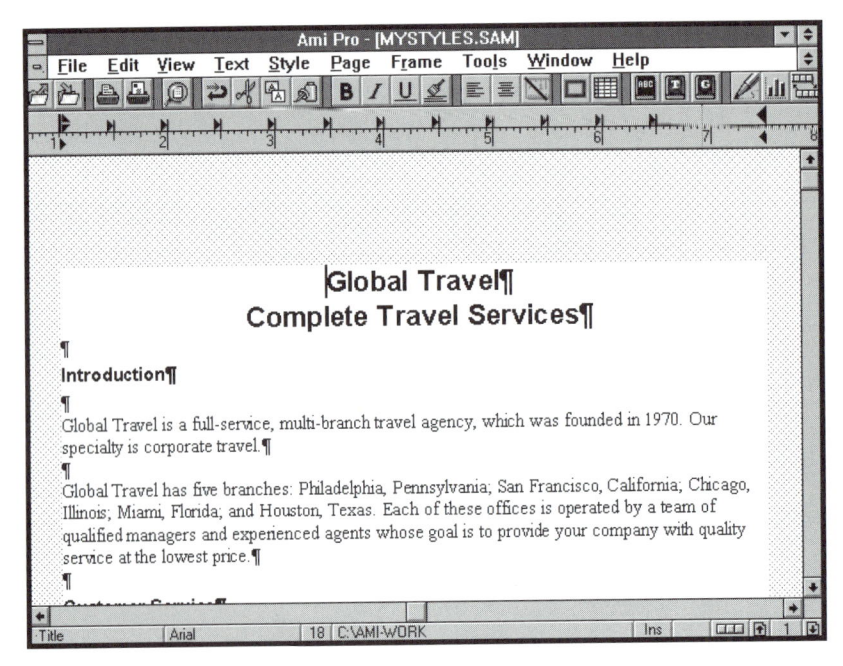

OVERRIDING STYLES

As you've learned, styles affect entire paragraphs at a time. However, you may want (for example) to apply text formatting to only a single word within a paragraph. In this case, you need to *override* the style assigned to that paragraph. You might also decide to override a style when you want to change text enhancements for only one or a few paragraphs within a document, *without* modifying or creating any styles. (You'll learn how to create your own styles later in this chapter.)

Don't think of overriding styles as something new; you've been overriding styles since Chapter 4. Whenever you applied text formatting or enhancements using the Text menu or SmartIcons, you overrode the default Body Text style. Think of overriding styles as applying an extra layer of appearance options on top of an existing style. For example, though the Body Text style is set by default to Times New Roman, you can change the typeface for any paragraph with that style by selecting the entire paragraph and then using the Text, Font command to change the font for just that paragraph.

Overriding a style in one paragraph does not affect any other paragraph with that same style.

Caution: Because text formatting and enhancements act as an extra layer of appearance options on top of a style, they can interfere with paragraph reformatting when you modify a style. For example, if you use the Text, Bold command or the Bold Text SmartIcon to apply the Bold text attribute to a paragraph, and then later assign a style that does not incorporate boldface formatting, the paragraph might still display in boldface. To remove the extra layer of boldface formatting, select the entire paragraph and then choose Text, Normal.

Let's override some styles:

1. Scroll to the three numbered paragraphs on page 3, below the heading *Newsletter*.
2. Select **Travel costs**, and then click on the **Bold Text SmartIcon** (or choose **Text, Bold**). Ami Pro applies the Bold text attribute to the selected text, but leaves the rest of the paragraph unchanged.
3. Use the same technique to apply the Bold text attribute to **Special fares** and **Travel basics** (located in the next two paragraphs).
4. Save your document.

CREATING STYLES

If Ami Pro does not provide the styles to meet your exact formatting needs, you can create your own styles. You can design a new style based on the elements of an existing style, or based on the formatting and enhancements of selected text. As with modified styles, whenever you create a new style, Ami Pro displays a dot in front of that style's name to remind you that the style is not one of the document's original styles.

Also, Ami Pro automatically assigns a function key to your new style, if one is available. (**Tip:** You can use Ami Pro's Style, Style Management command to manually assign and reassign function keys to styles. For more information on this command, see your Ami Pro documentation.)

Note: When you create a new style, Ami Pro does *not* assign that style automatically to the current paragraph; you must assign your new style manually. Once you've created a new style, you can assign and modify that style using the same techniques you've already learned for existing styles.

CREATING A NEW STYLE BASED ON SELECTED TEXT

Designing a new style based on selected text is called creating a style "by example." For example, if you've underlined, italicized, and centered a heading paragraph, you can create a style based on that paragraph, and then use the style to underline, italicize, and center other headings.

Follow these steps when you want to create a new style based on selected text:

- Select text that displays the appearance elements you want to include in your new style. Regardless of how much text you select, Ami Pro will base your style on the appearance elements of the first word in your selection.

- Choose Style, Create Style to open the Create Style dialog box.

- In the New Style text box, type a name for your new style. Be sure not to use the name of an existing style.

- Select Based On Selected Text.

- To create your new style and close the Create Style dialog box, click on Create. If you want to add other style elements that are not included in your selected text, click on Modify to open the Modify Style dialog box, select the desired elements, and then click on OK.

Let's create a new style now based on selected text:

1. Observe the three headings under *Additional Services* on page 3: *Newsletter*, *Telex*, and *Personal Vacations* (scroll down, if necessary).

2. Open and examine the styles list (click on the **Style Status button**). Other than the two you've already used, *Subhead* and *Title*, Ami Pro doesn't provide any predefined styles for headings.

CREATING STYLES • 263

3. Close the styles list (click on the **Style Status button** again), and then select the entire heading **Newsletter**.

4. Apply the **Underline** text attribute, and then change the heading's typeface to **Arial**.

5. Choose **Style, Create Style**, and then type **Subhead 2** in the New Style text box.

6. Examine the dialog box's Based On box. Here you can create a new style based on another style, or based on selected text.

7. Select **Based On Selected Text** (see Figure 9.8), and then click on **Create**. Ami Pro closes the Create Style dialog box.

Figure 9.8   **Creating a style based on selected text**

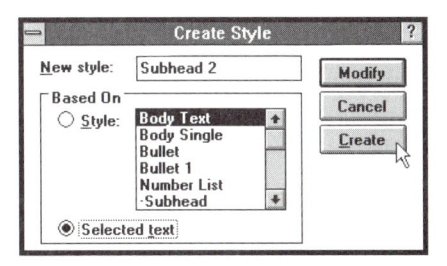

```
┌─────────────────────────────────────┐
│            Create Style         [?] │
│  New style:  [Subhead 2]   [Modify] │
│  ┌Based On─────────────┐   [Cancel] │
│  │ ○ Style: Body Text  │   [Create] │
│  │         Body Single │            │
│  │         Bullet      │            │
│  │         Bullet 1    │            │
│  │         Number List │            │
│  │         ·Subhead    │            │
│  │                     │            │
│  │ ⦿ Selected text     │            │
│  └─────────────────────┘            │
└─────────────────────────────────────┘
```

8. Open and examine the styles list. Notice that Ami Pro has added your new style to the bottom of the list, and has automatically assigned the F12 function key to that style. Because this is a new style, Ami Pro displays a dot between *F12* and *Subhead 2*.

9. Select **F12·Subhead 2** to assign your new style to the heading *Newsletter*.

10. Use **F12** to assign your Subhead 2 style to the headings *Telex* and *Personal Vacations*.

CREATING A NEW STYLE BASED ON ANOTHER STYLE

When you design a new style based on another style, you can recycle the work you've already invested in creating and/or modifying an existing style. For example, suppose you have a heading style that produces Arial 12-point boldfaced centered text, and you need a subheading style that produces Arial 12-point *underlined* centered text. You can create your new subheading style based on the existing heading style, and then simply remove the Bold attribute and add the Underline attribute.

Follow these steps when you want to create a new style based on an existing style:

- Choose Style, Create Style to open the Create Style dialog box.
- In the New Style text box, type a name for your new style.
- Select Based On Style, if necessary.
- In the Based On Style list box, select the style upon which you want to base your new style.
- If you want your new style to be an exact duplicate of the style upon which you are basing it, or if you want to wait until later to customize your new style, click on Create. If you want to modify your new style's elements right away, click on Modify to open the Modify Style dialog box, select the desired style elements, and then click on OK.

Note: Once you've finished creating a new style based on another style, Ami Pro breaks the link between those two styles. Therefore, if you later go back and change the original existing style, you will not affect your new style with that change.

Let's create a new style based on the existing Title style:

1. Move to the top of page 1, and look at the page's two-line heading. This heading might look better if the second line's font size were smaller.

2. Choose **Style, Create Style**, and then type **Title 2** in the New Style text box.

3. Verify that *Based On Style* is selected, and that ·*Title* is selected in the Based On Style list box. (If not, select these options now.) You will base your new Title 2 style on the existing Title style.

4. Click on **Modify** to open the Modify Style dialog box. Verify that *Modify Font* is selected, select **14** in the Size list box, and click on **OK**.

CREATING STYLES • 265

5. Place the insertion point in the second line of the two-line heading (*Complete Travel Services*), and then open and examine the style list. Ami Pro lists your Title 2 style, but because there are no more function keys beyond F12, Ami Pro has not assigned a function key.

6. Select ·**Title 2** to assign your newest style to *Complete Travel Services*. Ami Pro reduces the text's size (see Figure 9.9).

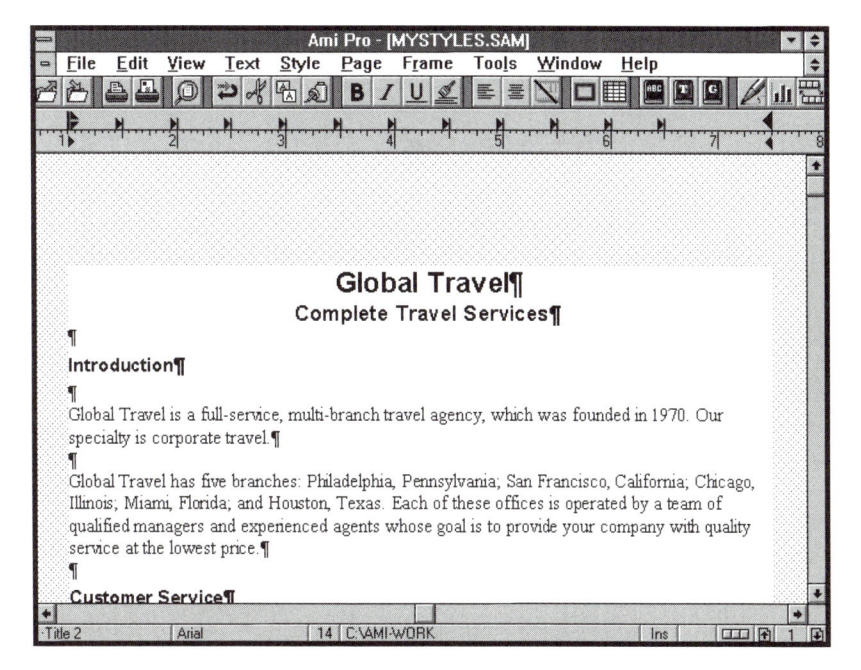

Figure 9.9 **MYSTYLES.SAM, after assigning the Title 2 style**

7. Assign your Title 2 style to the second line of the two-line headings on the tops of pages 2 and 3.

8. Save MYSTYLES.SAM.

9. Print the document, and then compare it to Figure 9.10.

10. Close the document.

Figure 9.10   Page 1 of MYSTYLES.SAM

Global Travel
Complete Travel Services

Introduction

Global Travel is a full-service, multi-branch travel agency, which was founded in 1970. Our specialty is corporate travel.

Global Travel has five branches: Philadelphia, Pennsylvania; San Francisco, California; Chicago, Illinois; Miami, Florida; and Houston, Texas. Each of these offices is operated by a team of qualified managers and experienced agents whose goal is to provide your company with quality service at the lowest price.

Customer Service

We at Global Travel feel that communication with our corporate accounts is essential for providing good service. Each corporate account is assigned to a specific account executive. Your account executive will be available to answer any questions and provide you with any information that you request.

The corporate travel division of Global Travel is designed to offer the best and most professional service available to your business travelers. We encourage you to tour our facility and meet our staff at your convenience.

International Travel

We offer complete international itinerary assistance. We maintain a supply of passport and visa applications so that we can provide the necessary papers to our clients with minimum delay. Our International Rate Program guarantees your fast and accurate pricing, no matter how complicated the itinerary.

Corporate Profiles

Your company profile will be stored in our computer, and individual profiles will be maintained on each frequent traveler. Each profile will contain information regarding passport information, seating preference, car rental preference, frequent-flyer membership number, and corporate discount numbers. This information ensures that we can provide frequent travelers, fast, cost-effective itineraries.

Figure 9.10   **Page 2 of MYSTYLES.SAM**

Global Travel
Complete Travel Services

Worldwide Services

The Global Travel Reservation Center will handle all of your weekend and after-hour reservations and changes. The reservation center can be dialed toll-free 24 hours a day. The worldwide service emergency numbers will be clearly marked on your travel itineraries.

Discounts

Global Travel guarantees the lowest air fares available. Due to the volume of tickets that we issue, several of the large air carriers offer us special discounts that we can pass on to our clients.

Our quality-control specialists check each of your tickets to guarantee that you have received the lowest rate available. In addition, each ticket is checked to ensure that it includes seating assignments and boarding passes before it is delivered to you.

Deliveries

Our courier makes daily deliveries, both in the morning and afternoon, to offices within 20 miles of our local branch. All of our offices, each located across from the local airport, have drive-up windows. If you make last minute travel plans with us you can pick up your ticket right at the drive-up window.

Auto Rentals

We guarantee the lowest prices on all car rentals. We will match the type of car with the information provided in the profile for each of your frequent travelers. Each car that is rented through Global Travel carries an extra $50,000 worth of liability insurance.

Hotel Accommodations

Our Corporate Hotel Program is the most competitive and comprehensive program in the world, offering corporate travelers cost savings and extra amenities in most business locations. Global Travel has access to more than 10,000 hotels worldwide, with a range of rooms from economy to luxury. This selection offers your corporate travelers the accommodations they want with a cost savings of 10-30% off the regular rates.

Figure 9.10 Page 3 of MYSTYLES.SAM

Global Travel
Complete Travel Services

Additional Services

Global Travel also provides the following services for our corporate customers:

Newsletter

All clients receive our monthly newsletter that covers a variety of travel topics, including:
1. **Travel costs** – we will keep you informed about the competition among the large air carriers that will affect your travel costs.
2. **Special fares** – we will keep you apprised of the many unadvertised special airline fares that we offer.
3. **Travel basics** – our newsletter will provide you with suggestions to make your corporate travel safer and more enjoyable.

Telex

Telex service is available for international hotel confirmations.

Personal Vacations

Our corporate clients are invited to discuss their vacation and personal travel plans with an agent from the Global Travel Vacation Division. Our Vacation Division is skilled in both domestic and international travel.

UNDERSTANDING STYLE SHEETS

You've now learned how to assign, modify, override, and create styles. But where do styles come from? The answer is *style sheets*. Each time you create a new document, Ami Pro uses a style sheet as a source for styles and other document characteristics, including

- *Page layouts*   Page size, orientation, margins, and so on
- *Contents* (sometimes called *boilerplate text*)   Text or other elements, such as letterhead text and/or a company logo, that you want to include in every document that is based on that style sheet
- *Macros*   Recorded sets of steps (like small computer programs within Ami Pro) that you can run whenever you create a document based on that style sheet

You can think of style sheets as templates, much like the patterns you might use when cutting fabric or wood. Style sheets provide elements that are common to a certain class of documents—such as interoffice memos or press releases—and therefore can increase your productivity and promote consistency within document classes.

Ami Pro supplies a variety of style sheets to help you meet your various document needs, for example, basic letters, appointment calendars, fax cover sheets, mailing labels, memos, press releases, and so on. For a description of each of these style sheets, see the *Style Sheet Guide* that shipped with your Ami Pro documentation.

USING STYLE SHEETS

When you create a new document by using the File, New command (you last used this command in Chapter 1), Ami Pro requires you to base the new document on a style sheet. By default, Ami Pro bases new documents on the Default - Most Frequently Used Paragraph Styles style sheet; however, you can instruct Ami Pro to use any available style sheet when creating a new document.

Follow these steps when you want to create a new document and specify a particular style sheet:

- Choose File, New to open the New dialog box.

- In the Style Sheet For New Document list box, select the desired style sheet. (You can view the style sheets in this list box either by description or by file name. To toggle between these two views, check or uncheck List By Description. For the most part, keep List By Description checked.)
- Click on OK.

Note: The New dialog box contains two options that you can use to control which elements Ami Pro will copy from the style sheet to your new document: With Contents and Run Macro. Ami Pro checks these options by default; for the most part, you should leave them that way.

Once you click on OK in the New dialog box, Ami Pro creates a new document based on the style sheet you selected. It copies the style sheet's page layout, and creates a link between your new document and the style sheet to provide access to that style sheet's styles. If you left the With Contents option checked, and the style sheet has any text and element contents, Ami Pro copies those contents into your new document. If you left Run Macro checked, and the style sheet is *automated* (that is, if it contains a macro), Ami Pro will run that macro. (You'll see an example of a macro at work later in this chapter.)

USING A STYLE SHEET TO CREATE A CALENDAR

Because style sheets can incorporate so many elements, they may seem somewhat confusing—that is, until you start to use them. In this next task, we'll create a new document based on one of Ami Pro's built-in style sheets—Calendar - Monthly, Automated—to create a one-month calendar. This style sheet is fairly complex; it has a nonstandard page layout, specialized styles, contents, and a macro. Practicing with it will show you how easy and convenient even the most complex style sheets can be. Let's start:

1. Choose **File, New**, verify that *List By Description* is checked, and then observe the New dialog box. As you saw in Chapter 1, Ami Pro normally creates new documents based on the Default - Most Frequently Used Paragraph Styles style sheet.

2. Scroll down through the Style Sheet For New Document list box. Ami Pro provides style sheets for a variety of documents, from envelopes and fax cover sheets to mailing labels and overheads.

3. Scroll back to the top of the Style Sheet For New Document list box, and then select **Calendar - Monthly, Automated** (see Figure 9.11).

Figure 9.11   **Using the Calendar - Monthly, Automated style sheet**

4. Verify that *With Contents* and *Run Macro* are selected, and then click on **OK**.

5. After a few moments, Ami Pro opens a Monthly Calendar dialog box asking you to specify the month and year for your calendar. (If your computer's internal clock is correct, Ami Pro automatically selects the current month and year.)

6. In the Month drop-down list box, select **October**.

7. In the Year drop-down list box, select **1994**.

8. Click on **OK**, and you'll see Ami Pro switch to Full Page view and build a calendar for October 1994 right on your screen, as shown in Figure 9.12. (If you wanted to, you could now switch to Custom view and fill in appointments on this calendar.)

9. Save the document as **mycalend**, and then close MYCALEND.SAM.

Figure 9.12   **The completed calendar**

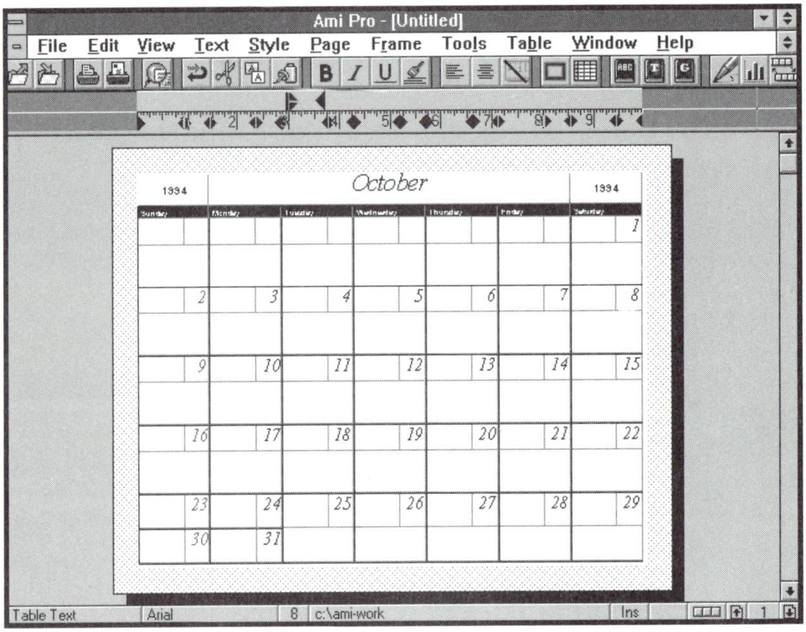

PRACTICE YOUR SKILLS

In this chapter, you learned how to assign, modify, override, and create paragraph styles. You also created a new document based on an automated style sheet. The following two Practice Your Skills activities give you the opportunity to practice some of these techniques. After each activity step, we've provided a chapter reference (in parentheses) to inform you where we introduced the relevant technique for that step.

Follow these steps to produce the final document shown in Figure 9.13 from the original document PRAC9A.SAM:

1. Open **prac9a.sam**. (Chapter 2)

2. Assign the **Title** style to the following heading paragraphs. (Chapter 9)

        Introduction
        Product Features
        Vendors

```
                Food Brokers
                Projected Quarterly Sales
```

3. Modify the Title style by changing the typeface to **Times New Roman**, and by removing the paragraph spacing above and below. (Chapter 9)

4. Apply the **Bullet 1** style to the following paragraphs, located on page 1 under the heading *Product Features*. (Chapter 9)

```
                organically grown
                flash-frozen on site
                naturally ripened
                grown with natural fertilizers
                no sugar added
```

5. Scroll to the bottom of page 1, and then select the entire first line of the tabbed table under the heading *Vendors*. (Chapter 3)

6. Apply the Bold and Underline text attributes to the selected text. (Chapter 4)

7. Create a new style, **Table Heading**, based on the selected text. (Chapter 9)

8. Assign your Table Heading style to the selected text.

9. Assign your Table Heading style to the first lines of the two tabbed tables on page 2 under the headings *Food Brokers* and *Projected Quarterly Sales*. (Chapter 9)

10. Save your document as **myprac9a**. (Chapter 1)

11. Print the document and compare it to Figure 9.13. (Chapter 1)

12. Close the document. (Chapter 1)

Follow these steps to produce the final document shown in Figure 9.14:

1. Create a new document based on the **Calendar - Weekly By Hour, With To Do List** style sheet. (Chapter 9)

2. In the Personal Information dialog box that Ami Pro opens, type your own personal information and then click on **OK**. (If you've used this style sheet before, you might need to skip to step 3.) (Chapter 1)

Figure 9.13   **MYPRAC9A.SAM**

Introduction

Moosie's Garden Patch announces the unveiling of a new food line in the Garden Patch series: the Fruit Patch. The Fruit Patch product line was developed through the cooperation and dedication of Drs. Eugenie Alfa and Vera Betta and their staffs after two years of intense work. The FDA recently approved the food and it will be released for public sale in three weeks.

The Fruit Patch includes a variety of organically grown fruit: the berries (cherries, strawberries, raspberries, blackberries, and blueberries), apricots, peaches, grapes, and plums.

Product Features

The Fruit Patch product line has been specially developed. The features that distinguish it as a high-quality organic product include:

- organically grown
- flash-frozen on site
- naturally ripened
- grown with natural fertilizers
- no sugar added

Vendors

Like our vegetable product line, we will sell the fruit product line directly to vendors who cater to the natural and organic market. Our present vendors are ready to include the new product line in their markets. The present buyers for our vendors follow:

VENDOR	**PHONE**	**BUYER NAME**
Trader Tom's	(206) 323-4511	Maura Murphy
Aunt Emily's Market	(818) 853-1562	Martino Brown
Hamlet Farms	(717) 654-1294	Judy Hughson

Figure 9.13   **MYPRAC9A.SAM (Continued)**

Food Brokers

The food brokers for the US regions are also selling both product lines. The brokers' reception to the new product is an overwhelming success. Each brokerage firm took in orders for over ten thousand boxes for the quarter. The present brokerages selling our product are listed below:

BROKERAGE	**REGION**	**CONTACT**
B & J's	West	Julie Dimes
Hout, Black, and Wallace	East	Wilma Kurtz
Price Farms Co.	South	Michael Meigs

Projected Quarterly Sales

Our finance department has been hard at work, determining sales projections for the next quarter. Those results are shown below in the table.

Vendors and Brokers	**Boxes Sold**	**Total Profit**
Price Farms Co.	13,500	9,315.00
Hout, Black, and Wallace	10,543	8,328.97
B & J's	9,888	8,800.32
Hamlet Farms	5,533	7,137.57
Aunt Emily's Market	3,998	5,957.02
Trader Tom's	1,500	2,535.00

3. In the Default Information dialog box that Ami Pro opens, verify that the information is correct, and then click on **OK**. (Chapter 1)

4. Save your document as **myprac9b**. (Chapter 1)

5. Print your document, and then compare it to Figure 9.14. The document should display *your* personal information and the current date. (Chapter 1)

6. Close the document. (Chapter 1)

SUMMARY

In this chapter, you learned how to assign styles with the Style Status button and function keys, modify a style's text-formatting and paragraph-spacing elements, create new styles based on selected text and on other styles, and use Ami Pro's built-in style sheets.

Here is a quick reference guide to the Ami Pro features introduced in this chapter:

Desired Result	How to Do It
Assign a style	Select paragraph(s), click on **Style Status button**, and then select style. Or select paragraph(s), and then press appropriate function key.
Open Modify Style dialog box	Choose **Style, Modify Style**. Or click in main document text with **right mouse button**.
Modify a style	Open Modify Style dialog box and select desired style from Style drop-down list box. Then select Modify option and choose desired style elements. Repeat last step as necessary, and then click on **OK**.
Override a style	Apply desired text formatting and/or enhancements to selected text.

Figure 9.14 **MYPRAC9B.SAM**

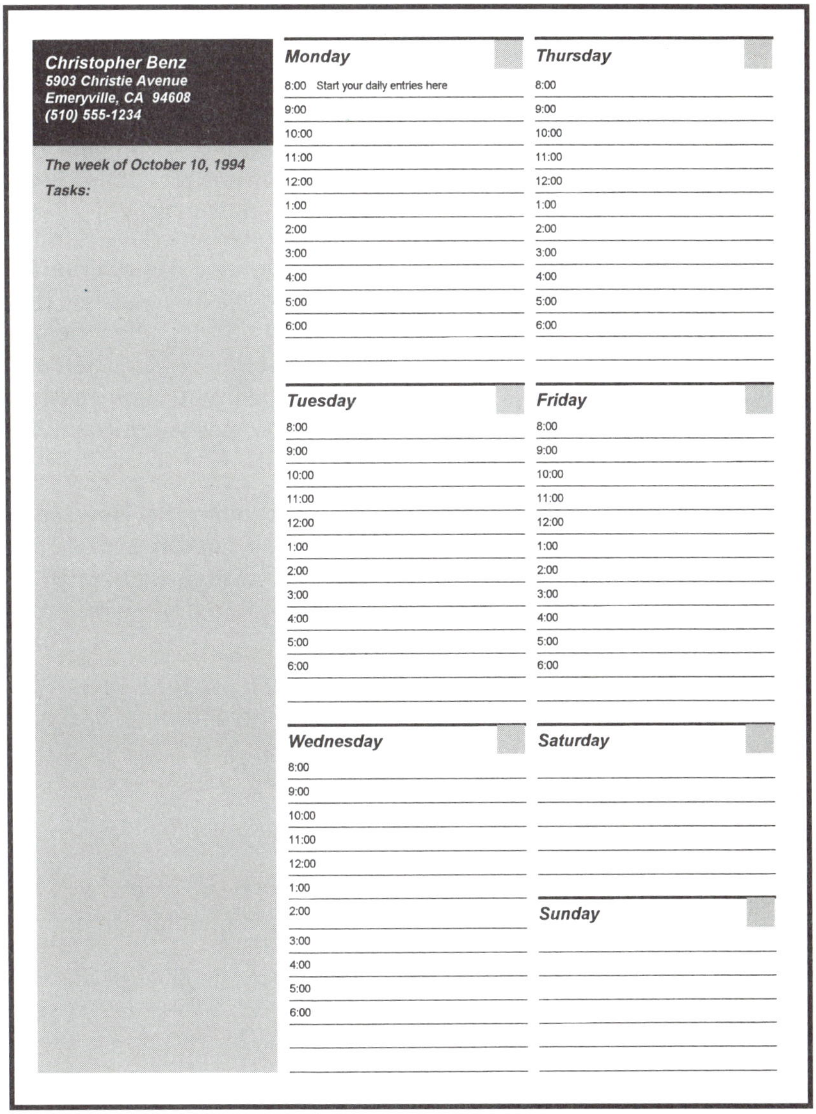

Christopher Benz
5903 Christie Avenue
Emeryville, CA 94608
(510) 555-1234

The week of October 10, 1994

Tasks:

Monday

8:00 Start your daily entries here
9:00
10:00
11:00
12:00
1:00
2:00
3:00
4:00
5:00
6:00

Tuesday

8:00
9:00
10:00
11:00
12:00
1:00
2:00
3:00
4:00
5:00
6:00

Wednesday

8:00
9:00
10:00
11:00
12:00
1:00
2:00
3:00
4:00
5:00
6:00

Thursday

8:00
9:00
10:00
11:00
12:00
1:00
2:00
3:00
4:00
5:00
6:00

Friday

8:00
9:00
10:00
11:00
12:00
1:00
2:00
3:00
4:00
5:00
6:00

Saturday

Sunday

Desired Result	How to Do It
Create new style based on selected text	Select text displaying desired appearance; choose **Style, Create Style**; type new style name in New Style text box; select **Based On Selected Text**; then click on **Create** or **Modify**. If you click on **Modify**, select additional style elements as desired, and then click on **OK**.
Create new style based on another style	Choose **Style, Create Style**; type new style name in New Style dialog box; select **Based On Style**; select base style in Based On Style list box; then click on **Create** or **Modify**. If you click on **Modify**, select additional style elements as desired, and then click on **OK**.
Create new document based on non-default style sheet	Choose **File, New**, select desired style sheet in Style Sheet For New Document list box, and then click on **OK**. If style sheet is automated, follow on-screen directions.

In the next chapter, you'll learn how to use tables to arrange text and numbers into rows and columns, and to perform calculations on numbers within tables.

IF YOU'RE STOPPING HERE

If you need to take a break here, please exit Ami Pro. If you want to proceed directly to the next chapter, do so now.

CHAPTER 10: WORKING WITH TABLES

Table Basics

Working with Numbers in a Table

Modifying a Table Layout

Changing the Appearance of Table Contents

You saw in Chapter 5 that you can use tabbed tables to arrange text and numbers in rows and columns. However, creating tabbed tables can be a tricky process, and tabbed tables are somewhat inflexible when you want to add or remove columns or rows of information. Fortunately, Ami Pro enables you to create tables *without* using tabs. As you'll see, these nontabbed tables make it easy for you to create good-looking tables quickly, and to modify and enhance them easily.

When you're done working through this chapter, you will know how to

- Create a table
- Enter text and numbers into a table
- Total columns or rows of numbers within a table
- Modify a table's layout
- Format text and numbers within a table

TABLE BASICS

Ami Pro's nontabbed tables, properly referred to simply as *tables*, consist of vertical *columns* and horizontal *rows* divided on screen by *table gridlines*, nonprinting vertical and horizontal lines that Ami Pro displays by default for your visual reference. (You'll learn later in this chapter how to set table lines that *do* print.) Within the table, at each intersection of a column and a row, are *cells*. (See Figure 10.1 for an illustration of these table components.)

Figure 10.1 **Table components**

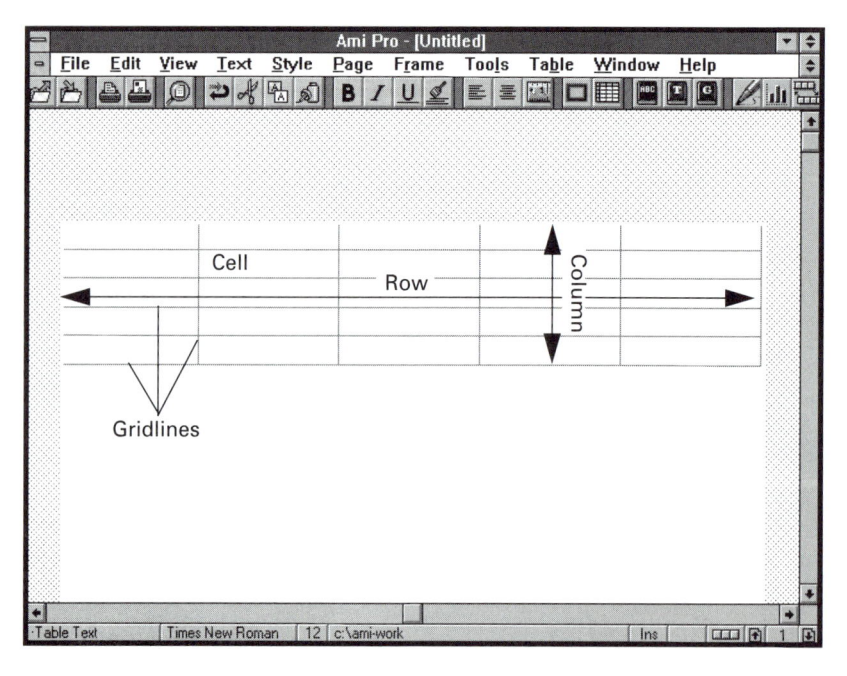

Ami Pro tables are similar in appearance and function to spreadsheets, so if you've used an electronic spreadsheet program such as Excel or 1-2-3, you might already be fairly familiar with Ami Pro's table terms. If you aren't familiar with electronic spreadsheet programs, think of a table as a tiled floor; each cell is like a single tile, and the gridlines are like the grout lines separating all the tiles.

You can use tables to set up grids of text and numbers (for example, the monthly calendar you created in Chapter 9); side-by-side columns (like the tables shown throughout this book); mailing labels; or in any situation that requires an orderly arrangement of data.

Note: Whenever the insertion point or current selection is inside a table, Ami Pro adds the Table menu to the menu bar. You'll learn how to use some Table menu commands later in this chapter.

CREATING A TABLE

Follow these steps when you want to create a table:

- Place the insertion point where you want to insert the table.
- Choose Tools, Tables to open the Create Table dialog box.
- Select the number of columns and rows that you want in your table. An Ami Pro table can contain up to 250 columns and 4,000 rows.
- Click on OK.

Ami Pro inserts a table with the number of columns and rows you specified, and places the insertion point in the table's upper-left cell. By default, Ami Pro makes the table as wide as the typing area so that the table stretches from the left to the right margin, and sizes each column's width equally according to the amount of available space; the greater the number of columns, the narrower each column will be.

Note: When the Create dialog box is open, you can also click on Layout to open the Modify Table Layout dialog box and select additional table layout options before creating your table. For now, however, we'll just let Ami Pro determine most of our table layout details. Later in this chapter, we'll show you how to open and use the Modify Table Layout box *after* you've created a table.

284 • WORKING WITH TABLES

If you are not running Ami Pro, please start it now. Let's create a table that has three columns and six rows:

1. Open **table.sam**.

2. Because we won't be using the current ruler in this chapter, hide the ruler by choosing **View, Hide Ruler**.

3. Scroll to the top of page 2, and then scroll down to position the heading *Discounts* at the top of the document window.

4. Place the insertion point in the second of the three blank lines below the paragraph beginning *Global Travel guarantees*.

5. Choose **Tools, Tables** and then examine the Create Table dialog box. Here is where you specify the number of columns and rows for your table (see Figure 10.2).

Figure 10.2 **The Create Table dialog box**

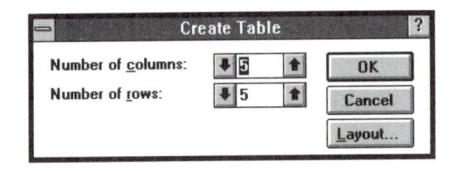

6. In the Number Of Columns box, type **3**.

7. In the Number Of Rows box, type **6**.

8. Click on **OK**. As shown in Figure 10.3, Ami Pro inserts an empty three-column, six-row table that is as wide as the typing area. Because the table is empty, all you can see are the table's nonprinting gridlines.

SPECIFYING TABLE VIEW PREFERENCES

As you learned earlier in this chapter, table gridlines do not print; Ami Pro displays them on screen for your visual reference only. If you'd prefer not to view gridlines, you can hide them. Here are the steps to turn table gridlines on or off:

- Choose View, View Preferences to open the View Preferences dialog box.

Figure 10.3   **The empty table**

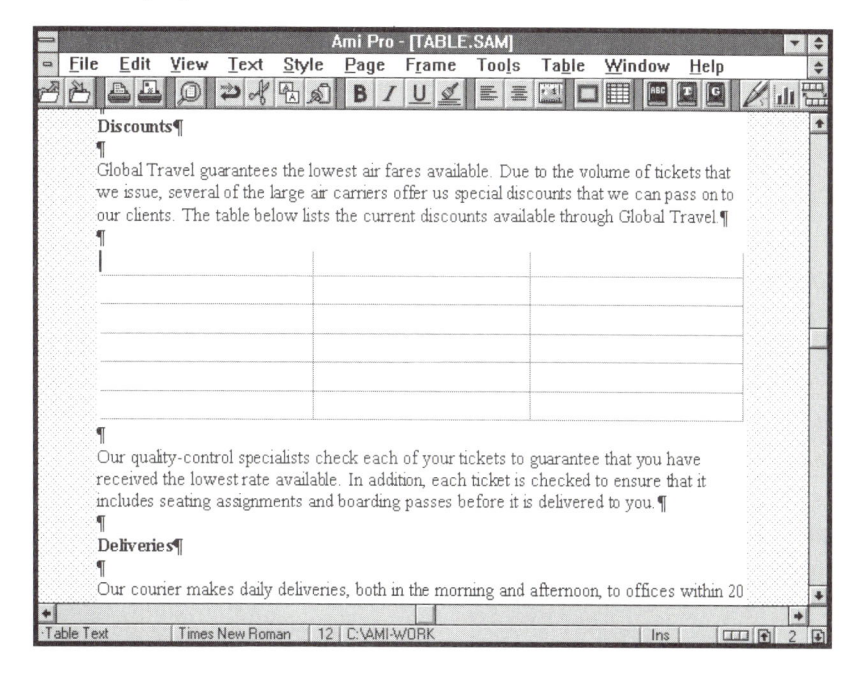

[Screenshot of Ami Pro - [TABLE.SAM] window showing a document titled "Discounts" with introductory text, an empty table with multiple rows and columns, followed by text about quality-control specialists and a "Deliveries" section.]

- Check or uncheck Table Gridlines, as appropriate.
- Click on OK.

Note: If you are currently displaying the Tables SmartIcon set (see Chapter 8 if you need a review of SmartIcon sets), you can also open the View Preferences dialog box by clicking on the *View Preferences SmartIcon*; it's the fifth SmartIcon from the left, displaying a pair of eyeglasses. Because the Tables SmartIcon set is designed specifically for working with tables, we'll display that set in the activities throughout this chapter.

When you're working with tables, you also might want to display *row and column headings*. Row and column headings act as a "road map" to Ami Pro's row and column identification system: Columns are referred to by letters (A, B, C) with the leftmost column always being A; and rows by numbers (1, 2, 3) with the topmost row always being 1. By combining a specific cell's row and column label, Ami Pro provides each cell with a unique *cell address*. For example, the cell at the intersection of column B and row 4 is called "cell B4." (Think of cell addresses as street intersections: "Meet me at the corner of Avenue B and 4th Street.") To keep cell references consistent, Ami Pro always refers to a cell first by its column letter, and then by its row number. Thus, the cell address for a cell in column B and row 4 is B4 and never 4B.

When row and column headings are displayed, Ami Pro clearly labels each row and column for you on screen. Ami Pro displays row and column headings only when the insertion point or current selection is inside a table. Row and column headings never print; Ami Pro displays them on screen for your visual reference only, as it does table gridlines.

Follow these steps when you want Ami Pro to display or hide row and column headings:

- Choose View, View Preferences or click on the View Preferences SmartIcon to open the View Preferences dialog box.
- Check or uncheck Table Row/Column Headings, as appropriate.
- Click on OK.

Let's work with the View Preferences dialog box now to see how to control Ami Pro's table-specific view preferences:

1. Display the **Tables** SmartIcon set. (Click on the status bar's **SmartIcon button**, and then select **Tables**.) This SmartIcon set contains a number of SmartIcons to help you work with tables.

2. Click on the **View Preferences SmartIcon** to open the View Preferences dialog box.

3. Uncheck **Table Gridlines**, click on **OK**, and then observe TABLE.SAM. Because the table you just created is empty and Ami Pro no longer displays gridlines, you see only a blank space in the table's position.

4. Reopen the View Preferences dialog box (click on the **View Preferences SmartIcon**), check **Table Gridlines**, check **Table Row/Column Headings**, and then click on **OK**.

5. Examine the table. Ami Pro displays the table's gridlines again, places letters across the top of the table, and places numbers along the table's left side (see Figure 10.4).

6. Observe the letters at the top of the table (*A*, *B*, *C*). These are the column headings; each letter identifies an individual column.

Figure 10.4   **Displaying gridlines and row/column headings**

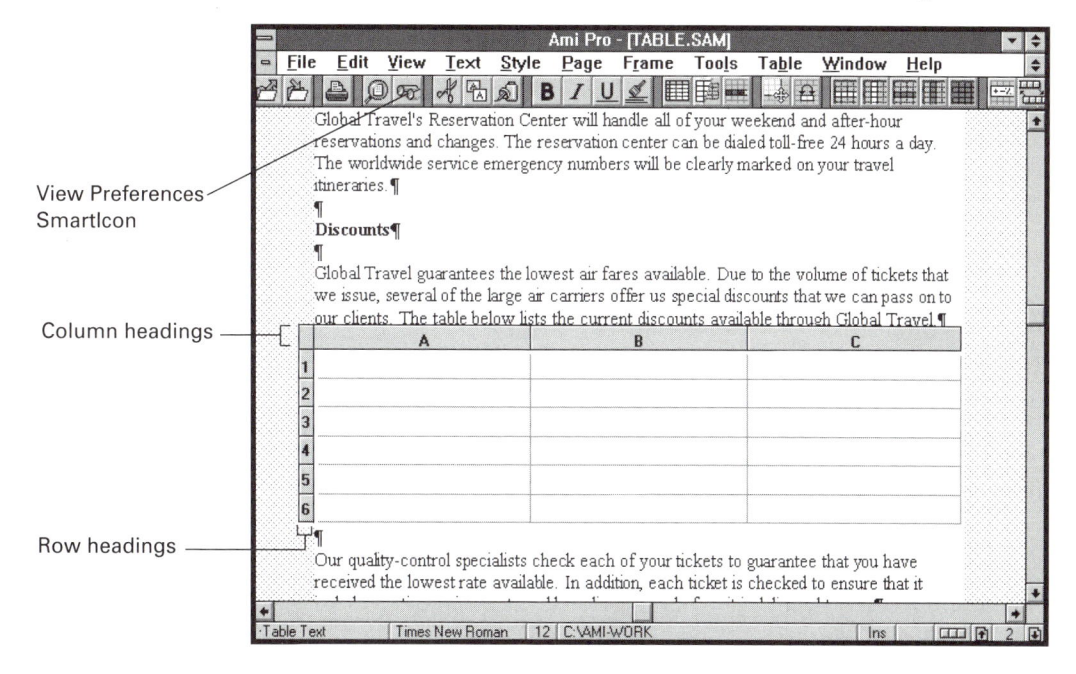

View Preferences SmartIcon

Column headings

Row headings

7. Observe the numbers to the left of the table (*1, 2, 3*, and so on). These are the row headings; each number identifies an individual row.

8. Observe the intersections of the columns and rows. Each intersection of a column and a row is a cell. For example, cell B2 is at the intersection of column B and row 2.

9. Click outside the table. Ami Pro displays column and row headings only when the insertion point or the current selection is inside the table. However, Ami Pro continues to display gridlines.

10. Click inside the table. Ami Pro displays the column and row headings again.

MOVING IN A TABLE

You can use either the mouse or the keyboard to move to any table cell. Using the mouse, simply position the I-beam anywhere over the cell, and then click. Table 10.1 lists some of Ami Pro's keyboard techniques for moving within a table. (See your Ami Pro documentation for other techniques.)

Table 10.1 **Keyboard Techniques for Moving in a Table**

Press:	To Move:
Tab	One cell to the right
Shift+Tab	One cell to the left
Ctrl+Up Arrow	Up one cell
Ctrl+Down Arrow	Down one cell

Note: Depending on the current cell's contents and the location of the insertion point within that cell, you may also be able to use one of the four arrow keys on your keyboard to move one cell up, down, left, or right. For example, if the current cell is empty or if the insertion point is at the very end of any text or numbers within that cell, you can use the Right Arrow key to move one cell to the right.

If the insertion point is in the last cell of a row, Tab moves the insertion point to the first cell of the next row. Likewise, if the insertion point is in the first cell of a row, Shift+Tab moves the insertion point to the last cell of the previous row.

If you use any keyboard technique to move up when the insertion point is in a table's first row, or down when the insertion point is in a table's last row, you will move the insertion point out of the table altogether. For example, if the insertion point is in cell A1 (the first cell in the first row) and you press Ctrl+Up Arrow, the insertion point moves out of the table.

Let's practice some of the techniques listed above to move around in the table you created in TABLE.SAM:

1. Click in cell A1 (that is, the cell at the intersection of column A and row 1) to place the insertion point in that cell.

2. Press **Tab** to move one cell to the right, to cell B1.

3. Press **Tab** twice to move to cell C1 and then to cell A2. Notice that when you Tab past the end of a table row, Ami Pro moves the insertion point to the beginning of the next row.

4. Press **Shift+Tab** twice to move to cell C1 and then to cell B1. Shift+Tab moves the insertion point in the opposite direction of Tab.

   5. Press **Ctrl+Down Arrow** to move to cell B2. (Because cell B1 is empty, you could also press Down Arrow to move to cell B2.)

   6. Press **Ctrl+Up Arrow** to move back up to cell B1. (Because cell B2 is empty, you could also use Up Arrow to move to cell B1.)

   7. Press **Ctrl+Up Arrow** again. Notice that when you move past the top (or bottom) row of a table, Ami Pro moves the insertion point outside the table and no longer displays the table's column and row headings.

   8. Click in cell A1 to move back into the table and display the column and row headings once again.

PRACTICE YOUR SKILLS

   1. Use **Tab** and **Ctrl+Down Arrow** to move to cell C6.
   2. Use **Shift+Tab** and **Ctrl+Up Arrow** to cell A3.
   3. Return to cell A1, using the method of your choice.

ENTERING TEXT IN A TABLE

It's easy to enter text in a table cell: Just place the insertion point in the cell, and then begin typing. When you finish typing in the cell, press Tab to move the insertion point to the next cell. By default, Ami Pro left-aligns all table text.

Enter some text into your table:

   1. In cell A1, type **Destination**, and then press **Tab** to move to cell B1.

   2. In cell B1, type **Standard Price**, and then press **Tab** to move to cell C1.

   3. In cell C1, type **Your Price**, and then press **Tab** to move to cell A2.

   4. In cell A2, type **Frankfurt, Germany (via London)**, and then examine row 2. Your text wraps to a second line, and Ami Pro automatically expands row 2's height to fit your text (see Figure 10.5).

290 • WORKING WITH TABLES

Figure 10.5 **Entering text in a table**

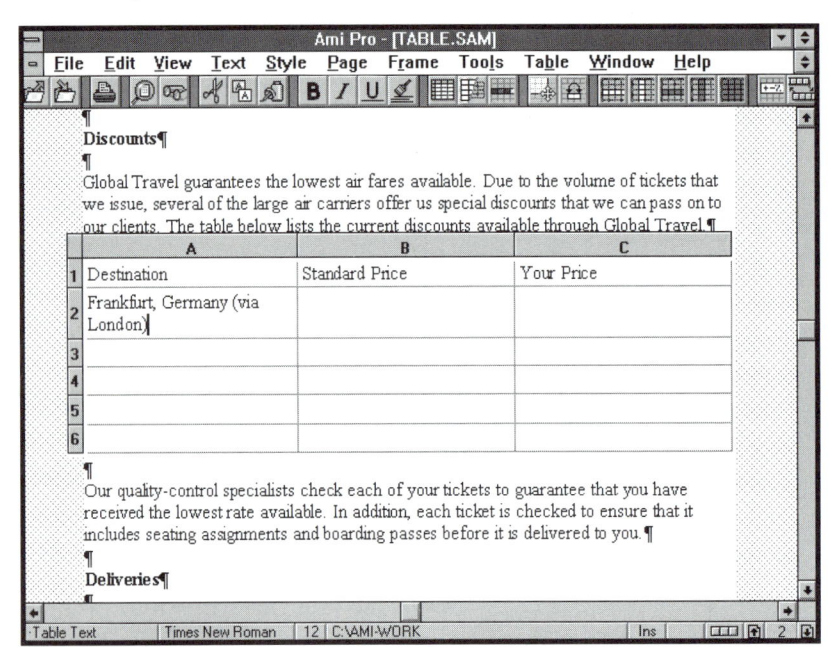

[Screenshot of Ami Pro - [TABLE.SAM] window showing a document with "Discounts" heading, introductory paragraph about Global Travel's lowest air fares, and a table with columns A (Destination), B (Standard Price), C (Your Price). Row 1 contains headers; Row 2 contains "Frankfurt, Germany (via London)"; Rows 3-6 are empty. Below the table is text about quality-control specialists checking tickets, followed by "Deliveries" heading.]

5. Save the document as **mytable**.

PRACTICE YOUR SKILLS

1. Type the following text into the specified table cells:

   Cell A3: **Paris, France (direct)**

   Cell A4: **Sydney, Australia (via Hawaii)**

   Cell A5: **New Delhi, India (via Madrid)**

2. Compare your table to Figure 10.6.
3. Save the document.

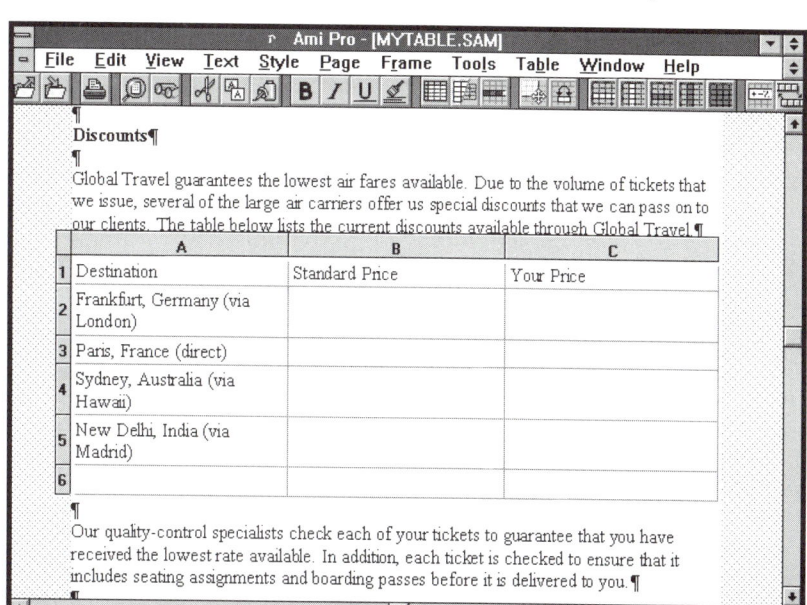

Figure 10.6   **The table, after typing text in cells A3, A4, and A5**

WORKING WITH NUMBERS IN A TABLE

One of the many advantages of tables over tabbed tables is the way tables handle numbers. When you enter a number into a table cell, and then move the insertion point out of that cell, Ami Pro automatically applies a *numeric format* to the number. You can either accept Ami Pro's default numeric format or select another one. Numeric formats determine the following:

- Whether numbers will contain *thousands separators*; for example, the comma in *5,689*

- How many decimal places will be displayed; for example, *5689* (no decimal places), *5689.0*, or *5689.00*

- Whether negative numbers will be preceded or followed by a minus sign, or will instead be displayed in red or within parentheses.

- Whether Ami Pro will add a currency symbol before or after the number, and what that currency symbol will be; for example, $ or £.

By default, Ami Pro adds thousands separators when appropriate; displays decimal points only when necessary (for example, *5689.1*, but not *5689.0*); displays a minus sign before negative numbers; and displays no currency symbols.

You can also perform calculations with table numbers. For example, you can add a column or a row of numbers and display that result in another table cell.

You'll learn how to control how Ami Pro's numeric format as well as how to perform calculations later in this chapter.

ENTERING NUMBERS

Here are a couple of simple rules for entering numbers in an Ami Pro table:

- Use only numeric digits (0, 1, 2, and so on) and decimal points.
- Do *not* use returns, commas, spaces, currency symbols, or any other characters. For example, you can type *1, 4639*, or *67.54*, but not *$1, 4,639*, or *67-54*.

When you enter a number following these rules, Ami Pro automatically applies a numeric format to that number (possibly adding currency symbols and commas for you), and allows you to use the numbers in calculations. Otherwise, Ami Pro leaves the numbers and characters as you typed them, and is unable to calculate with those numbers.

Whenever you type only numeric digits and decimal points in a table cell, Ami Pro defines that cell as a *numeric cell*; all other cells are *non-numeric cells*.

To enter a number in a table, place the insertion point in the desired cell, and then type the number. When you move out of the cell, Ami Pro right-aligns the number and applies a numeric format to it. If you move the insertion point into a numeric cell, Ami Pro temporarily left-aligns the number and removes the numeric format; this makes it easier for you to edit the number. To redisplay the numeric format, simply move the insertion point back out of that cell.

WORKING WITH NUMBERS IN A TABLE • 293

Let's practice entering numbers now, and see how Ami Pro handles them:

1. Move to cell B2, type **1259**, and then press **Tab** to move to cell C2.

2. Look at cell B2. Ami Pro has automatically right-aligned your number, and placed a comma as a thousands separator between the *1* and the *259* (see Figure 10.7).

Figure 10.7 **Entering a number in a table**

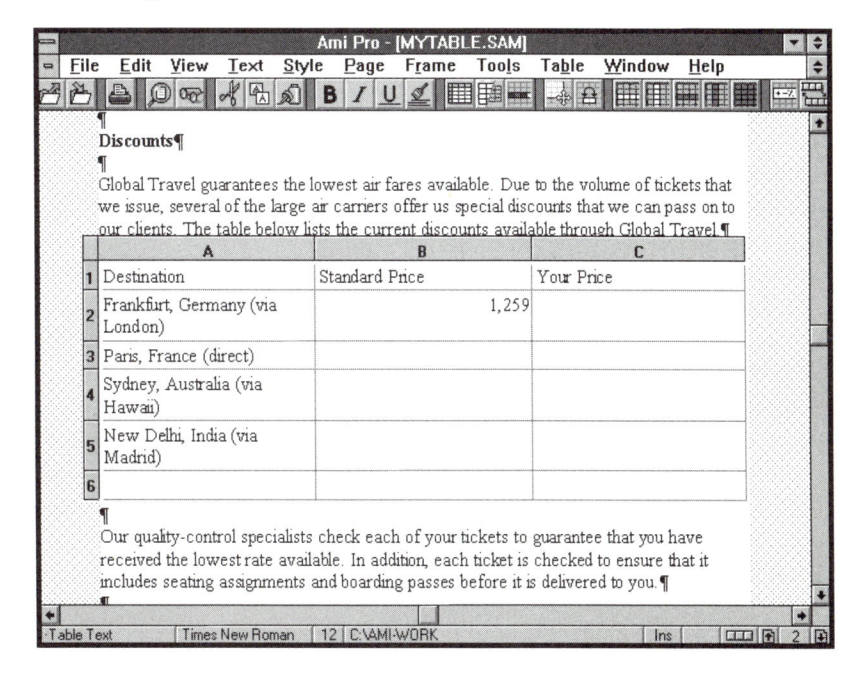

3. In cell C2, type **999.75**, and then press **Tab** to move to cell A3. Ami Pro right-aligns this number, as well.

PRACTICE YOUR SKILLS

1. Type the following numbers into the specified cells:

    Cell B3: **1175.99**

    Cell C3: **975**

294 • WORKING WITH TABLES

        Cell B4: **4350**

        Cell C4: **2250.15**

        Cell B5: **2340.25**

        Cell C5: **2100**

2. Move the insertion point to any cell not containing a number, and then compare your table's numbers to those in Figure 10.8. Notice that Ami Pro automatically adds thousands separators as needed; however, it does not decimally align the numbers. (We'll learn how to fix this alignment problem later in this chapter.)

3. Save MYTABLE.SAM.

Figure 10.8   **The table, after entering six more numbers**

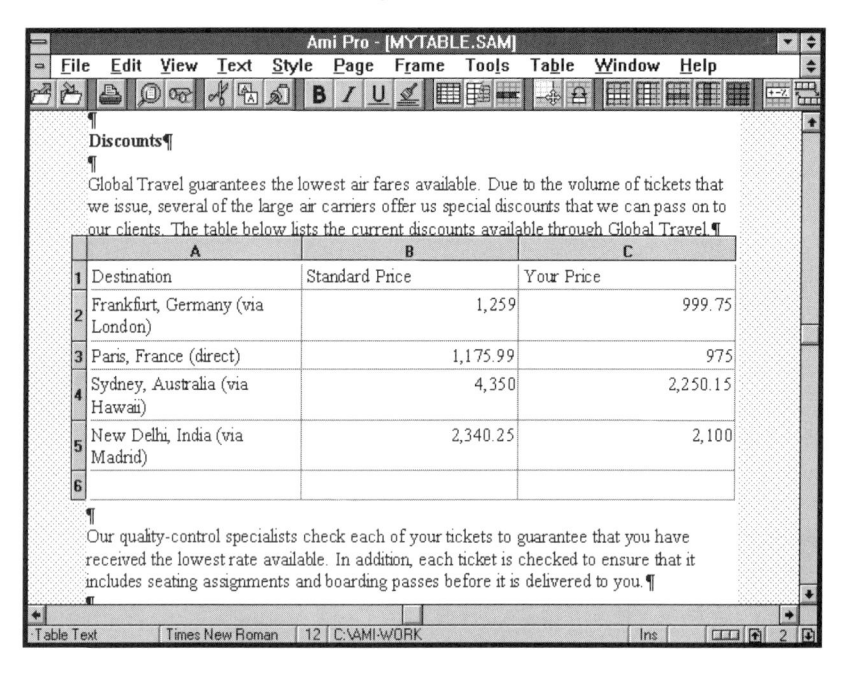

USING QUICK ADD

You can use the Table, Quick Add command to add (or *total*) the contents of every numeric cell in a column or a row. Follow these steps when you want to use Quick Add:

- Place the insertion point in the cell where you want the column or row total amount to appear. This cell *must* be in the same row or column as the cells you want to total.

- Choose Table, Quick Add, Column to total a column, or Table, Quick Add, Row to total a row. Ami Pro will place the total in the current cell.

Note: If the column or row you are totaling contains non-numeric cells intermixed with numeric cells, Quick Add might not display the correct total.

If you edit a number in a column or row that Quick Add has totaled, Ami Pro will recalculate a new total automatically once you move out of the cell you edited.

Let's use Quick Add now to total column B, and then see how Ami Pro automatically recalculates the total when you edit a number in that same column:

1. Observe the menu bar. Whenever the insertion point or current selection is in a table, Ami Pro provides a Table menu.

2. Move to cell A6, and then type **Totals** to identify the numbers that you are about to place in the table's bottom row.

3. Press **Tab** to move to cell B6.

4. Choose **Table, Quick Add, Column**, and then observe the number in cell B6: *9,125.24*. Ami Pro has totaled the existing numbers in column B (see Figure 10.9).

5. In cell B4, select **4350** (double-click on the number).

6. Type **2560** to replace *4350*, and then press **Tab** to move to cell C4.

7. Look at cell B6. Ami Pro has automatically recalculated the total to *7,335.24* to reflect the change you made in cell B4.

Figure 10.9 **Using Quick Add to total a column**

	A	B	C
1	Destination	Standard Price	Your Price
2	Frankfurt, Germany (via London)	1,259	999.75
3	Paris, France (direct)	1,175.99	975
4	Sydney, Australia (via Hawaii)	4,350	2,250.15
5	New Delhi, India (via Madrid)	2,340.25	2,100
6	Totals	9,125.24	

PRACTICE YOUR SKILLS

1. Move to cell C6, and then use **Table, Quick Add, Column** to calculate the total for column C.

2. In cell C3, replace *975* with **875**.

3. Move out of cell C3 so that Ami Pro recalculates the total in cell C6.

4. Compare your table to Figure 10.10.

MODIFYING A TABLE LAYOUT

After you create a table, you might want to modify it; you can change column widths, insert or delete columns or rows, add lines that print around certain cells, add a line that prints all the way around a table, and center the entire table.

You learned earlier in this chapter that you can use the Table Modify Layout dialog box to modify a table's layout. Ami Pro also offers a number of Table menu items, as well as SmartIcons in the

MODIFYING A TABLE LAYOUT • 297

Tables SmartIcon set, to help you meet your table modification needs. The next few sections will show you a variety of table modification options.

Figure 10.10   **The table, after totaling column C and editing cell C3**

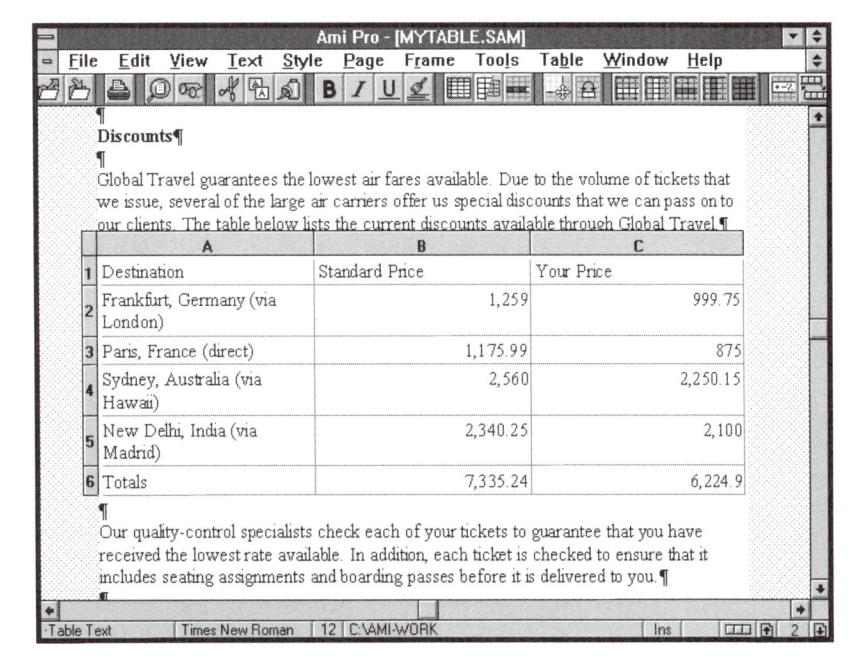

	A	B	C
1	Destination	Standard Price	Your Price
2	Frankfurt, Germany (via London)	1,259	999.75
3	Paris, France (direct)	1,175.99	875
4	Sydney, Australia (via Hawaii)	2,560	2,250.15
5	New Delhi, India (via Madrid)	2,340.25	2,100
6	Totals	7,335.24	6,224.9

TABLE SELECTION TECHNIQUES

As with controlling the appearance of characters and paragraphs, you often have to select a table or parts of a table in order to change its layout and appearance.

You can use both the mouse and the Table menu to select *ranges* of cells, columns, and rows, or even entire tables. (A range of cells is any square or rectangular group of contiguous cells. The cells included in a range are determined by the range's top-left cell and the bottom-right cell. For example, if you drag to select cells A1 through B2, Ami Pro will include cells B1 and A2 in that range.)

Table 10.2 lists table selection techniques using the Table menu. Table 10.3 lists table selection techniques using the mouse.

Table 10.2 **Table Selection Techniques with the Table Menu**

To Select	Do This
A row	Place the insertion point anywhere in the row you want to select; then choose Table, Select Row.
A column	Place the insertion point anywhere in the column you want to select; then choose Table, Select Column.
A table	Place the insertion point anywhere in the table; then choose Table, Select Entire Table.

Table 10.3 **Table Selection Techniques with the Mouse**

To Select	Do This
A row	Point to the left edge of the row's first cell. (You'll know you're in the correct place when the mouse pointer becomes a horizontal arrow.) Then click the mouse button.
A column	Point to the top edge of the column's first cell. (You'll know you're in the correct place when the mouse pointer becomes a vertical arrow.) Then click the mouse button.
A range of cells	Position the I-beam in the first cell you want to select; then drag to the last cell you want to select. Ami Pro selects a square or rectangular range of cells defined by those two cells.
Multiple rows	Point to the left edge of the first row you want to select; then drag down to the last row you want to select.
Multiple columns	Point to the top edge of the first column you want to select; then drag to the right to the last column you want to select.
A table	Select the table's first column; then drag to the last column. Or select the table's first row, and then drag to the last row.

MODIFYING A TABLE LAYOUT • 299

Note: You can use many of the text selection techniques you learned in Chapter 3 to select text and numbers within cells. However, you cannot select partial contents of multiple cells; whenever you select more than one cell, Ami Pro selects the entire contents of each cell in the range.

Let's practice some table selection techniques:

1. Move to cell A1, and then choose **Table**, **Select Column** to select column A.

2. Click anywhere else in the table to deselect column A.

3. Point to the top of column B, on the line *between* the column heading and cell B1. When the mouse pointer becomes a vertical arrow (see Figure 10.11), click the mouse button to select column B.

4. Place the insertion point in cell C4, and then choose **Table, Select Row** to select row 4.

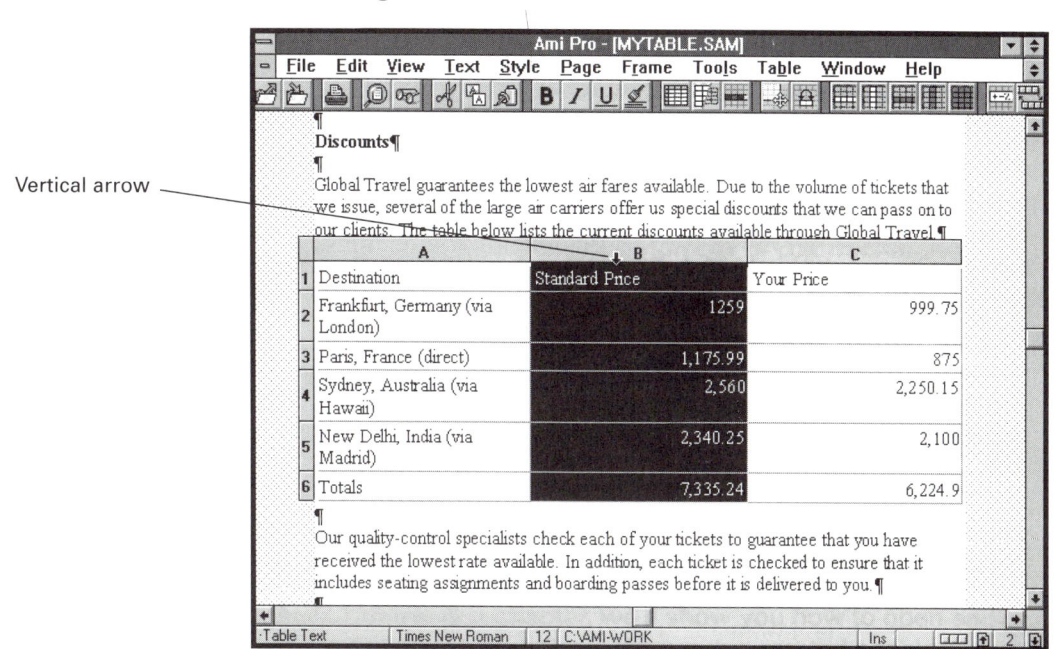

Figure 10.11 **Selecting a column with the mouse**

Vertical arrow

5. Point to the left edge of row 6, on the line between the row heading and cell A6. When the mouse pointer becomes a horizontal arrow, click to select row 6.

6. Point to the left edge of row 2 until the mouse pointer becomes a horizontal arrow. Then, to select rows 2 through 4, drag down through row 4.

7. Deselect, then position the I-beam in cell A2, and then drag to cell B4. This selects a rectangular range of six cells: A2, B2, A3, B3, A4, and B4.

8. Choose **Table, Select Entire Table** to select the entire table.

9. Deselect.

CHANGING COLUMN WIDTHS

When you create a table, Ami Pro sets equal column widths by default. If your table's contents don't fit neatly into these uniform columns, you can change each column's width individually through the Table menu, with a SmartIcon, or with the mouse. Each technique has its advantages:

- When you use the Table menu or the *Size Columns and Rows In A Table SmartIcon* (the 16th SmartIcon from the left in the Tables SmartIcon set, displaying a miniature table and a four-headed arrow), you can specify column widths numerically.

- When you use the mouse, you get to resize columns visually.

Note: You can also use the Modify Table Layout dialog box to change the width of *every* column in your table to a new set of uniform widths. However, if you have changed any individual column widths using the techniques described in this section, you can no longer use the Modify Table Layout dialog box to modify those columns' widths.

Follow these steps when you want to change the width of (*resize*) an individual column or multiple columns by using the Table menu or a SmartIcon:

- Select the column or columns that you want to resize.

- Choose Table, Column/Row Size or click on the Size Columns And Rows In A Table SmartIcon to open the Column/Row Size dialog box.

- In the Columns Width text box, specify the desired column width.
- Click on OK.

As you might expect, you can also use the Column/Row Size dialog box to change row heights. Because Ami Pro automatically adjusts row heights for you as necessary, however, you may not need to change row heights manually. For more information on changing row heights manually, see your Ami Pro documentation.

Follow these steps when you want to resize a column using the mouse:

- Position the I-beam over the vertical gridline at the right edge of the column you want to resize, until the I-beam becomes a four-headed arrow. (You can only resize one column at a time when using the mouse.) Do *not* point to the line between the column headings, but rather to the gridline between the table cells themselves.

- Drag to the right to widen the column, or drag to the left to narrow the column.

Caution: Whenever you widen a column, you must make sure that there is still some blank space between the edges of the table and the document's left and right margins. If the table already reaches from margin to margin, you must first narrow or delete other columns in order to narrow the overall table. (You'll learn how to delete columns shortly.)

Because the MYTABLE.SAM table already leaves no room between the edges of the table and the margins, let's use the mouse to first narrow column B, and then widen column A:

1. Position the I-beam over the vertical gridline between columns B and C, until the pointer becomes a four-headed arrow.

2. Drag the **vertical gridline** to the left until it is just to the right of the *e* in *Standard Price* (see Figure 10.12). When you release the mouse button, Ami Pro narrows column B and shifts column C to the left to narrow the entire table.

3. Position the I-beam over the vertical gridline between columns A and B, until the I-beam again becomes a four-headed arrow. Then drag to the right until the vertical gridline is between the *n* and *d* in *Standard*. When you release the mouse button, Ami Pro widens column A and shifts column B and C to the right, to widen the entire table.

302 • WORKING WITH TABLES

Figure 10.12 **Resizing a column with the mouse**

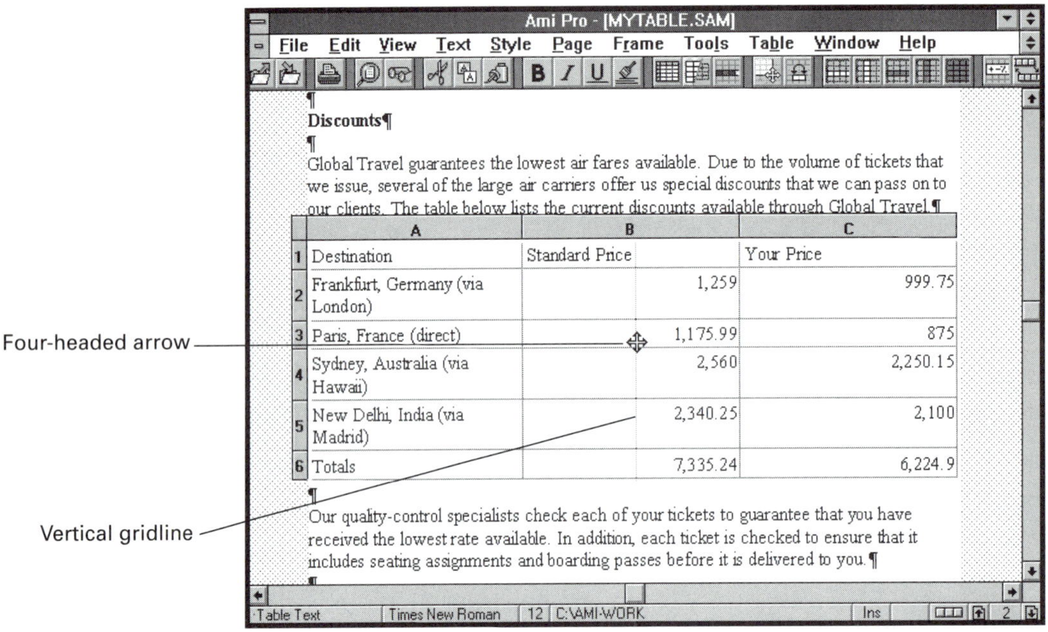

4. Examine column A. Because there is more room now, Ami Pro automatically "unwraps" the contents of each cell, so that each cell requires only one line.

Now let's use the Column/Row Size dialog box to make columns B and C exactly 1" wide.

1. Drag to select columns B and C.

2. Choose **Table**, **Column/Row Size** or click on the **Size Columns And Rows In A Table SmartIcon** to open the Column/Row Size dialog box.

3. In the Columns Width box, type **1**. Notice that Ami Pro automatically checks the Columns Width check box (see Figure 10.13).

4. Click on **OK**, and then observe your table. Ami Pro has resized both columns B and C to be exactly 1" wide.

5. Save MYTABLE.SAM.

MODIFYING A TABLE LAYOUT • 303

Figure 10.13 **The Column/Row Size dialog box**

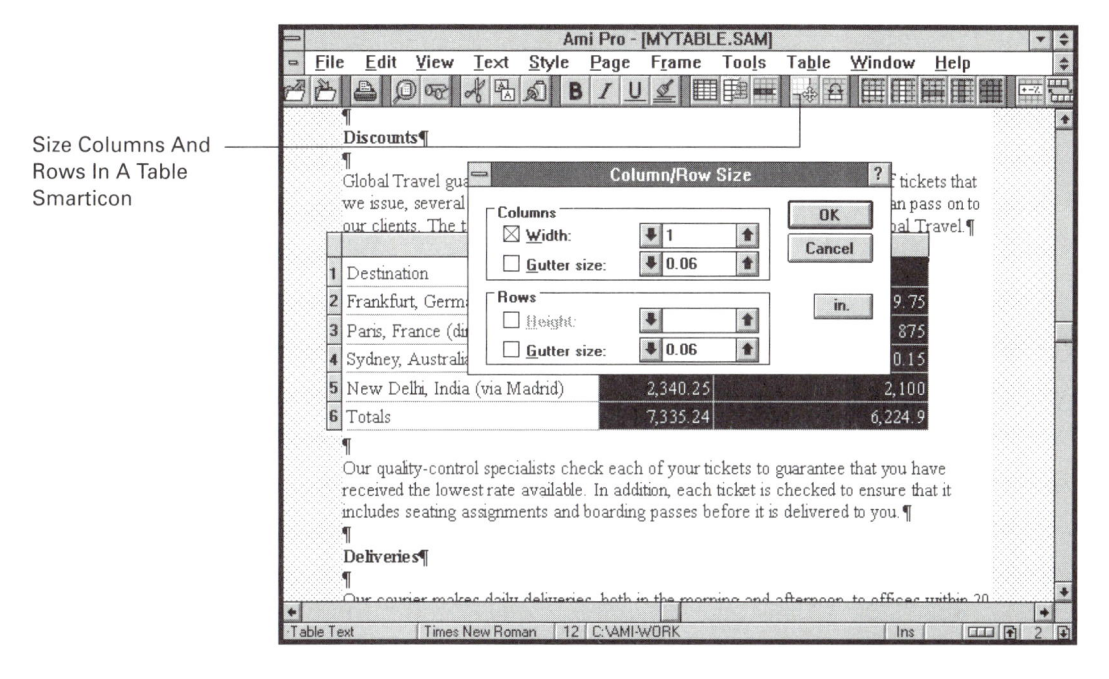

Size Columns And Rows In A Table Smarticon

INSERTING AND DELETING COLUMNS AND ROWS

Besides resizing columns and rows, you can also insert and delete them. Whenever you insert or delete columns or rows, Ami Pro automatically adjusts the numbers and/or letters of the columns and/or rows, as necessary.

Follow these steps when you want to insert columns or rows:

- If you are inserting columns, make sure there is enough blank space between the left and right document margins to accommodate the new columns.

- Place the insertion point anywhere in a column or row that is adjacent to where you want the new columns or rows inserted.

- Choose Table, Insert Column/Row to open the Insert Column/Row dialog box.

- Select Insert Columns or Insert Rows.

- In the Number To Insert box, specify the number of columns or rows you want to insert.
- Select Position Before or Position After to specify whether Ami Pro should insert the new columns or rows before or after the current column or row.
- Click on OK.

Follow these steps when you want to delete columns or rows:

- Place the insertion point anywhere in the column or row that you want to delete, or select multiple columns or rows.
- Choose Table, Delete Column/Row to open the Delete Column/Row dialog box.
- Select Delete Column or Delete Row.
- Click on OK. Ami Pro opens a dialog box to ask you to confirm your deletion. (**Caution:** You cannot undo column and row deletions.)
- Click on Yes. Ami Pro deletes the columns or rows, as well as any text or numbers they contain.

You can also delete an entire table by choosing Table, Delete Entire Table or by clicking on the *Delete Table SmartIcon* (the 22nd SmartIcon from the left in the Tables SmartIcon set, which displays a miniature shaded table).

Let's insert a fourth column in your table:

1. Move to anywhere in column C.
2. Choose **Table, Insert Column/Row** to open the Insert Column/Row dialog box (see Figure 10.14).

Figure 10.14   The Insert Column/Row dialog box

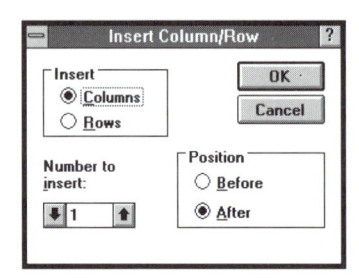

MODIFYING A TABLE LAYOUT • 305

3. Verify that *Insert Columns* is selected, that the Number To Insert box is set to *1*, and that *Position After* is selected.

4. Click on **OK**, and then observe your table. Ami Pro adds a column D that expands beyond the typing area, as shown in Figure 10.15. (You can't see the part of column D that reaches into the right margin, but notice that the *D* in the column header is not centered over the visible portion of the column. This indicates that column D is wider than it appears.)

Figure 10.15 **The table, after inserting a fourth column**

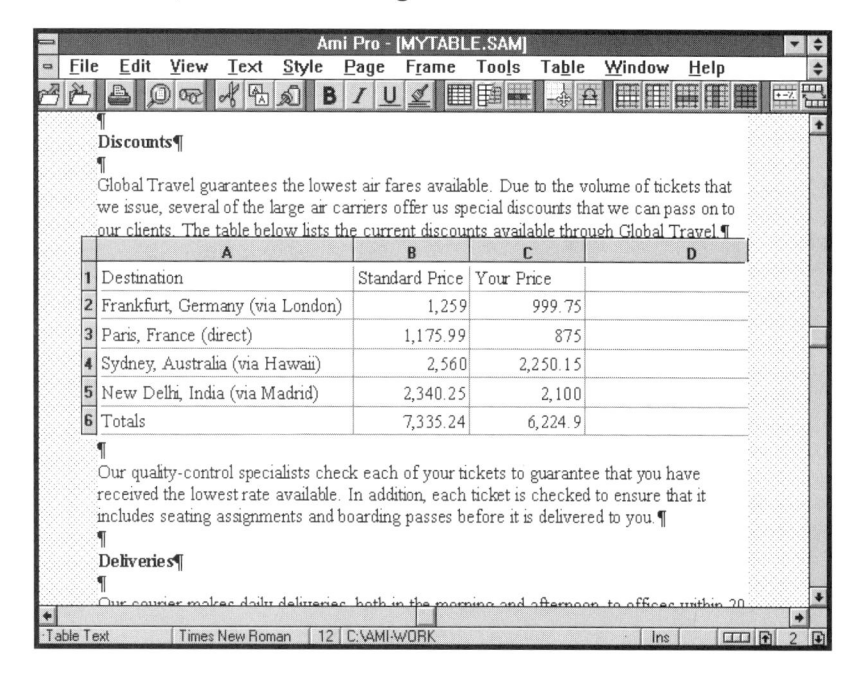

Now let's insert a couple of rows:

1. Move to anywhere in row 2.

2. Choose **Table, Insert Column/Row** to open the Insert Column/Row dialog box. Notice that this time, Ami Pro has selected *Insert Rows* and has dimmed *Insert Columns*. This is because there's no room to add another column to the table.

3. In the Number To Insert box, type **2**.

4. Select **Position Before**.

5. Verify that *Insert Rows* is selected, click on **OK**, and then observe the table. Row 2 has become row 4, and Ami Pro has added two rows above the original row 2.

Because we now have too many rows, let's delete one:

1. Move to anywhere in row 2, and then choose **Table, Delete Column/Row** to open the Delete Column/Row dialog box (see Figure 10.16).

Figure 10.16 **The Delete Column/Row dialog box**

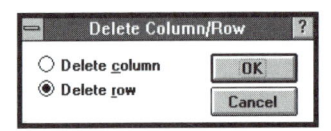

2. Verify that **Delete Row** is selected, and then click on **OK**. Ami Pro opens a dialog box that prompts:

    ```
    Deleting columns and rows in a table cannot
    be undone. Would you like to continue?
    ```

3. Click on **Yes** to close the dialog box and delete row 2. Notice that Ami Pro automatically renumbers the table's remaining rows.

PRACTICE YOUR SKILLS

1. Resize column D to be 1" wide.

2. Add the following text and numbers to the specified cells:

    Cell D1: **Savings**

    Cell D2: (leave blank)

    Cell D3: **295.25**

    Cell D4: **300.99**

    Cell D5: **309.85**

    Cell D6: **240.25**

MODIFYING A TABLE LAYOUT • 307

3. Use **Table, Quick Add, Column** to calculate a total for column D, to appear in cell D7.

4. Compare your table to Figure 10.17.

5. Save your document.

Figure 10.17 **The completed column D**

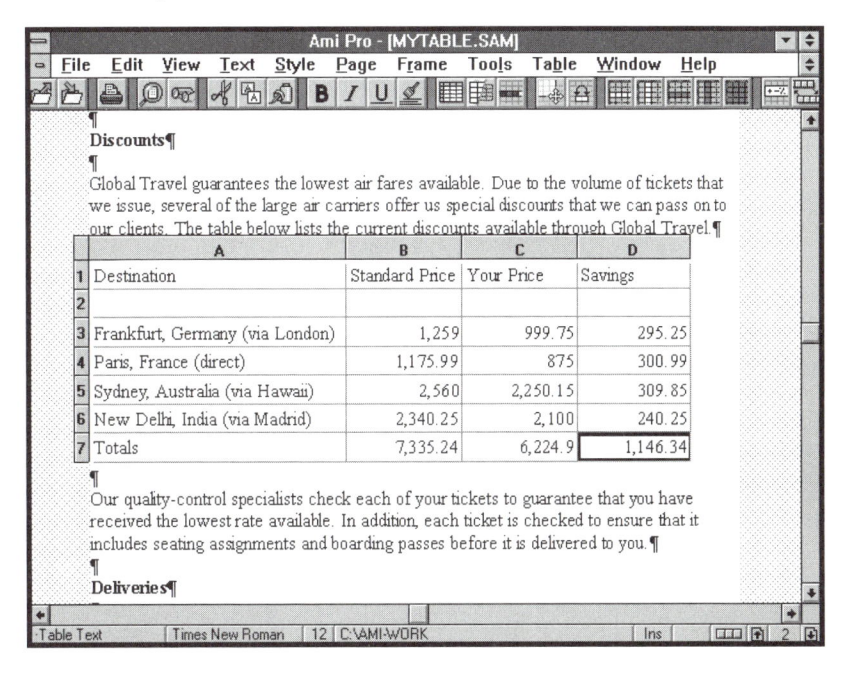

ADDING LINES TO SELECTED CELLS

You can enhance the appearance of tables by adding lines (and colors) to selected cells. You can add lines to any or all edges of a cell. Unlike table gridlines, the lines you add around cells do print. Be aware, however, that the table's gridlines can sometimes make lines difficult to see on screen. If this happens, use the View Preferences dialog box to turn off the gridlines.

Follow these steps when you want to add lines to selected cells:

- Select the cell(s) to which you want to add lines.

- Choose Table, Lines & Color or click on the *Modify Lines & Shades In A Table SmartIcon* (the 15th SmartIcon from the left in the Tables SmartIcon set, displaying a miniature table with multicolored cells) to open the Lines & Color dialog box.
- In the Line Position box, select the position for the lines: All, Left, Right, Top, Bottom, or Outline. (Line Position All adds lines to every edge of every selected cell; Line Position Outline adds a single line all the way around the selected cell range.)
- In the Line Style list box, select the desired line style.
- Click on OK.

Let's add some lines to your table now:

1. Observe the gridlines in your table. Ami Pro displays these gridlines on screen, but they do not print.
2. Open the View Preferences dialog box, uncheck **Table Gridlines**, and then click on **OK**. Ami Pro no longer displays the table gridlines.
3. Select row 1, and then choose **Table, Lines & Color** to open the Lines & Color dialog box (see Figure 10.18).
4. In the Line Position box, check **Line Position Bottom** to indicate that you want to add a line to the bottom edge of the selected cells.
5. In the Line Style box, select the third line style from the top.
6. Click on **OK**, and then observe the table. Ami Pro has placed a line along the bottom edge of every cell in row 1.
7. Select cells B7 through D7, and then click on the **Modify Lines & Shades In A Table SmartIcon** to open the Lines & Color dialog box.
8. Check **Line Position Top**, select the third line from the top in the Line Style box, and then click on **OK**. Ami Pro now displays a line above cells B7 through D7 (see Figure 10.19).

ADDING A LINE AROUND A TABLE

If you want to add a line around an entire table, one way to do it is to select the entire table, open the Lines and Color dialog box, select Line Position Outline, choose a line style, and then click on OK. However, if you later insert or delete rows or columns, you might

Figure 10.18   **The Lines & Color dialog box**

Modify Lines & Shades In A Table SmartIcon

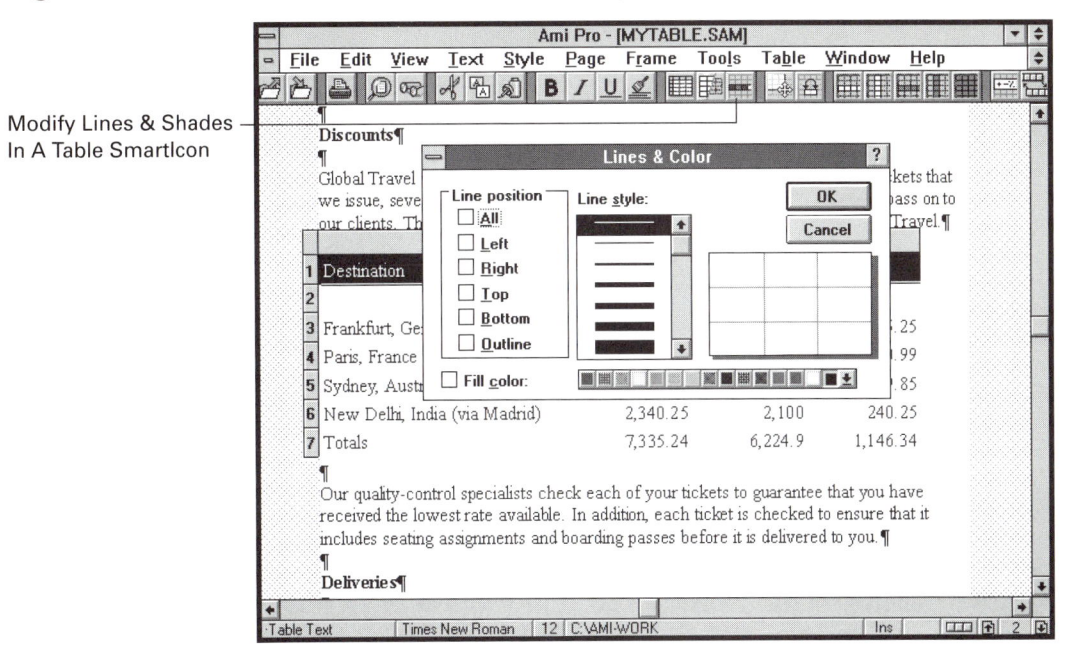

Figure 10.19   **The table, after adding lines to cells**

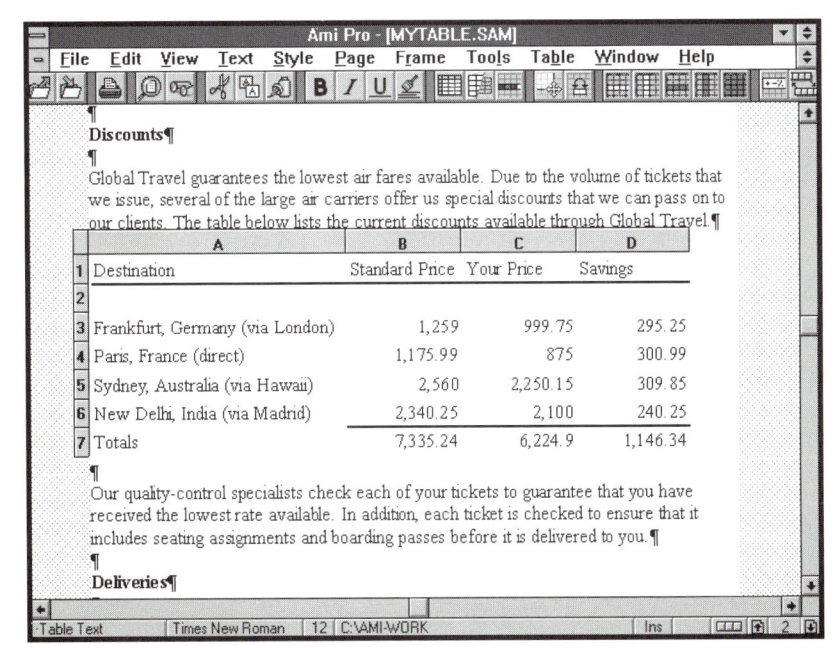

310 • **WORKING WITH TABLES**

get some undesirable results. Another alternative is to add a line around a table that will automatically adjust to any table modifications you make. To do this:

- Place the insertion point anywhere in the table.
- Choose Table, Modify Table Layout or click on the *Modify Table Layout SmartIcon* (the 14th SmartIcon from the left in the Tables SmartIcon set, displaying a diagonally split miniature table) to open the Modify Table Layout dialog box.
- Check Options Line Around Table.
- Click on OK.

Let's add a line around your table:

1. Choose **Table, Modify Table Layout** or click on the **Modify Table Layout SmartIcon** to open the Modify Table Layout dialog box (see Figure 10.20).

Figure 10.20 **The Modify Table Layout dialog box**

Modify Table Layout SmartIcon

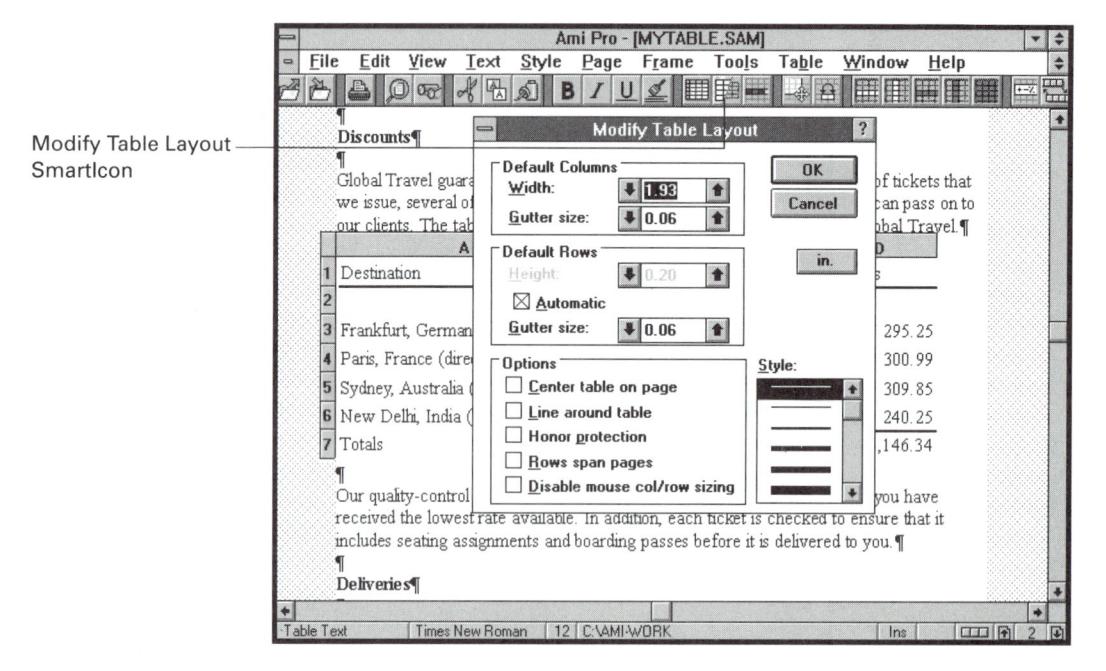

2. Check **Options Line Around Table**, and then click on **OK**.

3. Click outside the table, and then observe MYTABLE.SAM. Ami Pro has placed a thin line around the outside of the table.

CENTERING A TABLE

To enhance your table's appearance, you can center the table between the document's left and right margins. Follow these steps when you want to center a table:

- Place the insertion point anywhere in the table.
- Open the Modify Table Layout dialog box.
- Check Options Center Table On Page.
- Click on OK.

Let's center your table:

1. Click inside the table.

2. Open the Modify Table Layout dialog box (choose **Table, Modify Table Layout** or click on the **Modify Table Layout SmartIcon**).

3. In the Options box, check **Options Center Table On Page**, and then click on **OK**.

4. Click outside the table, and then observe your document. Ami Pro has centered the table between the left and right margins (see Figure 10.21).

5. Save MYTABLE.SAM.

CHANGING THE APPEARANCE OF TABLE CONTENTS

When you create a table in Ami Pro, Ami Pro automatically creates a Table Text style, and assigns that style to all of the text and numbers contained in that table.

To change the appearance of table contents, you can use any of these methods:

- Modify the Table Text style.
- Assign a different style to all cells or just selected cells.
- Apply text formatting and enhancements manually.

312 • WORKING WITH TABLES

Figure 10.21   **The table, centered**

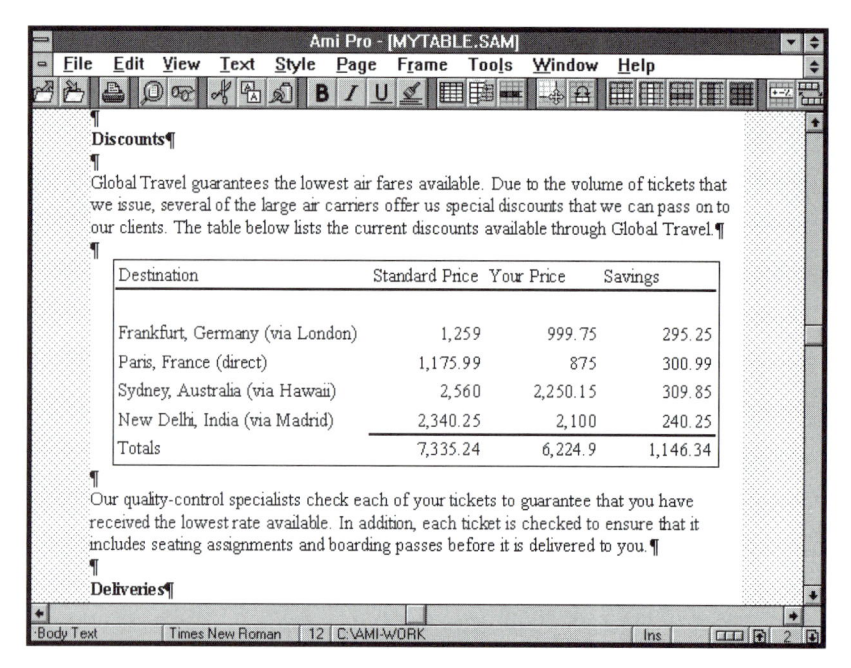

[Screenshot of Ami Pro - [MYTABLE.SAM] showing a document with the heading "Discounts" and a table of travel destinations with Standard Price, Your Price, and Savings columns:

Destination | Standard Price | Your Price | Savings
Frankfurt, Germany (via London) | 1,259 | 999.75 | 295.25
Paris, France (direct) | 1,175.99 | 875 | 300.99
Sydney, Australia (via Hawaii) | 2,560 | 2,250.15 | 309.85
New Delhi, India (via Madrid) | 2,340.25 | 2,100 | 240.25
Totals | 7,335.24 | 6,224.9 | 1,146.34]

APPLYING TEXT FORMATTING AND ENHANCEMENTS

You can apply text formatting and enhancements to the contents of a table just as you would apply them anywhere else in an Ami Pro document: Select the text or numbers, and then apply the formatting and enhancements.

Note: When you use paragraph alignment options in a table cell (left, right, center, or justified), Ami Pro aligns the text *within that cell*, and not according to indents or margins.

Let's apply some text formatting and enhancements to your table:

1. Select row 1.

2. Click on the **Bold Text SmartIcon** (or choose **Text, Bold**) to apply the Bold text attribute to all of the text in row 1. Notice that because boldface text generally is wider than normal text, Ami Pro needs to wrap *Standard Price* to two lines within cell B1.

3. Select **Totals** in cell A6, and then apply the Bold text attribute.

CHANGING THE APPEARANCE OF TABLE CONTENTS • 313

4. Select cells B1 through D1, and then choose **Text, Alignment, Right** to right-align the text within those cells.

MODIFYING THE TABLE TEXT STYLE

Through the Modify Style dialog box, you can modify the Table Text style as you would any other style. This dialog box provides a set of style elements applicable only to numbers within a table. These options were outlined earlier in this chapter under "Working with Numbers in a Table"; they help you to control how Ami Pro displays numbers within a table.

Follow these steps when you want to modify the style elements for table numbers:

- Open the Modify Style dialog box.
- Verify that the Table Text (or another appropriate) style is selected in the Style drop-down list box.
- Select Modify Table Format.
- Select the desired options.
- Click on OK.

Let's modify the Table Text style now to decrease the table contents' point size, and to format the table numbers as currency:

1. Click inside the table, and then observe the Style Status button. Ami Pro automatically assigns the Table Text style to the contents of every table cell.

2. Open the Modify Styles dialog box (choose **Style, Modify Style** or click over the table with the *right* mouse button). Then verify that *F12·Table Text* is selected in the Style drop-down list box.

3. Observe the right side of the dialog box. By default, Ami Pro sets the Table Text style's font to Times New Roman 12 point.

4. In the Size list box, select **10**, and then click on **OK**. Ami Pro reduces the size of all the table text.

5. Reopen the Modify Styles dialog box, verify that *F12·Table Text* is selected in the Style drop-down list box, and then select **Modify Table Format**.

314 • WORKING WITH TABLES

6. Examine the dialog box, which contains options that enable you to control the format of numbers within a table (see Figure 10.22).

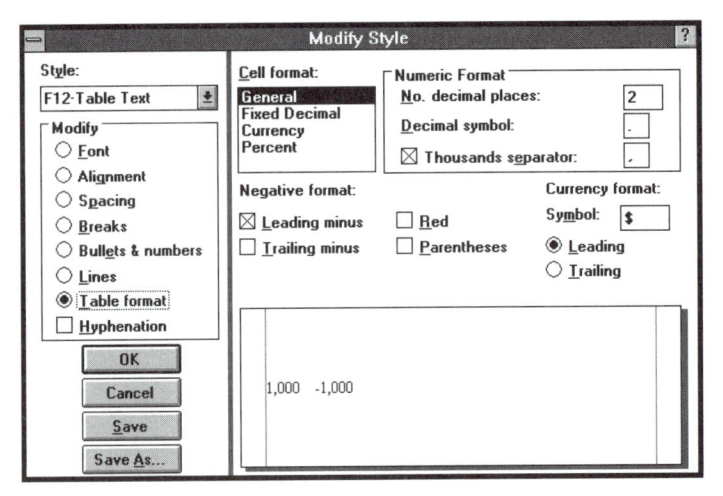

Figure 10.22   Viewing the Table Text style's Table Format elements

7. Observe the sample box in the dialog box's bottom-right corner. The sample numbers are formatted like the numbers in your table: They contain thousands separators, but have no currency symbols and only the necessary decimal places.

8. Observe the Cell Format list box. The current format is *General*, Ami Pro's default format.

9. In the Cell Format list box, select **Currency**. Notice that the samples now contain thousands separators, currency symbols, and two decimal places each.

10. Click on **OK**, and then look at your table numbers. Ami Pro has formatted them all as currency (see Figure 10.23).

Before we close MYTABLE.SAM, let's perform a little cleanup work so that Ami Pro's setup will be similar to the way it was when we started this chapter:

1. Open the View Preferences dialog box, check **Table Gridlines**, and then click on OK.

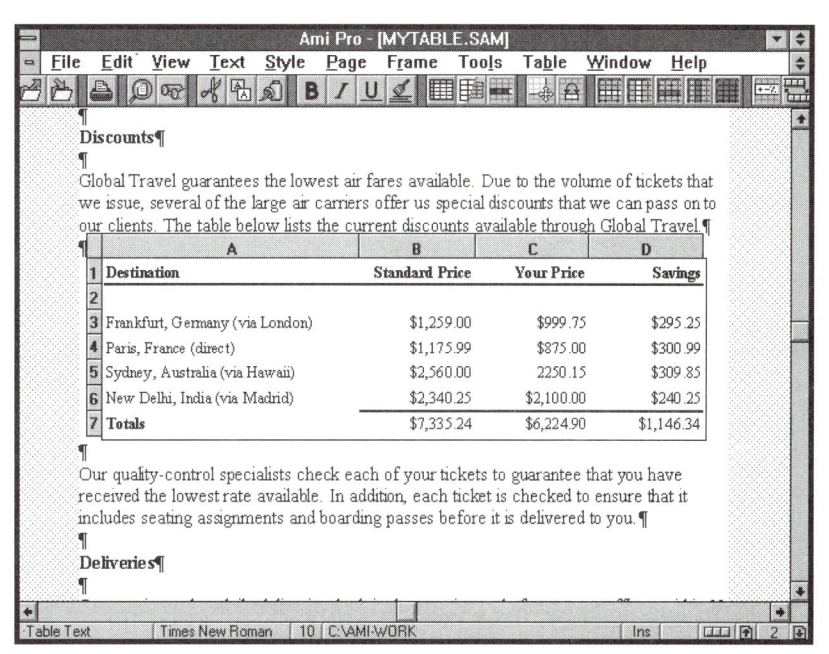

Figure 10.23 **The table, after modifying the Table Text style**

[Screenshot of Ami Pro - [MYTABLE.SAM] showing the following table content:]

Discounts¶

Global Travel guarantees the lowest air fares available. Due to the volume of tickets that we issue, several of the large air carriers offer us special discounts that we can pass on to our clients. The table below lists the current discounts available through Global Travel.¶

	A	B	C	D
1	Destination	Standard Price	Your Price	Savings
2				
3	Frankfurt, Germany (via London)	$1,259.00	$999.75	$295.25
4	Paris, France (direct)	$1,175.99	$875.00	$300.99
5	Sydney, Australia (via Hawaii)	$2,560.00	2250.15	$309.85
6	New Delhi, India (via Madrid)	$2,340.25	$2,100.00	$240.25
7	Totals	$7,335.24	$6,224.90	$1,146.34

Our quality-control specialists check each of your tickets to guarantee that you have received the lowest rate available. In addition, each ticket is checked to ensure that it includes seating assignments and boarding passes before it is delivered to you.¶

Deliveries¶

2. Redisplay the **Default** SmartIcon set.
3. Save and close **MYTABLE.SAM**.

PRACTICE YOUR SKILLS

In this chapter, you learned how to create and use tables to arrange information neatly in rows and columns, to add columns of numbers within a table, and to modify table layouts and the appearance of text and numbers within tables. The following two "Practice Your Skills" activities give you the opportunity to practice some of these techniques. After each activity step, we've provided a chapter reference (in parentheses) to inform you of where we introduced the relevant technique for that step.

Note: If you'd like to use the SmartIcons in the Tables SmartIcon set to complete these activities, feel free to do so. When you are finished, please redisplay the Default SmartIcon set.

Follow these steps to produce the final document shown in Figure 10.24 from the original PRAC10A.SAM document.

1. Open **prac10a.sam**. (Chapter 2)
2. Scroll to the bottom of the document, and then type the following information into the Projected Quarterly Sales table. (Chapter 10)

	Column A:	*Column B:*	*Column C:*
Row 3:	**Trader Tom's**	2300	1.49
Row 4:	**Aunt Emily's Market**	4900	1.29
Row 5:	**Hamlet Farms**	6500	1.09

3. Delete row 6 (the row for *Price Farms Co.*). (Chapter 10)
4. Right-align the contents of cells B1 and C1. (Chapter 10)
5. Apply the Bold text attribute to the contents of every cell in row 1. (Chapter 10)
6. Change the width for column B to 1". (Chapter 10)
7. Change the width for column C to 1¼". (Chapter 10)
8. In cell B9, use Quick Add to total column B. (Chapter 10)
9. Center the table on the page. (Chapter 10)
10. Modify the Table Text style to format the table's numbers as currency. (Chapter 10)
11. Save your document as **myprc10a**.
12. Print the document, and then compare it to Figure 10.24.
13. Close the document.

Follow these steps to produce the final document shown in Figure 10.25 from the original PRAC10B.SAM document:

1. Open **prac10b.sam**. (Chapter 2)
2. Move to the end of the document, and then create a table that contains three columns and seven rows. (Chapter 10)

Figure 10.24   MYPRC10A.SAM

The Garden Patch
Product Line Announcement

Introduction

The Garden Patch is pleased to announce the unveiling of a new food line in the Garden Patch series: the Fruit Patch. The Fruit Patch product line was developed after two years of intense work through the cooperation and dedication of Dr. Faye Shad and her staff. The FDA recently approved the food and it will be released for public sale in three weeks.

The Fruit Patch includes a variety of organically-grown fruit: berries (cherries, strawberries, raspberries, blackberries, and blueberries), apricots, peaches, grapes, and plums.

Projected Quarterly Sales

Our finance department has been hard at work, determining sales projections for the next quarter. The results are shown in the following table.

Projected Quarterly Sales

Vendors	Boxes Sold	Profit (per box)
Trader Tom's	2300	1.49
Aunt Emily's Market	4900	1.29
Hamlet Farms	6500	1.09
B and J's	10000	0.79
Hout and Wallace Inc.	11500	0.79
Total	35200	

Figure 10.25   **MYPRC10B.SAM**

The Garden Patch
Product Line Announcement

Introduction

The Garden Patch is pleased to announce the unveiling of a new food line in the Garden Patch series: the Fruit Patch. The Fruit Patch product line was developed after two years of intense work through the cooperation and dedication of Dr. Faye Shad and her staff. The FDA recently approved the food and it will be released for public sale in three weeks.

The Fruit Patch includes a variety of organically-grown fruit: berries (cherries, strawberries, raspberries, blackberries, and blueberries), apricots, peaches, grapes, and plums.

Projected Quarterly Sales

Our finance department has been hard at work, determining sales projections for the next quarter. The results are shown in the following table.

Projected Quarterly Sales Table

Vendors	Boxes Sold	Total Profit
Trader Tom's	2,300.00	$3,427.37
Aunt Emily's Market	4,600.00	$6,321.25
Hamlet Farms	6,500.00	$7,085.98
Totals	13400	$16,834.60

3. Type the following information into your table. (Chapter 10)

	Column A:	Column B:	Column C:
Row 1:	**Vendors**	**Boxes Sold**	**Total Profit**
Row 2:	(leave entire row blank)		
Row 3:	**Trader Tom's**	2300	3427.37
Row 4:	**Aunt Emily's Market**	4900	6321.25
Row 5:	**Hamlet Farms**	6500	7085.98
Row 6:	(leave entire row blank)		
Row 7:	**Totals**	(leave cell blank)	(leave cell blank)

4. In cells B7 and C7, use Quick Add to calculate the total for columns B and C. (Chapter 10)

5. Change the number in cell B4 from 4900 to **4600**. Then move from the cell, and watch the total in cell B7 recalculate. (Chapter 10)

6. Right-align the contents of cells B1 and C1. (Chapter 10)

7. Decrease the width of columns B and C to 1½" each. (Chapter 10)

8. Add a line to the bottom of row 1, using the fourth line style from the top of the Line Style list box. (Chapter 10)

9. Add a line above cells B7 and C7, using the third line style from the top of the Line Style list box. (Chapter 10)

10. Center and place a line around the table. (Chapter 10)

11. Create a new style, **Table Text 2**, based on the Table Text style, and then change the new style's table format to **Currency**. (Chapters 9 and 10)

12. Apply the **Table Text 2** style to column C. (Chapter 9)

13. Save your document as **myprc10b**. (Chapter 1)

320 • WORKING WITH TABLES

14. Print MYPRC10B.SAM, and then compare it to Figure 10.25. (Chapter 1)

15. Close the document. (Chapter 1)

SUMMARY

In this chapter, you learned how to create, move in, and enter text into tables; how to enter numbers into tables and use Quick Add to total columns of numbers; how to modify a table's layout by changing column widths, adding lines, and centering the table; and how to change the appearance of text and numbers contained within tables.

Here is a quick reference guide to the Ami Pro features introduced in this chapter:

Desired Result	How to Do It
Create a table	Choose **Tools, Tables**; specify number of columns and rows; and then click on **OK**.
Display or hide table gridlines	Open View Preferences dialog box; check or uncheck **Table Gridlines**; then click on **OK**.
Display or hide row and column headings	Open View Preferences dialog box; check or uncheck **Table Row/Column Headings**; then click on **OK**.
Move directly to any cell	Click in the cell.
Move one cell to the right	Press **Tab**.
Move one cell to the left	Press **Shift+Tab**.
Move up one cell	Press **Ctrl+Up Arrow**.
Move down one cell	Press **Ctrl+Down Arrow**.
Enter text in a table	Move to cell, and then type text.
Enter numbers in a table	Move to cell, and then type numbers and decimal points only.

Desired Result	How to Do It
Total a row or column	Move to any cell in column or row; then choose **Table, Quick Add, Column** or **Table, Quick Add, Row**.
Select a table row	Move to the row; then choose **Table, Select Row**. Or position I-beam on left end of row until horizontal arrow appears; then click.
Select a table column	Move to the column; then choose **Table, Select Column**. Or position I-beam on top of row until vertical arrow appears; then click.
Select a range of cells	Drag over the cells.
Select multiple rows	Point to the left edge of one row, and then drag.
Select multiple columns	Point to the left edge of one column, and then drag.
Select entire table	Choose **Table, Select Entire Table**. Or drag to select all rows or all columns.
Change column width with mouse	Position I-beam over vertical gridline to right of column until four-headed arrow appears; then drag.
Change column widths with Table menu	Select columns; choose **Table, Column/Row Size** or click on **Size Columns And Rows In A Table SmartIcon**; type new width in Column Widths box; then click on **OK**.
Insert columns or rows	Place insertion point in adjacent column/row, choose **Table, Insert Column/Row**; select **Insert Columns** or **Insert Rows**; in Number To Insert Box, specify number of columns/rows to insert; select **Position Before** or **Position After**; then click on **OK**.

322 • WORKING WITH TABLES

Desired Result	How to Do It
Delete columns or rows	Place insertion point in or select columns/rows; choose **Table, Delete Column/Row**; select **Delete Column** or **Delete Row**; click on **OK**; then click on **Yes**.
Add lines to cells	Select cells; choose **Table, Lines & Color** or click on **Modify Lines & Shades In A Table SmartIcon**; select desired Line Position option and line style; then click on **OK**.
Open Modify Table Layout dialog box	Choose **Table, Modify Table Layout** or click on **Modify Table Layout SmartIcon**.
Add line around table	Open Modify Table Layout dialog box; check **Options Line Around Table**; then click on **OK**.
Center a table	Open Modify Table Layout dialog box; check **Options Center Table On Page**; then click on **OK**.
Change appearance of table contents	Select contents; then apply text formatting and enhancements. Or modify Table Text style. Or apply a different style.
Format table numbers as currency	Open Modify Style dialog box; select style assigned to table numbers from Style drop-down list box; select **Modify Table Format**; select **Currency** in Cell Format list box; then click on **OK**.

In Chapter 11, you'll learn how to use Ami Pro to create form letters, labels, and envelopes.

IF YOU'RE STOPPING HERE

If you need to take a break here, please exit Ami Pro. If you want to proceed directly to the next chapter, please do so now.

CHAPTER 11: FORM LETTERS, LABELS, AND ENVELOPES

The Components of a Merge Operation

Creating Form Letters

Creating Mailing Labels

Creating an Envelope

In Ami Pro, *merging* (also known as *mail-merging*) is the process of combining information from two different documents to create customized printed documents. For example, you can merge a generic form letter together with a mailing list to produce a personalized form letter for each person on the list (just as the people who send you those $1,000,000 contest announcement letters do). Merging helps you avoid the tedium of manually generating many personalized letters. Other common uses for merging include creating mailing labels and personalizing interoffice memos and reports.

Ami Pro's File, Merge command helps to take you step by step through the merging process. This command will also help you organize your mailing lists and other such information, by enabling you to sort your information, say, by zip code.

For simple addressing when you're sending out a single letter, Ami Pro also enables you to print a single envelope based on the letter's inside address.

When you're done working through this chapter, you will know how to

- Create and edit the two component documents of a merge
- Use merging to generate form letters
- Sort merge data
- Use merging to generate mailing labels
- Create a single envelope

THE COMPONENTS OF A MERGE OPERATION

Before using Ami Pro's Print, Merge command, you should be familiar with the three components of the merge process: the *merge data file*, the *merge document*, and the *merged documents*. Figure 11.1 illustrates how these three components work together.

THE MERGE DATA FILE

The *merge data file* contains the variable information (you can use the terms *information* and *data* interchangeably) with which you will personalize the merged documents. Very often, a merge data file contains a list of names and addresses. Every merge data file contains three vital elements:

- *Fields*, which are categories of data. For example, you might put everyone's first name in a first-name field and everyone's last name in a last-name field.

- *Field names*, which identify each field. For example, you might use the field name First Name to identify the first-name field.

- *Records*, each of which contains a complete set of fields for a person or other subject. For example, one record in a name-and-address merge data file might contain one person's first name, last name, company name, street address, city, state, and zip code.

If you use the File, Merge command to create and edit your merge data files, Ami Pro enables you to work with your merge data on electronic index cards, which look very much like the rotary cardfiles that many of us use to organize our name-and-address data.

Figure 11.1 **The components of a merge**

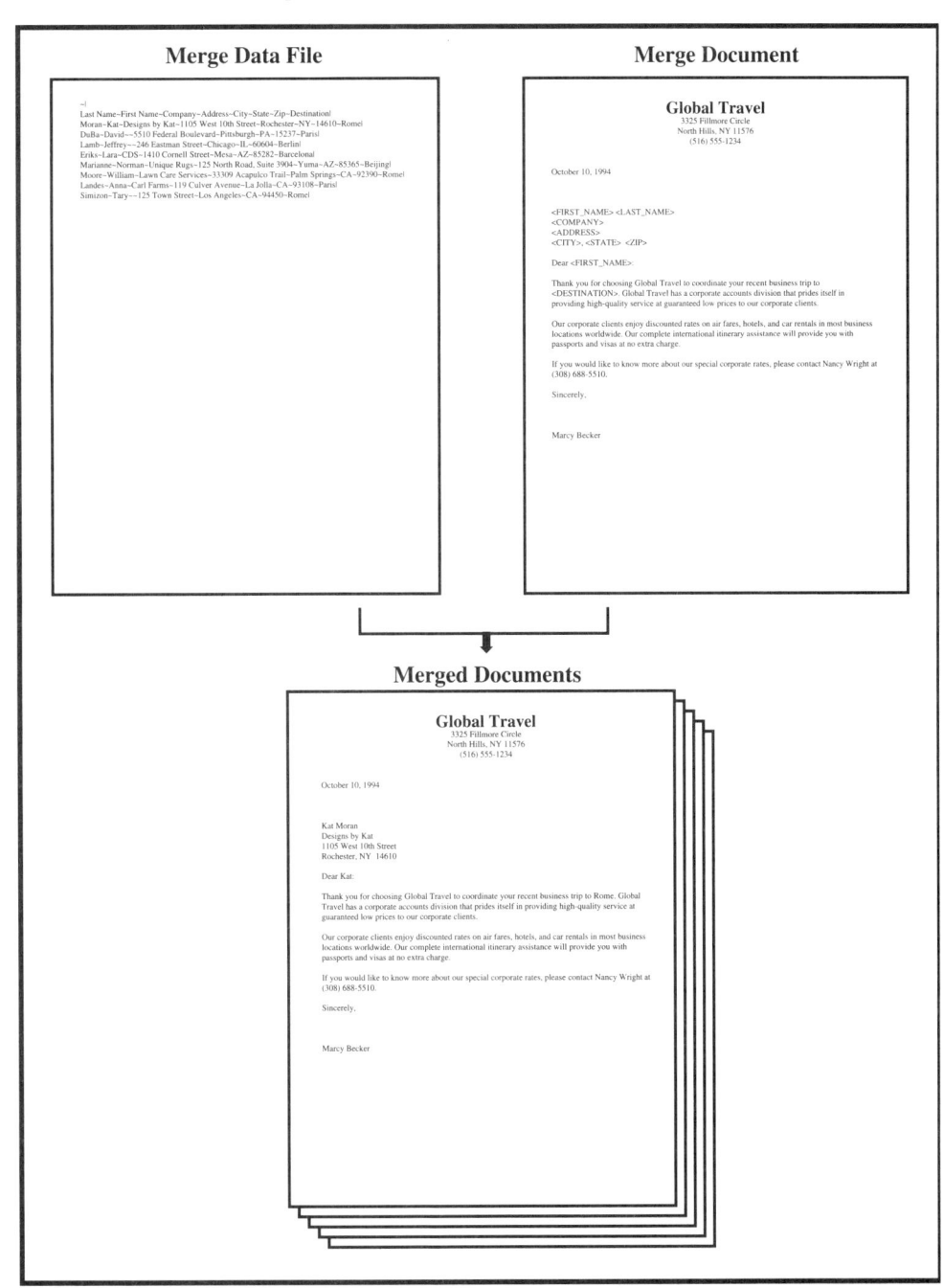

For each record in your merge data file, Ami Pro displays a corresponding index card that contains the data for every field in that record.

Like their paper-based counterparts, these electronic index cards even come complete with *tab dividers* that stick up from the top of each card to help you identify it when it is behind other cards. For example, a tab divider for Igor Bonski's card might say *Bonski*.

Besides using merge data files created through File, Merge, you can also use the following as merge data files:

- Ami Pro documents that contain tables
- Files created by database and spreadsheet applications, such as 1-2-3 for Windows or dBase
- Documents created in other word processing applications, such as Word for Windows or WordPerfect

In this chapter, we'll show you how to use File, Merge to create and edit merge data files. For information on using other types of merge data files, see your Ami Pro documentation.

THE MERGE DOCUMENT

The *merge document* contains the *standardized* (nonvariable) data in a merge, as well as *merge fields* that serve as placeholders for the variable data stored in the merge data file.

Merge documents for form letters can look a lot like fill-in-the-blanks forms, and Ami Pro essentially uses them that way. For example, a merge document for a form letter might start out like this:

    Dear <FIRST_NAME>:

In this example, *Dear*, the space following *Dear*, and the colon following *<FIRST_NAME>* are all standardized text; they'll print on every merged document, regardless of the data contained in the merge data file. *<FIRST_NAME>*, on the other hand, is a merge field that Ami Pro will see as a "blank" to be filled in; when merging, Ami Pro will look in the merge data file to find the personalized data to replace this merge field. After merging, the above example might print out as:

Dear Carol:

or

> Dear Michael:

By default, Ami Pro prints one personalized merged document for every record in a merge data file.

THE MERGED DOCUMENTS

When performing a merge, you can send the resulting merged documents directly to the printer, pause to view each merged document before printing, or save all the merged documents together on disk as a single Ami Pro document.

Tip: Because you usually can re-create your merged documents by performing another merge, you should in most cases avoid saving your merged documents. By not saving merged documents on disk, you save disk space and help ensure that the data in your merged documents is as current as possible.

CREATING FORM LETTERS

Producing form letters is one of the most common uses for merging. In this next section, we'll use form letters to show you the three steps of a merge:

- Creating and/or editing the merge data file
- Creating and/or editing the merge document
- Performing the merge

The File, Merge command opens the Welcome To Merge dialog box, which serves as a control center for your merge operations. You can issue the File, Merge command at any point in a merge operation; if your active document is a merge data file or a merge document, however, Ami Pro will sense this and might provide merge options customized to that current document. As we perform merges throughout this chapter, we'll return time and again to the Welcome To Merge dialog box to determine and then carry out the next step in the merging process.

Note: The File, Merge command is designed to take you through merging in one continuous procedure, but the aim of this section is to stop periodically and closely examine merge components and options along the way. As you work through the activities, it may seem that Ami Pro is making some poor guesses on how to proceed. Once you've learned the merge process in its entirety, however, you will find that File, Merge works very well in carrying you smoothly through the entire merge process.

CREATING A MERGE DATA FILE

Follow these steps when you want to use File, Merge to create a merge data file:

- Choose File, Merge to open the Welcome To Merge dialog box.

- Select the Select, Create Or Edit A Data File option (if necessary).

- Click on OK to open the Select Merge Data File dialog box.

- Click on New to create a new document and open the Create Data File dialog box.

- In the Field Name text box, type a field name, and then click on Add. Field names can contain letters, numbers, spaces, and many special characters; however, field names cannot *begin* with numbers, nor can they consist *only* of numbers. (Common field names include First Name, Last Name, Company, Address, City, State, and Zip.) Repeat this step as necessary, until you've named every field you think you'll need in your merge data file.

- Click on OK. Ami Pro will add the field names you specified to the merge data file, and then open a Data File dialog box, which displays blank electronic index cards so that you can start entering records.

- On the first blank card, type all the data for one record, and then click on Add. Ami Pro will add the data you typed to the merge data file, and then automatically display a new, blank card. Repeat this step as necessary until you have entered all of your records.

- Click on Close to close the dialog box and the merge data file. Ami Pro will prompt you to name and save the merge data file before closing it.

- Click on Yes to open the Save As dialog box. Then specify a name for the document and click on OK. Ami Pro will open the New dialog box to help you start creating your merge document.

- If you want to continue on to the next merge operation step and start working with a merge document, click on OK to create a new document; Ami Pro will automatically return you to the Welcome To Merge dialog box. Otherwise, click on Cancel.

As you work with the electronic index cards in the Data File dialog box, Ami Pro translates your field names and records into a *delimited* format, and places them in the document window behind the dialog box. Delimited is just a fancy way of saying that Ami Pro uses special characters to mark the ends of field names, fields within records, and records. By default, Ami Pro uses a *tilde* (~) as a *field delimiter* to mark the end of each field name and each field within a record, and a *vertical bar* (|) as a *record delimiter* to mark the end of each record.

For the most part, you don't have to worry about delimited formats and delimiters, because you can use File, Merge to translate the delimited format into the easier-to-use electronic index cards. However, since you often can see Ami Pro using the delimited format behind the Data File dialog box, it's good to know at least a little about what's happening back there. Also, as you'll see in the next activity, it's important sometimes to be able to recognize a merge data file when you see one.

Note: Because entering data for multiple records can be time consuming, in this next activity we'll only ask you to name fields and then enter one record—just so you can see how it's done. In the activity following this one, we'll have you open a merge data file that we provided on this book's Data Disk; this merge data file will mirror the file you'll be creating here, but it will contain more records.

If you are not running Ami Pro, please start it now. Let's create a merge data file:

1. Choose **File, Merge**, and then examine the Welcome To Merge dialog box (see Figure 11.2). This dialog box will guide you through the three steps of merging.

Figure 11.2 **The Welcome To Merge dialog box**

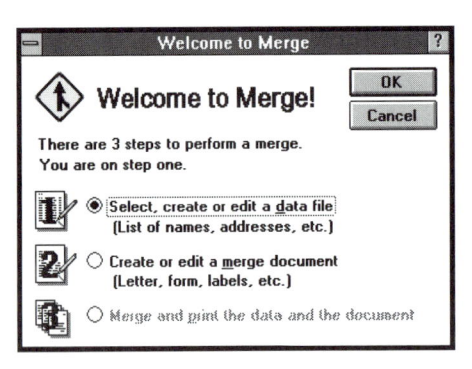

2. Verify that *Select, Create Or Edit A Data File* is selected, and then click on **OK**. Ami Pro opens the Select Merge Data File dialog box, enabling you to select or edit an existing merge data file, or to create a new one (see Figure 11.3).

Figure 11.3 **The Select Merge Data File dialog box**

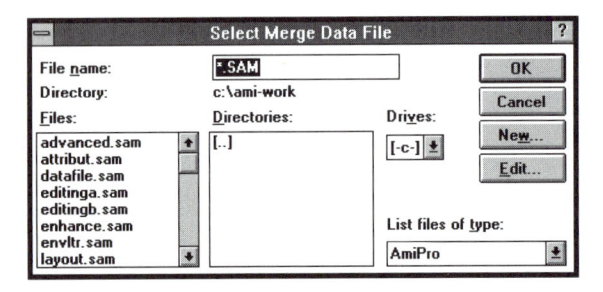

3. Click on **New** to indicate that you want to create a new merge data file. Ami Pro creates a new document (if you don't already have an untitled document open), and then opens the Create Data File dialog box, where you will provide field names for your data file.

4. In the Field Name text box, type **Last Name**, and then click on **Add**. Ami Pro adds *Last Name* to the Fields In Data File

list box, and leaves the insertion point in the Field Name text box, ready for you to type another field name.

5. Type the following field names in the Field Name text box, clicking on **Add** after entering each name:

   First Name

   Company

   Address

   City

   State

   Zip

   Destination

6. Observe the Fields In Data File list box. It should now list the eight field names you added (see Figure 11.4).

Figure 11.4 **Naming fields**

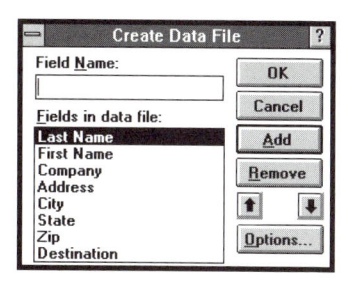

7. Click on **OK**. In the document window, Ami Pro adds the field names you specified, ending each field name with a tilde and each line with a vertical bar. When Ami Pro is finished, it opens the Data File - [Untitled] dialog box, which displays your field names along with corresponding text boxes on an electronic index card. This card enables you to enter all the data for one data record (see Figure 11.5).

Figure 11.5   **Electronic index cards**

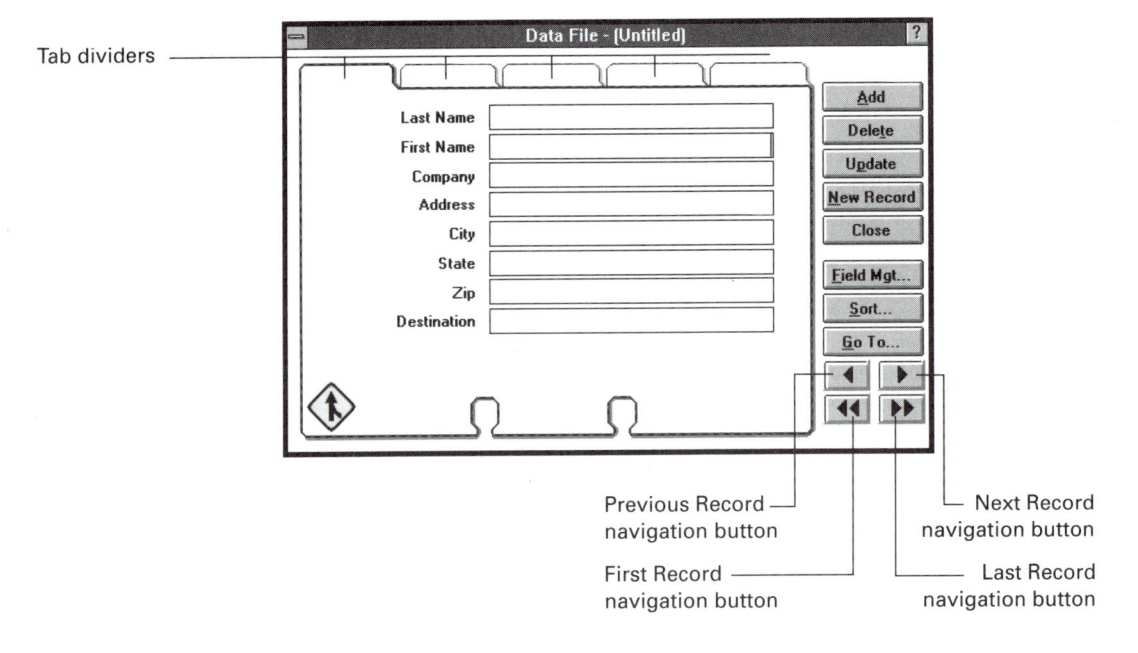

Tab dividers

Previous Record navigation button

Next Record navigation button

First Record navigation button

Last Record navigation button

8. Enter the following data to fill in the index card fields:

   Last Name: **Moran**

   First Name: **Kat**

   Company: **Designs by Kat**

   Address: **1105 West 10th Street**

   City: **Rochester**

   State: **NY**

   Zip: **14610**

   Destination: **Rome**

9. Click on **Add** to add your typed data as a record in your data file. In the document window behind the dialog box, Ami Pro adds a line for Kat Moran's record. Inside the dialog box, Ami Pro moves the card back one in the "stack" (notice that

Moran appears on the tab divider sticking up from the second card), and displays a new, blank card.

10. Rather than type in a lot of records, let's stop here. Click on **Close**. Ami Pro prompts:

    Save [Untitled]?

11. Click on **Yes** to open the Save As dialog box, type **mydata1** in the File Name text box, and then click on **OK**.

12. Ami Pro opens the New dialog box, assuming that you want to create your merge document. Since we'll be opening an existing merge document in the next activity, click on **Cancel**.

EDITING AN EXISTING MERGE DATA FILE

Once you've created a merge data file, you'll probably need to edit it at some point. You can open a delimited merge data file through File, Merge, and Ami Pro will automatically translate the delimited format into electronic index cards and display those cards in a Data File dialog box. Or you can open a delimited merge data file through File, Open or using the Open An Existing File SmartIcon; you will then need to use File, Merge to instruct Ami Pro to translate your data to index cards.

Note: If you prefer, you can also edit the merge data file's delimited text directly, though you might find it more difficult to keep track of your data.

Follow these steps when you want to open and translate a delimited merge data file through File, Merge:

- Choose File, Merge.
- Make sure that the Select, Create Or Edit A Data File option is selected, and then click on OK. Ami Pro opens the Select Merge Data File dialog box.
- Specify the appropriate drive and directory, if necessary.
- In the Files list box, select the merge data file's name.
- Click on Edit.

Follow these steps when you want to translate a delimited merge data file that is already open:

- Choose File, Merge.

- If necessary, select Edit The Data File. (The Edit The Data File option has replaced the Select, Create Or Edit A Data File option, because Ami Pro recognizes that you already have a merge data file open and adjusts the dialog box's first option to fit the situation.)
- Click on OK.

Once you've opened a delimited merge data file and translated the records into electronic index cards, you can use the Data File dialog box to edit your records. Ami Pro automatically displays the first record in your merge data file; to view other records, use one of these three methods:

- Use the tab dividers that stick up from the top of each card and are visible for the first five cards displayed. To move to a card whose tab divider is visible, click on the card's tab divider.
- Use the Go To button, which opens the Go To Record dialog box. You can use this dialog box much as you did the Find & Replace dialog box you learned about in Chapter 2, to move to a record that contains specific information. For example, you might want to move to the next record where the Last Name field is *Bonski*. You can also use the Go To Record dialog box to move to the merge data file's first or last record.
- Use the *navigation buttons*, which enable you to move to the first, last, previous, or next record. The *Previous Record navigation button* displays a single left-pointing triangle, the *Next Record navigation button* displays a single right-pointing triangle, the *First Record navigation button* displays two left-pointing triangles, and the *Next Record navigation button* displays two right-pointing triangles. (Refer back to Figure 11.5 for the locations of these buttons.)

Once you've displayed the record you want to edit, you can directly edit the data in any or all fields. Then click on the Update button to apply your changes to the merge data file, or the Add button to add your edited record as a new record to the merge data file.

If you want to delete the current record, click on the Delete button. Or, to enter a brand-new new record, click on the New Record button to display a new, blank card, enter the appropriate data, and then click on Update.

Once you've finished adding and editing records, click on Close to close the Data File dialog box and the merge data file. Ami Pro will prompt you to save your changes; click on Yes to do so. Because you used the File, Merge command, Ami Pro will then assume that you want to work with a merge document. To create a new merge document and return to the Welcome To Merge dialog box, click on OK; otherwise, click on Cancel.

As you'll see at the end of this next activity, after you edit records through the Data File dialog box, Ami Pro does not provide any opportunity for you to use File, Save As to save your edited merge data file with a new name. This is usually not a problem, because it usually makes little sense to maintain two copies of very similar merge data files. However, when you want to preserve your unedited merge data file and save your edited merge data file with a new name, follow these steps:

- Open the merge data file through File, Open or using the Open An Existing File SmartIcon.

- Save the document with a new name.

- *Then* use File, Merge to translate the records to electronic index cards.

We want you to preserve the merge data file we provided on this book's Data Disk, so we'll have you use the foregoing procedure in this next activity. Let's open and edit an existing merge data file:

1. Open and examine **datafile.sam**. This is how the data file you created in the last activity might look after you entered more records. Because Ami Pro does not automatically open a Data File dialog box to let you view your records on electronic index cards, the data is somewhat difficult to read (see Figure 11.6).

2. Save the document as **mydata2**.

3. Choose **File, Merge** to open the Welcome To Merge dialog box. Ami Pro recognizes that you already have a merge data file open, and offers you the choice of editing the merge data file or of moving on to creating or editing a merge document.

4. Verify that *Edit The Data File* is selected, and then click on **OK**. Ami Pro shrinks the document window, reads the data in MYDATA2.SAM, and then opens the Data File - MYDATA2.SAM dialog box to display the file's records on electronic index cards.

Figure 11.6 **Delimited data**

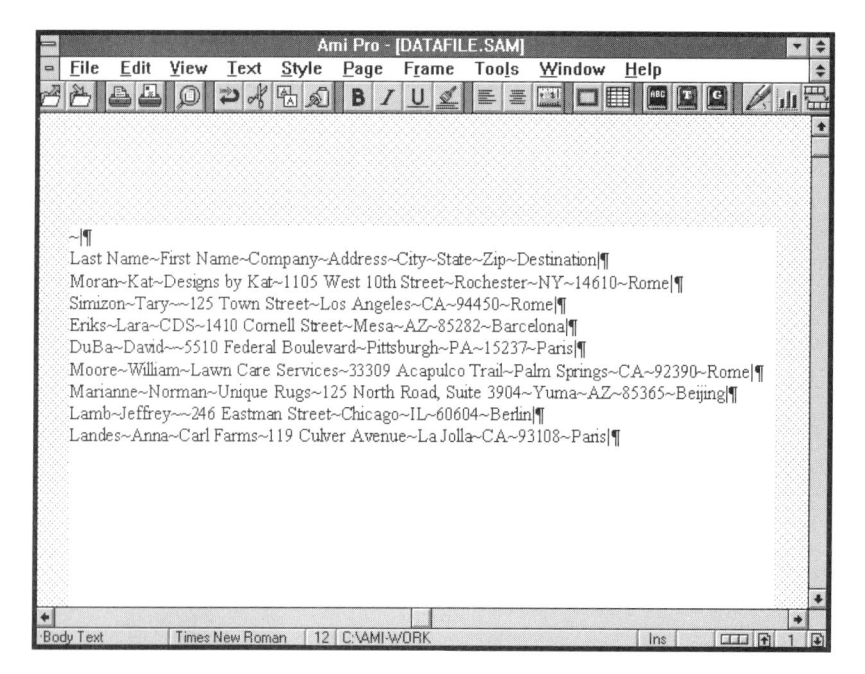

```
~|¶
Last Name~First Name~Company~Address~City~State~Zip~Destination|¶
Moran~Kat~Designs by Kat~1105 West 10th Street~Rochester~NY~14610~Rome|¶
Simizon~Tary~~125 Town Street~Los Angeles~CA~94450~Rome|¶
Eriks~Lara~CDS~1410 Cornell Street~Mesa~AZ~85282~Barcelona|¶
DuBa~David~~5510 Federal Boulevard~Pittsburgh~PA~15237~Paris|¶
Moore~William~Lawn Care Services~33309 Acapulco Trail~Palm Springs~CA~92390~Rome|¶
Marianne~Norman~Unique Rugs~125 North Road, Suite 3904~Yuma~AZ~85365~Beijing|¶
Lamb~Jeffrey~~246 Eastman Street~Chicago~IL~60604~Berlin|¶
Landes~Anna~Carl Farms~119 Culver Avenue~La Jolla~CA~93108~Paris|¶
```

5. Observe the navigation buttons in the dialog box's lower-right corner. You can use these to move to the previous, next, first, or last record in your data file (these buttons are labeled in Figure 11.5).

6. Click on the **Next Record navigation button** to display the next card: Tary Simizon's record. Notice that Tary's Company field is blank. Later in this chapter, we'll see how Ami Pro manages blank fields when merging files.

7. Click on the **Next Record navigation button** six more times, pausing between each click to view each of the records in MYDATA2.SAM. Notice that some of the other records, too, have blank Company fields.

8. When you reach the last record (Anna Landes's record), click on **New Record** to display a new, blank card.

9. On the new card, type in your own data; for the Destination field, type **Auckland**.

10. Click on **Add** to add your record to the merge data file. Ami Pro displays another blank card.

11. Click on **Close** to close the dialog box and the merge data file. Ami Pro prompts:

    ```
    MYDATA2.SAM has changed. Save changes?
    ```

12. Click on **Yes**. Once again, Ami Pro opens the New dialog box, assuming that you want to create a new merge document.

13. Click on **Cancel** to close the dialog box without creating a new document.

EDITING A MERGE DOCUMENT

Step two of a merge operation is creating and editing the merge document. To create a merge document, you can take any normal Ami Pro document, assign a merge data file to the document, and then insert merge fields from that merge data file.

When you work through File, Merge to create or open your merge documents, Ami Pro automatically asks you to assign a merge data file through the Select Merge Data File dialog box. Then Ami Pro automatically displays an Insert Merge Field dialog box, which lists all the available field names from the assigned merge data file. If, however, you create or open a merge document (or an intended merge document) through File, Open or using the Open An Existing File SmartIcon, you need to do at least some of this work manually. Follow these steps when you want to manually open the Insert Merge Field dialog box (that is, without using File, Merge) and assign a merge data file:

- From within the merge document (or intended merge document), choose Edit, Insert, Merge Field to open the Insert Merge Field dialog box.

- If the Insert Merge Field dialog box lists no field names, or if there is already a merge data file assigned to the merge document and you want to assign a different merge data file, click on Data File to open the Select Merge Data File dialog box. Then select the desired merge data file and click on OK. (Or, simply double-click on the merge data file's name.)

Once the Insert Merge Field dialog box is open, you are ready to insert merge fields into your merge document. This dialog box works somewhat differently from many Ami Pro dialog boxes: It stays on screen so that you can move freely between the document window and the dialog box.

Note: Regardless of how you typed field names in your merge data file, field names are displayed all in uppercase in the Insert Merge Field dialog box and in the merge document. In addition, spaces within field names are replaced with underscores. For example, if you have a field named First Name, Ami Pro will display the field name as FIRST_NAME. When you merge, however, Ami Pro inserts the variable data for each field exactly as you typed that data in your merge data file.

Follow these steps when you want to insert a merge field:

- Place the insertion point where you want to insert the merge field.

- Select the desired field name in the dialog box's Field Names list box, and then click on Insert. Or, simply double-click on the field name.

- Repeat the previous two steps as necessary to insert all of the desired merge fields.

Note: When Ami Pro inserts a merge field into a merge document, the merge field looks just like the field name, surrounded by *angle brackets* (< and >). Don't be fooled, however, into thinking that you can type the brackets and field names as merge fields yourself; Ami Pro only recognizes merge fields inserted through the Insert Merge Field dialog box.

If you want the fields in your merged document to be separated by spaces, commas, or other punctuation, type those characters *between* the merge fields. For example, if you want the last line of an address to read

    Orchard Park, NY 14127

then the corresponding line in your merge document should look something like this:

    <CITY>, <STATE> <ZIP>

Now let's open a partially created merge document, assign your MYDATA2.SAM merge data file to it, and then insert some merge fields to complete the document:

CREATING FORM LETTERS • 341

1. Open and examine **mergedoc.sam**. It is a one-page form letter. Notice the merge fields for the document's inside address: <FIRST_NAME>, <LAST_NAME>, and so on. We've already done a little of the work for you by inserting these merge fields to match the field names in MYDATA2.SAM.

2. Scroll down a few lines. We've also inserted a <FIRST_NAME> merge field in the letter's greeting and a <DESTINATION> merge field in the first multiple-line paragraph (see Figure 11.7).

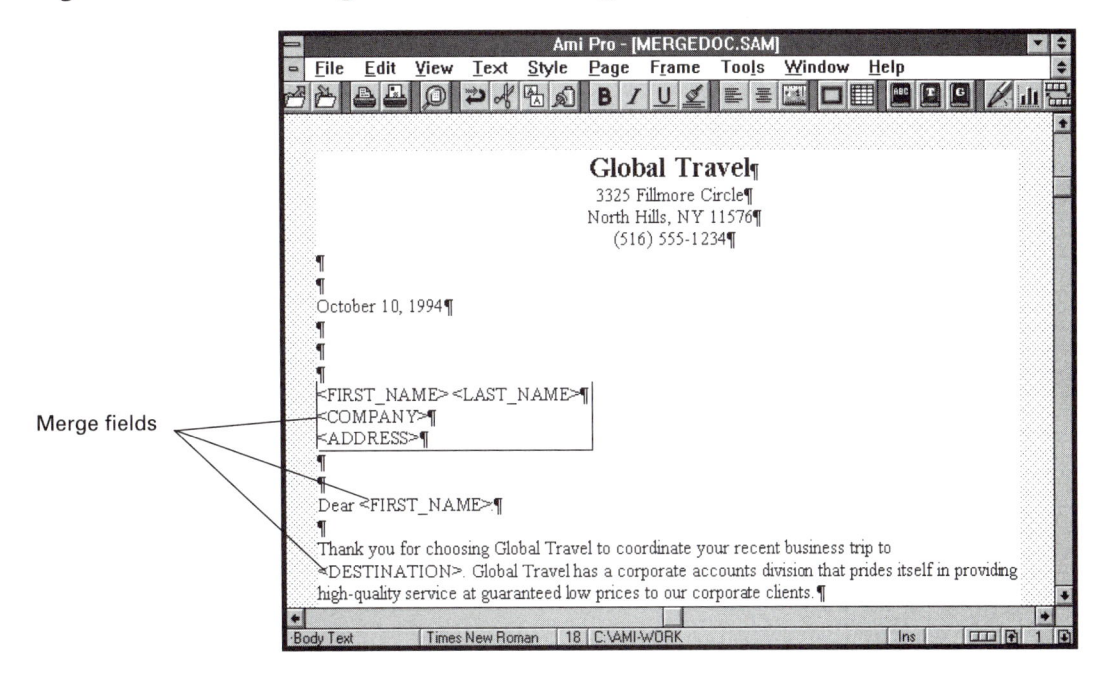

Figure 11.7   **Merge fields in a merge document**

[Screenshot of Ami Pro - [MERGEDOC.SAM] window showing the form letter with Global Travel letterhead, date October 10, 1994, and merge fields <FIRST_NAME> <LAST_NAME>, <COMPANY>, <ADDRESS>, Dear <FIRST_NAME>, and body text referencing <DESTINATION>. Labeled "Merge fields" with arrows pointing to the field placeholders.]

3. Choose **Edit, Insert, Merge Field**, and then examine the Insert Merge Field dialog box. Because Ami Pro does not know which merge data file you want to use for this merge document, it lists nothing in the Field Names list box.

4. In the Insert Merge Field dialog box, click on **Data File** to open the Select Merge Data File dialog box.

342 • FORM LETTERS, LABELS, AND ENVELOPES

5. In the File list box, select **mydata2.sam**, and then click on **OK**. (Or just double-click on **mydata2.sam**.) Ami Pro closes the Select Merge Data File dialog box.

6. Observe the Insert Merge Field dialog box. It now lists, in alphabetical order, all the field names from MYDATA2.SAM. Notice that Ami Pro has capitalized all the field names; for field names that include spaces, Ami Pro has replaced each space with an underscore.

7. Place the insertion point in the first blank line under <ADDRESS>. To complete the inside address, you need to add merge fields for the city, state, and zip code.

8. In the Insert Merge Field dialog box's Field Names list box, select **CITY**, and then click on **Insert**. (Or just double-click on **CITY**.) Ami Pro inserts a merge field for CITY at the insertion point (see Figure 11.8).

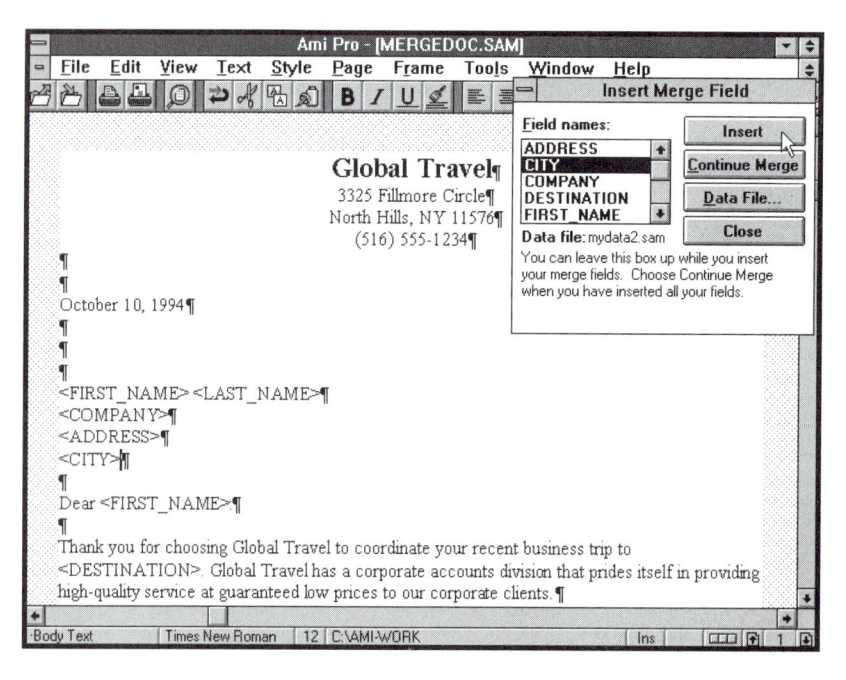

Figure 11.8   Inserting merge fields

9. Type a comma and then press **Spacebar** to insert a comma and a space after <CITY>.

10. Insert a merge field for **STATE**, press **Spacebar** twice, and then insert a merge field for **ZIP**. Your new line should now read

    <CITY>, <STATE>   <ZIP>

11. Click on **Close** to close the Insert Merge Field dialog box.

12. Save your merge document as **mymerge**.

MERGING THE FORM LETTERS

Once you've created and edited your merge data file and a merge document, the third and final step is the actual merging itself. You can start the merge from the merge document, the merge data file, or any other document.

Follow these steps when you want to start a merge from a merge document:

- Choose File, Merge to open the Welcome To Merge dialog box. If you've already assigned a merge data file to the merge document, Ami Pro selects the third and final option: Merge And Print The Data And The Document.

- Click on OK to open the Merge dialog box.

- To send your entire merge directly to the printer, select Merge & Print. To view (and possibly edit) each merged document before printing, select Merge, View & Print. To merge to a document on disk, select Merge & Save As, and then type a document name in the Merge & Save As text box.

- Click on OK.

Note: The Merge dialog box also provides options for *conditional merges* (which enable you to merge using only records that meet specific criteria), merging data to labels, changing your print options, and assigning a different merge data file. We'll look at merging data to labels later in this chapter. For more information on the other options in this dialog box, refer to your Ami Pro documentation.

If you select Merge, View & Print in the foregoing procedure, Ami Pro will merge the merge data file's first record with the merge document, and display the resulting merged document in the document window. Ami Pro will also display four command buttons in the Merge dialog box. Click on

- Print And View Next to print the current merged document and then merge and display the next merged document
- Skip And View Next to bypass the current merged document and then merge and display the next merged document
- Print All to print the current merged document and then merge and print all of the remaining merged documents, without displaying them first
- Cancel to stop merging

The Print And View Next and Skip And View Next options are good to use for running on-the-fly conditional merges. For example, if you want to print form letters for everyone in your merge data file except the one person who lives in Nebraska, you can view each document and choose *not* to print that merged document when it is displayed. These two options also enable you to edit merged documents before printing them. For instance, you might have only one or two merged documents to which you want to add some extra text; you can directly edit those documents when they are displayed, print them, and then continue with the rest of the merge.

MERGING RECORDS THAT CONTAIN BLANK FIELDS

It's not uncommon to have records with blank fields in your merge data file. For example, if you have a company name field, most records with a home address or for people who are not employed will probably have blank company name fields.

When Ami Pro encounters a blank field during a merge, it looks to see if the corresponding merge field in the merge document is in a paragraph by itself. If it is, Ami Pro reduces that paragraph's spacing to 0", which effectively removes any gap that would otherwise appear between the paragraphs above and below that merge field's paragraph.

Because some of your records contain blank Company fields, you'll see this feature in action during the merge.

CREATING FORM LETTERS • 345

Let's complete our merge now:

1. Verify that MYMERGE.SAM is still open, and then choose **File, Merge**. Because your merge document is already open, and you've already assigned MYDATA2.SAM as the merge data file, Ami Pro selects the third option: *Merge And Print The Data And The Document*.

2. Click on **OK**. Ami Pro opens the Merge dialog box.

3. Select **Merge, View & Print**, and then click on **OK**. Ami Pro merges the first form letter (for Kat Moran) and displays it in the document window. The Merge dialog box now enables you to print this form letter or skip to the next one (see Figure 11.9).

Figure 11.9 **Viewing a merged document**

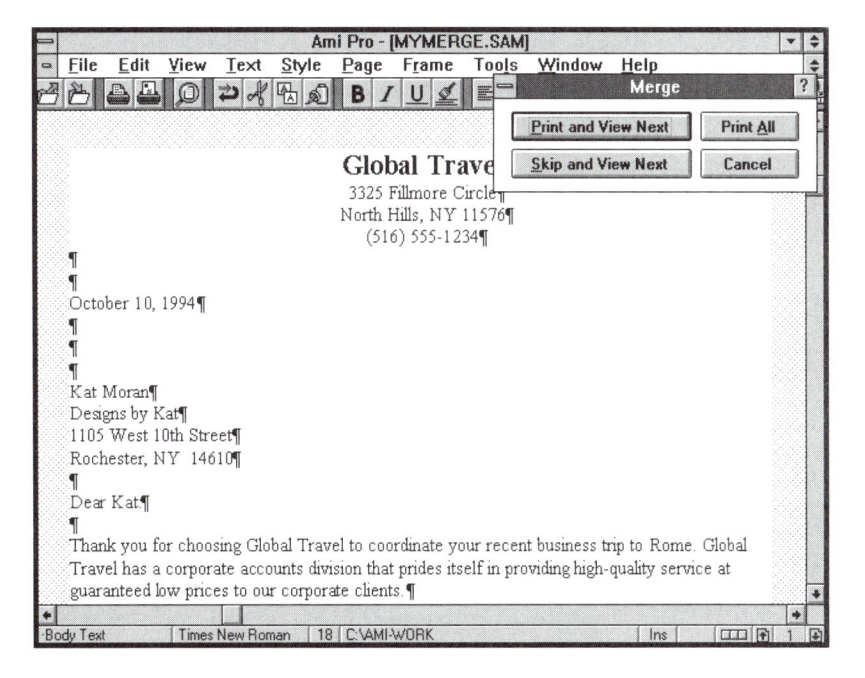

4. Examine the form letter. Into every merge field in the merge document, Ami Pro has merged data from Kat Moran's record.

5. If you want to conserve your printer paper, click on **Skip And View Next**. If you'd prefer to print the merged document, click on **Print And View Next** instead.

6. Observe the form letter for Tary Simizon. Remember from earlier in this chapter that Tary's Company field was blank. Notice how Ami Pro has automatically compensated for this by reducing to 0" the line spacing for the paragraph containing the COMPANY merge field. (You can see the return symbol for the 0" paragraph overlapping the *T* in *Tary.*) In this way, the form letter does not contain a gap between Tary's name and her street address.

PRACTICE YOUR SKILLS

1. View the rest of the form letters until Ami Pro closes the Merge dialog box. As you view the form letters, notice how Ami Pro has compensated for potential gaps for records with blank Company fields.

2. Save and then close MYMERGE.SAM.

CREATING MAILING LABELS

A merge operation to create mailing labels works much the same as one to produce form letters. You need a merge data file to supply the names and addresses, and a merge document to provide the proper layout for the labels. To create the mailing labels themselves, you simply merge these two documents.

In this section, you'll see how to sort a merge data file's records into zip code order, and then how to use one of Ami Pro's automated style sheets to help you create a merge document for your labels.

SORTING RECORDS IN A MERGE DATA FILE

When you want to create mailing labels (or any kind of merged document, for that matter), it's often useful to sort the records in your merge data file before performing the merge. For example, you might want to sort mailing labels by zip code in order to take advantage of the U.S. Postal Service's special rates for presorted mail. Or, if you use a hand-delivery service, you could sort by company name to make it easier to bundle together letters for people who work at the same company.

By default, Ami Pro stores records in the order they were entered, and creates merged documents in that same order.

If you use File, Merge to create and edit delimited merge data files, Ami Pro helps you to sort records easily from the Data File dialog box (the dialog box that displays electronic index cards). Follow these steps when you want to sort records in a delimited merge data file:

- Open the merge data file and the Data File dialog box. (For help with this, refer back to "Editing an Existing Merge Data File" earlier in this chapter.)

- Click on Sort to open the Sort Records dialog box.

- In the Sort By Field dialog box, select the field by which you want to sort.

- To sort fields that contain all letters, or a mixture of letters and numbers (such as street addresses), select Sort Type Alphanumeric. To sort fields that contain only numbers (such as zip codes), select Sort Type Numeric.

- To sort fields in *ascending order* (for example, from A to Z or from 1 to 100), select Sort Order Ascending. To sort fields in *descending order* (for example, from Z to A or from 100 to 1), select Sort Order Descending.

- Click on OK to sort all of the records according to your specifications.

After sorting, Ami Pro displays on the tab dividers for the first five electronic index cards the corresponding values for the sorted field. For example, if you sorted by company, the tab dividers will show the names of the companies for the first five records in your merge data file. This helps you to determine if Ami Pro sorted your records as you expected.

Once you've finished sorting records, click on Close and then on Yes to close the dialog box and to save and close the merge data file.

Let's sort the records in MYDATA2.SAM:

1. Open and observe **mydata2.sam**. The records are listed in the order in which they were entered.

348 • FORM LETTERS, LABELS, AND ENVELOPES

2. Choose **File, Merge**, verify that *Edit The Data File* is selected, and then click on **OK**. Ami Pro opens the Data File - MYDATA2-.SAM dialog box and displays the file's records on electronic index cards.

3. Click on **Sort**, and then examine the Sort Records dialog box (see Figure 11.10). You can sort records by any one field, alphanumerically or numerically, and in ascending or descending order.

Figure 11.10   **The Sort Records dialog box**

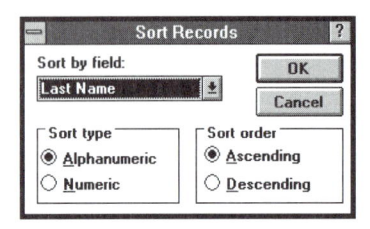

4. If necessary, select **Last Name** in the Sort By Field drop-down list box.

5. Verify that *Sort Type Alphanumeric* and *Sort Order Ascending* are selected, and then click on **OK**.

6. Observe the five visible tab dividers. You can see by these dividers that Ami Pro has sorted the records in ascending order by last name.

7. Click on **Sort** again, select **Zip** in the Sort By Field drop-down list box, select **Sort Type Numeric**, and then click on **OK**.

8. Observe the tab dividers. Ami Pro now displays zip codes to show that it sorted the records by the Zip field (see Figure 11.11).

   Note: Depending on the zip codes in your file, your Data File dialog box might differ somewhat from the figure.

9. Click on **Close**. Ami Pro prompts:

   ```
   MYDATA2.SAM has changed. Save changes?
   ```

10. Click on **Yes**. Once again, Ami Pro opens the New dialog box.

11. Click on **Cancel** to close the dialog box.

Figure 11.11   Records sorted by zip code

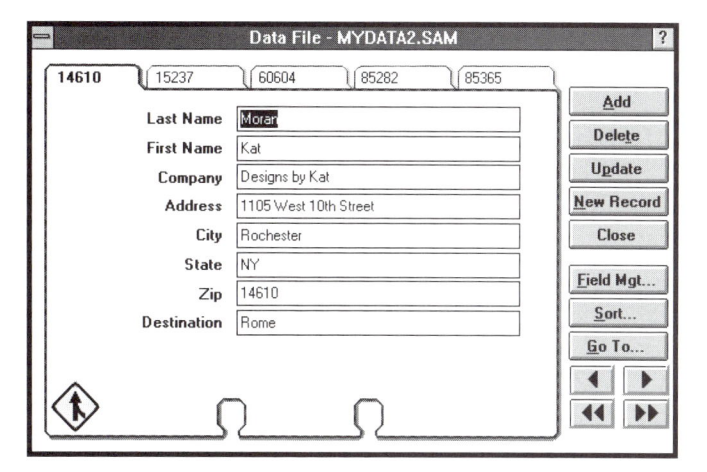

MERGING MAILING LABELS

Because setting up a mailing-label merge document with the correct label dimensions can be difficult to do manually, and because there are so many different types of labels, Ami Pro provides an automated style sheet to help you with this task. When you create a document based on this automated label style sheet, Ami Pro does the work of determining how to set up your merge document; all you have to do is tell Ami Pro what type of labels you are using.

Note: Ami Pro only provides automatic style sheet support for Avery brand labels. If you use another brand of labels, check the manufacturer's packaging for an Avery equivalency number. If there is no equivalency number, see your Ami Pro documentation for information on setting up merge documents for custom labels.

Follow these steps when you want to use Ami Pro's automated label style sheet for creating a label merge document:

- Choose File, New to open the New dialog box.

- Check List By Description (if necessary), and then select Label - Compatible With Avery® Laser Labels in the Style Sheet For New Document list box.

- Verify that With Contents and Run Macro are checked, and then click on OK.

- After loading and checking the label specifications, Ami Pro displays a sample label and then opens the Labels dialog box to enable you to select a label type. Select the appropriate type, and then click on Merge.

- Ami Pro sets up the current document for the label type you selected, and then opens the Select Merge Data File dialog box. Use this dialog box to choose the record source (that is, the merge data file) for your labels, and then click on OK. (Or, simply double-click on the merge data file's name.)

- Use the Insert Merge Field dialog box to add merge fields to the sample label. If you want to print standardized text on your labels, type that text, as well, on the sample label.

- If you want to continue on to merging your labels, click on Continue Merge. Otherwise, click on Cancel and skip the rest of this procedure.

- If you click on Continue Merge, Ami Pro opens the Welcome To Merge dialog box. Click on OK; Ami Pro opens the Merge dialog box and automatically selects Options As Labels for you. From here, you can complete the merge by clicking on OK.

Note: When merging labels, you cannot view them before printing; your only choices in the Merge dialog box are Merge & Print and Merge & Save As. If you need to edit your labels before printing them, choose Merge & Save As, type a document name in the Merge & Save As text box, click on OK, close the merge document, and then open the document you specified.

Let's use the automated label style sheet now to merge some mailing labels:

1. Open the New dialog box (select **File, New**), and then check **List By Description**, if necessary.

2. In the Style Sheet For New Document list box, select **Label - Compatible With Avery® Laser Labels**.

3. Verify that *With Contents* and *Run Macro* are checked, and then click on **OK**. Ami Pro displays a sample label, while the status bar informs you of Ami Pro's progress in loading and checking label specifications. Finally, Ami Pro opens the Labels dialog box.

CREATING MAILING LABELS • 351

4. Observe the dialog box. It lists the dozens of label types that Ami Pro supports.

5. In the Labels list box, select **Address - 5262**, and then click on **Merge**. Ami Pro adjusts the size of the sample label, and then opens the Select Merge Data File dialog box.

   Note: If *Address - 5262* is not available, select **Address - 4146** instead. If you do, your screen and printed labels may not exactly match this book's next two figures, but the steps should still work as described.

6. In the Files list box, double-click on **mydata2.sam** to specify the record source for your mailing labels. Ami Pro closes the Select Merge Data File dialog box, and then opens the Insert Merge Field dialog box.

7. Use the Insert Merge Field dialog box and your keyboard to create the sample label shown in Figure 11.12.

8. Click on **Continue Merge** to close the Insert Merge Field dialog box. Ami Pro opens the Welcome To Merge dialog box.

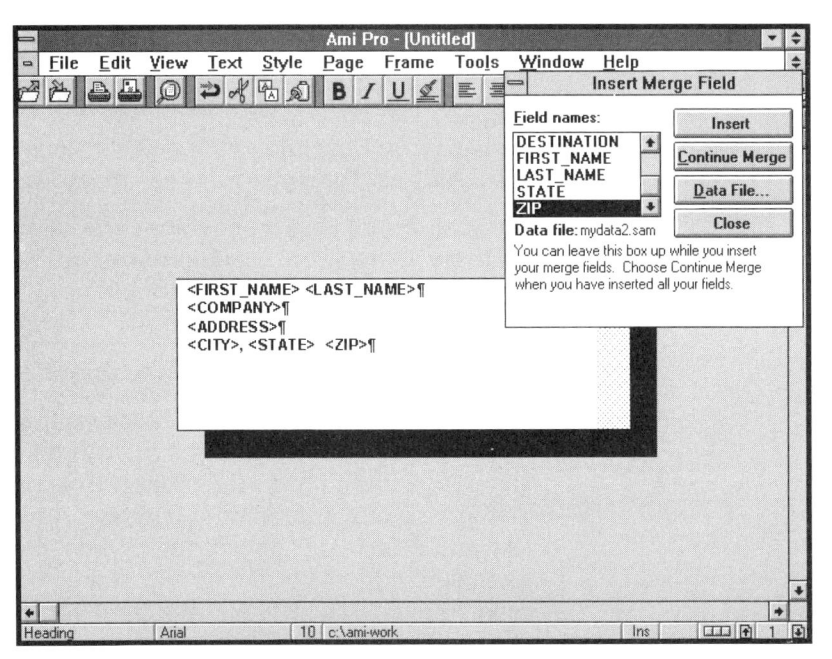

Figure 11.12 **The completed sample label**

9. Verify that *Merge And Print The Data And The Document* is selected, and then click on **OK**. Ami Pro opens the Merge dialog box.

10. Observe the dialog box. Because you used Ami Pro's automated label style sheet for creating this merge document, Ami Pro has automatically checked *Options As Labels*.

11. Verify that *Merge & Print* is selected, and then click on **OK** to send your merged labels directly to the printer. (Or, if you don't have a printer, click on **Cancel**.)

12. Compare your printout to Figure 11.13. Notice that your labels printed in ascending zip-code order. (Depending on your zip code, your labels may have printed in an order different from that shown in the figure.) Notice also that Ami Pro prints only nine labels, because MYDATA2.SAM only contains nine records.

13. Save your merge document as **mylabels**, and then close the document.

CREATING AN ENVELOPE

If you're creating a single letter, you probably don't want to go to the bother and waste of printing an entire sheet of labels. Instead, you can use Ami Pro's File, Print Envelope command to print a single envelope.

To use File, Print Envelope, your current document must contain an inside address for Ami Pro to use in addressing the envelope.

Note: If your printer has an envelope tray, Ami Pro will attempt to use that tray. Otherwise, it will use your printer's *manual feed* option, if it has one. If you have trouble printing an envelope, check your printer's documentation.

Follow these steps when you want to print a single envelope:

- Choose File, Print Envelope or click on the *Print Envelope SmartIcon* (the fourth SmartIcon from the left, displaying an envelope emerging from a printer) to open the Print Envelope dialog box. In the document window, Ami Pro will attempt to find and select your document's inside address. (If Ami Pro selects no address or the wrong address, click on Cancel, select the desired address, and then perform this step again.)

Figure 11.13 **The printed mailing labels**

Kat Moran
Designs by Kat
1105 West 10th Street
Rochester, NY 14610

David DuBa
5510 Federal Boulevard
Pittsburgh, PA 15237

Jeffrey Lamb
246 Eastman Street
Chicago, IL 60604

Lara Eriks
CDS
1410 Cornell Street
Mesa, AZ 85282

Norman Marianne
Unique Rugs
125 North Road, Suite 3904
Yuma, AZ 85365

William Moore
Lawn Care Services
33309 Acapulco Trail
Palm Springs, CA 92390

Anna Landes
Carl Farms
119 Culver Avenue
La Jolla, CA 93108

Tary Simizon
125 Town Street
Los Angeles, CA 94450

Christopher Benz
PC Learning Labs
5903 Christie Avenue
Emeryville, CA 94608

- In the Envelope Size box, select the desired envelope size. If the envelope size you want isn't listed in this box, open the More Envelope Sizes drop-down list box and look there for your desired envelope size. If you still can't find the size you want, type the appropriate dimensions in the two boxes below the More Envelope Sizes drop-down list box.

- Click on OK.

354 • FORM LETTERS, LABELS, AND ENVELOPES

Note: The Print Envelope dialog box also offers you a Print Return Address option to print your own return address in the upper-left corner of the envelope. For more information on this option, consult your Ami Pro documentation.

Let's open a document that has an inside address, and then create an envelope for the document:

1. Open and examine **envltr.sam**. It's a simple, one-page letter with an inside address.

2. Choose **File, Print Envelope** or click on the **Print Envelope SmartIcon**. Ami Pro automatically finds and selects the document's inside address, and then opens the Print Envelope dialog box (see Figure 11.14).

Figure 11.14   The Print Envelope dialog box

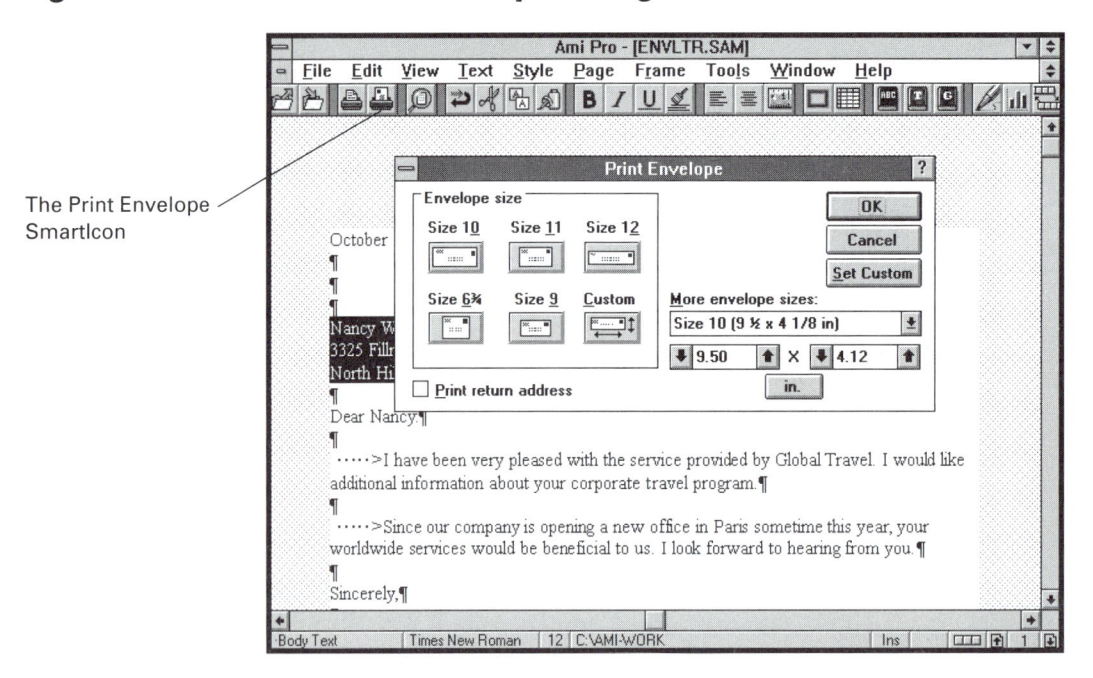

The Print Envelope SmartIcon

3. Select **Envelope Size Size 10** (the standard size for business envelopes), and then click on **OK**. (Or, if you don't have a printer, click on **Cancel**.) Ami Pro sends the envelope information to your printer.

4. Compare your printed envelope to Figure 11.15.

5. Close ENVLTR.SAM without saving changes.

Figure 11.15   **The printed envelope**

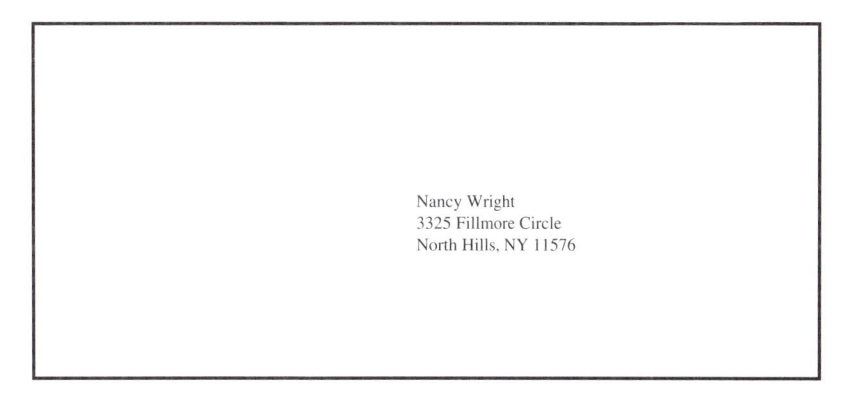

```
Nancy Wright
3325 Fillmore Circle
North Hills, NY 11576
```

SUMMARY

In this chapter, you learned how to use File, Merge to create form letters and mailing labels. You also learned how to sort records within a merge data file, and how to use File, Print Envelope to create and print a single envelope.

Here is a quick reference guide to the Ami Pro features introduced in this chapter:

Desired Result	How to Do It
Create a merge data file	Choose **File**, **Merge**; select **Select**, **Create Or Edit A Data File** (if necessary); click on **OK**; click on **New** and type field names, clicking on **Add** after each name; click on **OK**; fill in records on Data File dialog box index cards, clicking on **Add** after each record; click on **Close**; click on **Yes**; type name for merge data file; then click on **OK**.

Desired Result	How to Do It
Translate delimited data to electronic index cards	Choose **File**, **Merge**; select **Select**, **Create Or Edit A Data File** (if necessary); select merge data file name; then click on **Edit**. Or open merge data file; choose **File**, **Merge**; select **Edit The Data File** (if necessary); then click on **OK**.
Move to a new index card	Click on index card's **tab divider**. Or click on **Go To**; specify record; then click on **OK**. Or click on a **navigation button**.
Edit a record on an index card	Move to card; edit fields; then click on **Update**.
Create a brand-new index card and record	Click on **New Record**.
Delete an index card and record	Display card; then click on **Delete**.
Manually open the Insert Merge Field dialog box	Open merge document; then choose **Edit**, **Insert**, **Merge Field**.
Assign merge data file from Insert Merge Field dialog box	Click on **Data File**, select merge data file name; then click on **OK**.
Insert a merge field	Open merge document; open Insert Merge Field dialog box; place insertion point at desired location; select field name; then click on **Insert**.
Insert standardized text	Type text in merge document.

Desired Result	How to Do It
Merge from merge document	Open merge document; choose **File**, **Merge**; select **Merge And Print The Data And The Document**; click on **OK**; select **Merge & Print**, **Merge**, **View & Print**, or **Merge & Save As**; if you selected Merge & Save As, type name for merged document name; click on **OK**.
Sort delimited merge data file records	Translate file to index cards; click on **Sort**; select sort field, sort type, and sort order; click on **OK**.
Create mailing-label merge document	Choose **File**, **New**; verify that **List By Description** is checked; select **Label - Compatible With Avery**® Laser Labels; verify that **With Contents** and **Run Macro** are selected; select label type; click on **Merge**; select merge data file; build sample label with insert merge fields and standardized text; then click on **Continue Merge** or **Cancel**.
Create envelope	Open document containing envelope address; choose **File**, **Print Envelope** or click on **Print Envelope SmartIcon**; select envelope size; then click on **OK**.

In Chapter 12, you'll learn how to create a newsletter using frames, multiple columns, pictures, and full-page borders.

IF YOU'RE STOPPING HERE

If you need to take a break here, please exit Ami Pro. If you want to proceed directly to the next chapter, please do so now.

CHAPTER 12: CREATING A NEWSLETTER

Understanding Frames

Working with Multiple Columns

Working with Pictures

Adding a Line Around a Page

In this chapter, you'll learn some of the fundamentals of creating a newsletter with Ami Pro. To help you create professional-looking newsletters, Ami Pro provides many features usually associated with high-end desktop publishing programs such as PageMaker and QuarkXPress. These features include frames, multiple columns, the integration of text and pictures, and full-page borders.

When you're done working through this chapter, you will know how to

- Create and work with frames
- Create and work with multiple-column text
- Import pictures
- Add a line border around an entire page

Note: As you work through this chapter, bear in mind that creating a professional-looking newsletter is kind of like putting together a jigsaw puzzle when you don't have all the pieces (or maybe too many of them), and you have to construct some of your own. We at PC Learning Labs spent some advance time making sure that all the elements of the newsletter you are about to create work together smoothly and conveniently. When you start to create newsletters on your own, however, things might not work out so well. You might have to change your layout, add or remove text, change font sizes, and so on. Just remember when this happens that the old newspaper claim, "All the news that's fit to print," isn't quite so true as the more realistic adage, "All the news that fits, we print."

UNDERSTANDING FRAMES

In Ami Pro, *frames* are like minidocuments within documents: They come complete with their own margins and tabs, they can contain text, and they are independent of main document text formatting. For example, you can change the margins of your document without affecting the frame's own margins.

Frames give you the freedom to place just about any document element anywhere you want on a page. Suppose you have a line of text that you want to place in the left margin; you can use a frame to do so. If you'd like, you can also instruct Ami Pro to keep a frame exactly where you place it, regardless of what text you type above or below the frame—in a sense, the frame becomes a highly advanced, electronic Post-it note.

By default, Ami Pro makes room for a frame on the page by automatically *wrapping* text around the frame. For example, if you plunk a frame down in the middle of a page, Ami Pro automatically repositions the main document text so that the text displays on all sides of the frame, rather than staying hidden underneath

UNDERSTANDING FRAMES • 361

it. Figure 12.1 illustrates one way that Ami Pro can wrap text around a frame.

Figure 12.1 **Text wrapping around a frame**

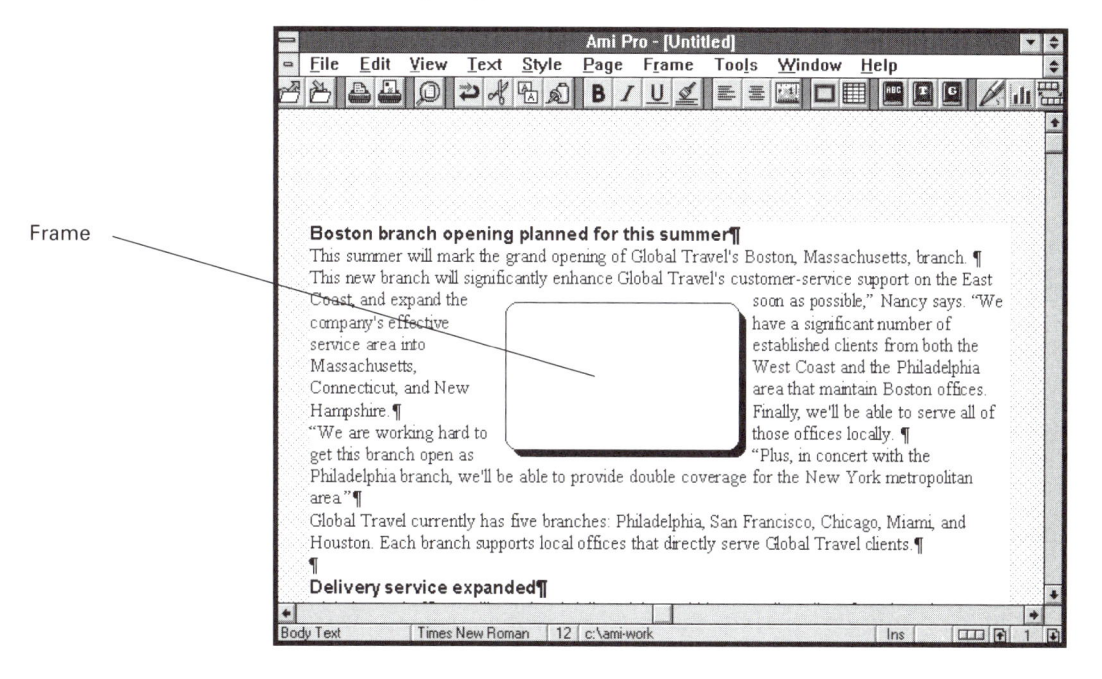

Frame

As you'll see later in this chapter, frames also enable you to incorporate graphic elements such as pictures into your documents.

Note: Frames are extremely flexible, and you can use them to create hundreds of document effects. Because of this flexibility, we cannot possibly show you everything there is to know about frames in a single chapter. Instead, we'll just show you the very basics; if this whets your appetite to learn more, refer to your Ami Pro documentation for further information about frames.

DISPLAYING THE VERTICAL RULER

When you work on complex documents such as newsletters, it's often useful to have a way of measuring document elements both horizontally *and* vertically. The current ruler provides a benchmark for horizontal measurements. To measure elements vertically, you can display the *vertical ruler*, which looks much like a "rotated" current ruler. Ami Pro displays the vertical ruler along the left side of the document window.

Follow these steps when you want to display the vertical ruler:

- Choose View, View Preferences to open the View Preferences dialog box.
- Check Vertical Ruler.
- Click on OK.

CREATING A FRAME

One way to create a frame is numerically, through the Create Frame dialog box. This dialog box enables you to specify the exact dimensions and page position for your frame.

Follow these steps when you want to create a frame numerically through the Create Frame dialog box:

- Move to the page where you want to create the frame.
- Choose Frame, Create Frame to open the Create Frame dialog box.
- Figure out how many inches down from the *top* edge of the page you want your frame to be, then type this number in the Position Down From Top box. If you want your frame to align with the document's top margin, type the height of the top margin in this box.
- Figure out how many inches in from the *left* edge of the page you want your frame to be, then type this number in the Position In From Left box. If you want your frame to align with the document's left margin, type the width of the left margin in this box.
- In the Size Width box, specify in inches how wide you want your frame to be.
- In the Size Height box, specify in inches how tall you want your frame to be.
- Click on OK.

Tip: Even though the Create Frame dialog box lists the Size options above the Position options, it's best to specify the Position options *before* you specify the Size options. Otherwise, Ami Pro might not let you specify the frame width and height you want. This is because the frame size you are trying to specify may not fit on the page at the location already specified by the Position options.

Once you finish creating a frame, Ami Pro displays your frame in the document window. By default, Ami Pro adds lines to every side of the frame, joins the lines with rounded corners, and creates a drop-shadow effect along the bottom and right frame lines.

As you'll learn later, you must select a frame before working with it. When you first create a frame, Ami Pro selects it for you. To select an unselected frame, click once anywhere inside the frame. To deselect a frame, press Esc or click anywhere outside the frame. While a frame is selected, it displays eight black *frame handles*, one at each corner and one halfway along each side. You can use these handles to resize the frame, as you'll see later.

If you are not running Ami Pro, please start it now. Before inserting a frame, let's open the document containing our newsletter text, NWSLTR.SAM, and then display the current and vertical rulers. This prepares your Ami Pro work environment for creating a newsletter:

1. Open **nwsltr.sam**.

2. Display the current ruler (choose **View, Show Ruler** or click on the **Show/Hide Ruler SmartIcon**).

3. Open the View Preferences dialog box (choose **View, View Preferences**), check **Vertical Ruler**, and then click on **OK**. Ami Pro now displays a vertical ruler along the left side of the document window (Figure 12.2).

4. Observe the current and vertical rulers. By having both rulers displayed, you can see (without opening the Modify Page Layout dialog box) that NWSLTR.SAM has a 1" left margin and a 1" top margin.

Now let's insert a frame at the top of the document:

1. Choose **Frame, Create Frame**, and then observe the Create Frame dialog box. This dialog box enables you to specify the exact size and position of your new frame (Figure 12.3).

Figure 12.2   **The vertical ruler**

Vertical ruler

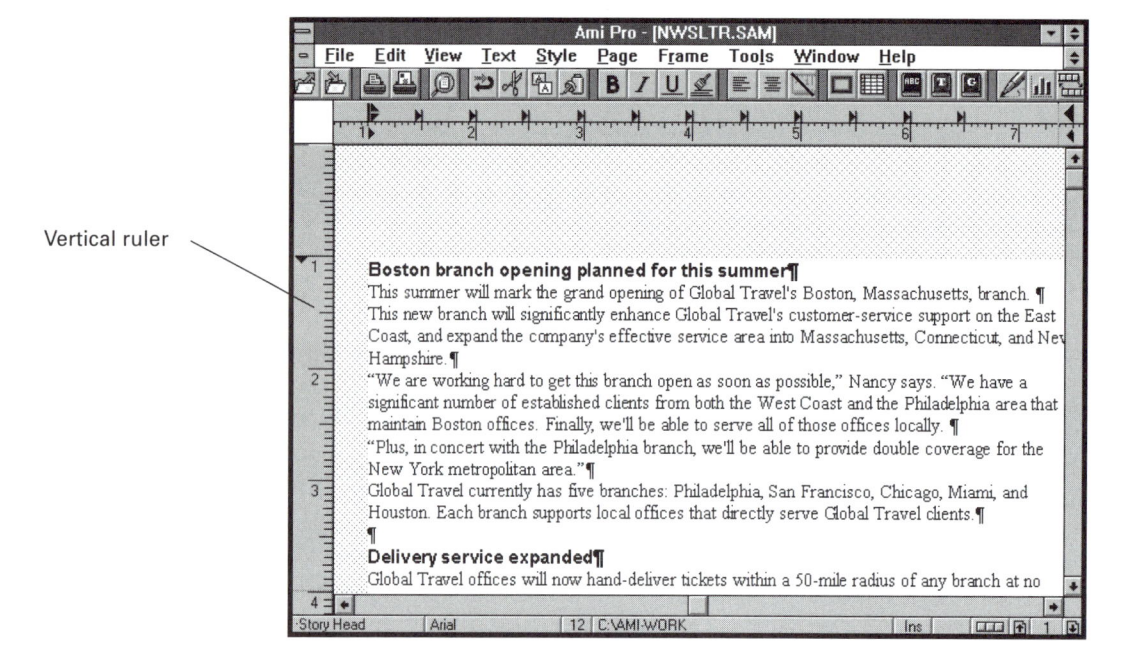

Figure 12.3   **The Create Frame dialog box**

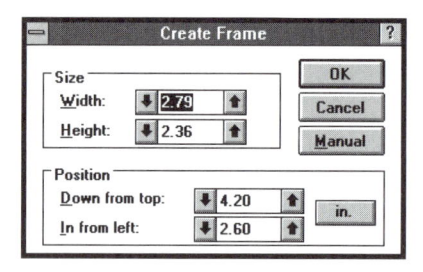

> 2. In the Position Down From Top box, type **1** to indicate that the frame should align with the typing area's top edge. (Remember, specify Position options *first*.)
>
> 3. In the Position In From Left box, type **1** to indicate that the frame should align with the typing area's left edge.
>
> 4. In the Size Width box, type **6.5** to indicate that the frame should be as wide as the typing area.

UNDERSTANDING FRAMES • 365

5. In the Size Height box, type **2** (if necessary).

6. Click on **OK**, and then observe your document. Ami Pro inserts a 6½"-by-2" frame at the top of the typing area, and automatically repositions all of the document's existing text to below the frame (see Figure 12.4).

Figure 12.4   **The inserted frame**

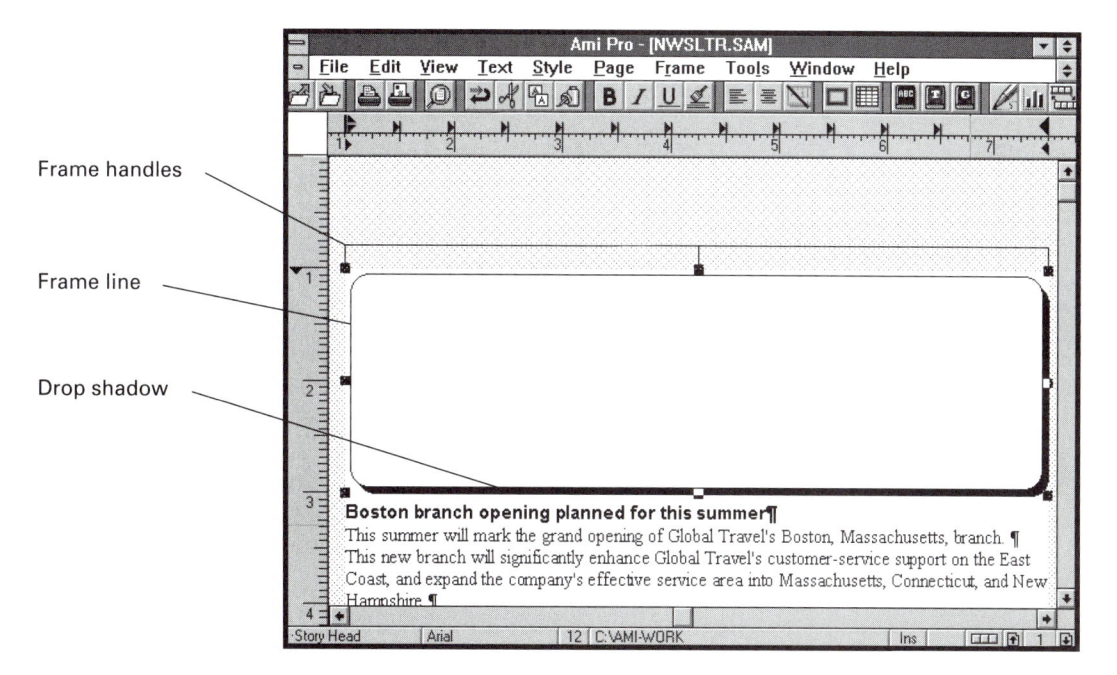

Frame handles
Frame line
Drop shadow

7. Observe the frame's lines. By default, the lines meet at rounded corners, and there is a drop shadow effect along the bottom and right of the frame. (You might need to scroll a little to the right to see the entire frame.)

8. Observe the frame's handles. When a frame is selected, Ami Pro displays eight black handles around the frame's perimeter.

9. Press **Esc** to deselect the frame. The frame handles disappear.

10. Click inside the frame to select it. Ami Pro redisplays the frame handles.

11. Save the document as **mynwsltr**.

TYPING TEXT IN A FRAME

As you've already learned, frames can contain text. By placing text in a frame, you help isolate that text from any changes you make in the main document text. As you'll see later in this chapter when we work with multiple-column text, frames enable you to have both multiple- and single-column text on a single page. This is important especially for newsletters, where you commonly have a *masthead* or *banner* that spans the width of the page, and multiple-column text on the rest of the page. (If you want to see an example of multiple- and single-column text, look ahead to Figure 12.15, which shows the completed newsletter.)

To type text into a frame, double-click inside the frame. Ami Pro changes the frame's handles from black to gray—to indicate that you've now selected the frame's *contents* and not the frame itself—and places the insertion point inside the frame. Entering text now is just the same as entering text in a new document; you simply type the text at the insertion point.

To control the appearance of framed text, you can use text formatting, enhancements, and/or styles.

After you've finished typing text in a frame, simply press Esc to deselect the frame contents and select the frame itself again.

Let's type some masthead text into your frame, and then apply some styles that we have designed especially for that text:

1. Double-click inside the frame. Ami Pro changes the frame handles to gray, and places the insertion point inside the frame.

2. Type **Going My Way?** and then press **Enter**. Ami Pro inserts a return and moves the insertion point down to a second line within the frame.

3. Type **A Global Travel publication**, press **Tab**, and then type **Spring Issue**.

4. Apply the **Title** style to the frame's first paragraph, and then apply the **Subtitle** style to the frame's second paragraph.

5. Press **Esc**. Ami Pro changes the gray frame handles back to black, indicating that the frame—not its contents—is selected (see Figure 12.5).

Figure 12.5   **The framed masthead text**

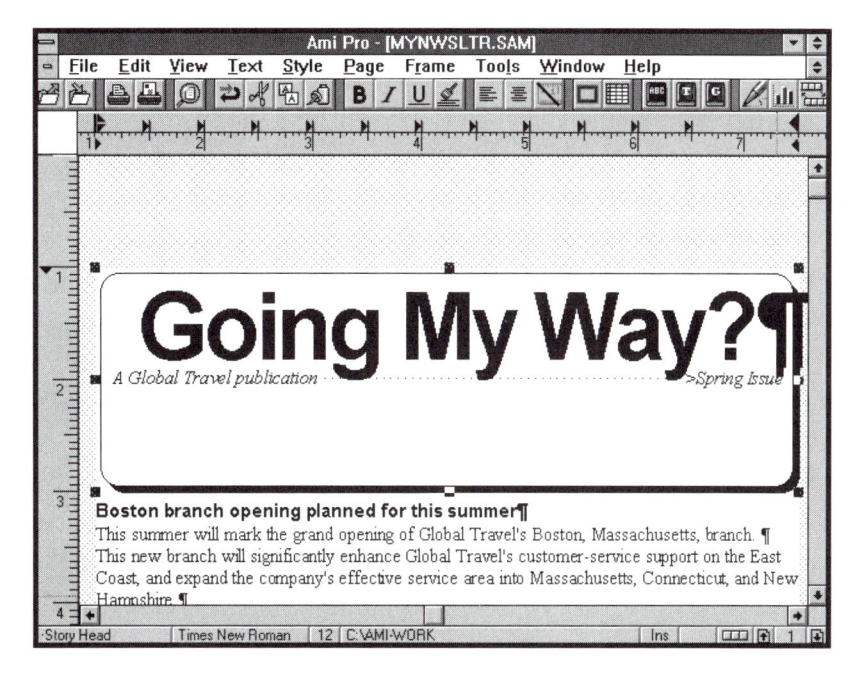

MODIFYING A FRAME LAYOUT

Once you've created a frame, you can modify its layout through the Modify Frame Layout dialog box. Options for modifying frames include changing the frame's dimensions and placement, changing how text wraps around the frame, altering the frame's margins and tabs, and adding or removing the frame's lines and drop shadow.

Follow these steps when you want to modify a frame's layout:

- Select the frame.

- Choose Frame, Modify Frame Layout or click the right mouse button inside the frame to open the Modify Frame Layout dialog box.

- In the Frame box, select the button for the category of frame options you want to change. When you do, Ami Pro displays those options in the rest of the dialog box.

- Change the frame options as desired, and then repeat this and the previous step if you want to change options in another category.
- Click on OK.

You can also resize frames with the mouse. Follow these steps when you want to resize a frame with the mouse:

- Select the frame.
- Position the mouse pointer over one of the frame's handles until the pointer changes to a double arrow.
- Drag the handle to change the frame's size.

In this next activity, we'll modify a frame's dimensions, lines, and drop shadow through the Modify Frame Layout dialog box. Later in this chapter, when we experiment with pictures, you'll have a chance to resize a frame using the mouse and the frame handles. For information on other frame modification options and techniques, refer to your Ami Pro documentation.

Let's modify our frame now by reducing its height, removing its lines and drop shadow, and then adding new lines:

1. Observe your frame. Notice that its height is too great for the text inside.

2. Verify that the frame is selected, and then choose **Frame, Modify Frame Layout** to open the Modify Frame Layout dialog box.

3. Observe the dialog box. Because *Frame Type* is selected on the dialog box's left side, the dialog box displays corresponding options, such as how text will wrap around frames and how frames will be positioned in relation to main document text (see Figure 12.6).

4. Select **Frame Size & Position**, and then observe the assortment of settings now displayed. There are options for controlling the frame's size and page position (these mirror the options you used when you first created the frame), and for controlling the frame's margins.

5. In the Size Height box, type **1.2**, and then click on **OK**. Ami Pro reduces your frame's height from 2" to 1.2", making the frame the perfect size to fit the text inside.

Figure 12.6   **The Modify Frame Layout dialog box**

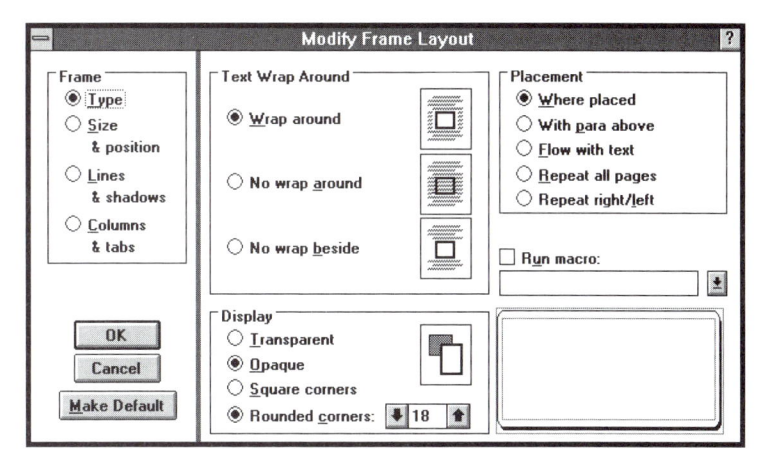

6. Open the View Preferences dialog box, uncheck **Tabs & Returns**, and then click on **OK**. Without the symbols for tabs and returns displayed, you can now see more clearly how the text looks within your frame.

7. Position the mouse pointer over the frame, and then click the *right* mouse button to reopen the Modify Frame Layout dialog box.

8. Select **Frame Lines & Shadow**, and then observe the Lines box. The *Lines All* option instructs Ami Pro to place lines on every side of your frame.

9. Observe the Shadow box. The *Shadow Normal* option instructs Ami Pro to add a medium-sized drop shadow to your frame.

10. Uncheck **Lines All**, select **Shadow None**, and then click on **OK**. Your frame no longer displays lines or a drop shadow.

11. Reopen the Modify Frame Layout dialog box (choose **Frame, Modify Frame Layout** or click over the frame with the *right* mouse button).

12. Select **Frame Lines and Shadows**, select **Lines Top** and **Lines Bottom**, select the fourth line down in the Style list box, and then click on **OK**. Ami Pro now displays thick lines at the top and bottom of your frame (see Figure 12.7).

13. Save MYNWSLTR.SAM.

Figure 12.7   **The completed masthead frame**

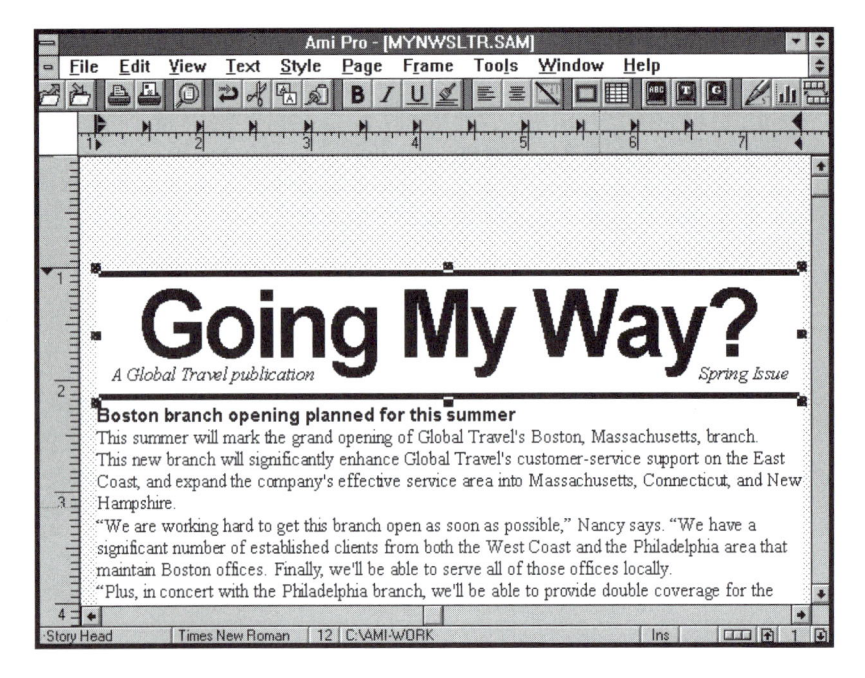

WORKING WITH MULTIPLE COLUMNS

If you've ever read a newspaper, you've seen how the text is typically arranged in multiple, side-by-side columns. Because lines of text in multiple columns are shorter, multiple-column text is often easier to read than single-column text that stretches from margin to margin. Multiple columns are also commonly used for newsletters, magazines, and other such publications where more than one story or article may appear on a single page.

CREATING MULTIPLE COLUMNS

Whenever you change single-column text to multiple-column text, Ami Pro rearranges the flow of text in a "snaking" pattern. That is, Ami Pro fills up one column, and then starts the text again at the top of the next column to the right, so that the text flows from top to bottom and then back to the top again—like a long snake.

You can specify multiple columns with the current ruler or through the Modify Page Layout dialog box.

Follow these steps when you want to set up multiple columns with the current ruler:

- Move to the page where you want to have text in multiple columns, making certain that the insertion point is in main document text.
- Activate the current ruler.
- On the current ruler's tab bar, change the number in the Cols box to any whole number from 2 to 8.
- Deactivate the current ruler.

Follow these steps when you want to set up multiple columns through the Modify Page Layout dialog box:

- Move to the page where you want to have text in multiple columns, making certain that the insertion point is in the main document text.
- Open the Modify Page Layout dialog box.
- Select Modify Margins & Columns (if necessary).
- For Number Of Columns, specify the number of columns you want.
- Click on OK.

By default, Ami Pro puts the main document text on every page of your document into the same number of columns. Although you *can*, for example, have single-column text on page 1 and multiple-column text on page 2, the main document text on any given page can be either single-column or multiple-column, but not both. This is why frames are useful: To create a page with both single- and multiple-column text, you simply use a frame to isolate some of the text. (If you'd like, you can even specify multiple-column text within a frame, through the Modify Frame Layout dialog box.)

Let's arrange all the main document text in our newsletter in three columns, and leave the framed masthead text in a single column:

1. Place the insertion point in the main document text (anywhere below your frame).

2. Switch to Full Page view (choose **View, Full Page** or click on the **Toggle Full Page/Layout View SmartIcon**), and then observe the document. All the text is in a single column.

3. Activate the **current ruler** (click on it). Ami Pro displays the current ruler's tab bar.

4. Observe the tab bar's Cols box. It is set to *1*.

5. Click twice on the Cols box's **up increment arrow** to change the number of columns to **3**, and then examine the document. Ami Pro has rearranged all the main document text into three side-by-side columns. The text in your frame, however, remains in a single column (see Figure 12.8).

Figure 12.8 **Creating multiple columns**

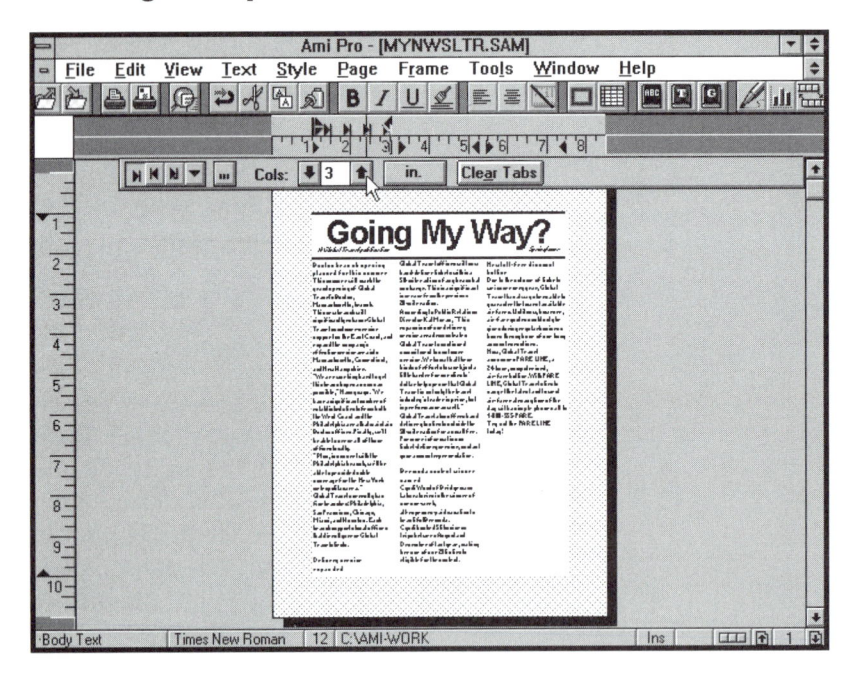

6. Deactivate the current ruler (press **Esc**).

7. Return to Custom view (choose **View, Custom 91%** or click on the **Toggle Full Page/Layout View SmartIcon**).

SPECIFYING GUTTER WIDTH

When you create multiple columns, Ami Pro places even amounts of space, called *gutters*, between the columns. By default, Ami Pro sets all gutter widths to .17". If you want to change this width, you can do so through the Modify Page Layout dialog box.

Follow these steps when you want to change the gutter width through this dialog box:

- Place the insertion point inside a column.
- Open the Modify Page Layout dialog box.
- Select Modify Margins & Columns (if necessary).
- Change the value in the Gutter Width box.
- Click on OK.

Note: When you use the Modify Page Layout dialog box to change gutter and column width, Ami Pro assigns your width specification uniformly to every gutter and column. If you'd prefer to create gutters and/or columns with uneven widths, you can do so through the current ruler. For more information on using the current ruler to modify gutter and column widths, consult your Ami Pro documentation.

Let's change your columns' gutter widths:

1. Observe your document. There is very little space between columns.
2. Open the Modify Page Layout dialog box (choose **Page, Modify Page Layout** or click in the left or right margin with the *right* mouse button).
3. Observe the Number Of Columns options. You can use either the current ruler *or* the Modify Page Layout dialog box to create multiple columns.
4. Look at the Gutter Width box. It is set to *0.17*.
5. Type .5 in the Gutter Width box, click on **OK**, and then observe your document. Ami Pro has increased the amount of space between all of the columns to ½"; now there appears to be *too* much space between the columns (see Figure 12.9).

374 • CREATING A NEWSLETTER

Figure 12.9   **MYNWSLTR.SAM, with ½" gutters**

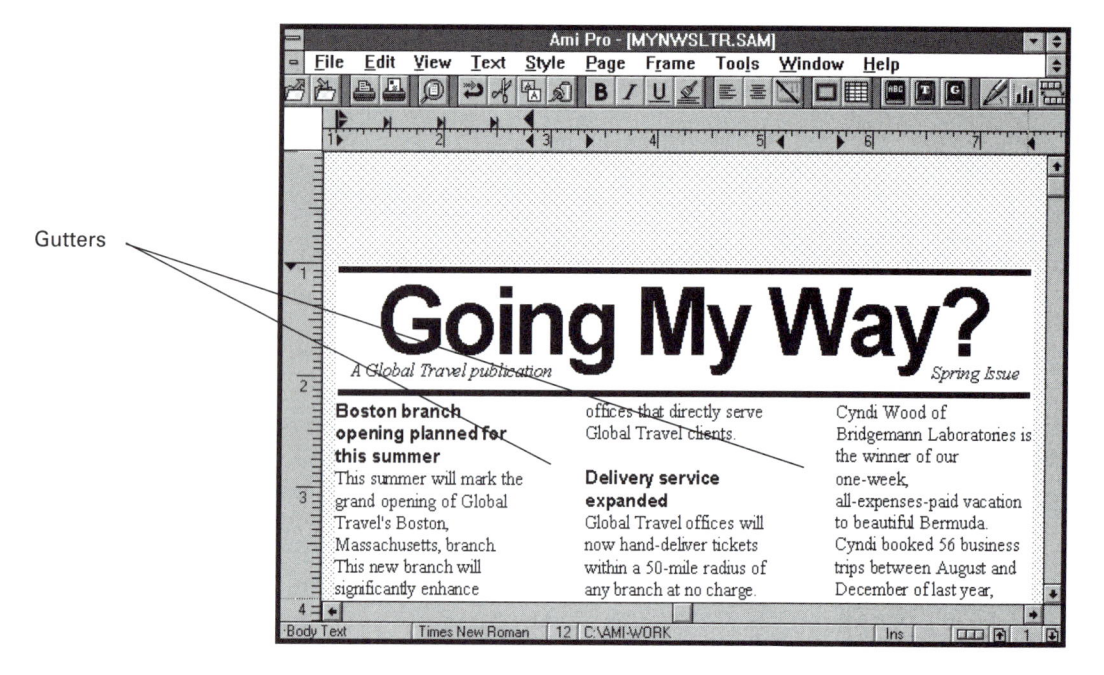

Gutters

6. Reopen the Modify Page Layout dialog box, type **.25** in the Gutter Width box, and then click on **OK**. Ami Pro decreases the amount of space between the columns to ¼", which looks more appropriate.

INSERTING A MANUAL COLUMN BREAK

Ami Pro breaks columns as it breaks pages; that is, when the program runs out of room for text in one column, it starts the text at the top of the next column. If you're not happy with how Ami Pro has ended a column, you can insert a *manual column break* to end the column exactly where *you* want it to end.

Follow these steps when you want to insert a manual column break:

- Place the insertion point in the paragraph *preceding* the paragraph that you want at the top of the next column.

- Choose Page, Breaks to open the Breaks dialog box.

- Select Insert Column Break.
- Click on OK.

Tip: Before you start inserting manual column breaks, note that you should insert them as late in the editing and formatting process as possible, just as for manual page breaks. Otherwise, edits such as added text or changed margins might make it necessary for you to remove and then reinsert your column breaks manually after editing.

Follow these steps when you want to remove a manual column break:

- Place the insertion point in the last paragraph of the column that ends with a manual column break.
- Choose Page, Breaks to open the Breaks dialog box.
- Choose Remove Column Break.
- Click on OK.

Note: You can display symbols for manual column breaks by checking Marks in the View Preferences dialog box.

Let's insert some manual column breaks:

1. Scroll to and examine the bottom of the page. The heading for the newsletter's second story, *Delivery service expanded*, begins at the bottom of the first column.
2. Place the insertion point in the blank line above *Delivery service expanded*, and then choose **Page, Breaks** to open the Breaks dialog box.
3. Select **Insert Column Break**, and then click on **OK**.
4. Scroll to the top of your document. Notice that Ami Pro has moved the story's first line to the top of the second column (see Figure 12.10).

PRACTICE YOUR SKILLS

1. Scroll to the bottom of the second column.
2. Place the insertion point in the blank line above the story heading, *Bermuda contest winner named*.
3. Insert a manual column break.

Figure 12.10 **MYNWSLTR.SAM, after inserting a manual column break**

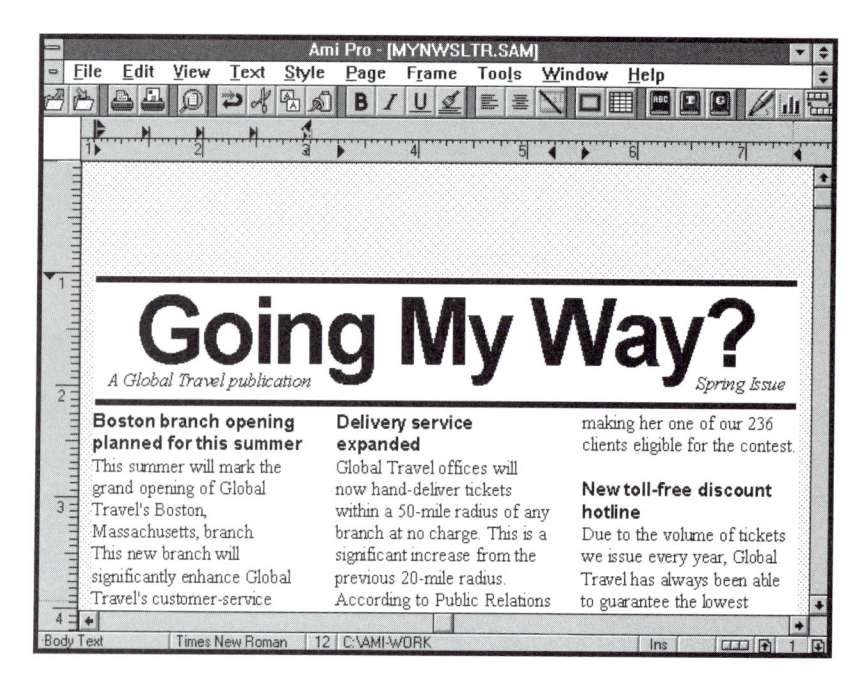

4. Scroll to the top of the document and verify that Ami Pro has moved the story heading to the top of the third column.
5. Save MYNWSLTR.SAM.

JUSTIFYING AND HYPHENATING TEXT

To provide a neater appearance for multiple-column text, you might want to justify it. This way, each column will have even (not ragged) right and left edges, which provides a good visual separation between columns. (For a review of justified text, refer back to Chapter 5.)

To justify text, you can first select the text and then choose Text, Alignment, Justify; or you can modify the text's style through the Modify Style dialog box.

When you justify multiple-column text, Ami Pro often inserts wide gaps between words in an effort to make the words stretch across the column. To help alleviate this problem, you can *hyphenate* the text, breaking words in two with a hyphen (-). (The text in this book is often hyphenated at the right margin.) Up to now, we have worked exclusively with unhyphenated text: Ami Pro has ended each line with a whole word rather than with a hyphenated word. By hyphenating text, you can decrease the interword gaps by fitting as many characters as possible on a single line.

Follow these steps when you want to hyphenate text:

- Open the Modify Style dialog box.
- Select the style assigned to the text you want to hyphenate. (Ami Pro will automatically hyphenate all the text based on this style.)
- Check Modify Hyphenation.
- Click on OK.

Note: If you don't like the way Ami Pro has hyphenated your text, you can override Ami Pro's hyphenation, insert your own hyphens, and/or change Ami Pro's hyphenation settings. For more information on controlling hyphenation, see your Ami Pro documentation.

Let's hyphenate all the body text in your newsletter stories:

1. Observe the three columns of text. These columns might look tidier as justified text.

2. Place the insertion point in the paragraph beginning *This summer will mark* (located at the top of the first column), and then observe the Style Status button. The Body Text style has been assigned to the body text paragraphs of every newsletter story.

3. Open the Modify Style dialog box (choose **Style, Modify Style** or click over the text with the *right* mouse button). Then verify that *F2-Body Text* is selected in the Style drop-down list box.

4. Select **Modify Alignment**, select **Alignment Justify**, and then click on **OK**. Ami Pro justifies the text in every column.

5. Scroll down through your document and observe the justified text. In some lines, Ami Pro has had to insert large gaps between words to make the lines reach from one side of a column to the other.

6. Reopen the Modify Style dialog box, verify that *F2·Body Text* is selected in the Style drop-down list box, check **Modify Hyphenation**, and then click on **OK**.

7. Scroll through and observe your document again. Ami Pro has automatically hyphenated the body text as necessary, thereby reducing or eliminating many of the gaps (see Figure 12.11).

8. Save your document.

Figure 12.11   Justified and hyphenated text

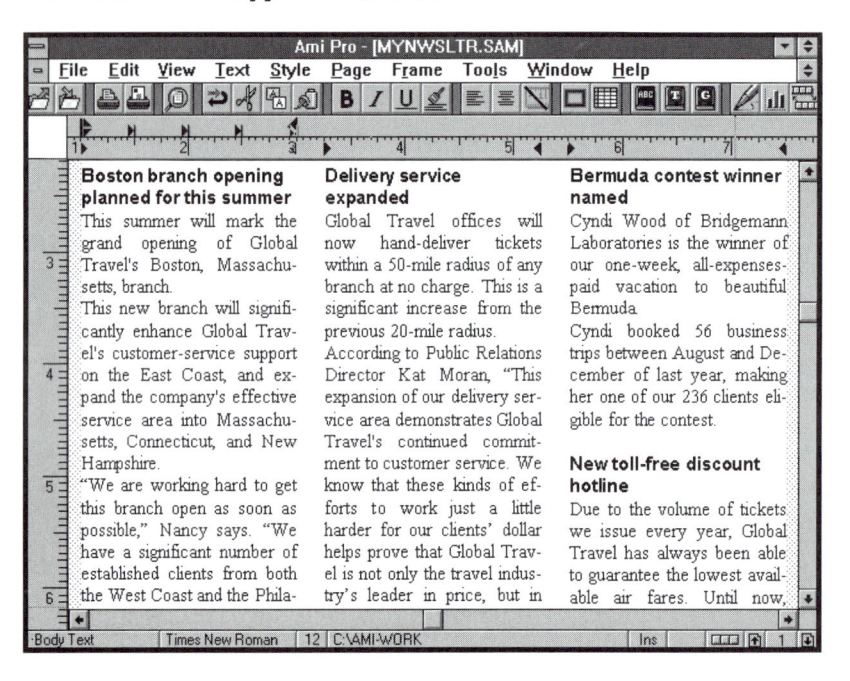

WORKING WITH PICTURES

"A picture is worth a thousand words," goes the old saying, so why not put one in your newsletter and save yourself a lot of typing? Pictures (also known as *graphics*) can dramatically increase the impact, sense, and readability of printed pieces. Rather than describe how something looks, you can illustrate it. Pictures can also prove useful for filling awkward empty spaces on a page.

IMPORTING A PICTURE

Ami Pro can import a wide variety of pictures, including

- *Objets d'art* you've created yourself in a graphics program such as Windows Paintbrush, CorelDRAW!, or Ami Pro's own AmiDraw
- Images you've scanned using a computer scanner
- One of the many pieces of clip art that are included with Ami Pro

Follow these steps when you want to import a picture into your document:

- Place the insertion point where you want to insert the picture.
- Choose File, Import Picture to open the Import Picture dialog box.
- In the File Type list box, specify what type of file the picture is in. For Ami Pro clip art, choose AmiDraw.
- Use the Drives drop-down list box and Directories list box as necessary to select the drive and directory that contain your picture. By default, Ami Pro will select the directory where it stores its own clip art (C:\AMIPRO\DRAWSYM, or something similar).
- In the Files list box, select the file containing your picture.
- Click on OK.

When Ami Pro imports a picture, it automatically creates a frame for that picture, and places the picture inside. If you want to modify the picture frame's size, placement, or other features, use the Modify Frame Layout dialog box and/or your mouse. Because your picture is inside a frame, you have much the same flexibility with pictures as you do with framed text.

Note: Ami Pro provides tools for creating, modifying, and enhancing pictures, including its own AmiDraw program. For more information on working with pictures, see your Ami Pro documentation.

Let's insert a picture now to fill a blank space in your newsletter:

1. Switch to Full Page view, and then observe your document. Because of the manual column break you inserted at the bottom of the second column, that column ends far short of the bottom margin.

2. Return to Custom view, and then scroll to and observe the bottom of the second column. A picture would fill this empty space nicely.

3. Place the insertion point in the blank line at the bottom of the second column (directly under the *your* in *your account representative*.).

4. Choose **File, Import Picture**, and then observe the Import Picture dialog box (see Figure 12.12). By default, Ami Pro looks in the C:\AMIPRO\DRAWSYM directory for AmiDraw pictures. (If you installed Ami Pro on a drive other than C, Ami Pro might look instead in the \AMIPRO\DRAWSYM directory on that drive.)

Figure 12.12   The Import Picture dialog box

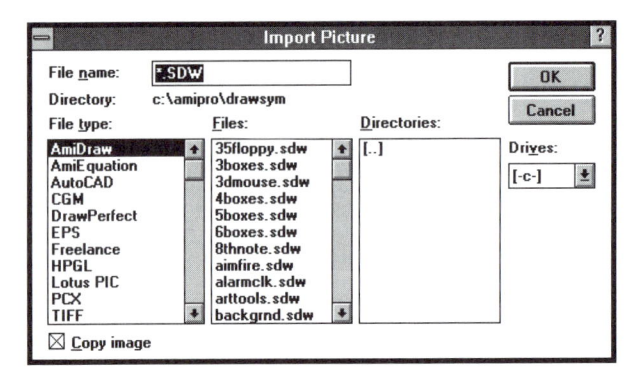

5. Observe the Files list box. It lists the dozens of pictures that install along with Ami Pro.

6. Scroll down in the Files list box, select **globe.sdw**, and then click on **OK** to import the picture into your document.

7. Observe your document. Ami Pro has imported a picture of a globe, and has placed it in its own frame at the bottom of the second column (see Figure 12.13).

8. Save MYNWSLTR.SAM.

Figure 12.13   **The imported picture**

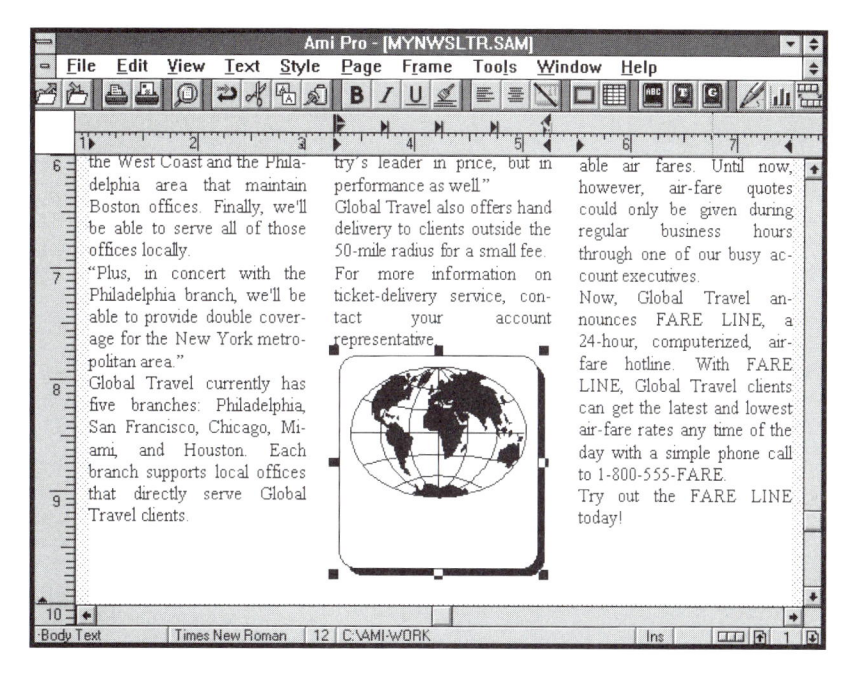

SIZING A PICTURE FRAME

Since Ami Pro created a frame that's too tall for the picture you imported, let's resize it using the mouse and a frame handle:

1. If it is not still selected, select the picture frame again.

2. Scroll down, if necessary, to see the entire frame.

3. Place the mouse pointer over the frame's bottom-center handle; the pointer changes to a vertical double arrow.

4. Begin to drag the frame handle upward. As you drag, Ami Pro displays a dotted outline to indicate the frame's changing size (see Figure 12.14).

5. Drag upward until the bottom of the dotted outline aligns with the bottom of the text in the first and third columns. Then release the mouse button. The picture now fits well inside the frame, and the frame aligns with the bottom of the first and third columns.

Figure 12.14   **Sizing a frame with the mouse**

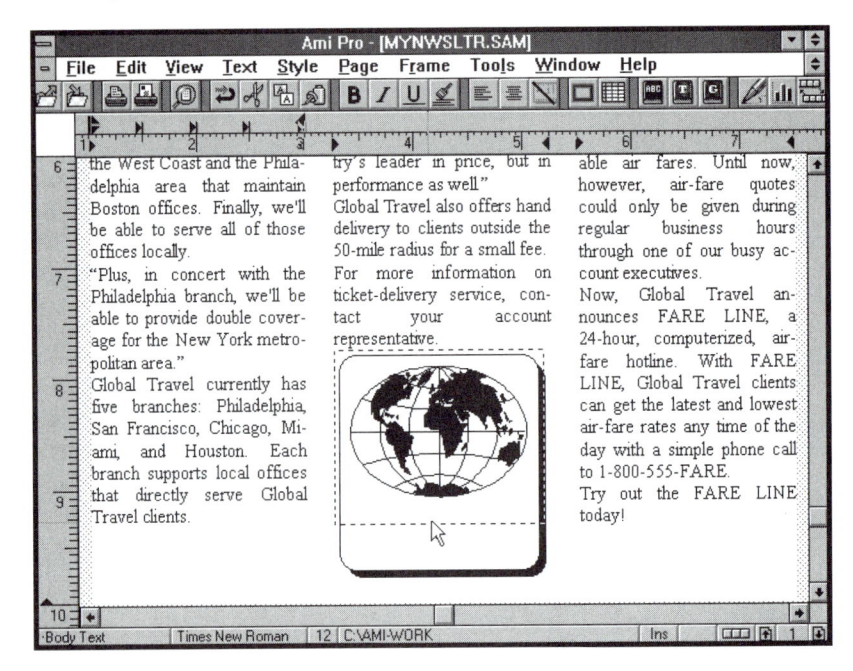

6. Deselect the frame, switch to Full Page view, and then observe your document. The framed picture makes the newsletter look more visually balanced.

ADDING A LINE AROUND A PAGE

One final touch you might want to add to a newsletter (or any document, for that matter), is a line (border) all the way around the page. This can give your newsletter a neat, boxed look.

To place a border around a page:

- Open the Modify Page Layout dialog box.
- Select Modify Lines.
- Select Around Page All. (Or, if you'd prefer, you can add lines just to the top, bottom, left, and/or right sides of the page.)
- In the Style list box, select the desired line style.

- If desired, choose an option in the Position box. By default, Ami Pro selects Position Middle, which places the border along each margin's midpoint. With the other options you can move the border closer to either the typing area or the paper's edge.
- Click on OK.

By default, Ami Pro adds a border around every page in the document.

Note: If the border around a page doesn't print, check your printer's documentation. You might have placed the border on a part of the page on which the printer can't print.

Let's add a border around your one-page newsletter:

1. Open the Modify Page Layout dialog box, select **Modify Lines**, and then observe the dialog box. The options here enable you to add a border around the page.

2. Check **Around Page All**, and then click on **OK**. Ami Pro adds a thin line inside the margins all the way around the page.

3. Open the View Preferences dialog box, uncheck **Margins In Color**, and then click on **OK**. You can now see much more clearly how your newsletter will look when printed (see Figure 12.15).

4. Save MYNWSLTR.SAM.

Before you finish this chapter, let's take a moment to set the Ami Pro work environment back to the way it was when we started this chapter:

1. Open the View Preferences dialog box, check **Margins In Color**, check **Tabs & Returns**, uncheck **Vertical Ruler**, and then click on **OK**.

2. Hide the current ruler (choose **View, Hide Ruler** or click on the **Show/Hide Ruler SmartIcon**).

3. Return to Custom view.

4. Close MYNWSLTR.SAM.

Figure 12.15 **The completed newsletter**

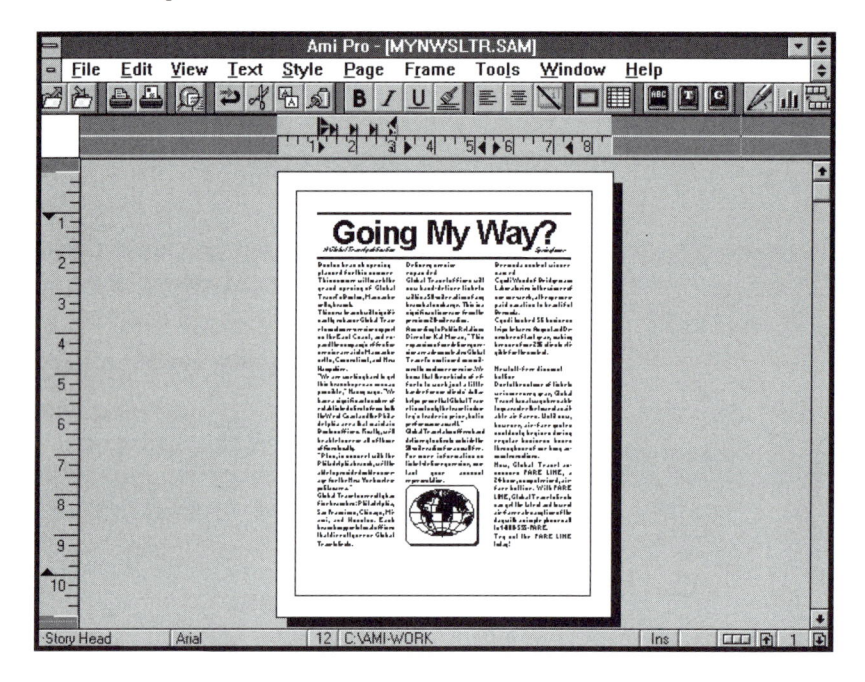

SUMMARY

In this chapter, you learned how to use frames, multiple columns, pictures, and full-page borders to create a newsletter.

Congratulations! Having completed this chapter, you've now developed a solid foundation of Ami Pro skills. You are now prepared to take all that you've learned and apply it to your own documents. Remember, to keep and master the skills you've acquired, you must now supply the most important ingredient: *practice*.

Good luck!

Here is a quick reference guide to the Ami Pro features introduced in this chapter:

Desired Result	**How to Do It**
Display the vertical ruler	Choose **View, View Preferences**; check **Vertical Ruler**; then click on **OK**.

Desired Result	How to Do It
Create a frame numerically	Move to desired page; choose **Frame, Create Frame**; specify frame's position and dimensions; then click on **OK**.
Select a frame	Click inside frame.
Deselect a frame	Click outside frame, or press **Esc**.
Type text in a frame	Double-click inside frame; then type text.
Open Modify Frame Layout dialog box	Select frame; then choose **Frame, Modify Frame Layout**. Or select frame and then click inside it with *right* mouse button.
Modify a frame layout	Select frame; open Modify Frame Layout dialog box; select option category; select desired options; click on **OK**.
Modify a frame's size with the mouse	Select frame and then drag a **frame handle**.
Create multiple columns	Place insertion point in desired text stream; activate **current ruler**; change number in tab bar's Cols box. Or, place insertion point in desired text stream; open Modify Page Layout dialog box; select **Modify Margins & Columns**; select desired number of columns; then click on **OK**.
Change gutter width	Place insertion point inside column; open Modify Page Layout dialog box; select **Modify Margins & Columns**; change value in Gutter Width box; then click on **OK**.
Insert a manual column break	Place insertion point in paragraph preceding the paragraph for new column; choose **Page, Breaks**; select **Insert Column Break**; then click on **OK**.

Desired Result	How to Do It
Remove a manual column break	Place insertion point in last paragraph of column ending with break; choose **Page, Breaks**; select **Remove Column Break**; then click on **OK**.
Hyphenate text	Open Modify Style dialog box; select style assigned to desired text; check **Modify Hyphenation**; then click on **OK**.
Import a picture	Place insertion point; choose **File, Import Picture**; select picture file type; select picture file; then click on **OK**.
Add a border around a page	Move to page; open Modify Page Layout dialog box; select **Modify Lines**; select **Around Page All**; select line style and position (if desired); then click on **OK**.
Remove margin coloring	Choose **View, View Preferences**; uncheck **Margins In Color**; then click on **OK**.

Following this chapter are three appendices:

- Appendix A, "Installation," walks you through an Ami Pro 3.0 installation.

- Appendix B, "Keyboard Shortcut Reference," lists many keyboard shortcuts available in Ami Pro and Windows.

- Appendix C, "Exchanging Documents with Other Programs," discusses how you can use Ami Pro to open files created in other computer applications and how you can save Ami Pro documents so that other applications can use them.

APPENDIX A: INSTALLATION

Preparing Your
Computer for Ami
Pro Installation

Installing Ami Pro
3.0 on Your
Computer

This appendix provides instructions for installing or reinstalling Ami Pro 3.0 on your computer.

To be certain that Ami Pro will run as described in this book, you should use the *Complete Ami Pro Install* option when installing Ami Pro (we will describe the procedure for doing so later in this appendix). If you already have installed Ami Pro, you may want to *reinstall* it to make certain that Ami Pro is completely installed. Otherwise, some Ami Pro features described in this book may not be available to you.

Note: To get you up and running in Ami Pro as quickly as possible, we have used terms in this appendix that you may not understand. Please bear with us. Most of the terms introduced here are explained early in the book.

PREPARING YOUR COMPUTER FOR AMI PRO INSTALLATION

There are three requirements that you must meet before you begin to install Ami Pro 3.0:

- DOS version 3.1 or higher must be installed on your computer. If it is not, install it now. (For help, see your DOS documentation.)

- Windows version 3.0 or higher must be installed on your computer. If it is not, install it now. (For help, see your Windows documentation.) As noted in this book's Introduction, we *strongly* recommend that you install Windows 3.1, if possible, rather than Windows 3.0.

- There must be enough free space (18 megabytes) on your hard drive to store all of Ami Pro's program files and the temporary files that Ami Pro creates while running.

Note: If you are *reinstalling* Ami Pro, you may need less than 18 megabytes of free space. This is because Ami Pro's installation program will replace Ami Pro program files already stored on your hard drive, thereby reducing the overall amount of *new* space needed.

Perform the following steps to meet the third requirement above:

1. You need to have your computer on and running in DOS. If Windows is running, you need to exit to DOS. To do this, click on **File** in the Program Manager window, click on **Exit Windows...** in the File menu, and then click on **OK**.

2. At the DOS prompt, type **c:** (or, if you intend to install Ami Pro on a hard drive other than C, type the letter of that drive, followed by a colon). Then press **Enter**.

3. Type **dir**, and then press **Enter**. DOS lists the files contained in the current directory and, at the very end of this list, reports the number of free bytes.

4. Observe the number of free bytes. You need at least 18 megabytes (just over 18,000,000 bytes) of free hard-drive space to install and run Ami Pro.

5. If the number of free bytes is over 18,000,000, skip the rest of this activity. If the number is very close to or under 18,000,000, delete enough files from your hard drive to free the space required for the Ami Pro installation. *Be sure to back up any files that you want to save before deleting them!*

6. Type **dir** and then press **Enter** again. DOS should now report over 18,000,000 free bytes. (If it does not, return to step 5.)

INSTALLING AMI PRO 3.0 ON YOUR COMPUTER

Now that you've met the three requirements above, you can begin the actual Ami Pro 3.0 installation or reinstallation.

Note: If you are installing Ami Pro using Windows 3.0, the following procedure may not work exactly as described. If this happens, follow the installation program's on-screen directions as necessary.

1. From DOS, type **win** and press **Enter** to start Windows.

2. Insert the disk labeled *Install (Disk 1)* in the appropriate floppy disk drive.

3. If necessary, activate the **Program Manager window**. (If Program Manager is running as an icon, double-click on the icon to open and activate Program Manager in a window. If Program Manager is running in a window, click on the title bar of the window to activate it.)

4. In the Program Manager window, click on **File** and then on **Run...** to open the Run dialog box.

5. Type **a:install** if the Install disk is in drive A, or **b:install** if the disk is in drive B. Then click on **OK** to begin the Ami Pro installation program.

6. After a moment, the Ami Pro installation program opens a window entitled *Ami Pro Install Program*, followed by a dialog box entitled *Name And Initials*. (If you are reinstalling Ami Pro, skip to step 10.)

7. Type your name in the Name text box. As you do, Ami Pro automatically adds your initials to the Initials text box.

8. If your initials are incorrect, press **Tab** to move to the Initials text box, and then type the correct initials.

9. Click on **OK**.

10. The installation program next opens the Main Menu dialog box, providing three options: *Install Ami Pro*, *Install Ami Pro On Server*, and *View What's New In 3.0*. For the purposes of this book, click on the large button to the left of **Install Ami Pro**. (If you work on a network and would like instead to install Ami Pro on a network server, check with your network administrator before clicking on the button next to *Install Ami Pro On Server*.)

11. Next you'll see an Install Choices dialog box that enables you to install Ami Pro completely or only partially. Click on the button for **Complete Ami Pro Install**.

12. The installation program next opens a Windows Or NewWave Installation dialog box, giving you the choice to install Ami Pro for use with Windows or NewWave. Since we designed this book for running Ami Pro with Windows, click on **Windows**.

13. Next you'll see a Specifying The Program Directory dialog box that enables you to specify where to install Ami Pro. This dialog box also shows how much hard drive space the installation will require and how much space is available. By default, the installation program suggests installing Ami Pro in *C:\AMIPRO*. If desired, you can type a different location for installing Ami Pro, and then click on **OK**; otherwise, just click on **OK**.

14. If you are reinstalling Ami Pro, the installation program next opens an Overwrite Existing Paths dialog box. Click on **OK** to accept the dialog box's defaults.

15. The installation program next opens a Transferring Files dialog box to show you the per-disk and overall installation progress. As it installs Ami Pro, the installation program also provides some general information about Ami Pro's features.

16. Follow the on-screen directions to remove the current installation disk and insert subsequent disks. Click on **OK** after inserting each disk.

17. After the installation program finishes with the last installation disk, it opens a WordPerfect SwitchKit Installation dialog box. (This SwitchKit is designed for people switching to Ami Pro from the WordPerfect word processing program.) Click on **Do Not Install SwitchKit**.

18. The installation program next opens an Ami Pro Install Program dialog box to inform you that the installation is complete. Click on **OK** to close this dialog box.

19. When you are returned to the Main Menu dialog box, click on **Exit Install**.

20. The Ami Pro Install Program window closes, returning you to the Program Manager window. There you will find a window entitled *Lotus Applications* that contains two Ami Pro icons: *Ami Pro 3.0* and *Dialog Editor*. (If you reinstalled Ami Pro, there may be two of each icon.)

21. Remove the last installation disk and put all your installation disks in a safe place.

Do *not* start Ami Pro at this point; you will learn how to start Ami Pro in Chapter 1. Return now to the "Before You Start" section in this book's Introduction, and then continue on to Chapter 1.

APPENDIX B: KEYBOARD SHORTCUT REFERENCE

Movement

Text Selection

Menu Commands

This appendix lists a number of keyboard shortcuts available in Ami Pro. In some cases, you may find these shortcuts easier to use than their mouse-based counterparts.

MOVEMENT

To Move	Use This Keyboard Shortcut
One character to the left	Left Arrow
One character to the right	Right Arrow
One line up	Up Arrow
One line down	Down Arrow
One word to the left	Ctrl+Left Arrow
One word to the right	Ctrl+Right Arrow
To the end of a line	End
To the beginning of a line	Home
To the beginning of the current or previous sentence	Ctrl+, (comma)
To the beginning of the next sentence	Ctrl+. (period)
To the end of a paragraph	Ctrl+Down Arrow
To the beginning of a paragraph	Ctrl+Up Arrow
Down one screen	PgDn
Up one screen	PgUp
Down one page	Ctrl+PgDn
Up one page	Ctrl+PgUp
To the top of a document	Ctrl+Home
To the end of a document	Ctrl+End

TEXT SELECTION

To select text with the keyboard, place the insertion point at one end of the text, press and hold Shift, use any of the movement shortcuts listed above, and then release Shift.

MENU COMMANDS

To Issue This Command	Use This Keyboard Shortcut
File, Open	Ctrl+O
File, Save	Ctrl+S
File, Print	Ctrl+P
Edit, Undo	Ctrl+Z
Edit, Cut	Ctrl+X
Edit, Copy	Ctrl+C
Edit, Paste	Ctrl+V
Edit, Find & Replace	Ctrl+F
Edit, Go To (opens Go To dialog box)	Ctrl+G
Edit, Go To (does not open Go To dialog box)	Ctrl+H
View, Full Page	Ctrl+D
View, Show SmartIcons or View, Hide SmartIcons	Ctrl+Q
Text, Alignment, Left	Ctrl+L
Text, Alignment, Center	Ctrl+E
Text, Alignment, Right	Ctrl+R
Text, Alignment, Justify	Ctrl+J
Text, Normal	Ctrl+N
Text, Bold	Ctrl+B
Text, Italic	Ctrl+I
Text, Underline	Ctrl+U
Text, Word Underline	Ctrl+W

KEYBOARD SHORTCUT REFERENCE

To Issue This Command	Use This Keyboard Shortcut
Text, Fast Format	Ctrl+T
Style, Modify Style	Ctrl+A

Note: To help you remember these keyboard shortcuts, Ami Pro lists them on the menus, to the right of each corresponding menu item. Because of limited space, Ami Pro uses a caret (^) as shorthand for Ctrl. For example, the keyboard shortcut for Style, Modify Style is listed as ^A rather than as *Ctrl+A*.

APPENDIX C: EXCHANGING DOCUMENTS WITH OTHER PROGRAMS

Opening Non-Ami Pro 3.0 Files

Saving Ami Pro 3.0 Documents in Other File Formats

Importing and Exporting for Unsupported Programs

Loss of Formatting When Importing and Exporting

Ami Pro 3.0 has a number of *import file filters* that enable it to open document files created in many other word processing programs, as well as files created by many spreadsheet and database programs. Ami Pro also has *export file filters* that enable Ami Pro to save its documents in a file format that other programs can use. Because of these import and export abilities, you can exchange information electronically with many other computer users, regardless of what programs they use. For example, you can open a coworker's Word for Windows document in Ami Pro, edit the document, save the document in Word for Windows format, and then hand the edited document back to your coworker.

This appendix lists the various programs supported by Ami Pro's file filters, and shows you how to open and save files in non-Ami Pro 3.0 formats.

OPENING NON-AMI PRO 3.0 FILES

Follow these steps when you want to open a non-Ami Pro 3.0 file:

- Open the Open dialog box (choose File, Open, or click on the Open An Existing File SmartIcon, or press Ctrl+O).

- In the List Files Of Type drop-down list box, select the appropriate file format. Ami Pro will then list in the Files list box any files that have the corresponding file name extension. For example, if you choose to open a Word for Windows document, which uses the .DOC file name extension, Ami Pro will list only those files that end with .DOC, rather than those that end with .SAM.

- If necessary, select the drive and directory where the file is stored. If you've imported this type of file before, Ami Pro will automatically select the same location from which you last imported a file of that type.

- Select the desired file in the Files list box; or type the file name (with its extension) in the File Name text box.

- Click on OK.

- For certain file formats, Ami Pro will next open an Import or Import Options dialog box to enable you to specify exactly how Ami Pro should import the selected file. If one of these dialog boxes opens, consult your Ami Pro documentation for information on the import options available for that specific file format. Then specify the desired option or options and click on OK.

Ami Pro opens the file as an untitled document. You can edit, print, and save this document as you would any standard Ami Pro document. When you name and save the document, Ami Pro by default will save it in Ami Pro 3.0 format. To save the file in its original or some other non-Ami Pro 3.0 format, refer to the procedure in the next section, "Saving Ami Pro 3.0 Documents in Other File Formats."

Note: If you open an ASCII-format file (usually, files that end with .TXT), Ami Pro will retain that file's original name. When you then save that file, Ami Pro by default will resave it as ASCII text. If you plan to import ASCII files, see your Ami Pro documentation for more details on opening, saving, and working with ASCII files.

Here is a list of non-Ami Pro 3.0 file types that Ami Pro can open:

1-2-3

1-2-3 for Windows

Advance Write

Ami Pro (previous versions)

ASCII

dBase

DCA/FFT

DCA/RFT

DIF

DisplayWrite

E-Mail

Enable

Excel

Executive MemoMaker

Manuscript

MultiMate

Navy DIF

Paradox

PeachText

Rich Text Format

Samna Word

SmartWare

SuperCalc

Symphony

Windows Write

Word for DOS

Word for Windows

WordPerfect

WordStar

SAVING AMI PRO 3.0 DOCUMENTS IN OTHER FILE FORMATS

Follow these steps when you want to save an Ami Pro 3.0 document in a non-Ami Pro 3.0 file format:

- Open the Save As dialog box (choose File, Save As).

- In the List Files Of Type drop-down list box, select the desired file format. Or, if you want to save the file in Ami Pro 1.2 format, check Ami Pro 1.2 Format.

- If necessary, select the drive and directory where you want to save the file. If you've exported this type of file before, Ami Pro will automatically select the same location to which you last exported a file of that type.

- In the File Name text box, type a name for your file. (Remember, file names must be one to eight characters, and cannot include spaces or some special characters.)

- Click on OK.

- For certain file formats, Ami Pro will open an Export or an Export Options dialog box to enable you to specify exactly how Ami Pro should export your document. If one of these dialog boxes opens, consult your Ami Pro documentation for information on the export options available for that specific file format. Then specify the desired option or options and click on OK.

Ami Pro saves the current document in the format you specified, leaving a copy of the original document in the active document window. If you want to save the document in Ami Pro 3.0 format, as well, save the document. Otherwise, just close the document window without saving changes.

Once you've saved a document in a non-Ami Pro 3.0 file format, you can open it in the program that uses this file format (for example,

SAVING AMI PRO 3.0 DOCUMENTS IN OTHER FILE FORMATS • 405

WordPerfect). Then you can edit, print, save, or close the file exactly as you would any standard file in that program.

Here is a list of non-Ami Pro 3.0 file types to which Ami Pro can export:

Advance Write

Ami Pro (previous versions)

ASCII

DCA/FFT

DCA/RFT

DisplayWrite

E-Mail

Enable

Executive MemoMaker

MultiMate

Navy DIF

PeachText

Rich Text Format

Samna Word

Windows Write

Word for DOS

Word for Windows

WordPerfect

WordStar

IMPORTING AND EXPORTING FOR UNSUPPORTED PROGRAMS

Although you can see from the long lists in this appendix that Ami Pro's import and export filters support a wide variety of file formats from other programs, one of the applications you use may not be listed or may be supported for import only and not for export. If this is the case, you may be able to use one of the following three options to transfer your information:

- Create and use an *interim file format* that both programs support. For example, if another program can export to Rich Text Format, save the file in that format and then import the interim file into Ami Pro. Conversely, if your other program can read Rich Text Format files, you can export to that format from Ami Pro.

- Among Windows applications, use the Windows Clipboard to copy and paste information. If you have an 80386-based (or higher) computer, you can even copy and paste between Windows and non-Windows applications. For more information on using the Windows Clipboard to transfer information between applications, see your Windows documentation.

- Call Ami Pro's support line to see if they have filters for your application that did not ship with your original Ami Pro package.

LOSS OF FORMATTING WHEN IMPORTING AND EXPORTING

Ami Pro's import and export filters are a good way to transfer information between one application and another. However, no import or export filter is perfect. Because each program supports a specific set of features, some formatting information may be lost when you import and export files. For instance, if you export an Ami Pro document that contains a table to another word processing program format that does not support tables, your table-formatting information will be lost.

For details on which formatting information will be retained and which will be lost during importing and exporting, see your Ami Pro documentation.

INDEX

angle brackets, 340

Applications program group, 8

application windows, 13–16

ascending sort order, 347

attributes, text. *See* text attributes

automatic page breaks, 185

A

alignment. *See also* tabs
- of headers, 172
- of paragraphs, 151–155
- of text with tabs, 20–21

Ami Pro
- application windows, 13–16
- document windows, 13–16
- exiting, 31
- installing, 389–393
- introduction to, 7–12
- navigating in, 35–68, 396
- setting defaults, 9–12
- starting, 8
- tutorial, 8

Ami Pro 3.0 icon, 393

B

Backspace key, 21–22

banner, 366

blank fields, merging records with, 344–346

blocks of text, deleting, 76–78

Body Text (Style Status) button, 250

boilerplate text, 269

bold text, 106, 109

Bold Text SmartIcon, 261

Breaks dialog box, 188

bullets, 224–226
- for paragraphs, 226
- styles for, 225

buttons, navigation, 336

C

calendar, creating, 270–272

Cancel button (dialog box), 17

capitalization of text, 104

cells (in tables), 282

    adding lines to, 307–308

    addresses of, 285–286

    numeric and non-numeric, 292

centered paragraphs, 154

centering headers, 172

centering a table, 311–312

Center Selected Text SmartIcon, 152–153

center tab, 130–131

Center Tab button, 137

check boxes, 11

checking grammar, 206–212

checking spelling, 198–204

clearing tabs, 134–135, 138–140

Clear Tabs button, 131, 134

clicking the mouse, 5

Clipboard, 88, 223

closing a document, 30

column breaks, inserting, 374–376

Column Row/Size dialog box, 301–303

columns in tables, 282. *See also* multiple columns

    changing column widths, 300–303

    headings for, 285, 287

    inserting, 303–304

    selecting, 298

    totaling, 295–296

commands

    dimmed, 17

    shortcuts for, 397–398

    using menu bar to issue, 16–18

conditional merges, 343

context-sensitive Help, 59–60

Control menu box, 5, 7, 15

copy arrow, 219

copying text, 88, 90–91

    between documents, 221–224

    with Drag & Drop, 218–221

Copy To The Clipboard SmartIcon, 89

Create Frame dialog box, 364

Create Style dialog box, 262–263
Create Table dialog box, 283–284
creating a new document, 30–31
Ctrl+Enter, 148–151
current date, entering, 4
current page, printing, 191
current ruler, 126–129
   displaying, 127–129
   indent markers, 141
   margins, 141
   setting custom tabs in, 131–136
   setting indents, 142–143
   tab bar, 132
   using to change margins, 180–182
Current Set drop-down list box, 231
current time, entering, 4
Custom view, 55–57
Cut To The Clipboard SmartIcon, 88–89

D

Date Created, 173
Date Of Last Revision, 173
dates
   entering current, 4
   examples of date styles, 173
   in headers and footers, 173–175
default document path, changing, 40–41
defaults, setting, 9–12
default tabs, 129
definition window, 57, 59
Delete Column/Row dialog box, 306
Delete key, 74–76
deleting
   blocks of text, 76–78
   manual page breaks, 189–190
   text, 21–22, 74–76
delimited data, 338
delimited format, 331
descending sort order, 347
dialog boxes, 10
   Cancel button, 17
   Help icon, 60
Dialog Editor icon, 393

dimmed commands, 17
Directories list box, 27
directory, 24
Document Description text box, 27–28
document margins. *See* margins
document path, 39–41
Document Path button, 41–42
documents
  closing, 30
  copying text between, 221–224
  creating new, 30–31
  exchanging with other programs, 401–406
  moving through, 46–51, 396
  naming, 26–28
  opening, 36–39, 72–74
  paginating, 185–190
  printing, 28–30
  proofing, 197–214
  retrieving saved, 36
  saving, 24–28
  saving in other formats, 404–405
  saving modified, 61
  scrolling through, 43–46
  source and target, 222
  viewing, 55–57
document windows, 2, 13–16, 221–222
  elements of, 5–6, 13–16
  floating, 233
  positioning SmartIcons in, 235
  typing area, 18–19
double-clicking the mouse, 4–5
down increment arrow, 11
Down Page Arrow button, 50
Drag & Drop, 218–221
dragging with the mouse, 17
  a floating SmartIcon set, 236
  selecting text by, 76–78
drives, specifying, 39–41
Drives list box, 27
drop-down list arrow, 12
drop-down list box, 12

E

editing
- basic techniques for, 72–79
- headers and footers, 176–178
- merge data files, 335–339
- merge documents, 339–343
- text, 71–100

Editing SmartIcon set, 233

Edit menu, 17
- Copy, 90
- Find & Replace, 51–55, 85–88
- Go To, 48–49
- Paste, 90
- Undo, 91–92

ellipsis (...) in menu items, 17

Enlarged view, 55

entering text, basics of, 18–20

Enter key, 19–20

envelopes, printing, 352–355

exchanging documents with other programs, 401–406

exiting Ami Pro, 31

export file filters, 401

exporting files, 404–406

extending a selection, 84

extensions, file name, 25

F

Face button, 112–114

Facing Pages view, 55

Fast Format dialog box, 115–116

Fast Format feature, 115–120

field delimiters, 331

field names, 326, 333

fields, 326
- blank, 344–346
- merge, 328
- naming, 326, 333

File menu
- Open, 36–39
- Save, 25–26
- Save As, 24–25

file name extensions, 25

file names, 26

files. *See also* documents
- exporting, 404–406

importing, 401–406

opening non-Ami Pro 3.0, 402–404

Files list box, navigating in, 38

finding text attributes, 227–230

Find & Replace, 51–55, 85–88, 227–230

Find & Replace Attributes dialog box, 227–229

Find & Replace Options dialog box, 53

fixed headers and footers, 170

floating headers and footers, 170

floating SmartIcon set, dragging, 236

floating window, 233

Font dialog box, 111–112

fonts, 104, 110–114

footers

changing margins for, 182–185

creating, 170–171, 173

dates in, 173–175

editing, 176–177

page numbers in, 175–176

types of, 170

formats

lost when importing and exporting, 406

numeric, 291

formatting text, 103–122. *See also* text attributes

modifying formats, 255–257

in tables, 312–313

form letters, 328–346

creating, 329–343

creating a merge data file, 330–335

merging, 343–344

frame handles, 363

frame layout, modifying, 367–370

frames (picture), 360–370

creating, 362–365

masthead frame, 366–370

sizing, 381–382

typing text in, 366–367

wrapping text around, 360–361

Full Page view, 55–56, 185–186

function keys, using to assign styles, 252–254

G

Go To dialog box, 49

Grammar Check, 206–212
- dialog box, 210
- SmartIcon, 207, 209
- starting, 207
- using, 207–208
- using readability statistics, 208–212

graphical user interface, 2

graphics, working with, 378–382

gridlines (table), 282, 287

gutters, 373

gutter width, specifying, 373–374

H

handles, frame, 363

hanging indents, setting, 140, 146–150

hard page breaks, 185

hard returns, 149–150

headers
- aligning, 172
- changing margins for, 182–185
- creating, 170–172
- dates in, 173–175
- editing, 176–178
- page numbers in, 175–176
- types of, 170

Headers & Footers dialog box, 171

headings, row and column, 285, 287

Help, 57–60

Help messages, one-line, 17
- hand, 58
- icon, 59–60
- table of contents, 57–58

Help windows, 57, 212

highlighting an item, 17, 26

homonyms, 211

horizontal scroll bar, 44

hyphenating text, 376–378

I

I-beam, 19

icons, 4. *See also* SmartIcons

    spacer, 237–238

    Windows program, 5

import file filters, 401

importing files, 401–406

Import Picture dialog box, 379–380

indentations. *See* indents

Indention dialog box, 144–145

indent markers, 129, 141

Indent Rest marker, 147

indents

    hanging, 140–141, 146–150

    setting with the current ruler, 142–143

    setting with the Indention dialog box, 144–145

index cards, electronic, 334

Insert Bullet dialog box, 225

Insert Column/Row dialog box, 304

Insert Date/Time dialog box, 174

insertion point, 18–19, 42

installation (Ami Pro), 389–393

italicized text, 107, 109

J

justifying text, 376–378

K

keyboard movement techniques, 46–47

keyboard shortcuts, 395–398

keys

    to assign styles, 252–254

    for moving in a table, 288

L

labels, mailing. *See* mailing labels

laying out pages, 169–194, 269

Leader Character button, 132

leading, 155

leading text (with page numbers), 175

Left Align Selected Text SmartIcon, 152

left-indented paragraph, 143

left margin. *See* margins

left tab, 130–131

letters, form. *See* form letters

line breaks, setting, 140

lines

    adding around tables, 308–311

    adding to table cells, 307–308

    drawing around a page, 382–383

Lines & Color dialog box, 309

line spacing

    changing, 155–157

    one-and-a-half, 157

    vs. paragraph spacing, 258

list box (drop-down), 12

lists, bulleted, 224–226

Load Defaults dialog box, 12

Lotus Applications program group, 8

M

macros, 269

mailing labels

    creating, 346–352

    merging, 349–352

    printing, 352–355

mail-merging. *See* merging

main document text, 198

manual column break, inserting, 374–376

manual feed (printer), 352

manual page breaks, 185

    inserting, 187–189

    removing, 189–190

    symbol, 189

margin markers, 129, 180–182

margins, 140–141. *See also* current ruler

    changing, 177–185

    changing header and footer, 182–185

    using current ruler to change, 180–182

masthead, 366–370

Maximize button, 6–7, 15

menu bar, 6–7, 16–18

menu commands, shortcuts for, 397–398

menu items, 10

menus, Windows, 5

merge data files, 326–329. *See also* merge documents; merging

   creating, 330–335

   editing, 335–339

   sorting records in, 346–349

merged documents, 326–328

merge documents, 326–328. *See also* merge data files; merging

   editing, 339–343

   merge fields in, 328, 341–342

   viewing, 345

merge fields, 328, 341–342

merging (merge operations), 325–329. *See also* merge data files; merge documents

   components of, 326–328

   form letters, 343–344

   mailing labels, 349–352

   records containing blank fields, 344–346

Minimize button, 6–7

Modify Frame Layout dialog box, 367–369

Modify Lines & Shades In A Table SmartIcon, 308

Modify Page Layout dialog box, 179–180

Modify Style dialog box, 254–256, 313–314

Modify Table Layout dialog box, 300, 310

monitor, 7

mouse

   clicking, 5

   double-clicking, 4–5

   dragging, 17

   left button, 5

   right button, 73

mouse pointer, 4

   changed to Help hand, 58

   changed to question mark, 59

   in Program Manager window, 7

move arrow, 218

moving

   with Drag & Drop, 218–220

   to a page, 48–51

   shortcut keys for, 396

   tabs, 137–139

   text, 88–89

   through a document, 46–51

multiple columns
    creating, 370–372
    specifying gutter width, 373–374
    working with, 370–378

multitasking, 3

N

Name and Initials dialog box, 391

naming a document, 26–28

naming fields, 333

navigating in Ami Pro, 35–68

navigation buttons, 336

New dialog box, 30

new line
    adding to a tabbed table, 133–134
    creating, 148–151

newsletters
    creating, 359–386
    and frames, 360–370

Next Icon Set SmartIcon, 231–233

non-Ami Pro 3.0 files, opening, 402–404

non-numeric cells, 292

nonprinting symbols, displaying, 22–23

numbers (page)
    styles for, 175
    using in headers and footers, 175–176

numbers (in tables)
    entering, 292–294
    format, 291
    working with, 291–296

numeric cells, 292

numeric format, 291

numeric tab, 130–131

Num Lock key, 74

O

one-line Help messages, 17

on-line Help. *See* Help

Open dialog box, 37

Open An Existing File SmartIcon, 72–74

opening a document, 36–39, 72–74

P

Page Arrow buttons, 49–50

page break
   inserting, 187–189
   removing, 189–190
   symbol, 189
   types of, 185

page-layout rulers, 126

page layouts, 169–194, 269

Page Numbering dialog box, 176

page numbers
   styles for, 175
   using in headers and footers, 175–176

pages
   drawing lines around, 382–383
   moving to, 48–51

Page Status button, 48

paginating a document, 185–190

paragraph alignment, 151–155

paragraphs
   bulleted, 226
   centered, 154
   changing alignment of, 151–155
   creating a new line, 148–151
   with hanging indents, 140, 146–150
   selecting for text enhancements, 129

paragraph selection shortcuts, 129

paragraph spacing, 248
   vs. line spacing, 258
   modifying, 258–260

paragraph-style rulers, 126

paragraph styles. *See* styles (paragraph)

Paste Clipboard Contents SmartIcon, 89

path, document, 39–41

picture frame, sizing, 381–382

pictures, working with, 378–382

point-and-shoot Help, 59

pointer, mouse. *See* mouse pointer

Point Size button, 112–114

point size (text), 110

Print dialog box, 28–29, 191

Print Envelope dialog box, 354

Print Envelope SmartIcon, 352

printers, manual feed, 352
printing
   controlling, 190–192
   the current page, 191
   documents, 28–30
   envelopes, 352–355
   mailing labels, 353
Print SmartIcon, 190–192
program group icon, 6–7
program group, 6–7
program icon 5, 6–7
   for Ami Pro, 8
Program Manager, 4–7
proofing documents, 197–214

Q

question mark, mouse pointer as, 59
Quick Add, 295–296

R

RAM (random-access memory), 3

ranges, selecting in tables, 297–300
readability statistics (Grammar Check), 208–212
   dialog box, 208–209, 211
   Help window, 212
record delimiter, 331
record navigation buttons, 336
records (merge), 326
   containing blank fields, 344–346
   sorting in a merge data file, 346–349
   sorted by zip code, 349
reinstallation (Ami Pro), 389–390
repeated words, finding, 203–204
replacement text, 85
replacing text, 78–79. *See also* Find & Replace
resizing table columns, 300–303
Restore button, 14–15
retrieving a saved document, 36
returns, hard, 149–150
return symbol, 23
reverse video, 17
right-indented paragraph, 143
Right Margin marker, 181–182

right margin. *See* margins

right mouse button, 73

right tab, 130–131

row headings (in tables), 285, 287

rows (in tables), 282
- inserting, 303, 305–306
- selecting, 298

rulers
- current, 126–129
- displaying the current, 127–129
- types of, 126

ruler (vertical), 361–362, 364

rules (horizontal lines), 249

S

saved document, retrieving, 36

saving
- Ami Pro 3.0 documents in other formats, 404–405
- documents, 24–28
- modified documents, 61

scroll arrows, 44

scroll bars, 14

scrolling through a document, 43–46, 396

search text, 51, 85

selected (highlighted) items, 26

selecting text, 396
- for deleting, 76–78
- extending a selection, 84
- selecting a sentence, 82
- techniques for, 79–84
- for text enhancement, 129

Select Merge Data File dialog box, 332

sentence, selecting, 82

separators for thousands, 291

shortcut keys, 395–398

Show/Hide Ruler SmartIcon, 127
- adding to a set, 241–242
- moving, 238–239
- removing, 240

Size Columns And Rows In A Table SmartIcon, 300, 302

SmartIcons, 14. *See also* SmartIcon sets
- adding to sets, 241–242
- Bold Text, 261

Center Selected Text, 152–153

customizing, 230–242

displaying the names of, 73

Grammar Check, 207, 209

Left Align Selected Text, 152

Modify Lines & Shades In A Table, 308

moving, 238–239

Next Icon Set, 231–233

Print, 190–192

Print Envelope, 352

removing from sets, 239–240

reordering in sets, 237–239

Show/Hide Ruler, 127

Size Columns And Rows In A Table, 300, 302

Spell Check, 198, 202

Tables, 297

Thesaurus, 205

Toggle Fast Format, 115–117

Toggle Full Page/Layout View, 186

using to open a document, 72–74

using for text attributes, 108–110

View Preferences, 285

SmartIcons button, 231–233

SmartIcons dialog box, 234

SmartIcon sets. *See also* SmartIcons

   adding icons to, 241–242

   displaying a list of, 232

   dragging, 236

   positioning, 233–236

   removing icons from, 239–240

   reordering icons in, 237–239

   switching, 231–233

snaking text, 370

sorting records in a merge data file, 346–349

sort orders, 347

Sort Records dialog box, 348

source document, 222

spacer icons, 237–238

spacing

   changing line spacing, 155–157

   modifying paragraph spacing, 258–260

   one-and-a-half, 157

   paragraph, 248

paragraph vs. line, 258

Spacing dialog box, 155–156

spacing elements, 259

special effects for text, 104

Spell Check, 198–204

    dialog box, 201–202

    setting options, 203

    SmartIcon, 192, 202

    starting, 198–199

    using, 199–204

standardized data, 328

Standard view, 55

starting Ami Pro, 8

starting Windows, 3–5

status bar, 14

    using to change fonts, 112–114

    using to move to a page, 49–51

styles box, 249

style sheets, 247, 269–272

styles list, 251

styles (paragraph), 247–268

    assigning, 249–254

    creating, 261–268

    elements of, 248

    modifying, 254–261

    modifying spacing elements, 258–260

    overriding, 260–261

    using function keys to assign, 252–254

Style Status button, 249–253, 262–263

subdirectory, 24

submenu, 152

symbols, displaying nonprinting, 22–23

synonyms, finding and placing, 204–206

system date, 4, 173

system time, 4

T

tab bar, 131–132

tabbed tables. *See also* table contents; tables

    adding a line to, 133–134

    aligned, 140

    clearing tabs in, 134–135

    misaligned, 138

setting tabs in, 135–137

tab buttons, 132, 134

tab characters, 21, 131

tab leader, 132

table contents. *See also* tabbed tables; tables

   changing the appearance of, 311–315

   modifying the text style, 313–315

table of contents (Help), 57–58

table gridlines, 282, 287

Table Modify Layout dialog box, 296

tables, 281–322. *See also* tabbed tables; table contents

   adding a line around, 308–311

   adding lines to cells, 307–308

   applying text formatting in, 312–313

   basics of, 282–291

   cell addresses, 285–286

   centering, 311–312

   changing column widths in, 300–303

   components of, 282

   creating, 283–284

   deleting columns and rows, 303–307

   entering numbers in, 292–294

   entering text in, 289–291

   inserting columns and rows, 303–307

   modifying layout of, 296–311

   moving in, 287–289

   row and column headings for, 285, 287

   selection techniques, 297–300

   totaling in, 295–296

   viewing, 284–287

   working with numbers in, 291–296

Tables SmartIcon set, 297

Table Text style, 314–315

tabs, 20–21

   clearing, 138–140

   clearing in tabbed table, 134–135

   default, 129

   moving custom, 137–139

   setting in the current ruler, 131–136

INDEX • 425

setting in tabbed table, 135–137
types of, 130–131
working with, 130–140
tab symbol, 23, 133
target document, 222
text attributes, 104
   applying, 105–110
   finding and replacing, 227–230
   using SmartIcons for, 108–110
text blocks, deleting, 76–78
text box, 24
text enhancements, 125–166
   applying in tables, 312–313
   selecting paragraphs for, 129
text formatting, 103–122
   applying in tables, 312–313
   modifying, 255–257
Text menu, using for attributes, 105–107
text selection. *See* selecting text
text stream, 198
text tightness, 248
Thesaurus, 204–206
   dialog box, 206

SmartIcon, 205
thousands separators, 291
tightness, text, 248
tilde (~), 331
time, entering current, 4
title bar, 6–7, 17
Title style, 258–260
Today's Date, 173
toggle, 41
Toggle Fast Format SmartIcons, 115–117
Toggle Full Page/Layout View SmartIcon, 186
totaling in tables, 295–296
tutorial (Ami Pro), 8
typefaces, 104
typing area (document window), 18–19

U

underlined text, 107, 109
Undo Last Command Or Action SmartIcon, 91–92
undo operations, 91–92

Untitled window, 13
up increment arrow, 11
Up Page Arrow button, 50
User Setup dialog box, 11

V

vertical bar (|), 331
vertical ruler, 361–362, 364
vertical scroll bar, 44
viewing a document, 55–57
viewing a table, 284–287
View menu, 9
View Preferences, 55, 284–287
View Preferences dialog box, 10, 284–286
View Preferences SmartIcon, 285

W

Welcome To Merge dialog box, 331–332
Window menu, 223–224
Windows application, 2
Windows Applications program group, 8
windows (document), 2, 13–16, 221–222
   elements of, 5–6, 13–16
   floating, 233
   positioning SmartIcons in, 235
   typing area, 18–19
Windows (Microsoft)
   Clipboard, 88, 223
   introduction to, 2–7
   program groups, 6–7, 8
   Program Manager window, 5–7
   starting, 3–5
words, finding, 203–207
word wrap, 19–20
wrapping text around a frame, 360–361
WYSIWYG feature, 18

Z

zip codes, records sorted by, 349

Ziff-Davis Press Survey of Readers

Please help us in our effort to produce the best books on personal computing. For your assistance, we would be pleased to send you a FREE catalog featuring the complete line of Ziff-Davis Press books.

1. How did you first learn about this book?

Recommended by a friend .... ☐ -1 (5)
Recommended by store personnel .... ☐ -2
Saw in Ziff-Davis Press catalog .... ☐ -3
Received advertisement in the mail .... ☐ -4
Saw the book on bookshelf at store .... ☐ -5
Read book review in: _____ ☐ -6
Saw an advertisement in: _____ ☐ -7
Other (Please specify): _____ ☐ -8

2. Which THREE of the following factors most influenced your decision to purchase this book? (Please check up to THREE.)

Front or back cover information on book ... ☐ -1 (6)
Logo of magazine affiliated with book ..... ☐ -2
Special approach to the content .... ☐ -3
Completeness of content .... ☐ -4
Author's reputation .... ☐ -5
Publisher's reputation .... ☐ -6
Book cover design or layout .... ☐ -7
Index or table of contents of book .... ☐ -8
Price of book .... ☐ -9
Special effects, graphics, illustrations ..... ☐ -0
Other (Please specify): _____ ☐ -x

3. How many computer books have you purchased in the last six months? _____ (7-10)

4. On a scale of 1 to 5, where 5 is excellent, 4 is above average, 3 is average, 2 is below average, and 1 is poor, please rate each of the following aspects of this book below. (Please circle your answer.)

Depth/completeness of coverage	5	4	3	2	1	(11)
Organization of material	5	4	3	2	1	(12)
Ease of finding topic	5	4	3	2	1	(13)
Special features/time saving tips	5	4	3	2	1	(14)
Appropriate level of writing	5	4	3	2	1	(15)
Usefulness of table of contents	5	4	3	2	1	(16)
Usefulness of index	5	4	3	2	1	(17)
Usefulness of accompanying disk	5	4	3	2	1	(18)
Usefulness of illustrations/graphics	5	4	3	2	1	(19)
Cover design and attractiveness	5	4	3	2	1	(20)
Overall design and layout of book	5	4	3	2	1	(21)
Overall satisfaction with book	5	4	3	2	1	(22)

5. Which of the following computer publications do you read regularly; that is, 3 out of 4 issues?

Byte .... ☐ -1 (23)
Computer Shopper .... ☐ -2
Corporate Computing .... ☐ -3
Dr. Dobb's Journal .... ☐ -4
LAN Magazine .... ☐ -5
MacWEEK .... ☐ -6
MacUser .... ☐ -7
PC Computing .... ☐ -8
PC Magazine .... ☐ -9
PC WEEK .... ☐ -0
Windows Sources .... ☐ -x
Other (Please specify): _____ ☐ -y

Please turn page.

6. What is your level of experience with personal computers? With the subject of this book?

	With PCs	With subject of book
Beginner...............	☐ -1 (24)	☐ -1 (25)
Intermediate...........	☐ -2	☐ -2
Advanced..............	☐ -3	☐ -3

7. Which of the following best describes your job title?

Officer (CEO/President/VP/owner)........ ☐ -1 (26)
Director/head........................... ☐ -2
Manager/supervisor..................... ☐ -3
Administration/staff..................... ☐ -4
Teacher/educator/trainer................. ☐ -5
Lawyer/doctor/medical professional....... ☐ -6
Engineer/technician..................... ☐ -7
Consultant............................. ☐ -8
Not employed/student/retired............ ☐ -9
Other (Please specify): _____ ☐ -0

8. What is your age?

Under 20............................. ☐ -1 (27)
21-29................................ ☐ -2
30-39................................ ☐ -3
40-49................................ ☐ -4
50-59................................ ☐ -5
60 or over........................... ☐ -6

9. Are you:

Male................................. ☐ -1 (28)
Female............................... ☐ -2

Thank you for your assistance with this important information! Please write your address below to receive our free catalog.

Name: _____
Address: _____
City/State/Zip: _____

Fold here to mail.

134X-01-01

BUSINESS REPLY MAIL
FIRST CLASS MAIL   PERMIT NO. 1612   OAKLAND, CA

POSTAGE WILL BE PAID BY ADDRESSEE

Ziff-Davis Press
5903 Christie Avenue
Emeryville, CA 94608-1925
Attn: Marketing

NO POSTAGE NECESSARY IF MAILED IN THE UNITED STATES

■ TO RECEIVE 5$\frac{1}{4}$-INCH DISK(S)

The Ziff-Davis Press software contained on the 3$\frac{1}{2}$-inch disk included with this book is also available in 5$\frac{1}{4}$-inch format. If you would like to receive the software in the 5$\frac{1}{4}$-inch format, please return the 3$\frac{1}{2}$-inch disk with your name and address to:

Disk Exchange
Ziff-Davis Press
5903 Christie Avenue
Emeryville, CA 94608

■ END-USER LICENSE AGREEMENT

READ THIS AGREEMENT CAREFULLY BEFORE BUYING THIS BOOK. BY BUYING THE BOOK AND USING THE PROGRAM LISTINGS, DISKS, AND PROGRAMS REFERRED TO BELOW, YOU ACCEPT THE TERMS OF THIS AGREEMENT.

The program listings included in this book and the programs included on the diskette(s) contained in the package on the opposite page ("Disks") are proprietary products of Ziff-Davis Press and/or third party suppliers ("Suppliers"). The program listings and programs are hereinafter collectively referred to as the "Programs." Ziff-Davis Press and the Suppliers retain ownership of the Disks and copyright to the Programs, as their respective interests may appear. The Programs and the copy of the Disks provided are licensed (not sold) to you under the conditions set forth herein.

License. You may use the Disks on any compatible computer, provided that the Disks are used on only one computer and by one user at a time.

Restrictions. You may not commercially distribute the Disks or the Programs or otherwise reproduce, publish, or distribute or otherwise use the Disks or the Programs in any manner that may infringe any copyright or other proprietary right of Ziff-Davis Press, the Suppliers, or any other party or assign, sublicense, or otherwise transfer the Disks or this agreement to any other party unless such party agrees to accept the terms and conditions of this agreement. This license and your right to use the Disks and the Programs automatically terminates if you fail to comply with any provision of this agreement.

U.S. GOVERNMENT RESTRICTED RIGHTS. The disks and the programs are provided with **RESTRICTED RIGHTS**. Use, duplication, or disclosure by the Government is subject to restrictions as set forth in subparagraph (c)(1)(ii) of the Rights in Technical Data and Computer Software Clause at DFARS (48 CFR 252.277-7013). The Proprietor of the compilation of the Programs and the Disks is Ziff-Davis Press, 5903 Christie Avenue, Emeryville, CA 94608.

Limited Warranty. Ziff-Davis Press warrants the physical Disks to be free of defects in materials and workmanship under normal use for a period of 30 days from the purchase date. If Ziff-Davis Press receives written notification within the warranty period of defects in materials or workmanship in the physical Disks, and such notification is determined by Ziff-Davis Press to be correct, Ziff-Davis Press will, at its option, replace the defective Disks or refund a prorata portion of the purchase price of the book. **THESE ARE YOUR SOLE REMEDIES FOR ANY BREACH OF WARRANTY.**

EXCEPT AS SPECIFICALLY PROVIDED ABOVE, THE DISKS AND THE PROGRAMS ARE PROVIDED "AS IS" WITHOUT ANY WARRANTY OF ANY KIND. NEITHER ZIFF-DAVIS PRESS NOR THE SUPPLIERS MAKE ANY WARRANTY OF ANY KIND AS TO THE ACCURACY OR COMPLETENESS OF THE DISKS OR THE PROGRAMS OR THE RESULTS TO BE OBTAINED FROM USING THE DISKS OR THE PROGRAMS AND NEITHER ZIFF-DAVIS PRESS NOR THE SUPPLIERS SHALL BE RESPONSIBLE FOR ANY CLAIMS ATTRIBUTABLE TO ERRORS, OMISSIONS, OR OTHER INACCURACIES IN THE DISKS OR THE PROGRAMS. THE ENTIRE RISK AS TO THE RESULTS AND PERFORMANCE OF THE DISKS AND THE PROGRAMS IS ASSUMED BY THE USER. FURTHER, NEITHER ZIFF-DAVIS PRESS NOR THE SUPPLIERS MAKE ANY REPRESENTATIONS OR WARRANTIES, EITHER EXPRESS OR IMPLIED, WITH RESPECT TO THE DISKS OR THE PROGRAMS, INCLUDING BUT NOT LIMITED TO, THE QUALITY, PERFORMANCE, MERCHANTABILITY, OR FITNESS FOR A PARTICULAR PURPOSE OF THE DISKS OR THE PROGRAMS. IN NO EVENT SHALL ZIFF-DAVIS PRESS OR THE SUPPLIERS BE LIABLE FOR DIRECT, INDIRECT, SPECIAL, INCIDENTAL, OR CONSEQUENTIAL DAMAGES ARISING OUT THE USE OF OR INABILITY TO USE THE DISKS OR THE PROGRAMS OR FOR ANY LOSS OR DAMAGE OF ANY NATURE CAUSED TO ANY PERSON OR PROPERTY AS A RESULT OF THE USE OF THE DISKS OR THE PROGRAMS, EVEN IF ZIFF-DAVIS PRESS OR THE SUPPLIERS HAVE BEEN SPECIFICALLY ADVISED OF THE POSSIBILITY OF SUCH DAMAGES. NEITHER ZIFF-DAVIS PRESS NOR THE SUPPLIERS ARE RESPONSIBLE FOR ANY COSTS INCLUDING, BUT NOT LIMITED TO, THOSE INCURRED AS A RESULT OF LOST PROFITS OR REVENUE, LOSS OF USE OF THE DISKS OR THE PROGRAMS, LOSS OF DATA, THE COSTS OF RECOVERING SOFTWARE OR DATA, OR THIRD-PARTY CLAIMS. IN NO EVENT WILL ZIFF-DAVIS PRESS' OR THE SUPPLIERS' LIABILITY FOR ANY DAMAGES TO YOU OR ANY OTHER PARTY EVER EXCEED THE PRICE OF THIS BOOK. NO SALES PERSON OR OTHER REPRESENTATIVE OF ANY PARTY INVOLVED IN THE DISTRIBUTION OF THE DISKS IS AUTHORIZED TO MAKE ANY MODIFICATIONS OR ADDITIONS TO THIS LIMITED WARRANTY.

Some states do not allow the exclusion or limitation of implied warranties or limitation of liability for incidental or consequential damages, so the above limitation or exclusion may not apply to you.

General. Ziff-Davis Press and the Suppliers retain all rights not expressly granted. Nothing in this license constitutes a waiver of the rights of Ziff-Davis Press or the Suppliers under the U.S. Copyright Act or any other Federal or State Law, international treaty, or foreign law.